Burns

A Study of the Poems and Songs

BURNS

A Study of the Poems and Songs

THOMAS CRAWFORD

STANFORD UNIVERSITY PRESS

STANFORD, CALIFORNIA

Stanford University Press
Stanford, California
© Copyright 1960 by T. Crawford
All rights reserved
Original edition 1960
Reprinted 1965

Printed in the United States of America

Preface

Of the many people who helped me in the writing and revision of this book I should like especially to thank Mr J. K. Walton, of Trinity College, Dublin, who first urged me to begin it; Professor S. Musgrove, who encouraged me throughout; Dr Elizabeth Sheppard, who assisted with the glossary and Appendix I; Mr M. K. Joseph and the Rev. J. A. Cumming, who commented on parts of an early draft; Mr Allen Curnow, who read the proofs; Mr D. D. Murison, editor of *The Scottish National Dictionary*, who settled the meaning of some obsolete words and phrases; Dr W. V. Falkenhahn, who summarised all available Russian material and translated the Russian quotations; and—above all—Mr R. L. C. Lorimer, the ideal editor for a book on Burns.

My thanks are also due to Mr Charles Brasch for permission to reprint those parts of Chapters V and VI which originally appeared in *Landfall: a New Zealand Quarterly*; to the University of New Zealand, for a research grant with which I purchased microfilm material; to Mr Samuel Marshak, Professor S. Orlov and Miss S. Kolmakova for sending me Russian works on Burns; to Herr W. Michelsen of Hamburg for compiling a bibliography of German secondary sources; and to Miss Pat Gulliver for typing most of the manuscript.

I should like to thank the authors and publishers mentioned below for permission to quote as follows: *The Aberdeen Journal* (and D. Wyllie & Son, Aberdeen), from A. Keith, *Burns and Folk-Song*; Mr J. K. Baxter, from *The Fire and the Anvil*; A. & C. Black, Ltd, from H. G. Graham, *The Social Life of Scotland in the Eighteenth Century*; Professor B. H. Bronson, from *Some Aspects of Music and Literature in the Eighteenth Century*; the Editor of *The Burns Chronicle*, from Dr A. M. Kinghorn, "Burns and his Early Critics" (1954), and from Dr Wen Yuan-Ning, reprint of a B.B.C. broadcast (1945); Mr J. R. Campbell, from *Burns the Democrat*; Cassell & Co., Ltd, from *Scottish Poetry: a Critical Survey*, ed. J. Kinsley, and from Cervantes, *Three Exemplary Novels* (tr. S. Putnam); the Clarendon Press, Oxford, from Professor J. de Lancey Ferguson's edition of Burns's *Letters*, Professor J. Y. T. Greig's edition of Hume's *Letters*, and W. P. Ker, *On Modern Literature*; James Clarke, Ltd, from Calvin, *Institutes* (tr. Beveridge); the

Columbia University Press, from H. N. Fairchild, *Religious Trends in English Poetry*; Mr James Craigie, from Sir William Craigie, *A Primer of Burns*, and from Sir William's essay, "The Present State of the Scottish Tongue"; Dr David Daiches and Cassell and Co., Ltd, from *Robert Burns*; J. M. Dent and Sons, Ltd, from Frank Walker, *Hugo Wolf*; Martin F. Dick, Esq., from J. C. Dick, *The Songs of Robert Burns*; G. Duckworth, Ltd, from R. Capell, *Schubert's Songs*; Mme A. E. Elistratova, from *Robert Burns*; Messrs Faber & Faber, Ltd, from T. S. Eliot, *Triumphal March*, and from J. Handley, *Scottish Agriculture in the Eighteenth Century*; Professor J. de Lancey Ferguson and the Oxford University Press, New York, from *Pride and Passion*; Gowans and Gray, Ltd, Glasgow, from *Robert Burns's Commonplace Book* 1783-1785; the Hamburg Staata-und-Universitäts-bibliothek, from O. Ritter, *Quellenstudien zu Robert Burns* and *Neue Quellenfunde*; the Harvill Press, Ltd, from S. Moreux, *Béla Bartók*; W. Heffer, Ltd, from A. B. Jamieson, *Burns and Religion*; W. Heinemann, Ltd, from *Boswell's London Journal*, *Boswell in Holland*, the 18-vol. edition of the Boswell Papers, and from J. Reeves, *The Idiom of the People*; Miss Christina Keith and Robert Hale, Ltd, from *The Russet Coat*; Dr Arnold Kettle and The Hutchinson University Library, from *An Introduction to the English Novel*; William Kimber, Ltd, from *Boswell's Column* (ed. Margery Bailey); Lawrence & Wishart, Ltd, from S. Finkelstein, *How Music Expresses Ideas*, and from A. L. Morton, *The English Utopia*; W. Maclellan, Glasgow, from *New Judgments: Robert Burns*; Macmillan and Co., Ltd, London, from M. J. E. Brown, *Schubert: A Critical Biography*, and from W. P. Ker, *Collected Essays*; The Macmillan Co., New York, from *His Very Self and Voice, Collected Conversations of Lord Byron*, ed. E. J. Lovell, Jr; John Murray, Ltd, London, from L. A. Marchand, *Byron: A Biography*; the Oxford University Press, London, from *The Letters of Gerard Manley Hopkins to Robert Bridges* (ed. C. C. Abbott); the Oxford University Press, New York, from J. T. Macneill, *The History and Character of Calvinism*; Mme Raït-Kovaleva, from introduction to S. Marshak, *Robert Burns in Translation*; Dr John Strawhorn, from "The Background to Burns" in *Ayrshire Archaeological and National History Society Collections*; R. D. Thornton, from *The Tuneful Flame: Songs of Robert Burns as he sang them*; *Unitarian Register*, Boston (*The Christian Register*), from W. Walsh, "Robert Burns, a Unitarian Forerunner"; the University Press, Cambridge, from J. S. Whale, *The Protestant Tradition*; the University of Chicago Press, from Aeschylus, *Agamemnon* (tr. Lattimore); the University of Chicago Press and the Editors of *Modern Philology*, from Marion Witt, "The Making of an Elegy: Yeats's 'In Memory of Major Robert Gregory'"; University of North Carolina Press, from Professor R. T. Fitzhugh, *Robert Burns: His Associates and Contemporaries*.

With very few exceptions, all quotations from Burns's poems are from the Henley and Henderson ("Centenary" edition), and unless otherwise stated all page and volume references in the notes are to this edition. Very occasionally, and in the interests of clarity, I have substituted the punctuation of some other edition for Henley and Henderson's.

Auckland, 1959   T. C.

Contents

In Politics if thou would'st mix,
And mean thy fortunes be,
Bear this in mind, be deaf and blind,
Let great folks hear and see.

Attributed to Robert Burns 1793

To the greater poets everything they see has its relation to the national life, and through that to the universal and divine life : nothing is an isolated artistic moment ; there is a unity everywhere ; everything fulfills a purpose that is not its own ; the hailstone is a journeyman of God ; the grass blade carries the universe upon its point. But to this universalism, this seeing of unity everywhere, you can only attain through what is near you, your nation, or, if you be no traveller, your village and the cobwebs on your walls. You can no more have the greater poetry without a nation than religion without symbols. One can only reach out to the universe with a gloved hand—that glove is one's nation, the only thing one knows even a little of.

W. B. Yeats, 2 Sept. 1888

Introductory

THE bicentenary of Robert Burns's birth provides an excellent opportunity for re-examining current critical judgments upon his poems. Some of the most popular of these can be traced back to the late nineteenth century, and in particular to Angellier, the greatest of all Continental students of the poet, who in 1893 put forward the view that "Burns was the culminating point in a native literature which now seems at an end. He was the most glowing, the most succulent, and the last fruit on the highest branch of the old Scottish tree."[1]

This opinion naturally leads to another, that his best work is in Scots, and that when he turns to English he becomes invariably tedious and second-rate. Yet many of the critics espousing such views are great admirers of the songs, some of the best of which are in English, admittedly as pronounced in Scotland, but including only a few distinctively Scots words. It would seem, then, that Burns could write well in the southern literary tongue at least when he had a tune on his lips; and if then, why not on other occasions? Burns did, indeed, write some good narrative, descriptive and elegiac poetry in English. The non-dialectal verses of "The Vision" and "The Brigs of Ayr" are at least as good as "Sweet Afton" and "Husband, Husband, cease your Strife," while even the "Ode for General Washington's Birthday" has its points.

Poems like "The Cotter's Saturday Night" and the "English" sections of "The Vision" have been undervalued for over fifty years because primitivist critics have been obsessed by the vigour and expressiveness of "Lallans." There is a real need to give them once more the praise which is their due, reinterpreting them in the light of modern revaluations of eighteenth-century poetry—a process which was recently begun

---

[1] A. Angellier, *Robert Burns: La Vie, les oeuvres*, henceforth cited as Angellier, 2 vols., Paris 1893, VOL. II, p. 401 : "Burns a été le point culminant d'une littérature indigène qui semble close maintenant. Il a été le plus brillant, le plus savoureux, le dernier fruit, sur le plus haut rameau du vieil arbre écossais."

by David Daiches and Christina Keith, and which can be
expected to continue after this bicentenary year. The total
effect of much modern writing on Burns has been to emphasise
what is old and traditional in his work to the detriment of
what is new, and there has been a tendency to ignore the
content of his poems while concentrating either upon their
language or upon what Burns borrowed from Ramsay and
Fergusson, Thomson and Pope. There is no longer any need to
demonstrate Burns's indebtedness to the Scots (or the English)
literary tradition, except incidentally, as part of a wider purpose—to reveal Burns the innovator ; nor is there any reason
to fulminate against the imbecilities of the Burns Cult : these
jobs have been well done, and today the critic's task is of quite
a different nature. The present study arose, at least in part,
as a reaction against James K. Baxter's attempt to interpret
Burns in terms of the doctrine of the Poetic Mask. Indeed,
from one point of view, it may be regarded as an extended
meditation upon the following statement of Mr Baxter's :

> In attempting to assess the significance of a poem, one must
> realize that nearly all poetry is dramatic in character. The
> catharsis which a reader experiences could not occur if he felt
> the self that the poem expresses to be entirely actual ; rather,
> the self is the projection of complex associations in the poet's
> mind, and the poem enables the reader to make the same pro-
> jection. The *I* of a poem may not exist. Thus, if one regarded
> the work of Burns as a poetic *credo*, one would have to conclude
> that he was either insincere or schizophrenic. . . . But the
> problem arises from a false conception of the poet's rôle. If
> Burns had been permanently committed to any one attitude, he
> could not have attained the objectivity necessary to write at all.[2]

Though I am willing to express qualified agreement with
Mr Baxter at some points, I am inclined to contradict him at
others. Both as a man and as a poet, Burns did in fact exhibit
that insincerity and schizophrenia which Mr Baxter would
deny him. He sometimes liked to strike rhetorical attitudes, to
"let great folks hear" in both of the senses in which it is possible
to take these four words, but most of his poems are made out of
a highly inconsistent man's battle with the world. Even on the

[2] J. K. Baxter, *The Fire and the Anvil*, Wellington, N.Z., 1955, pp. 48–9.

occasions when he did create a *persona*, its function was to body forth some mood or trait or experience of his own, or of the people round about him.

I believe that the approach from or to a tradition must always fail to bring us to the heart of Burns as a poet unless it is combined with a detailed examination of how he felt and thought about real people and about his actual surroundings. Nor is the "New Criticism," at least in its purest form, enough for Burns; he cannot be judged except by some amalgam of biography and careful scrutiny of individual poems. And yet, paradoxically enough, there is very little about his life in the present volume. I assume that my readers are already familiar with the bare outlines of Burns's story, and my usual method has been to work outwards from the poems to society, rather than the other way round. Nevertheless, there are certain interpretations of the biographical evidence which are crucial for the understanding of his work.

One of these is his shifting relation to an upper-class or educated audience at different stages of his career. In the Kilmarnock poems, he or his advisers let great folks hear what they perhaps desired to hear, and only sometimes (as in "A Dream") what might be dangerous to print. But in the "English" poetry written under the spell of the Edinburgh visit, which by no means includes all his "English" pieces, he tried to be a national poet of the kind that Hugh Blair and Dr John Moore wanted him to become: at the same time, he wished to love Clarinda like a Man of Feeling, and in his Border and Highland tours to experience the correct responses to wild and noble prospects. He knew from the beginning that his stay in Edinburgh could not last long, and he saw through the pretensions of cultivated mediocrity; yet for a short time he played with the idea of turning himself into a man who saw and felt like a town-bred lawyer or schoolmaster. His return to the countryside was associated with the open acknowledgment of Jean Armour as his wife. Upper-class women might be refined, but they were not for him, except as an excuse for airing his "skinless sensibility";[3] but for the solider kind of

---

[3] R. T. Fitzhugh, *Robert Burns, his Associates and Contemporaries*, N. Carolina 1943, p. 7.

love, the love that is generous and does not count the cost, he had to go to his own people, as even in Edinburgh he went to servant-girls like May Cameron and Jenny Clow.[4] Though, at Ellisland, he was once more able to create at full stretch, removal from Ayrshire meant that he could no longer produce *genre* pictures of the old sort, for he found it impossible to know Dumfries men and women as he had known the people of his native Kyle. Inevitably, his later work is more abstract (in the sense in which music itself is abstract), and also of more universal appeal than the poems written before 1786, so that by and large Burns's evolution as a poet may be termed a development from the particular to the general. In his last years, while letting the whole world hear Scotland's tunes and passions, he also, with his private voice, "let great folks hear" the song of democratic rebellion. One should not forget that from the end of 1792 there were some things Burns dared not say too openly; not for nothing did he make his minstrel sing, "I winna ventur't in my rhymes."[5]

Burns was a letter-writer almost before he was a poet, and he was brought up on the epistolary dogma that one should suit one's style to the needs and personality of one's correspondents. The same rhetorical principles are also to be found in his poetry, so that what the followers of I. A. Richards call "tone" is of peculiar importance in evaluating his work. "Death and Dr Hornbook" and "The Address to the Deil" gain their effect from sudden transitions in the mood and attitude of both Burns (or the "I" of the poem) and the supernatural visitant, while in the course of its two hundred and twenty-four lines "Tam o' Shanter" deploys no fewer than three distinct attitudes. The idea of tone is at least as rewarding to the reader of Burns as the concept of the *persona*.

Detailed analysis of Burns's poetry tends to remove emphasis from pride and passion and place it on thought and wit. Now thought and wit must be about something; and in this case

---

[4] J. De Lancey Ferguson, *Pride and Passion*, henceforth cited as Ferguson, N.Y. 1939, pp. 113ff.

[5] "As I stood by yon roofless Tower," in *The Poetry of Robert Burns*, edd. W. E. Henley and T. F. Henderson (the "Centenary Edition"), henceforth cited as H. & H., 4 vols., Edinburgh 1896–7, VOL. III, pp. 144 (406). Unless otherwise stated, all further references in the footnotes are to volume and page in this edition.

they are about the kind of man Burns believed himself to be, and the actual world, whether local, national, or European, in which he found himself. Four great events colour all Burns's life and work : the agrarian changes in late eighteenth-century Ayrshire; the American Revolution; the conflict between extremists and moderates within the Scottish Church, which was a specific and local extension of the general European movement known as "the Enlightenment"; and the French Revolution. They are just as important, in any attempt to understand Burns, as the Scots literary tradition, the English Augustan poets, or the eighteenth-century song-books, and I have given them as much prominence as my method allows.

Taken together, Burns's poems and letters can still be regarded as "a continuous revelation of personality." But that personality was not such an uncomplicated one as was once thought, for it required both rhetoric and self-dramatisation to give itself full expression. Burns wrote, patched or transmitted some of the most personal lyrics in the language ; but he was also a political poet, and if this aspect of his achievement is distorted or played down, he must inevitably be assigned a false place in literary history.

I

The Young Poet

URNS was not quite fifteen when he produced his first song,
"O, once I lov'd a Bonie Lass."[1] At that time the family
were renting Mount Oliphant, a seventy-five-acre farm
("between eighty and ninety English statute measure," according to Robert's younger brother Gilbert) on the outskirts of
Ayr; and they were finding it hard to make ends meet.
Gilbert records his memories of this time as follows:

> We lived very sparingly. For several years butcher's meat was a
> stranger in the house, while all the members of the family
> exerted themselves to the utmost of their strength, and rather
> beyond it, in the labours of the farm. My brother at the age of
> thirteen assisted in threshing the crop of corn, and at fifteen was
> the principal labourer on the farm, for we had no hired servant,
> male or female. The anguish of mind we felt at our tender years,
> under these straits and difficulties, was very great. To think of
> our father growing old (for he was now above fifty) broken down
> with the long continued fatigues of his life, with a wife and five
> other children, and in a declining state of circumstances, these
> reflections produced in my brother's mind and mine sensations
> of the deepest distress. I doubt not but the hard labour and
> sorrow of this period of his life, was in a great measure the cause
> of that depression of spirits with which Robert was so often
> afflicted through his whole life afterwards.[2]

Yet these hardships left absolutely no mark on the song;
peasants, and above all young peasants, are sometimes able to
enjoy themselves even in the shadow of famine itself. The
poem is about a real girl in a real situation—Nelly Kirkpatrick,
"a bonie, sweet, sonsie lass" of fourteen who was his neighbour
in the harvest field. "I remember I composed it in a wild

[1] III. 197 (442).
[2] Gilbert Burns to Mrs F. A. Dunlop in *The Works of Robert Burns*, ed. J.
Currie, henceforth cited as Currie, 4 vols., Liverpool 1800, VOL. I, pp. 61, 71.

enthusiasm of passion," he wrote in his commonplace-book ;[3] and his emotion was none the less powerful for being harnessed to a convention of rural courtship. It often happened in that age of folk dance and folk music that lovers sang songs to their mistresses with as sweet and proud a grace as the sonneteers of an earlier time and a higher social class. The Ayrshire of those days must have been almost as much a nest of singing birds as Elizabethan England is reputed to have been : not even the Kirk could stamp out the singing and making of songs, and (who knows ?) even Holy Willie himself may have been known to "roar a ditty up" in his hot youth. Burns was doing nothing out of the ordinary when he wrote "O, once I lov'd." One of his companions had already sung to Nelly Kirkpatrick a song of local composition, though he had not made it himself; Robert simply wished to go one better by producing something of his very own.[4]

"O, once I lov'd" differs from anonymous folk-songs only in that we know who the author was. If we are to believe Burns's account of how he came to write it, it was intended for oral delivery and to be sung to a tune, *I am a man un-married*, which has unfortunately not survived. Right in this very first work of his, Burns's vocabulary is both Scots and English. The poem does not move from a Scottish beginning to an apparently English conclusion, as is common in many of his later works, but from English to Scots and then back to English again. Long before he came up against the advice of the Edinburgh *literati*, who told him to learn classical mythology and write in heroic couplets, he found himself poised between two languages, two mental worlds. "O, once I lov'd" owes whatever character it possesses to the alternation between them ; and the point of beginning and return, the centre of its statement, is quite definitely English. Though words like "virtue, reputation, qualities," or metaphors like "it's innocence and modesty that polishes the dart," are from the common stock of art-song, they had in all probability become folk

[3] *Robert Burns's Commonplace Book 1783–1785*, edd. J. C. Ewing and D. Cook, henceforth cited as R. B.'s *Commonplace Book*, Glasgow 1938, p. 5.
[4] See Burns's autobiographical letter to [Dr John Moore], 2 Aug. 1787, in *The Letters of Robert Burns*, ed. J. De Lancey Ferguson, henceforth cited as *Letters*, 2 vols., Oxford 1931, VOL. I, p. 108.

material by the time they reached Burns. The traditional melody, the modification of the original verse-pattern ("four-teeners"), presumably to fit the tune, and the final "O" of the poem, at once conventional and reminiscent of the primitive emotional cry, are more evidently among the attributes of folk song.[5]

It is important to remember that the Ayrshire peasantry were hardly strangers to abstract English diction or even to concepts like "Cupid's arrows." Their language was a mixture of dialect and Standard English, as spoken in Scotland; their culture, too, was mixed. For generations, farmers and labourers had been familiar with the Authorised Version of the Bible, English theological works, and interminable sermons full of words like "effectual calling"; for generations, youngsters had adapted songs and broadsheet ballads, both Scots and English, for their own use. Burns, therefore, did not start off from an uncontaminated folk culture, shining and incorruptible in its original purity; he began with a mixture of Scots and English. William Burnes, the poet's father, is said to have possessed an exceptionally good English pronunciation for one in his walk of life,[6] which perhaps implies that there were other small farmers in the district who could speak some sort of "Modified Standard," at least on special occasions, though not so well as he. All the evidence goes to show that the community from which Burns sprang was composed of men and women who were accustomed to shifting from one level of usage to another. "High English" was apparently reserved for such activities as theological discussion, business correspondence and the writing of certain kinds of love-letter; small wonder then that there clung to it some of that artificiality which always adheres to a polite language which is considerably removed from familiar speech.

In his juvenilia Burns early showed that preoccupation with injustice, exploitation and the power of wealth which haunts much of his later poetry. It was, indeed, a natural response to his father's difficulties. To quote his own words, "we fell into

---

[5] See O. Ritter, *Quellenstudien zu Robert Burns 1773–1791*, henceforth cited as Ritter, Berlin 1901, pp. 1–5.
[6] J. Murdoch to J. C. Walker, in Currie, 1. 97.

the hands of a Factor who sat for the picture I have drawn of
one in my Tale of two dogs. . . . There was a freedom in his
[my father's] lease in two years more, and to weather these two
years we retrenched expenses.—We lived very poorly."[7] By
what must have seemed a tremendous stroke of luck Robert's
father, William Burnes (or Burness, as he sometimes spelt the
name) secured the lease of Lochlie in the parish of Tarbolton
from an Ayr merchant who also helped him to stock the farm ;
there the family moved at Whitsun 1777. At first it seemed as if
the new venture would be successful, but in the end bad weather
and economic crisis destroyed William Burnes. As Gilbert put
it later, "No writing had ever been made out of the conditions
of the lease, a misunderstanding took place respecting them ;
the subjects in dispute were submitted to arbitration, and the
decision involved my father's affairs in ruin."[8] Actually the
merchant went so far as to take out "a warrant of sequestration
against the plenishings of Lochlea,"[9] and William died of consumption early in 1784 ; had he lived, it is probable that he
would have been imprisoned for debt by those whom Robert
called "the rapacious hell-hounds that growl in the kennel of
justice."[10]

"O Tibbie, I hae seen the Day,"[11] written when he was
about seventeen, is a riposte on a stand-offish opinionated
minx who had looked down her nose at him because he was
poorer than she. It is a considerable advance on "O, once I
lov'd." The language is much more Scottish than in his first
poem, because subject and point-of-view alike demand it. The
values of the song are those of the local community of young
lovers, in contrast to the money-grubbing snobbishness of
Tibbie, and vernacular Scots is therefore in place as the
language of democracy and invective. The "yellow dirt" that
poisons personal relationships may be found in innumerable
Scottish songs of the eighteenth century[12] (indeed, the phrase
itself occurs in Pope),[13] but it fits in perfectly with what Burns

[7] To [Moore], 2 Aug. 1787, in *Letters*, I. 107.
[8] Gilbert Burns to Mrs Dunlop, in Currie, I. 72.
[9] See J. Strawhorn, "The Background to Burns," henceforth cited as Strawhorn, in *Ayrshire Archaeological and Natural History Society Collections*, 1950–4, p. 166.
[10] To [Moore], 2 Aug. 1787, *Letters*, I. 113.   [11] III. 37 (333).
[12] Ritter, pp. 5 ff.   [13] *Essay on Man*, IV, I. 279.

had already proved upon his pulses—that some bonnie lasses prefer men of means to men of sense. The final stanza is a humorous and defiant assertion of what was to prove a permanent conviction, that human beings are important because of their own inner worth, even though they own nothing but the shirts they stand up in :

> There lives a lass beside yon park,
> I'd rather hae her in her sark
> Than you wi' a' your thousand mark,
> That gars you look sae high.

In his early years at Lochlie and Irvine, the little seaport which was the scene of his unsuccessful attempt to set up in business as a flax-dresser in 1781, Burns appears to have been obsessed by the knowledge that he had greater gifts than most of those around him, but little chance of putting them to use unless after a cruel and exhausting struggle. "A Ruined Farmer"[14] is perhaps the first of the dramatic lyrics in which he penetrated the mind of another person : in this case his own father, driven bankrupt in the battle to make ends meet. But however documentary its intention may be, the poem presents the farmer's situation altogether too abstractly; it is rhetorical, artificial and curiously rigid, like a stuffed animal in a glass case. Another piece which has come down from this time, "Tragic Fragment,"[15] exhibits many themes which were to recur in later works : hatred of the oppressor; the heroic resistance of indomitable yet ordinary men; and the consciousness that just beyond the circle of the respectable are the "lower depths" inhabited by beggars and vagabonds, here seen as vicious and corrupt, not anarchistic and defiant, as in "The Jolly Beggars." Typical of later attitudes is his protagonist's "me-too" reflexion :

> Oh ! but for friends and interposing Heaven,
> I had been driven forth, like you forlorn,
> The most detested, worthless wretch among you ![16]

[14] IV. I (81). [15] II. 233 (423).
[16] So H. & H., following R. H. Cromek, *Reliques of Robert Burns,* henceforth cited as Cromek, London 1808; of the MSS, *A* and *C* read "Oh! but for kind, though ill-requited friends," and *B* reads "Oh! but for heaven and interposing friends. . . ."

When Burns turned to song again towards the end of the Lochlie period, it was to show himself the possessor of a supreme lyrical gift. "The Lass of Cessnock Banks"[17] is the first of his great songs : a predominantly English poem whose conventional diction is tinctured by only the faintest colouring of Scots. It is generally believed to have been composed for Alison Begbie, the girl to whom he made his first offer of marriage ; indeed it corresponds in tone to five letters addressed to "My dear A." or "My dear E.," which were apparently penned at the same time.[18] Most editors and biographers assume that "My dear A." or "E.," Alison (or Ellison) Begbie, and the "Lass of Cessnock Banks" were one and the same person. Certainly, there is a peculiar atmosphere of strained and artificial compliment in both letters and poem. The letters are those of a man trying to feel what he thinks he ought to feel, because a higher class has decreed that "refined" emotions are better than those experienced by the swinish multitude in their cottages and barns ; they are among Burns's first essays in sensibility and significantly enough they are deliberate imitations of English epistolary models—perhaps of those in his old school reading-book, Arthur Masson's *Collection of English Prose and Verse*, or else of that "collection of letters by the Wits of Queen Ann's reign" which made such an impression on him when he first came across it.[19]

Like the letters to "My dear A.," "The Lass of Cessnock Banks" is stylised, traditional and exquisitely beautiful. A woman's body is identified with the pastoral scene, and there are images of the passing day from morning to evening seen in terms of the sun's movement. The sun itself glints upon the poem, as do the "twa sparkling, rogueish een" of the chorus, which fascinated the rustic love poet in the same way as, centuries before, a girl's eyes had enraptured courtly gentlemen like Petrarch and Ronsard and Wyatt and Sir Philip Sidney.

---

[17] iv. 3 (82).

[18] *Letters*, I. 5–11. Some of these letters may, however, have been drafts written by Burns as chief love-adviser to the "lads of the village." Cp. Ferguson, p. 69, and *Letters*, II. 338.

[19] Cp. F. B. Snyder, *The Life of Robert Burns*, henceforth cited as Snyder, N.Y. 1932, pp. 43–4, 72 ; D. Daiches, *Robert Burns*, henceforth cited as Daiches, London 1952, pp. 60, 365, n.

Running water flows through Burns's lines; dew, mist, the
rainbow, mountains and thorns (both the hawthorn and the
rose) appear, together with the colours of blood and of the
fairest skin, of snow and sheep and cherries and roses. One
thinks of Marvell musing within a formal seventeenth-century
garden :

> No white nor red was ever seen
> So am'rous as this lovely green.[20]

Both poets succeed in giving a sexual significance to the natural
scene, though in very different ways.

A full catalogue of the poem's images would read like a
conducted tour of the Archetypes with a visit to Arcadia
thrown in for good measure. Even the briefest analysis must
note the dominance of gems, linked with twinkling, with dewdrops and with flashing eyes. In the sixth stanza, the girl's
head is a mountain and her hair a mist, while in the seventh :

> Her forehead's like the show'ry bow,
> When gleaming sunbeams intervene,
> And gild the distant mountain's brow—
> An' she has twa sparkling, rogueish een !

The rose to which her cheeks are compared is not so much
organic as petrified—a stone flower or a rose in a stained glass
window, a "crimson gem." If we accept a plausible emen-
dation in the ninth stanza, the girl's breast is compared to
snow—perhaps, by association, to snow on mountains, and the
streamlets become both mountain torrents and founts of
amplitude and abundance.[21]

In the tenth stanza, the theme of shelter ("cherries. . . .
that sunny walls from Boreas screen") is introduced for the first
time, and then in the eleventh there is a return to the imagery
of hills (". . . . sheep . . . That slowly mount the rising steep").
The flower reappears in an especially sensuous form, parti-

[20] Andrew Marvell, "The Garden," ll. 17–18.

[21] The poem was published by Cromek "from the oral communication of a
lady residing in Glasgow," but corrected by the Aldine Editor (1839) from an
original MS. In the st. ix, p. 1, for "Her teeth are" Scott Douglas substituted "Her
bosom is." As H. & H. point out (IV. 83), this alteration has no authority : but
surely it is imaginatively probable.

cularised as the bean,[22] and associated, one feels, with a kiss, while the individual dewdrops or streams of earlier verses have now become the all-encompassing seas. In the thirteenth stanza, the generalised "birds" of the fifth stanza reappear as the more concrete "thrush," and the shelter theme is once more brought forward in the form of the mate who "sits nestling in the bush."

The last stanza of all is at first sight conventionally Petrarchan :

> But it's not her air, her form, her face,
> Tho' matching Beauty's fabled Queen :
> 'Tis the mind that shines in ev'ry grace—
> An' chiefly in her rogueish een !

The idea is commonplace, and previous critics have pointed out the resemblance to a well-known song by the Cavalier lyrist Thomas Carew :

> He that loves a rosy cheek
> Or a coral lip admires . . .
> But a smooth and steadfast mind
> Gentle thoughts and calm desires . . .
> Where these are not I despise
> Lovely cheeks, or lips, or eyes.[23]

But the contrast with Carew's lines is no less significant. Burns is interested not so much in a "smooth and steadfast mind" as in an inborn quality of intellect capable of alliance with the stormiest of thoughts and with desires that are anything but calm. One feels that his heroine possesses the feminine equivalents of the innate sense and worth of his masculine ideal, the Honest Man—a response induced by the repetition in stanza after stanza of the burden "An' she has twa sparkling, rogueish een !"

"The Lass of Cessnock Banks" is unified by means of interwoven traditional images that provide a pattern as satisfying as those of many more pretentious poems that trade on what Yeats called "the fascination of what's difficult."[24] Right at its centre are the girl's eyes, the source of the recurrent pictures of water and light; the head in which they are set gives us the

---

[22] Cp. "The Lass o' Ballochmyle," iv. 16 (37), st. i, l. 3 : "The zephyr wanton'd round the bean."   [23] Cp. H. & H., iv. 83 and iii. 374.
[24] Yeats, *Collected Poems*, London 1939, p. 104.

mountain imagery. Conventional or not, the last verse is the summation of the poem, the goal to which it has been irresistibly moving. Throughout, Burns has been conscious of a woman's body, but only as informed and dominated by mind. It is for this reason that there is such emphasis on the head and its associated features of brows, hair and teeth. The head, after all, is the seat of the intellect; the eyes, mentioned in the refrain at the end of every verse, are windows of the mind, twinkling with a rogueishness that implies both humour and the conscious control of physical desire. Finally, it is rather an "English" poem; its Scottishness is largely a matter of intonation and idiom, or of isolated Scots words such as "twa" and "een," whose function is to add a delicate touch of intimacy to the otherwise all-pervasive English diction.

It is possible that Burns's brief infatuation for Alison Begbie was also responsible for "And I'll kiss thee yet,"[25] a delightful exercise in the folk idiom, as well as for the finest of his early songs, "Mary Morison."[26] In the first stanza of "Mary Morison," all the preoccupations of his early years—his hatred of money, his conviction that sexual love can make the poor man superior to the rich—are fused into poetic unity. In "And I'll kiss thee yet," he had identified his sweetheart with "countless treasure"; now her smiles and glances "make the miser's treasure poor," and were he to win her he would be able to endure the dust and toil of a slave's life. The Ayrshire ploughman has been transmuted into something rich and strange, a cross between the Helot of ancient times and a negro slave on one of the West Indian plantations, an effect secured by the combination of "weary slave" with "sun to sun"; the labour is not simply day-labour, but labour performed in the heat of a most un-Scottish summer.

In the second stanza Burns conveys with absolute simplicity the obsessive, compulsive nature of love. Every aspect of the music and the dance except their movement is excluded, in complete contrast to the timeless stillness of the "trysted hour"

[25] III. 34 (330, 499).
[26] III. 286 (499). It is perhaps worth mentioning that when Burns sent it to Thomson on 20 Mar. 1793, he directed that the song should be sung to the tune *Duncan Davison*, not the one to which it is usually sung today. Cp. Dick, *The Songs of Robert Burns*, henceforth cited as *Songs*, London 1903, p. 371.

with which the first verse begins. The motions of the dancing company lead on naturally to the swift bird's flight of fancy, so that in the fourth line of this second stanza— "I sat, but neither heard nor saw"—the transition back to stillness again comes as a positive shock to the reader. It is a sudden passing from one opposite to another—we may regard it either as absolute quiet at the centre of movement, or as movement surrounding the still centre; and it conveys to the reader the trance-like quality of Burns's vision of the absent one. Just as in the first stanza agricultural labour is transformed by metaphorical associations with other lands and times, so in the second the environment is denuded of all qualities except those which it shares with an aristocratic entertainment. We are at liberty to imagine any lighted hall, and probably the hall we picture is both larger and grander than the one Burns actually saw. Everything ephemeral and transitory is shut out, and only the permanent and *general* remains; yet the general comes to us through an image of the particular (in this case, the "lighted ha' ") which we construct for ourselves.

The third stanza is even simpler than the other two. It is the traditional complaint of the lover who would die for his mistress, who is in danger of having his heart broken, and who asks that, at the very least, the beloved substitute pity for disdain. Half way through there is a subtle reminiscence of the money or exchange theme which was present in Burns's mind when he began—

> If love for love thou wilt na gie. . . .

But the verse, and therefore the whole poem, is rescued from triteness by the delicacy and sensitivity of the two final lines:

> A thought ungentle canna be
> The thought o' Mary Morison.

The exchange of "love for love" is real, personal, and (in the context of the poem) *gentle*—a very different thing from the "stoure" of market exchange. If the woman refuses to enter into the give-and-take of love, then she can and indeed ought to bestow upon her wooer the other but still human and generous emotion of pity. The movement of the piece is from market-exchange to its negation; from gold (an idea implied but not crudely or even directly stated at the beginning) towards spontaneous and humane feeling.[27] This development of mood is completely integrated with the melancholy and elegiac tone of the poem.

In "Mary Morison," as in all Burns's best poems, the form corresponds perfectly to the content. When it is a case of complete interweaving of Scots and English into a seamless garment of image and emotion, it is not enough to speak of "considerable influence from the English tradition."[28] The stanza is that of the octosyllabic ballade, which was brought into Scottish poetry by Robert Henryson, who borrowed it from Chaucer. No sooner was it introduced than it became one of the national measures—a thoroughly Scottish form, called "Ballat Royal" by King James VI, who prescribed it "for any heich and graue subiectis, specially drawin out of learnit authoris." Burns probably got it from Allan Ramsay's *Ever Green* miscellany, which contains some twenty poems written in the form.[29]

The living rhythm of "Mary Morison" of course differs in detail from its underlying pattern of iambic octosyllabics. The first four lines of the second stanza contain many more heavy beats than the first stanza, thus adding to the slow, meditative, mournful effect :

> Yestreen, when to the trembling string
> The dance gaed thro' the lighted ha',
> To thee my fancy took its wing,
> I sat, but neither heard nor saw.

[27] The contrast between love and money, together with the idea that true wealth consists in giving one's affections to another human being, is often found in folk-song, and is so old that it is embedded in most of the European languages. *Trésor* is a common French term of endearment, and so is *Schatz* (treasure) in German. Quite recently it has been pointed out that "Love's Wealth" is a basic theme of early Shakespearian comedy, of the Sonnets, and of *Romeo and Juliet.* Thus the motto on the leaden casket in *The Merchant of Venice*, II. vi, is "who chooseth me must give and hazard all he hath," while Juliet says (II. vi, 32–4) :

> They are but beggars that can count their worth ;
> But my true love is grown to such excess,
> I cannot sum up sum of half my wealth.

Cp. J. R. Brown, *Shakespeare and his Comedies*, London 1957, *passim.* As the allusions in his correspondence prove, Burns was widely read in Shakespeare.

[28] Daiches, p. 61.   [29] Cp. H. & H., I. 371–2, III. 500.

The contradiction between these heavy beats and the actual
hurly-burly of the dance itself prepares for the stock-stillness of
"I sat, but neither heard nor saw," and intensifies our image
of the motionless lover by sheer contrast. At the same time,
the alliteration of "Ye*str*een . . . *tr*embling *str*ing," and the
internal rhyme "trembl*ing* str*ing*," create a singularly precise
auditory image of Scottish fiddle-music. The complete unity
of Scots and English is demonstrated by still another fact—the
existence of definite parallels to particular lines and sentiments
in Shakespeare, Pope, Thomson, Shenstone, Henry Mackenzie,
Crawford's "Beneath a Beech's grateful Shade," Sempill's
"Old longsyne," Mitchell's "Charming Chloe, look with
Pity," and the ballad of "William and Margaret."[30] Only
three of the authors in this list, Shakespeare, Pope and Shenstone, are not of Scottish birth, so that most of the apparently
"English" influences may well reflect specifically Scottish love-
feelings even when their expression is linguistically English.
Furthermore, the Scottish component of the amalgam is
apparent in rhythm and intonation even when the work is
simply read as a poem : when it is sung to the tune for which
Burns originally intended it, the fusion of Scottish and English
is seen to be complete.

At the time of the collapse of his flax-dressing project at
Irvine in 1781–2, Burns experienced something approaching
the violence and intensity of a nervous breakdown. "The
weakness of my nerves," he wrote to his father on 27 Dec.
1781,[31] "has so debilitated my mind that I dare not, either
review past events, or look forward into futurity ; for the least
anxiety, or perturbation in my breast, produces most unhappy
effects on my whole frame." He was not yet twenty-three, but
he spoke of being tired of "this weary life," maintaining that
he could "contentedly & gladly resign it. . . . As for this world
I despair of ever making a figure in it. . . . I foresee that very
probably Poverty & Obscurity await me & I am, in some
measure prepared & daily preparing to meet & welcome them."
Small wonder then that Burns's poetry during this period was
often shot through with melancholy, despondency and guilt,

[30] Ritter, pp. 23–6. Ritter mentions other parallels which do not, however,
affect my general argument.   [31] *Letters*, I. 4–5.

and that in later life he drew on the experiences of these years in order to give expression to similar moods. His was by no means the hypochondria of the rich, who

> . . . when nae real ills perplex them,
> They mak enow themselves to vex them,[32]

but the voice at once of profound personal sorrow and of the dull misery of the mass of the people. To these years belong "Winter: A Dirge" (?1781), "Prayer under the Pressure of Violent Anguish" (1781–2), "Paraphrase of the First Psalm" (1781–2), "The Ninetieth Psalm Versified" (1781–2), "Raging Fortune" (1781–2), "A Prayer in the Prospect of Death" (1781–2), "Remorse" (?1783) and "Man was made to Mourn" (?1785).[33]

"Winter: A Dirge"[34] is probably the earliest of these pieces; indeed, it may quite possibly go back to an even earlier period than the Irvine venture. The obvious resemblance to much minor eighteenth-century nature poetry does not mean that the poem is entirely derivative, for it reflects Burns's own delight in the winter scene—and this despite the funereal implications of the sub-title. Characteristically, the poem's scope includes the whole of nature; it embraces animals as well as scenery, thus demonstrating that here, as in so many other works, Burns was not merely a typical Scot but a typical man of the Enlightenment. The last stanza appears to accept the doctrine of predestination, which he was already disposed to reject in the early 1780s:

> Thou Pow'r Supreme, whose mighty scheme
> These woes of mine fulfil, . . .[35]

In the "Prayer under the Pressure of violent Anguish"[36] there is a development away from the orthodox determination

---

[32] "The Twa Dogs": 1. 9 (318).

[33] Here I have followed H. & H.'s dating.　　　　　　[34] 1. 134 (374).

[35] David Sillar, in his recollections of the poet's Tarbolton days, says that Burns had a reputation for theological heresy in the 1780s (R. Chambers, *Life and Works of Burns*, henceforth cited as Chambers, 4 vols., Edinburgh and London 1856, 1. 46). According to the autobiographical letter to Moore (*Letters*, 1. 112), Burns held heretical opinions even before this time. It follows, therefore, that there is no doctrinal reason why "Winter: A Dirge" could not have been written before 1781.　　　　　　[36] 1. 233 (406).

to bear evils merely because they are God's will; Burns's treatment of the problem of evil contains undertones of revolt. He does not whine or grovel in front of the Almighty, but faces up to Him like a man :

> But, if I must afflicted be
> To suit some wise design,
> Then man my soul with firm resolves
> To bear and not repine !

The "Paraphrase of the First Psalm"[37] begins with sentiments that not even Holy Willie himself could quarrel with, only to end in its turn on a note for which there is no authority in Burns's models :

> For why? that God the good adore
> Hath giv'n them peace and rest,
> But hath decreed that wicked men
> Shall ne'er be truly blest.[38]

[37] I. 232 (406).

[38] In the A.V. the fifth and sixth verses of Ps. I are as follows :

Therefore the ungodly shall not stand in the judgment, nor sinners in the congregation of the righteous.

For the Lord knoweth the way of the righteous : but the way of the ungodly shall perish.

In the metrical version, with which Burns would of course be familiar, the sixth verse runs :

> For why? the way of godly men
> Unto the Lord is known :
> Whereas the way of wicked men
> Shall quite be overthrown.

Alexander Scott renders the same passage thus :

> For air and lait the Lord weill wait
> The wayiss of vertewus men ;
> And every gait off wicket stait
> Sall perreiss owt of ken.

And the version in Allan Ramsay's *The Ever Green, being a Collection of Scots Poems, Wrote by the Ingenious before 1600*, 2 vols., Edinburgh 1724, II. 216, is in similar strain :

> For quhy? The Lord quha beirs Record,
> He knaws the richteous Conversation ay,
> But godles Gaits, quhilk he so haits,
> Sall quickly perreiss, and bot Dout decay.

In Burns's version God has "decreed" what fate shall befall the wicked, in true Calvinistic fashion ; but at the same time the sinner does not perish, and his punishment seems confined to this world ; at least, there seems to be some ambiguity attached to "shall ne'er be truly blest."

And "The Ninetieth Psalm Versified"[39] is not illumined
by any faith in a future existence with which to comfort the
afflicted spirit; indeed, its mood is strangely reminiscent of
Thomas Hardy brooding over the hopelessness of human
life in face of the malevolence of an inscrutable fate. In "A
Prayer in the Prospect of Death,"[40] the poet pleads that God
made Robert Burns's passions, and therefore if Robert abuses
them the blame is in part God's. Evidently the attempt to get
free of Calvinist orthodoxy played a not inconsiderable part in
Burns's melancholy, just as it did in the case of his older and
more aristocratic contemporary, James Boswell.[41] In this poem
his theology seems to have developed further in the direction
of a liberal deism. God is now all-good, a God of forgiveness
rather than of vengeance, but in spite of that His presence is
still, in the first stanza, a "dread" one. In "Stanzas written in
Prospect of Death,"[42] dread is completely victorious; the
Liberal God has turned back into an "angry god," an Avenger.
The poet is as "guilty of guilt" as any of Kafka's heroes or any
young existentialist; he is plainly terrified by the image of the
Deity armed with his "sin-avenging rod." If God forgives him
and his life is spared, he knows that in all probability he will sin
again. God exerts a "controlling power" over the vagaries of
the material universe; and Burns prays the "great Governor
of all below" to use it to help him to confine those "headlong
furious passions" of his. Behind these "Stanzas," indeed behind
this whole group of poems, there lies a conflict between reason,
society, and the moral law (identified with God), on the one
hand, and, on the other, the passions, which played the same
part in Burns's experience as did "the dark gods" in that of
D. H. Lawrence and his followers in the nineteen-twenties and
thirties; in essence it is the same struggle as that which runs
through Hardy's *Tess*, and although Burns does not in these
poems come out on the side of the passions, the sombre mood
is nevertheless very similar to Hardy's. None of these devotional poems is specifically Christian; in "A Prayer in
Prospect of Death," for example, Burns rests all his hope on

[39] I. 234 (407).   [40] I. 135 (375).
[41] See Boswell's journals, *passim*; *e.g.*, esp., *Boswell in Holland 1763-4*, ed.
F. A. Pottle, London 1952, pp. 88, 178-9, 188, 191, 196, 307.   [42] I. 229 (404).

the Father's goodness, not on redemption by Christ, and his thought seems to move from an almost Jewish Old-Testament religion to "the daring path Spinoza trod,"[43] without any intermediary stage of Christian conviction. Sometimes Burns did feel drawn towards the *personality* of Christ, that "amiablest of characters";[44] but he did not give memorable poetical expression to such emotions. In Burns's imagination, the Devil was always a far more vital symbol than Christ.

In "Tho' Fickle Fortune,"[45] an eight-lined poem of this group, the buckler or trust is neither a fearsome nor a forgiving God but the poet's own heart; and should prudence fail to bring success, then the remedy is a stoical and non-religious resignation :

> Then come, Misfortune, I bid thee welcome—
> I'll meet thee with an undaunted mind !

Some of these "hypochondriacal" pieces are poetically worthless, but the ones written in psalm metre are real poems in their own right, although they are little known. "Raging Fortune,"[46] for example, presents the contrast between innocence and experience, between simple happiness and a life blighted by Fortune, in terms of traditional pastoral imagery, and it does it extremely well :

> My stem was fair, my bud was green,
>   My blossom sweet did blow ;
> The dew fell fresh, the sun rose mild,
>   And made my branches grow.
>
> But luckless Fortune's northern storms
>   Laid a' my blossoms low !
> But luckless Fortune's northern storms
>   Laid a' my blossoms low ![47]

---

[43] Burns used the phrase, which comes from John Brown, "Essay on Satire," in writing to James Candlish, 21 Mar. 1787, in *Letters*, 1. 79.

[44] Cp. below, p. 47.   [45] iv. 6 (83).   [46] iv. 7 (84).

[47] Burns may have been indebted to "Ossian" for the central image of "Raging Fortune," but "The Flowers of the Forest" was a more likely stimulus (Ritter, pp. 33–4). "Raging Fortune" was originally intended for an air of Burns's own composition "in the old Scotch style," not for a psalm tune. See *Commonplace Book*, p. 42.

"Man was made to Mourn,"[48] the finest fruit of Burns's melancholy, is often sneered at by those who like to wrap their political antipathies in an aesthetic garb. One may agree that it is rhetorical, but that does not mean that its emotions are necessarily false, any more than the rhetoric of Dryden's plays or of Shakespeare's *Henry VI* or *Richard III* is evidence of artistic insincerity. The poem is an excellent example of Burns's relation to his sources. Writing to Mrs Dunlop on 16 Aug. 1788, Burns mentions an old grand-uncle who had gone blind, and whose "most voluptuous enjoyment was to sit down & cry, while my Mother would sing the simple old song of, *The Life & Age of Man.*"[49] The song began thus :

> 'Twas in the sixteenth-hunder year
>   Of God and fifty-three
> Frae Christ was born, that bought us dear,
>   As writings testifie ;
> On January the sixteenth day,
>   As I did lie alone,
> With many a sob and sigh did say,
>   Ah ! man was made to moan ![50]

According to Gilbert Burns, "He [Robert] used to remark to me, that he could not well conceive a more mortifying picture of human life than a man seeking work. In casting about in his mind how this sentiment might be brought forward, the elegy *Man was made to Mourn* was composed."[51] It is out of such materials, then, that the poem is made—recollections of a suffering grand-uncle, his own miseries, and the tribulations of practically the whole population of Ayrshire in the difficult years 1781–4.

It is a commonplace that subsistence agriculture cannot provide a surplus large enough to withstand drought or hurricane or flood; and during the eighteenth century Scotland experienced conditions of near famine in 1740, 1756, 1778, 1796, and 1799–1800, years when the weather was more than ordinarily atrocious. These crises were a legacy from the primitive feudal system of cultivation, but they had the incidental effect of furthering the agrarian revolution by bankrupting marginal

---

[48] I. 130 (372).
[49] *Letters*, I. 246.
[50] As quoted in I. 373.
[51] Chambers, I. 158.

farmers and consolidating the position of those who remained. One of the worst of these spells of bad weather took place in the years 1782–3, immediately after Robert's return from Irvine and before his father's death.[52]

On 21 Jun. 1783 Robert described the economic state of Ayrshire in these terms :

> Our m[arkets] are exceedingly high; oatmeal 17 & 18d. p^r peck, & [not to] be got even at that price. We have indeed been [pr]etty well supplied with quantities of white pease from England & elsewhere, but that resource is likely to fail us; & what will become of us then, particularly the very poorest sort, Heaven only knows.—This country, till of late, was flourishing incredibly in the Manufactures of Silk, Lawn & Carpet Weaving, and we are still carrying on a good deal in that way but much reduced from what it was; we had also a fine trade in the Shoe way, but now entirely ruined, & hundreds driven to a starving condition on account of it.—Farming is also at a very low ebb with us.[53]

Over thirty years later, Sir John Sinclair could remember how widespread the general pessimism had been. In a paragraph which makes special mention of Burns's county, Sinclair says :

> Even in Ayrshire the snow fell before the corns were cut down; the greatest part were in the fields, and much destroyed by frost. . . . This calamity . . . occasioned, in some districts, a great decrease of population; in other a diminution of births in the succeeding year. It increased the numbers of the poor; impaired the constitution of multitudes in the lower orders, and entailed on them consumption and other fatal disorders. Even where no remarkable sickness followed, the hardships and difficulties to which the people were reduced by such a calamity, made them neglect those rural amusements in which they formerly delighted, and to contract a dull and melancholy look, which continued for several years after.[54]

The consumption which killed William Burnes was probably

---

[52] J. E. Handley, *Scottish Farming in the Eighteenth Century*, London 1953, p. 35.
[53] R. B. to [J. Burness], 21 Jun. 1783, in *Letters*, I. 15.
[54] Sinclair, *Analysis of the Statistical Account of Scotland*, Edinburgh 1823, PT. II, Appendix II ("On the Famines"), pp. 40 ff.

a legacy of this crisis, and so too were Robert's most pessimistic poems, of which "Man was made to Mourn" is a late but outstanding example. Though the first stanza, which sets the scene, perhaps contains an echo of Shenstone, it also looks forward to Wordsworth:

> I spied a man, whose aged step
>   Seem'd weary, worn with care,
> His face was furrow'd o'er with years,
>   And hoary was his hair.[55]

The second stanza, on the contrary, looks backwards to a typically medieval conception—the Seven Ages of Man. It would seem that Burns had got from his mother or perhaps from the old grand-uncle himself the platitudes that young men, lecherous and full of pride, are ruled by pleasure, while the middle-aged have greed for money as their ruling passion. (He could equally well have gained such ideas from Pope,[56] or Shakespeare,[57] or from simple observation.) But when, in the third stanza, the old man points out the moors

> 'Where hundreds labour to support
>   A haughty lordling's pride,'

he is voicing an anti-aristocratic conviction which might not have been phrased so bluntly in the Middle Ages, except in periods of peasant revolt. Even in Queen Anne's days, although the pride of magnates was a stock butt for scribblers, it was not (Swift excepted) customary to deal so ruthlessly with economic exploitation. The conventional description of human life as a progress from licentious youth to neglected old

---

[55] Cp. Shenstone, Elegy VII, sts. iv–v:
> As led by Orwell's winding banks I stray'd . . . .
> Instant, a grateful form appear'd confest;
> White were his locks. . . .

[56] *Essay on Man*, ii, ll. 275–82.

[57] *As You Like It*, ii. vii, 139–66. And cp. Shenstone, Elegy VII, st. vi:
> 'Stranger,' he said, 'amid this peeling rain,
> Benighted, lonesome, whither wouldst thou stray?
> Does wealth, or power, thy weary step constrain?
> Reveal thy wish, and let me point the way.'

The parallel was noted by J. Logie Robertson ("Hugh Haliburton") *Furth in Field*, London 1894, p. 258.

age is used again in the seventh stanza to bring out the contrast between the few who revel in luxury (not all the rich, be it noted, are "truly blest") and the many who are afflicted by physical want. Burns does not confine his gaze to Ayrshire or even to Scotland; his centre of perception is "a small room with large windows"[58] looking out upon the sufferings of the whole world, for he speaks of "crowds in ev'ry land" who learn the universal lesson "that Man was made to mourn." Spiritual woes, however, are even worse than bodily ills, and our greatest miseries are often self-inflicted ones. In the seventh stanza an age-old paradox obsesses the poet:

> 'Many and sharp the num'rous ills
>   Inwoven with our frame!
> More pointed still we make ourselves
>   Regret, remorse, and shame!
> And Man, whose heav'n-erected face
>   The smiles of love adorn,—
> Man's inhumanity to man
>   Makes countless thousands mourn!'

The thought is that of a meditative eighteenth-century Lear sharing something of Blake's understanding that the manacles which prevent the reign of universal love are at least in part "mind-forged."[59]

The eighth stanza is the centre of the whole poem—the image of a man pleading with an employer for work:

> 'See yonder poor, o'erlabour'd wight,
>   So abject, mean, and vile,
> Who begs a brother of the earth
>   To give him leave to toil;

[58] This phrase is the title of a poem by Allen Curnow.
[59] And cp. Young, *Night Thoughts*, "Night III, ll. 211–8; v. l. 163; and VIII, ll. 102–4):

> Man, hard of heart to man! . . . .
> Man is to man the sorest, surest ill.
> Inhumanity is caught from men.
> Turn the world's history; what find we there?
>   man's revenge . . . .
> And endless inhumanities on man.

These parallels are noted by Ritter, p. 59. In this, as in so many other poems, Burns owes as much to the English literary tradition as he does to that of his own country.

And see his lordly fellow-worm
The poor petition spurn,
Unmindful, tho' a weeping wife
And helpless offspring mourn.'

Burns here passes to what is new and even revolutionary in the poem. Not only were such scenes common during the contemporary agrarian revolution in Ayrshire, but they are typical of the lives of many who have worked for wages in the last hundred and fifty years in country and in town. The reader is here presented with a specifically working-class predicament, perhaps for the first time in our literature. It is significant that Gilbert Burns reported his brother as tracing the origin of the poem, not to the plight of a small farmer about to be evicted, so much as to the misery of the unemployed wage-earner : the poem deals with a situation common to both classes.[60]

This central and all-important eighth stanza is content simply to present the human truth of the situation ; strangely enough (at least to a modern reader, unused perhaps to eighteenth-century conventions) the rhetoric does not in the least detract from the starkness of the picture. The following stanzas fit the growing pains of a new economic system into the pattern of universal human suffering. The ninth stanza in particular puts the independence theme (so common in Burns) fairly and squarely in its historical context, for personal integrity appears as the direct opposite of a society dominated by landlords :

'If I'm design'd yon lordling's slave—
By Nature's law design'd—
Why was an independent wish
E'er planted in my mind ?
If not, why am I subject to
His cruelty, or scorn ?
Or why has Man the will and pow'r
To make his fellow mourn ?'[61]

[60] See above, p. 17 ; and cp. Chambers, 1. 158.

[61] If we did not have Burns's own statement (to [Mrs Dunlop], 28 Apr. 1788, in *Letters*, 1. 220) that he had not read Dryden until early in 1788 it would be tempting to follow Ritter's suggestion (p. 60) that the following lines from *Aureng-Zebe* (III. i) are a source of this stanza :

Why am I thus to slavery designed,
And yet am cheated with a freeborn mind ?

At first sight it might seem as if Burns were simply attacking
feudalism, from the standpoint of the middle class. But in
actual fact the landowners in lowland Scotland in the eighteenth
century were simultaneously both feudal and capitalist. They
seemed feudal to the urban middle classes, who tended to
oppose them politically; but they appeared in an altogether
different light to their tenants, since they were the main agents
of a change which substituted production for the market for
subsistence agriculture. Behind the calculating money-grubber
stood the landlord, in the countryside at least—as Burns well
knew from the events of his father's last years. When he opposes
independence to landlordism, Burns is therefore taking a stand
not against one form of class oppression only, but implicitly
against all exploitation of one group of people by another. It
is the agricultural labourer as well as the market-conscious
tenant farmer who speaks in the ninth stanza; indeed, the
whole poem is based on feelings common to both classes.

The tenth stanza attempts to qualify the unrelieved sombre-
ness of Burn's vision by the suggestion that perhaps the "I" of
the poem is biassed, and there are after all some compensatory
joys in human life. It is a good instance of conversational
common-sense reasoning in verse, lightening the picture in
preparation for the greater shadow of the final stanza:

> 'O Death! the poor man's dearest friend,
>   The kindest and the best!
> Welcome the hour my agèd limbs
>   Are laid with thee at rest!
> The great, the wealthy fear thy blow,
>   From pomp and pleasure torn;
> But oh! a blest relief to those
>   That weary-laden mourn!'[62]

[62] Cp. Ecclesiasticus, XLI. 1–2:
> O death, how bitter is the remembrance of thee to a man
>   that liveth at rest in his possessions,
> Unto the man that hath nothing to vex him, and that
>   hath prosperity in all things:
> Yea, unto him that is yet able to receive meat!
> O death, acceptable is thy sentence unto the needy,
> And unto him whose strength faileth, that is now in
>   the last age,
> And is vexed with all things,
> And to him that despaireth, and hath lost patience!   (cont. opposite

The mood is only superficially akin to that of an upper-class melancholiac like Burns's older contemporary, James Boswell. "He ruminates upon all the evils that can happen to man," says Boswell of the Hypochondriac, "and wonders that he has ever had a moment's tranquillity, as he never was nor ever can be secure. . . . In all other distresses there is the relief of hope. But it is the peculiar woe of melancholy, that hope hides itself in the dark cloud." Thus far, Boswell and Burns might seem to share similar feelings. But there is a profound and dismal pity behind Burns's poem which implies an aim he often stated in his letters : to "wipe away all tears from all eyes." Burns's gloom is humanitarian, Boswell's destructive. The "corrosive imagination" of Boswell's Hypochondriac "destroys to his own view all that he contemplates. . . . Even his humanity towards the distressed is apt to be made of no avail. For as he cannot even have the idea of happiness, it appears to him immaterial whether they be relieved or not."[63] Burns's imagination, on the contrary, is corrosive only of hypocrisy and social evil; even his depression, his melancholia, resembles that of the nineteenth-century working class, evoking comparison with *The Ragged Trousered Philanthropists*[64] rather than with *The Anatomy of Melancholy*.

"Man was made to Mourn" has been unjustly decried by readers who feel that Burns's vernacular poems are the only ones that count. It is in my opinion one of his best pieces, not-

Another possible source is Goldsmith's *Vicar of Wakefield*, VOL. II, ch. x : "Then let us take comfort now, for we shall soon be at our journey's end ; we shall soon lay down the heavy burthen laid by heaven upon us ; and though death, the only friend of the wretched, for a little while mocks the weary traveller with the view, and like his horizon, still flies before him ; yet the time will certainly and shortly come, when we shall cease from our toil ; when the luxurious great ones of the world shall no more tread us to the earth ; when we shall think with pleasure of our sufferings below ; when we shall be surrounded with all our friends, or such as deserved our friendship ; when our bliss shall be unutterable, and still, to crown all, unending."

But Burns has nothing of the Christian comfort of Goldsmith's conclusion. His ideas—despite all parallels, even with the Bible itself—remain fresh, because they sprang in the first instance from his own experience, which is today most often echoed in the lives of the landless labourers and poor peasants of some European and most Oriental countries.

[63] *Boswell's Column*, ed. M. Bailey, London 1951, pp. 209–10.
[64] R. Tressell, *The Ragged Trousered Philanthropists*, unabridged edn., London 1955, p. 358.

withstanding its Scots-English diction; and it gains rather than loses from the repetition of certain key words, such as "pleasure" (three times), "youthful" (four times), "poor" (four times), "weary" (four times), "age" or "aged" (three times), or such combinations as "prest with cares and woes" or "with cares and sorrows worn." Much of our delight in reading it comes from these recurring, and partially varied, sounds and concepts.

When "Man was made to mourn" has been used four times in the refrain, and thus established as normal for the poem, the variations begin. Because of our slight surprise at not meeting the expected phrase, the very first of these ("Makes countless thousands mourn") is the most effective of all; and afterwards Burns is careful never to return to the original refrain. Instead he gives us: "And helpless offspring mourn"; "To make his fellow mourn?"; "To comfort those that mourn!"; "That weary-laden mourn!" Furthermore, the poem demonstrates Burns's mastery of verbal music in Scots-English, which is just as great as in other poems where Braid Scots predominates.[65]

The mood of "Man was made to Mourn" has much in common with that which inspired such English poems of the century as Johnson's "Vanity of Human Wishes" and Gray's "Elegy"; but Burns's universality consists in the fact that he looks backwards and forwards at one and the same time— backwards to Ecclesiasticus, and forward to such writers as Robert Tressell.

[65] For further details, see below, Appendix I, § I, pp. 352–3.

II

Calvin's Well

WHAT is more petty, more embarrassingly local, than the wind of controversy that will sometimes blow through a vestry or convulse a church committee, while lewd outsiders and hardened scoffers split their sides at the antics of the Lord's anointed and the follies of the faithful? Can one imagine anything less inherently likely to produce great literature than such parish squabbling? Yet Trollope's Barchester novels (not to speak of Galt's *Annals of the Parish*) were made out of such material, and so were Burns's anti-Calvinist poems. These achieve the anatomy of a nation's mind, and something in addition; for there is in their scenes and characters an element typical not just of Scotland but of the entire modern world from the seventeenth century to the present day and from Chatanooga to Kamchatka. Hypocrisy has come to supplement Pride and Lust and Greed and the others as the eighth Deadly Sin; and nowhere, not even in Molière's *Tartuffe* or Balzac's *Comédie humaine* can one find a more out-and-out dissection of dissimulation and pretence than in Burns's Kirk satires.

Referring to his boyhood and adolescence, Robert wrote:

Polemical divinity about this time was putting the country half-mad; and I, ambitious of shining in conversation parties on Sundays between sermons, funerals, &c. used in a few years more to puzzle Calvinism with so much heat and indiscretion that I raised a hue and cry of heresy against me which has not ceased to this hour.[1]

"A few years more" refers to the period of the Kirk satires. These broadsides and propaganda salvoes were early works, written contemporaneously with the first epistles, and show Burns in agreement with the very landlords whom on other

[1] To Moore, 2 Aug. 1787, in *Letters*, I. 107.

issues he attacked. It was the "paughty feudal thane" who as a rule supported the liberal clergy, while the humble cotter preferred the narrow zeal of traditional Calvinism. Politically, Burns was often a democrat; ecclesiastically, he was on the side of the minority—"the best people." In each case, his attitude seemed to him to be sane, logical, and consonant with right reason, even although it meant giving simultaneous support to two mutually antagonistic social groups; but the point is worth bearing in mind by those who like to think of history as always moving forward along a straight arterial road with the wheel firmly in the grip of the "Progressive Forces" and the reactionaries bound and gagged in the back seat. In this case it was the democrats who were against freedom, and the hereditary landlords who stood for enlightenment.

The dogmatic Calvinism of the Kirk has not only seared deeply into the Scottish character; it has also shaped, moulded and tempered that protective armour which most Scots use to conceal the violent irrationality of their being, so that even today business men and shop-stewards from north of the Border share an inner passion and an outer hardness that make them seem different from their southern neighbours. Fundamental to Calvinist theory is the conviction of the absolute and all-encompassing dominion of God, to know whom, in the sense of glorifying and enjoying Him, is man's overmastering duty and the purpose of his life on earth. Man, poor weak creature that he is, is in himself utterly corrupt and supremely culpable; this is a necessary consequence of the Fall, when Adam infected all his posterity with deadly pestilence, so that even the newly-born are corrupted, not by another's error, but by their own innate sin. "For," to quote Calvin's own inimitable words, "although they have not yet produced the fruits of their own unrighteousness, they have the seed implanted in them. Nay, their whole nature is, as it were, a seed-bed of sin, and therefore cannot but be odious and abominable to God."[2] In the language of modern genetics, sin is an inherited, not an acquired, characteristic, and its natural and inevitable consequence is the wrath of God.

---

[2] Calvin, *Institutes of the Christian Religion*, henceforth cited as *Inst.*, II. i, 8 (tr. Beveridge, London 1949, I. 217–8).

In the words of Thomas Boston, whose *Fourfold State* was a popular work of divinity among Scottish laymen all through the eighteenth century, "Everything in God is perfect of its kind, and therefore no wrath can be so perfectly fierce as His ; the wonted force of the rage of lions, leopards, and she-bears deprived of their whelps, is not sufficient to give a scanty view of the power of the wrath of God."[3] Although much has been written by modern critics and social historians about Calvinist hell-fire preaching, it does not seem to be generally realised that true Calvinism did not assert the literal existence of material torments. Boston, in the passage just quoted, uses lions and leopards and she-bears in a figurative sense only, and Calvin himself is most explicit on this point :

> Moreover, as language cannot describe the severity of the divine vengeance on the reprobate, their pains and torments are figured to us by corporeal things, such as darkness, wailing and gnashing of teeth, unextinguishable fire, the ever-gnawing worm. . . . And whenever the prophets strike terror by means of corporeal figures, although in respect of our dull understanding there is no extravagance in their language, yet they give preludes of the future judgment in the sun and the moon, and the whole fabric of the world.[4]

Naturally, perhaps inevitably, the laity and even some of the clergy themselves came to hold that the Deity's most magnificent and all-perfect wrath was actually manifest in physical torments that took place in an enormous torture chamber, known as Hell. The Rev. J. Mackinlay, a contemporary and indeed a victim of Burns's, whose induction to the Laigh Kirk in Kilmarnock was the signal for "The Ordination,"[5] appeared to believe in a Hell of a very literal sort. One Sunday, before he was due to arrive to preach his sermon, a seat broke, and there was a rending noise. When somebody called out that the church was collapsing, the entire congregation rushed in a panic for the doors, with the result that thirty persons were killed in the crush. Next week Mackinlay

---

[3] Boston, *Human Nature in its Fourfold State*, Edinburgh 1720, p. 126 ; quoted in H. G. Graham, *The Social Life of Scotland in the Eighteenth Century*, henceforth cited as Graham, 2 vols., London 1899, II. 134–5.

[4] *Inst.*, III. xxv, 12 (Beveridge, II. 275–6). [5] See below, pp. 62 ff.

preached a sermon in which he presented the calamity as God's
judgment on the sins of the congregation, asking his hearers to
take thought on what would have happened to them if they
had been among the victims of the accident. "Would you have
been with Lazarus in heaven, enjoying the felicity of the
righteous," he asked, "or with the rich man in Hell, enduring
that terrible misery, which shall ever increase, and know no
end ?" There is no indication that Mackinlay did not conceive
of both Heaven and Hell as places, or of the bliss and torment
there endured as essentially physical states.[6]

Hell as conceived by the Rev. Ralph Erskine appears to
have been of the same essentially corporeal kind. Preaching
in Dunfermline in 1727, some sixty years before Mackinlay,
Erskine said :

> O what a bed is there ! no feathers, but fire ; no friends, but
> furies ; no ease, but fetters ; no daylight, but darkness ; no
> clock to pass away the time, but endless eternity ; fire eternal is
> always burning and never dying away. O who can endure ever-
> lasting flame ? It shall not be quenched night or day. The
> smoke thereof shall go up for ever and ever. The wicked shall
> be crowded like bricks in a fiery furnace. Good Lord, what a
> world of miseries hath seized on miserable sinners ! Their
> executioners are devils ; the dungeon fills ; the earth stands
> open ; the furnace is burning to receive you. O, how will these
> poor souls quake and tremble ! Every part of their body will
> bear a part in their woeful ditty : eyes weeping, hands wringing,
> breasts beating, heads aching with voices crying.[7]

Eternal punishment of the sort which popular preachers
translated into images of fire and brimstone for the edification
of the vulgar, but whose real nature was essentially spiritual,
was in Calvin's view the just fate of all humanity ; but in His
infinite mercy God had decided to save—not the whole human
race, but a few only, known as "the elect"—and to confer upon
these chosen ones an eternity of blessedness. After all, it is a
matter of daily experience that some men have faith while
others do not ; and faith does not proceed in the first instance

[6] Memoir prefaced to J. Mackinlay, *Select Sermons*, Kilmarnock 1843 ; quoted
in A. B. Jamieson, *Burns and Religion*, Cambridge 1931, pp. 19–20.

[7] Ralph Erskine, *Christ's Coming in Clouds to Judgment*, quoted in Graham, II. 135.

from the believer, but is on the contrary the gift of God, bestowed on whom it pleases Him to save.

> We have not [says Calvin] the least hesitation to admit what Paul strenuously maintains, that all, without exception, are depraved and given over to wickedness. . . . Therefore, while we all labour naturally under the same disease, those only recover health to whom the Lord is pleased to put forth his healing hand. The others whom, in just judgment, he passes over, pine and rot away till they are consumed. And this is the only reason why some persevere to the end, and others, after beginning their course, fall away. Perseverance is the gift of God, which he does not lavish promiscuously on all, but imparts to whom he pleases. If it is asked how the difference arises—why some steadily persevere, and others prove deficient in steadfastness—we can give no other reason than that the Lord, by his mighty power, strengthens and sustains the former, so that they perish not, while he does not furnish the same assistance to the latter, but leaves them to be monuments of instability.[8]

It is "by the mercy of God, not their own exertions," that believers "are predestinated, called, and justified."[9]

It follows logically and inevitably from Calvin's premises that those who do not have faith in God, who do not experience union with Christ, who do not live good lives (for it is a sign of God's grace when a man is enabled to act virtuously), have been predestined from all eternity to perpetual damnation. Election and reprobation are facts, according to Calvin; they are what he himself was forced to recognise as a "horrible decree (*decretum horribile*)";[10] and they are attested by many well-known passages in Scripture which cannot be explained away on any other supposition.[11] "Ye have not chosen me but I have chosen you." "Many are called but few are chosen." "All that the Father hath given me shall come unto me; and him that cometh unto me I will in no wise cast out." "No man can come to me except the Father draw him." "So then God hath mercy on whom he will; and whom he will he hardeneth." "That which Israel seeketh for, that he obtained not; but the

[8] *Inst.*, ii. v. 3 (Beveridge, i. 275).   [9] *Inst.*, ii. v. 2 (Beveridge, i. 274).
[10] Quoted in J. S. Whale, *The Protestant Tradition*, henceforth cited as Whale, Cambridge 1955, p. 142.   [11] Calvin, *Inst.*, iii. xxi–v (Beveridge, ii. 202–58).

elect obtained it, and the rest were hardened." But the most terrible of all the quotations which can be used to buttress the doctrine of absolute predestination, a text which seems full of the grandeur and awesomeness of original Calvinism itself, is perhaps the following: "Jacob have I loved, but Esau have I hated."[12]

Even the elect of God could not be assured the blessings of eternal life without a bloody sacrifice. The victim's sufferings had at the very least to equal those which the elect would have had to endure if God had not decided to bestow His grace upon them, although according to some—a minority group within the Scottish Church—Christ died for all men, not just for the chosen, and therefore the suffering experienced by Him must have been "equal to that which humanity past, present, and to come deserve to bear"; therefore (according to the smaller party), he went through agony for the reprobate, those who were in any case predestined to eternal torment, as well as for the elect. Furthermore, "this transcendent or infinite vicarious agony could only be borne by One who was at once God and man; for the very least sin being committed against an infinite God is therefore infinite in its guilt, and deserves punishment infinite in its extent."[13]

In all varieties of Calvinism there is a special relationship between the elect and Christ. A man could not know he was one of the chosen until he had "gotten a grip of Christ," an operation which it was impossible to carry out without the direct aid of the Holy Spirit. When the believer is at one with Christ, he feels an inner quickening of spiritual life which assures him of his salvation, an intense emotional reinforcement of his previous intellectual conviction. Not only does he know that he is saved; he feels it in his bones. It is by means of faith, too, that he "receives justification" (i.e. becomes righteous in the judgment of God) and his sins are forgiven him. Christ's righteousness is imputed to him "for reconciliation and eternal salvation," which constitutes his "effectual calling" to salvation; and by these means he is kept faithful and holy to the end of his days.[14]

---

[12] Cp. Whale, *loc. cit.*   [13] Graham, II. 141–2.
[14] Calvin, *Inst.*, III. xiii. 1–3; xxiv. 1–3 (Beveridge, II. 68–70, 240–3).

Logically, these doctrines are open to a terrible perversion :
the idea that once God has chosen him, it does not matter a jot
whether a man lives a good life or not—he will still be saved
because he is one of the elect, predestined to that honour from
before the beginning of things. And the repetition in sermon
after sermon and tract after tract that mere good works were
of no value by themselves could only serve to strengthen that
impression. Persistent preaching of the value of moral duties
was given the name of "legality" ; and so much was it detested
that it was sometimes declared to be "the cleanest road to
Hell." Towards the end of the century, Adam Gib stoutly
maintained that "the immediate preaching of moral duties is
quite vain. Gospel hearers should be called to the performance
of duties only in the way of betaking themselves to Christ by
faith. It is calling them to what is absolutely impracticable and
leading to eternal perdition."[15]

There is, however, nothing in the original fount and origin
of the doctrine, nothing in Calvin's *Institutes* themselves, to
warrant the idea that a man may sin as much as he pleases—
especially if he takes good care not to be found out. On the
contrary,

> God works in his elect in two ways : inwardly, by his Spirit ;
> outwardly, by his Word. By his Spirit illuminating their minds,
> and training their hearts to the practice of righteousness, he
> makes them new creatures, while, by his Word, he stimulates
> them to long and seek for this renovation[16]. . . . When God erects
> his kingdom in them [the godly], he, by means of his Spirit,
> curbs their will, that it may not follow its natural bent, and be
> carried hither and thither by vagrant lusts ; bends, frames,
> trains, and guides it according to the rule of his justice, so as to
> incline it to righteousness and holiness, and stablishes it and
> strengthens it by the energy of his Spirit, that it may not stumble
> or fall.[17]

A good life is a sign that a man is of the chosen : "To wish is
from nature, to wish well is from grace." Once faith exists,
good works and therefore duties follow as an inevitable conse-

---

[15] Cp. Ralph Erskine, *Gospel Sonnets*, and Adam Gib, *Sacred Contemplations*,
Edinburgh 1786, p. 354, quoted in Graham, II. 144.
[16] Calvin, *Inst.*, II. v, 5 (Beveridge, I. 277).   [17] II. v, 14 (Beveridge, I. 287).

quence; the Christian life "is laden with responsibilities, and these extend to every task and every hour."[18]

In spite of the fact that their distortions of the original doctrine were against the general tenor of the *Institutes*, certain seventeenth-century theologians actually and in all seriousness made the monstrous deductions which appear in the caricatures of Calvinism purveyed by its opponents. One writer of this sort was E. Fisher, whose *Marrow of Divinity*, published in England as early as 1646, exhorts the faithful in these terms:

> No, assure yourself that your God in Christ will never un-son you, nor yet as touching your eternal salvation will He love you even a whit the less *though you commit never so many* and great sins; for this is certain, that as no good in you did move Him to justify you and give you eternal life, so no evil in you can move Him to take it away being once given.[19]

In 1720, this seventeenth-century tract was republished by certain of the more uncompromising of the Scottish clergy, only to be promptly condemned by the General Assembly of the Church of Scotland as containing doctrine unsound and dangerous. One of its heresies, according to the Assembly, was the view that personal holiness is not necessary to salvation, since it is the fact of election alone that counts. Also rejected was the view that a believer (by definition, one of the Chosen) does not allow himself to be motivated by the fear of punishment or the hope of reward, together with the equally pernicious opinion that the elect need not necessarily frame their conduct in accordance with God's Law. It is only fair to notice that the "Marrow Men" denied that such doctrines were in the book; but whether they were present or not is immaterial to the reader of Burns. The important thing is that they were rejected lock, stock and barrel by the supreme governing body of the Kirk sixty-five years before Burns wrote "Holy Willie's Prayer" and thirty-nine years before his birth.[20]

It follows, therefore, that those writers are wrong who claim that Burns played a major part in destroying the narrower

---

[18] J. T. McNeill, *The History and Character of Calvinism*, henceforth cited as *Calvinism*, N.Y. 1954, p. 221.

[19] Fisher, *Marrow of Divinity*, ch. iii; quoted in Graham, II. 147.

[20] Graham, II. 146–7.

form of Scottish Calvinism—or, at least, its antinomian[21] distortions. Not only had the General Assembly, in 1720, declared
such views to be heretical, but in the ensuing half century the
gloomier side of orthodoxy itself had been increasingly criti-
cised by the liberal or "New Licht" party within the Church.
There is a sense in which all Scottish eighteenth-century
literature—sceptical philosophy and classical economics and
the works of the northern sentimentalists as well as vernacular
poetry—was a reaction against root-and-branch predestinarian
ideas. The Church came to be divided between two types of
preacher, the Evangelicals, or "high-fliers," who revelled in
emotion, and the Moderates, or "legal men," who gave out
allegedly dry, logical sermons about moral duties and were
supposed to be infected by deism. Cultural diffusion from
England and France and the material progress of society itself
alike compelled some relaxation of the old, grim faith, and
liberalism would doubtless have triumphed even if Robert
Burns had never existed.

Nevertheless, the opposite view—that Burns's ecclesiastical
satires had no political or social effects whatsoever—cannot
with justice be maintained. They reinforced existing pressures,
especially in Ayrshire, where orthodox ideas were particularly
tenacious, and they were influential among the lower classes,
always more fanatical than their "betters." The works of
Thomas Boston and other traditional divines were continually
reprinted throughout the century for the use of men and women
of all classes.[22] In 1762—to take one example only—a translation of Calvin's *Institutes* was published in Glasgow. There
were 481 subscribers, only a few of whom (namely some of the
66 whose occupations are not stated in the list at the end of the
book) may conceivably have been landed proprietors. Of the
rest, there was a minority of merchants, vintners, innkeepers,
excise-officers, farmers, and "writers" (solicitors), with one
solitary schoolmaster: but the great bulk of the subscribers
were tradesmen or artisans—farrier, skinner, weaver, wright,

[21] *Antinomianism*—the doctrine of those Protestant sectaries who maintained
that the moral law is not binding on Christians.
[22] See *Cambridge Bibliography of English Literature*, Cambridge 1940, II. 994, and
D.N.B., II. 886–8.

mason, candlemaker, "coalier" and hammerman were typical occupations. Although some subscribers came from as far afield as Edinburgh, the overwhelming majority were from Glasgow and its environs : clear evidence of the popularity of doctrinal Calvinism at mid-century among the population of an expanding merchant city, as well as of a certain lack of support for the old ideas amongst the educated and the upper classes.[23]

Moreover, it is comparatively easy to adopt a new philosophy intellectually, but surprisingly difficult to free oneself from the emotions and the taboos generated by previous beliefs and age-old traditions. Even among the most vociferous exponents of enlightenment, there must have been many doubts, many heart-searchings, many fits of despair generated by the consciousness of intolerable tensions. One can imagine the form such questioning would take. Perhaps the faith of our childhood is true after all, and our inability to make up our minds, our own character-defects, our loose living, our liberal and progressive opinions themselves, are nothing but the outward and visible marks of our damnation ? Possibly there is no hope for us, no hope whatsoever ? May not Boston and Calvin and Knox be proved right at the last day, and we be banished with Davy Hume and the mass of the unregenerate to an eternity of spiritual torture ?

There exist, fortunately, three records which are extremely revealing in this respect—James Boswell's journals, David Hume's letters, and Clarinda's letters to Burns. Boswell belonged to the same strongly Covenanting region as Burns himself, and was therefore exposed in childhood to similar pressures ; but the class from which he came experienced the Enlightenment at least a generation earlier than the peasantry. Consequently Boswell went through in the early 1760s much the same mental evolution that Burns was to undergo twenty years later—the rejection of old-style Calvinism in favour of a gentler and more humanitarian creed. Like Burns, he suffered from the "hypochondria," or recurrent fits of neurotic depression ; and—significantly enough—a surprisingly large

[23] See Calvin, *The Institution of the Christian Religion*, Bryce and Maclean, Glasgow 1762, pp. 782–6.

number of references to melancholy in the early journals or letters occur in close proximity to remarks about Presbyterianism. Thus on 15 May 1763 Boswell found that "the whole vulgar idea of the Presbyterian worship, made me very gloomy." Writing to his friend Temple on 22 May 1764, he exclaimed :

> What variety of woe have I not endured ! Above all, what have I not endured from dismal notions of religion ! . . . My misery is that, like my friend Dempster, I am convinced by the last book which I have read. I have a horror at myself for doubting thus. I think of death, and I shudder. You know how sadly I was educated. The meanest and most frightful Presbyterian notions at times recur upon me.

What these notions were is made plain in a slightly earlier letter of 23 Mar. 1764 :

> I have been tormenting myself with abstract questions concerning Liberty and Necessity, the attributes of the Deity, and the origin of Evil. I have truly a dark disposition. I must be patient. I may yet become quite clear. I have rather a hard task of it. I have no friend to whom I can disclose my anxieties and receive immediate relief.[24]

A letter of Hume's to Gilbert Elliot of Minto, dated 10 Mar. 1751, on the subject of an early draft of his *Dialogues*, seems to reflect a similar—though much milder—spiritual crisis :

> Any Propensity you imagine I have to the other Side [*i.e.* to scepticism], crept in upon me against my Will : And tis not long ago that I burn'd an old Manuscript Book, wrote before I was twenty [*i.e.*, presumably, in 1729–31] ; which contain'd, Page after Page, the gradual Progress of my Thoughts on that head. It began with an anxious Search after Arguments, to confirm the common Opinion : Doubts stole in, dissipated, return'd, were again dissipated, return'd again ; and it was a perpetual Struggle of a restless Imagination against Inclination, perhaps against Reason.[25]

[24] *Boswell's London Journal 1762–3,* ed. Pottle, London 1950, p. 259 ; *Boswell in Holland 1763–4,* ed. Pottle, London 1952, pp. 246, 190.
[25] To Gilbert Elliot of Minto, 10 March 1751, in *Letters of David Hume,* ed. J. Y. T. Greig, 2 vols., Oxford 1932, VOL. I, p. 154. That (as suggested to me by

His early arguments against faith are presented as the products of "Imagination," and the "common opinion" as being in tune with "Inclination," and perhaps with "Reason" : whereas in Boswell's case, it is the "dismal notions of religion" on which Imagination dwells, and "Reason" and "Inclination" which tend towards emancipation from traditional beliefs. As a young man, Hume appears to have been as prone to "the hypochondria" as Boswell or Burns, with this difference that—in keeping with his more equable temperament—his melancholy was much less violent than theirs :

> The small Distance betwixt me & perfect Health makes me the more uneasy in my present Situation. Tis a Weakness rather than a Lowness of Spirits which troubles me, & there seems to be as great a Difference betwixt my Distemper & common Vapors, as betwixt Vapors & Madness.[26]

In the very next paragraph Hume compares his condition in 1734 to the "dark night of the soul" so beloved of mystical writers. He insists on ascribing his symptoms of 1729–31, during the years of his emancipation from Calvinism, to physical causes ; but in view of his letter to Elliot and of the conversation reported by Boswell it seems possible that they were at least aggravated by mental struggles and feelings of repressed guilt of the sort which plagued many Scots of his century. If so, it is a further point that Hume has in common with Burns, and perhaps also with Byron, another Calvinist subject who had his moments of anxiety and despair.[27]

Mr R. L. C. Lorimer) the "common opinion" for which Hume in 1729–31 was trying to find arguments was in fact Calvinism is to some extent confirmed by Boswell's account of his conversation with Hume, on 7 Jul. 1776, only a few weeks before he died : "I asked him if he was not religious when he was young. He said he was, and he used to read the *Whole Duty of Man* [an anonymous but rather moderate Calvinist work first published in 1658] ; that he made an abstract from the Catalogue of vices at the end of it, and examined himself by this, leaving out Murder and Theft and such vices as he had no chance of committing, having no inclination to commit them." (*Private Papers of James Boswell*, ed. G. Scott and F. A. Pottle, Yale 1931, VOL. XII, pp. 227–32 ; quoted in *Hume's Dialogues concerning Natural Religion*, ed. N. Kemp Smith, Edinburgh, 1935, p. 76.) The mature Hume's detestation of Calvinism is well-known.

   [26] To [? Dr George Cheyne], Mar. or Apr. 1734, in Hume, *Letters*, I. 17.

   [27] Byron's feelings of guilt, unlike Hume's, appear to have been the reverse of "repressed." Thus, Lady Byron said to Henry Crabb Robinson, 5 Mar. 1855 : "I could not but conclude he [Byron] was a believer in the inspiration of the

If Boswell's journals reveal the strains and stresses of emancipation from Calvinism, and Hume's correspondence at least hints at similar difficulties, the letters of Clarinda (Mrs Maclehose) exhibit all the force and tenacity of the traditional faith. Clarinda was a sensitive, well-educated middle-class woman. The exact contemporary of Burns, she had been brought up, not in the fanatical Western country districts, but in Glasgow and Edinburgh—yet she actually became converted to Calvinism in the 1780s. She wrote to Burns that she had been bred to Arminianism (a belief which rejected absolute pre-destination), but that experience and the influence of a "dear, valued friend" had made her reject it for the faith of Knox and the Covenanters. Emancipation had apparently brought con-fusion and conflict, whereas acceptance of the ancient dogmas meant inner certitude and peace.

Comparing her settled position with Burns's own, on 7 Jan. 1788 she confessed :

> One thing alone hurt me, though I regretted many—your avowal of being an enemy to Calvinism. I guessed it was so by some of your pieces; but the confirmation of it gave me a shock. . . . You will not wonder at this, when I inform you that I am a strict Calvinist, *one or two* dark tenets excepted, which I never meddle with. . . . Were I to narrate my past life as honestly as you have done, you would soon be convinced that neither of us could hope to be justified by our good works.

On 13 Jan. 1788, she pointed the contrast between them in even more unmistakable terms :

Bible, and had the gloomiest Calvinistic tenets . . . Judge, then, how I must hate the creed which made him see God as an Avenger, not a Father ! . . . I, like all connected with him, was broken against the rock of predestination." (*His Very Self and Voice, Collected Conversations of Lord Byron*, ed. E. J. Lovell, Jr., N.Y. 1954, pp. 450–1.) Basing his reconstruction largely upon "The True Story of Lady Byron's Life" in Harriet Beecher Stowe, *Lady Byron Vindicated*, London 1870, p.302, the most recent of Byron's biographers, L. A. Marchand, (in *Byron: a Biography*, 3 vols., London 1957, VOL. II, p. 515) reinterprets Byron's mood in 1815 as follows : "Voltairean skepticism, which before marriage she had believed was the source of his Satanic pose, she now saw influenced only the surface of his intelligence ; whereas deeply ingrained in his unconscious mind a gloomy Calvinism made him feel that the majority of men and himself in particular had the mark of Cain on them and were slated for damnation. After exhausting his powers of reason, wit, and ridicule in trying to refute the arguments of religion, he would often say with violence : 'The worst of it is, I *do believe*'."

In most points we seem to agree : only I found all my hopes of pardon and acceptance with Heaven upon the merit of Christ's atonement,—whereas you do upon a good life.

And on 19–20. Jan. she burst out :

Oh, Sylvander, who would go on fighting with themselves, resolving and resolving, while they can thus fly to their Father's house?[28]

Thus strict orthodoxy was hardly a dead thing in the Edinburgh of 1788 ; indeed, it was still very much alive under the surface nearly forty years later, when James Hogg wrote the *Private Memoirs and Confessions of a Justified Sinner*[29]—no mere work of antiquarian reconstruction, but a passionate satire upon forces which still existed beneath the surface of the Scottish mind.

Although Burns did not by his own unaided efforts bring about the collapse of Calvinism, yet neither was he fighting battles long since won, nor kicking at a completely open door. His work was in accord with the spirit of the age, and he had many precursors ; but its main value does not lie in its direct historical effects so much as in the enduring creations of universal hypocrisy he was able to fashion from a particular Scottish dilemma.[30] Burns used a local religious situation as the raw materials of poems ; and it is as poems, not as polemics, that the ecclesiastical satires must be judged today.

[28] In *The Life and Works of Robert Burns*, ed. Robert Chambers, revised by William Wallace, henceforth cited as C. & W., 4 vols., Edinburgh and London 1896, VOL. II, pp. 242, 251, 260.

[29] 1824 ; Cresset Library, London 1947, with introd. by André Gide.

[30] Although this dilemma—the conflict between Calvinism and rationa religion—received its most extreme expression in Scotland, it was by no means confined to that country : which explains, perhaps, why Scottish literature is so "typical" of the north-European eighteenth century, and why Byron, a poet whose childhood was exposed to the influence of Scottish Calvinism, occupies such a central position in the *European* romantic movement. And the dilemma was as much social as national ; it was part of the evolution of the middle-class mind, at any rate in Great Britain. Cp. H. N. Fairchild, *Religious Trends in English Poetry*, 3 vols., N.Y. 1939–42, henceforth cited as Fairchild, I (1700–40). 545–6, 571–2. Fairchild maintains that sentimentalism, with its libertarian and melancholy sides, derives from an older Calvinism ; sentimental attitudes are simply Calvinist (or "bourgeois") reactions to the eighteenth-century compromise, and the sentimentalist's mind is as divided as the Calvinist's ever was. Fairchild's book is valuable in that it reminds us that anti-Calvinism was an English, and even a general north-European, phenomenon.

It was the Moderates—preachers influenced by such Scottish and English philosophers as Shaftesbury, Hutcheson, Kames and Thomas Reid, and backed by the lairds who often appointed them to churches against the wishes of their congregations—who did most to undermine narrow Calvinism; and it was this party to which Robert lent the support of his pen. In the list of Burns's library as supplied by the sons of the poet, the philosophical and theological sections are particularly impressive. Significantly enough, there were many works by the leaders of the new school, or older books of a broadly humane cast : Hugh Blair, Tillotson, Sherlock, Hume, Montaigne, Lord Kames, Adam Smith and Dugald Stewart were all represented. But the list also contains the titles of many "high-flying" or Evangelical volumes, such as Boston's *Crook in the Lot* and *Fourfold State*, Wellwood's *Glimpse of Glory*, the *Works* of John Knox, "Sermons, many volumes," the *Solemn League and Covenant*, the (Westminster) *Confession of Faith*, and "sundry large volumes, Folio 4to and 8vo, containing many tracts connected with the Church of Geneva and the reformation in General." It is obvious from the books owned by him at his death that Burns was in a position to know both orthodox and unorthodox theology, as well as what in Scotland at any rate passed for "New Philosophy."[31]

It seems highly probable that a few of these theological works had belonged to his father, William Burnes, whose interests were of a decidedly devotional kind. There is a *Manual of Religious Belief in the Form of a Dialogue between Father and Son*,[32] the manuscript of which was owned in 1875 by Gilbert Burns junior, the youngest son of the poet's brother. According to family tradition it was compiled by William Burnes himself; and it is significant that Currie, who knew of its existence in 1800, believed it to have been written by the elder Burns. The document (again according to family tradition) was not in William's handwriting but in that of John Murdoch, the tutor of the Burns children.[33] The *Manual* may therefore be entirely Murdoch's composition, in which case one could

---

[31] *The Works of Robert Burns*, 2 vols., Glasgow 1874, I. ccxlvii.
[32] Kilmarnock 1875; henceforth cited as *Manual*. Also in C. & W., I. 455 ff.
[33] *Manual*, pp. xiv, xix; Currie, I. 84.

describe it as an imaginative reconstruction of William's beliefs; alternatively, it may be a heightened and "improved"
version of a dialogue originally written by the poet's father; or
finally—and this is what both Currie and Gilbert Burns firmly
believed—it may be a faithful and accurate transcript of what
William Burnes actually composed. Whichever of these possibilities is the correct one, the evidential value of the document
is unimpaired, since it must necessarily contain ideas to which
Burns was exposed during his earliest years. It does not matter
whether he got them from his tutor or from his own father, so
long as we can be sure that he heard them.

Now the beliefs expounded in the *Manual* are most definitely
not of the extreme Calvinist or Auld Licht variety; on the
contrary, they have a strong liberal tinge, with great stress on
the value of subjective experience and struggle, on reason, on
love (the Sermon on the Mount is often quoted), and on the
achievement of righteousness as the result of a conflict between
the animal and rational parts of man's nature. This last preoccupation is especially interesting, since in a slightly different
form it haunted Robert all his life. The father in the dialogue
states that repentance is absolutely necessary to salvation, and
when the son asks him to define repentance more fully he
replies in these terms:

> I not only mean a sorrowing for sin, but a labouring to see the
> malignant nature of it; as setting nature at variance with herself,
> by placing the animal part before the rational, and thereby
> putting ourselves on a level with the brute beasts, the conse-
> quence of which will be an intestine war in the human frame,
> until the rational part be entirely weakened, which is spiritual
> death, which in the nature of the thing renders us unfit for the
> society of God's spiritual kingdom, and to see the beauty of
> holiness.

The subjective life of man is thus a continual struggle between
animal instinct and controlling reason, like the inner existence
of Bunyan's Christian. The dialogue continues:

> On the contrary, setting the rational part above the animal,
> though it promote a war in the human frame, every conflict
> and victory affords us grateful reflection, and tends to compose

the mind more and more, not to the utter destruction of the
animal part, but to the real and true enjoyment of them [*sic*],
by placing Nature in the order that its Creator designed it,
which in the natural consequences of the thing, promotes
spiritual life, and renders us more and more fit for Christ's
spiritual kingdom; and not only so, but gives animal life pleasure
and joy, that we never could have had without it.

Spiritual life seems to the writer a battle to attain inner peace
and order, whose aim is to "exalt the mind above those
irregular passions that jar, and are contrary one to another,
and distract the mind by contrary pursuits." The final result
of this conflict, the desired end, is "uniformity of pursuits,"
which rests firmly upon the conviction "that all our interests
are under the care of our Heavenly Father. This gives a relish
to animal life itself, this joy that no man intermeddleth with,
and which is peculiar to a Christian or holy life; and its comforts and blessings the whole Scripture is a comment upon,
especially our Lord's Sermon upon the Mount . . . and its
progress in the parable of the Sower."[34]

For all its liberality and rationality, this little theological
manual commonly ascribed to William Burnes is concerned
with the same sort of antinomies that are revealed alike in
Robert's own life, in some of Smollett's novels, and in such
literary characters as Holy Willie or Hogg's Justified Sinner.
There is a sense in which all that is best in Burns is either an
extension, a qualification or a direct negative of positions
stated or implied in the *Manual*, for sometimes he was content
to body forth those "irregular passions" which the father of the
dialogue had harmonised and subdued; sometimes he expressed the desire to bring them under the sway of reason and
the will; and sometimes he pilloried those "cits" whose "inner
regularity and order" (qualities approved in the dialogue)
were in daily life compatible with meanness and the exploitation of other human beings.

The great opposition which underlies the *Manual*, that
between the instincts and the rational will, was a common preoccupation of seventeenth and eighteenth-century Scotsmen.
It is found in one of the devoutest mid-seventeenth-century

[34] *Manual*, xlvii–l.

Covenanters, Major Thomas Weir, who seems to have lived, at least in imagination, a double life. According to Arnot, he "was accused of having exceeded the common depravity of mankind, was dreaded for his sorceries, and admired for his *gift* of prayer." At the age of seventy he made public confession of his misdeeds. After months of scandal a minister "whom they esteemed more forward than wise" divulged the matter to the civil authorities; an inquiry was instituted, and at his trial in 1670, Weir was found guilty of adultery, incest and other horrible crimes, for which he died impenitent, having previously renounced all hope of Heaven.[35] At the beginning of the eighteenth century, the same opposition is found in men like James Erskine, Lord Grange (1679–1754), and his friends, who "passed their time in alternate scenes of exercises of religion and debauchery, spending the days in prayer and pious meditation, and their nights in lewdness and revelling";[36] in Duncan Forbes of Culloden (1685–1747), Lord President of the Court of Session, an amateur theologian, and a heavy drinker,[37] and, at a theoretical level, in David Hume's famous philosophical dictum that "reason is, and ought only to be, the slave of the passions."[38]

The conflict is seen at its most hypocritical in Burns's contemporary William Brodie, Deacon of the Incorporation of Edinburgh Wrights and Masons. This apparently respectable and honest citizen nightly frequented a low gambling den in Fleshmarket Close, a fact which he was able to hide only too successfully from the well-to-do merchants and tradespeople with whom he normally associated. He became the leader of a small gang of burglars, two of whom turned King's Evidence after a particularly daring robbery, for which Brodie was tried

[35] H. Arnot, *A Collection and Abridgment of Celebrated Criminal Trials in Scotland* (1536–1784), Edinburgh 1785, pp. 359 f.; D.N.B., xx. 1062–3; M. Summers, *The History of Witchcraft and Demonology*, London 1926, pp. 34 ff.

[36] A. Carlyle, *Autobiography*, ed. J. Hill Burton, Edinburgh 1860, p. 15, quoted in Graham, ii. 45.

[37] *D.N.B.*, vii. 384–6; G. Menary, *The Life and Letters of Duncan Forbes of Culloden*, London 1936, pp. 92 ff., 384 f., 393 ff.; and for the future Lord President's own entertaining account of his very bibulous journey from Edinburgh to Inverness in April 1715, see *Major Fraser's Manuscript*, ed. A. Fergusson, Edinburgh 1889, ii. 159 ff.

[38] *Treatise*, bk. ii, pt. iii, § iii (ed. Selby-Bigge, Oxford 1888, repr. 1955, p. 415).

and executed in 1788.[39] Hypocrisy, vice contrasting with virtue as opposite sides of the same medal, dual personality—all these seem inevitably and ineffaceably Scottish. It is perhaps not entirely accidental that it was a Scotsman who wrote *Dr Jekyll and Mr Hyde*, or that one of the most deeply imaginative explorations of mental division and moral evil ever written, James Hogg's *Private Memoirs and Confessions of a Justified Sinner*, should be in part a satire upon old-fashioned Calvinism.[40] It is here, at its most national, that Scottish literature comes nearest to being universal—in Hogg's tragical treatment of "darkness at noon," and in Burns's satirical explorations of the same condition.

The works of Burns, like Shakespeare's and the Bible, have been used to buttress and support almost every conceivable shade of religious opinion from the orthodox to the merely eccentric; it has been said that he was a freethinker, a moderate Christian, a Unitarian and—in spite of everything—a Calvinist. One of his own contemporaries, the minister of Newton-on-Ayr ("Peebles frae the water-fitt" of "The Holy Fair") complained that in his poetry and his life "sinfulness, gross immoralities, and irreligion" are "celebrated, extenuated, vindicated: the worst of passions indulged and gratified: the sacred truths of religion treated with levity, and made the song of the drunkard and the abandoned profligate"—a charge which was occasionally repeated by pious souls during the nineteenth century.[41] The rationalists accepted this accusation of faith-

---

[39] See *Trial of Deacon Brodie*, ed. W. Roughead, W.S., henceforth cited as Roughead, in Notable Scottish Trials, Glasgow and Edinburgh 1906. Roughead (p. 25) points out that Richmond's lodgings, where Burns stayed during the winter of 1786-7, were in the Lawnmarket opposite Deacon Brodie's house, and suggests that Burns, Nasmyth and Deacon Brodie may well have "foregathered with other kindred spirits at Johnnie Dowie's tavern in Libberton's Wynd."

[40] Cp. above, p. 38, n. 29, and K. Wittig, *The Scottish Tradition in Literature*, henceforth cited as Wittig, Edinburgh 1958, pp. 247 ff. Roughead (p. 10) points out that, as early as 1864 Stevenson "prepared the draft of a play, which . . . finally took shape in the melodrama *Deacon Brodie, or the Double Life*, written in collaboration with . . . W. E. Henley, and published in 1892. It may even be that the conception of Dr Jekyll and Mr Hyde was suggested to Stevenson by his study of the dual nature so strikingly exemplified in his earlier 'hero'."

[41] [W. Peebles], *Burnomania: The Celebrity of Robert Burns considered: in a Discourse addressed to all real Christians of every Denomination*, Edinburgh 1811, p. 9; [G. Gleig], *A Critique on the Poems of Robert Burns*, Edinburgh 1812, p. 22.

lessness only to glory in it. "Burns had thought himself out of all cut and dried religions," wrote John S. Clarke on one occasion; "he rejected all forms of Christianity by doubting its cardinal tenets."[42] In complete contrast to this opinion, J. R. Campbell (a writer whose own beliefs appear to be on the sceptical side) maintains that "on one thing Burns never wavered—the existence of a good, benevolent God. This he deduced less from theology than from philosophy—from the character of the human mind. . . . Burns worshipped a God of Love and Human Brotherhood."[43] Another twentieth-century writer, William Walsh, pushes this view to the point where he sees Burns as "an early confessor of the Unitarianism to be preached, a few years after his death, by William Ellery Channing," a doctrine whose leading characteristics were "humane sympathies" and "belief in the dignity of human nature";[44] while A. B. Jamieson, the most thorough of all investigators into Burns's religious views, holds that at heart Robert was more of a Calvinist than he knew. "Holy Willie's Prayer" thus becomes the ridicule of "his own sincerest feelings and profoundest experiences . . . no doubt, he often came nearer to the true meaning of Calvin than the Auld Lichts themselves."[45]

Burns was not the chameleon poet taking the hue of whatever doctrine he happened to light upon, but rather a man moving towards self-mastery and self-knowledge through the testing and rejection of successive experiences and beliefs. Intellectually as well as morally, Burns's life was an exploration in the spirit of the *Manual*—a voyage cut short by early death, so that we do not really know what the final harbour would have been. As Jamieson well says, "he attempted self-conquest, according to the teaching of his father, and also to see things as they really are."[46] Unfortunately, most of his prose statements about religion were made after his visit to Edin-

---

[42] J. S. Clarke, *The Story of Robert Burns*, Glasgow [? 1917], p. 7.

[43] J. R. Campbell, *Burns the Democrat*, Glasgow 1945, pp. 21–2.

[44] W. Walsh, "Robert Burns, a Unitarian Forerunner," in *The Christian Register*, Boston, 26 Dec. 1929, pp. 1043–4. This benevolent humanitarianism was as much the product of eighteenth-century deism and the sentimental movement as it was a forerunner of nineteenth-century Unitarianism. See Fairchild, *passim*.

[45] Jamieson, *Burns and Religion*, pp. 48, 76.   [46] *Op. cit.*, p. 108.

burgh, and cannot therefore be taken as exact reflexions of his state of mind in 1784–6, during which period the ecclesiastical satires were composed. It appears that as a child he was deeply religious, for in his autobiographical letter to Dr Moore he speaks of the "enthusiastic, idiot piety" of his early years.[47] In adolescence and early manhood (if one may make a plausible deduction from the juvenilia) he was both attracted and repelled by the traditional creed. In view of William Burnes's liberal tendencies, Jamieson may well be right in suggesting that Robert did not feel the full impact of orthodox Calvinism until the family moved away from Ayr, and that he adopted the fully developed moderate or "legal" position only after an intense inner struggle. Traces of such a conflict are to be found in the early poems in psalm metre ; but, as we have seen, Robert had already adopted a theologically Moderate attitude, complete with "a certain satirical seasoning," by the time he was twenty-three. There is evidence that at some period in his youth or early manhood he had been attracted by deism or even by outright atheism, for to James Candlish, who had been one of his boyhood friends, he wrote as follows :

> I likewise, since you and I were first acquainted, in the pride of despising old women's stories, ventured in "the daring path Spinoza trod" ; but experience of the weakness, not the strength, of human powers, made me glad to grasp at revealed religion.[48]

The letter is dated 21 Mar. 1787—an indication that at this time Burns did not wish to count himself an infidel even when writing to a professedly irreligious person like Candlish.

Though he sometimes confided his religious views to others, his main references to this topic occur in letters to Clarinda and to his aristocratic friend Mrs Dunlop. Always he is consistently against Calvinist Doctrine. As he wrote to Clarinda on 8 Jan. 1788 :

> A mind pervaded, actuated, and governed by purity, truth, and charity, though it does not *merit* heaven, yet is an absolutely necessary prerequisite, without which heaven can neither be

---

[47] *Letters*, I. 106. Burns's position at this time was remarkably similar to Hume's on his death-bed, as reported by Boswell (above, p. 36, n. 25).

[48] *Letters*, I. 79.

obtained nor enjoyed ; and, by Divine promise, such a mind
shall never fail of attaining "everlasting life" : hence the im-
pure, the deceiving, and the uncharitable exclude themselves
from eternal bliss, by their unfitness for enjoying it. . . . [Christ],
except for our own obstinacy and misconduct, will bring us all,
through various ways, and by various means, to bliss at last. . . .
My creed is pretty nearly expressed in the last clause of Jamie
Deans's grace, an honest weaver in Ayrshire : "Lord, grant that
we may lead a gude life ! for a gude life maks a gude end ; at
least it helps weel !"[49]

An even more uncompromising rejection of Calvinism occurs
in a letter to Miss Rachel Dunlop dated 2 Aug. 1788 :

I am in perpetual warfare with that doctrine of our Reverend
Priesthood, that "we are born into this world bond slaves of
iniquity & heirs of perdition, wholly inclined" to that which is
evil and wholly disinclined to that which is good untill [sic] by
a kind of Spiritual Filtration or rectifying process Called effectual
Calling &c.—The whole business is reversed, and our con-
nections above & below completely change place.—I believe
in my conscience that the case is just quite contrary—We come
into this world with a heart & disposition to do good for it,
untill by dashing a large mixture of base Alloy called Prudence
alias Selfishness, the too precious Metal of the Soul is brought
down to the blackguard Sterling of ordinary currency. . . .[50]

Burns vacillated greatly on the question of life after death,
sometimes accepting the idea of a future existence, sometimes
doubting the very possibility. To Robert Muir, the Kilmarnock
wine-merchant, he wrote on 7 Mar. 1788 :

[49] To [Mrs Maclehose], 8 Jan. 1788, in *Letters*, I. 159. It is perhaps of interest
that this passage contains one of the few references to Christ in the Burns correspondence ; and that Burns's conception of Him is the very reverse of "Christ the
Tiger."

[50] To [Miss Rachel Dunlop], 2 Aug. 1788, in *Letters*, I. 242. For the doctrine of
Effectual Calling, see the Westminster Confession, ch. x : "I. All those whom
God hath predestinated unto life, and those only, he is pleased, in his appointed and
accepted time, effectually to call, by his word and Spirit, out of that state of sin and
death in which they are by nature, to grace and salvation by Jesus Christ. . . . II.
This effectual call is of God's free and special grace alone, not from any thing at all
foreseen in man ; who is altogether passive therein, until, being quickened and
renewed by the Holy Spirit, he is thereby enabled to answer this call, and to
embrace the grace offered and conveyed in it."

—The close of life indeed, to a reasoning eye is, "dark as was chaos, ere the infant sun
"Was roll'd together, or had try'd his beams
"Athwart the gloom profound"—
But an honest man has nothing to fear.—If we lie down in the grave, the whole man a piece of broke machinery, to moulder with the clods of the valley—be it so ; at least there is an end of pain, care, woes and wants : if that part of us called Mind, does survive the apparent destruction of the man—away with old-wife prejudices and tales ! Every age and every nation has had a different set of stories ; and as the many are always weak, of consequence they have often, perhaps always been deceived : a man, conscious of having acted an honest part among his fellow-creatures ; even granting that he may have been the sport, at times, of passions and instincts ; he goes to a great unknown Being who could have no other end in giving him existence but to make him happy ; who gave him those passions and instincts, and well knows their force.—[51]

On 13 Dec. 1789, he apostrophised the Saviour as follows :

Jesus Christ, thou amiablest of characters, I trust thou art no Imposter [*sic*], & that thy revelation of blissful scenes of existence beyond death and the grave, is not one of the many impositions which time after time have been palmed off on credulous mankind.[52]

Seven months later, on 9 Jul. 1790, he was inclined to accept the future life not on grounds of revelation but because of proofs "wrought out of our own heads & hearts," which have for him "the conviction of an intuitive truth" ; but later still, on 22 Aug. 1792, he could report that "still the damned dogmas of reasoning Philosophy throw in their doubts."[53] In the years before his death, the will to believe appears to have become stronger. On 25 Feb. 1794 he wrote to Alexander Cunningham of "those *senses of the mind*, if I may be allowed the expression, which connect us with, and link us to, those awful obscure realities—an all-powerful and equally beneficent God, and a world to come, beyond death and the grave," and

---

[51] To Muir, 7 Mar. 1788 in *Letters*, I. 207.
[52] To Mrs Dunlop, 13 Dec. 1789, in *Letters*, I. 374.
[53] To Mrs Dunlop, 9 Jul. 1790 and 22 Aug. 1792, in *Letters*, II. 26, 118.

which had the effect of pouring "the balm of comfort into the wound which time can never cure."[54] His last statement on the topic, made on 29 Dec. 1794, some eighteen months before his death, is both agonised and ambiguous. It is full of an almost passionate yearning for certainty but nevertheless fails to communicate the impression of a final conviction :

> What a transient business is life !—Very lately I was a boy ; but t'other day I was a young man ; & I already begin to feel the rigid fibre & stiffening joints of Old Age coming fast o'er my frame.—With all my follies of youth, & I fear, a few vices of manhood, still I congratulate myself on having had in early days religion strongly impressed on my mind.—I have nothing to say to any body, as, to which Sect they belong, or what Creed they believe ; but I look on the Man who is firmly persuaded of Infinite Wisdom & Goodness superintending & directing every circumstance that can happen in his lot—I felicitate such a man as having a solid foundation for his mental enjoyment ; a firm prop & sure stay, in the hour of difficulty, trouble & distress ; & a never-failing anchor of hope, when he looks beyond the grave.—[55]

One cannot by any stretch of the imagination call this either orthodox or atheistic ; perhaps a sane yet reverent agnosticism is the only name for it.

Burns appears to have been a pious child, a doubting adolescent and (possibly) an irreligious young man. After 1787 he increasingly felt the need for faith (especially the concept of a future life), but even towards the very end of his days he could never accept traditional views for very long ; his doubts just would not be stilled. Deeply revering his father's moderate faith, and emotionally responsive to traditional Calvinism in the very moment of rejecting it, he was indeed the ideal person to make poetry out of the contemporary religious scene.

---

[54] To [A. Cunningham], 25 Feb. 1794, in *Letters*, ii. 235.
[55] To [Mrs Dunlop], 20 Dec. 1794–12 Jan. 1795, in *Letters*, ii. 281.

III

The Kirk's Alarm

IN Burns's Ayrshire the Church was divided into the same parties as in other regions of Scotland, but the contestants loathed each other with a passion hardly to be matched elsewhere. On the one hand were the last-ditch Calvinists, "the lads in black," as Robert contemptuously called them ; on the other those whom their enemies termed Arminians and Socinians. The Arminians were opposed to absolute predestination, believing amongst other things that Christ's atonement was made for the entire human race and that man may both resist God's call and relapse from a state of grace once he has attained it.[1] The Socinians were anti-Trinitarians who, in the opinion of their Evangelical opponents, denied the divinity of Christ and interpreted the Bible in accordance with human reason, holding that salvation was attained by imitating Christ's virtue.[2] In the eyes of the orthodox, both groups were highly suspect—next door to infidels and atheists.

The views of the local Moderates can be traced back to the rationalist morality of English deism ; in point of fact, a single work provided them with a great part of their theories, namely *The Scripture Doctrine of Original Sin*, by John Taylor of Norwich. Taylor maintained that there is nothing in the Bible to warrant the concept of original sin ; according to him, "the consequences of Adam's first transgression upon us are labour, sorrow, and mortality." He also said :

> ". . . we cannot conclude that any other evil or death came upon mankind in consequence . . . besides that death from which mankind shall be delivered at the resurrection ; whatever that death be . . . . furthermore, God in Christ hath bestowed upon us mercy and gifts, privileges and advantages, both in this and a future world, abundantly beyond the reversing of any evils we are subject to in consequence of Adam's sin."[3]

[1] P. Schaff, *A History of the Creeds of Christendom*, 3 vols., London 1877, VOL. I, pp. 509 ff.   [2] Cp. McNeill, *Calvinism*, pp. 356, 370.   [3] Chambers, I. 356.

The laity were as much involved in these speculations as their pastors, and one John Goldie, a wine-merchant of Kilmarnock, had the temerity to set down his opinions in print. He brought out his *Essays on various Important Subjects, Moral and Divine : being an Attempt to distinguish True from False Religion* in 1779 and a second edition in 1785,[4] which led Burns to write his epistle "To John Goldie"[5] in August of that year. In a gloriously comic personification, Orthodoxy (identified with evangelicalism and emotional religion) and her sister Superstition are depicted as sick unto death. Superstition, indeed, is so ill that it seems advisable to call in her physician, "Black Jock" Russell, a minister of the older doctrine, in order to examine her urine :

> Poor gapin, glowrin Superstition !
> Wae's me, she's in a sad condition !
> Fye ! bring Black Jock, her state physician,
>   To see her water !
> Alas ! there's ground for great suspicion
>   She'll ne'er get better.

> Enthusiasm's past redemption
> Gane in a gallopin consumption :
> Not a' her quacks wi' a' their gumption
>   Can ever mend her ;
> Her feeble pulse gies strong presumption
>   She'll soon surrender.

The man who in other contexts praised "Nature's fire" and uninhibited passion here scorns Enthusiasm, the religion of feeling, in favour of an apparently bleak and rational faith. Yet in the defence of Reason all the warmth of his emotional being was engaged. He specifically links Taylor with Goldie as the main inspirers of the new ideas in Ayrshire, ironically suggesting that if this were not the enlightened eighteenth century but the good old theocratic days, Goldie's opponents would have burnt him alive :

> 'Tis you an' Taylor are the chief
> To blame for a' this black mischíef ;

---

[4] C. & W., i. 169–70, 460–1.   [5] II. 70 (355).

> But, gin the Lord's ain folk gat leave,
> A toom tar barrel
> An' twa red peats wad bring relief,
> And end the quarrel.

"Black Jock" is also one of the main figures in "The Twa Herds : or, The Holy Tulyie [squabble], An unco mournfu' Tale,"[6] Burns's first published work and the earliest of the ecclesiastical satires ; the other was the Rev. Alexander Moodie of Riccarton. One of the other ministers in Kilmarnock, a certain Lindsay, was a notorious liberal. It would therefore have been becoming, as well as politic, for the high-fliers Russell and Moodie to have stuck together. But the exact opposite happened and the two stalwarts fell out :

> The twa best herds in a' the wast,
> That e'er gae gospel horn a blast
> These five an' twenty simmers past—
> O, dool to tell !—
> Hae had a bitter, black out-cast
> Atween themsel.

They took a dispute about parish boundaries to the Presbytery, where they proceeded to abuse each other like a pair of drunken fishwives, to the scandal of their supporters and the huge amusement of their opponents. Burns fits his satire into an obvious allegorical framework in which ministers are shepherds while evil-doers are polecats, badgers and foxes, developing still further the technique used in the second and third stanzas of the "Epistle to John Rankine"[7]—the apparent assumption of the standards, beliefs and language of the opposite party :

> What flock wi' Moodie's flock could rank,
> Sae hale an' hearty every shank ?
> Nae poison'd, soor Arminian stank
> He let them taste ;
> But Calvin's fountainhead they drank—
> O, sic a feast ![8]

---

[6] II. 20 (314). In Scots, *herd* = "one who tends flocks."   [7] I. 176 (384).

[8] In the MS in the B.M., ll. 3 and 4 of this fifth stanza read :
> Nae poison'd Ariminian stank
> He loot them taste,

while, as printed by Stewart and Meikle, Glasgow 1796, 1799 and 1801, l. 5 reads :
> Frae Calvin's well, ay clear, they drank.

It is from the Stewart and Meikle reading that I took the title of my second chapter.

The third-last and second-last stanzas show up very acutely an interesting contradiction in Burns's system of ideas. The flocks are ironically urged

> To cowe the lairds,
> An' get[9] the brutes the power themsels
> To chuse their herds!

—a practice for which Burns had nothing but ridicule and contempt, however democratic his political views may have been. If the faithful will only unite to impose their will on their parishes:

> Then Orthodoxy yet may prance,
> An' Learning in a woody dance,
> An' that fell cur[10] ca'd Common-sense,
> That bites sae sair,
> Be banish'd o'er the sea to France—
> Let him bark there!

To the Auld Licht supporter into whose mouth the poem is put, France is a heathenish land, almost as remote as the moon; to Burns, it is a place of learning, so that the actual effect of the stanza is to identify *his* position with that of the Enlightenment.

His next attempt proved to be one of the finest satires of all time, "Holy Willie's Prayer."[11] Auld Licht ministers and elders were adherents not only of an ancient and forbidding theology but also of a tyrannical system of Church government involving detailed supervision of the morals and sex-habits of every parish. Burns's own landlord and personal friend, the lawyer Gavin Hamilton, was a New Licht layman who had been so contumacious as to stay away from church, "having been absent two Sundays in the past, and three in the present month." It was further complained against him "that on the third Sunday of the present month, he set out on a journey to Carrick, although admonished against so doing by the minister; that he habitually, if not totally, neglects the worship of God in his family; and, finally, that he had written an abusive letter to the session." According to the Kirk Session's records, five servants previously employed by Hamilton and three still in

---

[9] Stewart (1796 and 1799) reads "gie."   [10] Ms reads "cur'st."   [11] ii. 25 (320).

his service at the time of the dispute were willing to give evidence against their master : evidently the lower orders did not like Sabbath-breakers. The matter was taken to a higher court, the Presbytery of Ayr, where judgment was delivered in Hamilton's favour, thanks partly to the eloquent pleading of another of Burns's friends, Robert Aiken ("Orator Bob"). The Presbytery ordered Mauchline Kirk Session to strike out of its minutes those passages which Hamilton considered offensive ; finally, in 1785, a higher body than even the Presbytery, the Synod, granted him "a certificate of being free from all ground of church censure." The Lord's folk had been sorely routed, and the victory had gone to Belial and the Mammon of Unrighteousness. One of Hamilton's most zealous opponents in this business was a certain William Fisher, an influential Mauchline elder whose own life did not always seem completely virtuous when measured by the godless standards of legality. Long after the Hamilton case, Fisher was said to have stolen from "the plate," and he died, miserably, in a ditch. Burns's own intervention in the dispute was to make of the real William Fisher the towering figure of Holy Willie, the comic counterpart of Hogg's Robert Wringhim.[12]

"Holy Willie's Prayer" may be interpreted either as a mean sycophant's confidential transaction with the Deity or as a piece of sublimely egotistical declamation reverberating from Mauchline to the outermost galaxies. Although the former interpretation is suggested by the epigraph, Pope's line "And send the godly in a pet to pray," a close reading of the poem reveals an imaginative synthesis of the two apparently opposite conceptions. Burns puts himself under the skin of his protagonist and speaks in his very tone of voice in order to make his satire all the more destructive, indicating with remorseless economy of language both the inhumanity and the devilish splendour of unmitigated Calvinism :

> When from my mither's womb I fell,
> Thou might hae plung'd me deep in hell
> To gnash my gooms, and weep, and wail,
>   In burning lakes,
> Whare damnèd devils roar and yell,
>   Chain'd to their stakes.

[12] Chambers, I. 135, 138; Snyder, pp. 108–9.

Yet I am here, a chosen sample,
To show Thy grace is great and ample :
I'm here a pillar o' Thy temple,
 Strong as a rock,
A guide, a buckler, and example
 To a' Thy flock ![13]

In spite of his own similes, Holy Willie is no petrified paragon—nothing so firmly founded as a hewn pillar, a buckler or a lifeless rock. The humour consists in the exquisitely ludicrous contrast between pretensions and reality. Willie aspires to the monolithic majesty of stone but, poor forked radish that he is, constantly assailed by the lusts of the flesh, he every now and then experiences an irresistible urge to make the beast with two backs with seductive hizzies like Meg or "Leezie's lass." The war between the rational and animal parts of man's nature which runs through the "Dialogue between Father and Son" was well known to Holy Willie. But even that internecine strife was probably part of God's plan for the salvation of William Fisher :

Maybe Thou lets this fleshly thorn
Buffet Thy servant e'en and morn,
Lest he owre proud and high should turn
 That he's sae gifted :
If sae, Thy han' maun e'en be borne
 Until Thou lift it.[14]

No doubt, years before, Willie had "gotten a grip of Christ" and experienced that subjective intensification of spiritual life which guaranteed his membership of the Church Invisible as one

[13] The textual variants in the different editions and MSS of these stanzas are of small importance. But after st. v, in his edition of 1802, Stewart inserted a stanza which H. & H. do not include in the main body of the poem :

O Lord, Thou kens what zeal I bear
When drinkers drink, an' swearers swear,
An' singin hear an dancin there
 Wi' great an' sma' ;
For I am keepit by Thy fear
 Free frae them a'.

I have taken these lines into account in my remarks on Burns's repetition of key words and phrases, below, p. 60.

[14] In this ninth stanza, Stewart reads "Beset Thy servant," "high and proud," and "*Cause* he's sae gifted."

of the elect of God. As the Westminster Confession puts it :[15]

> True believers may have the assurance of their salvation divers ways shaken, diminished, and intermitted ; as, by negligence in preserving of it ; by falling into some special sin, which woundeth the conscience, and grieveth the Spirit ; by some sudden or vehement temptation ; by God's withdrawing the light of his countenance, and suffering even such as fear him to walk in darkness, and to have no light : yet are they never utterly destitute of that seed of God, and life of faith, that love of Christ and the brethren, that sincerity of heart and conscience of duty, out of which, by the operation of the Spirit, this assurance may in due time be revived, and by which, in the mean time, they are supported from utter despair.

As a "true believer," Willie would never experience utter despair ; all he had to do was to wait until God should once more show him the light of His countenance.

A surprising number of God's elect were concentrated in Mauchline and the surrounding district :

> Lord, bless Thy chosen in this place,
> For here Thou has a chosen race !
> But God confound their stubborn face
>   An' blast their name,
> Wha bring Thy elders to disgrace
>   An' open shame !

In contrast to the elect—that is, to those who thought like William Fisher—were the unregenerate New Licht sinners, with Gavin Hamilton at their head. Willie was not content with the doctrinal assurance that, as the Westminster Confession has it,[16] "Others not elected, although they may be called by the ministry of the word, and may have some common operations of the Spirit, yet they never truly come unto Christ, and therefore cannot be saved" ; he wanted Hamilton to be punished in this world as well as hereafter by some miraculous interference with the course of nature :

> Curse Thou his basket and his store,
>   Kail an' potatoes !

The most terrible mundane affliction he could conceive of was to be injured in the purse.

---

[15] xviii. iv.   [16] x. iv.

In the next two stanzas, the comedy resides in a clash between the sublime pretensions of the elect and their miserable snivelling when successfully challenged by an assembly of Moderates. Willie is nowhere smaller than in the second of these stanzas :

> Lord, hear my earnest cry and pray'r,
> Against that Presbyt'ry of Ayr !
> Thy strong right hand, Lord, make it bare
>   Upo' their heads !
> Lord, visit them, an' dinna spare,
>   For their misdeeds !

> O Lord, my God ! that glib-tongu'd Aiken,
> My vera heart and flesh are quakin
> To think how we stood sweatin, shakin,
>   An' pish'd wi' dread,
> While he, wi' hingin lip an' snakin,
>   Held up his head.

But immediately afterwards Willie, as he lashes Robert Aiken, expands to become a gigantic embodiment of abstract Hypocrisy, terrifying in his stupidity and self-confidence. Alone with God, he becomes almost His equal, but even in that dread presence he does not forget to ask for a share of that material prosperity which, if a popular interpretation of history is correct,[17] was one of the consequences of historical Calvinism:

> Lord, in Thy day o' vengeance try him !
> Lord, visit him wha did employ him !
> And pass not in Thy mercy by them,
>   Nor hear their pray'r,
> But for Thy people's sake destroy them,
>   An' dinna spare !

> But, Lord, remember me and mine
> Wi' mercies temporal and divine,
> That I for grace an' gear may shine
>   Excell'd by nane ;
> An' a' the glory shall be Thine—
>   Amen, Amen !

[17] Cp. M. Weber, *The Protestant Ethic and the Spirit of Capitalism*, tr. Talcott Parsons, London 1930, *passim*.

It may be that in writing "Holy Willie's Prayer" Burns's purpose was simply to expose the meanness, the essential little-ness of Fisher and the Auld Licht diehards of Mauchline. If so, what he actually achieved was rather different from what he had intended. Holy Willie, for all his parochial mingling of kail and potatoes with the awful purposes of God, is not without a kind of reflected grandeur derived from the magnificence of his dreadful doctrine. Though lacking the cosmic devilishness of a Major Weir or a Robert Wringhim, he too has a certain breadth and stature ; there is a largeness about his pettiness that arises perhaps from the typicality of his inner conflicts and their rationalisations. Burns has made of him not merely a butt for satirical attack but a great comic character, who is amusing not because he is a man behaving as a thing but because he is "the man who thinks he is God" acting in a merely human way. Yet even so he turns into a thing without knowing it, in the very moment of making himself the equal of Supreme Power. When Willie likens himself to an object as unyielding as a pillar or a metal shield, it is almost as if Burns were aware that there is an inanimate, robot-like quality about a Superman ; you cannot aspire to become more than human without at the same time running the risk of turning yourself into stone or steel.

The opposing poles of Willie's nature are revealed in the language of the poem, which oscillates between the elevated diction of the saints[18] and the backyard Scots of a small-town backslider in a way that is, surely, parody of a very special sort —the ironically heightened reflexion of men's actual speech. Parody usually proceeds from love ; but although he delights

[18] Christina Keith, *The Russet Coat*, henceforth cited as C. Keith, London 1956, p. 74, states that in the doctrinal passages of "Holy Willie's Prayer" Burns used "the clearest English at his command—an English so clear and so superlatively difficult of attainment that no Holy Willie could ever have acquired it." In fact it is not English, but Scots-English : English spoken with a Scottish accent, and by no means incompatible with a sprinkling of vernacular words. Moreover, as shown by the Scriptural parallels that Ritter (pp. 66–7) has noted, it corresponds very closely with the English of the Authorised Version ; and the real Willie could perfectly well have acquired it, for he must have heard it every Sunday of his life, and read something very like it on Saturday nights, and often on week-days too. For details of Scots-English as used in "Holy Willie's Prayer," see Appendix I, § 2 (below, pp. 353 f.) ; and for the Scriptural parallels noted by Ritter, see Appendix II (below, pp. 363 f.).

in the verbal idiosyncrasies of his opponent, Burns certainly
does not *love* Willie.

Particular phrases such as "grace an' gear" and "temporal
and divine" unite sacred and profane concepts exactly as the
Auld Lichts' speech appears to have done in real life ;[19] and
the mordant intellectual wit with which Burns fuses the sordid
and the sublime is as destructive as anything in Dryden or
Pope. Burns's antitheses are not merely verbal; they are a
matter of *ideas*, and their merciless irony strips bare the perverse
barbarity of Willie's distorted Calvinism :

> Sends ane to Heaven an' ten to Hell
> A' for Thy glory,
> And no for onie guid or ill
> They've done before Thee.

It is a doctrine, not just a man, that Burns pillories when he
makes Willie say :

> I, wha deserv'd most just damnation
> For broken laws
> Sax thousand years ere my creation,
> Thro' Adam's cause![20]

For Burns, at this period, damnation could never be right, still
less could there be degrees of justice in such a matter. It
follows, then, that it is wrong to say that Burns never attacks a
theory but only its practitioners. In this poem at least, theory
and practice are inseparable, and Willie is what he is because
of the doctrine, just as the doctrine (or its perversion in Auld
Licht hands) is suspect because it tends to produce people like
Willie.

In "Holy Willie's Prayer," antithesis does not operate only
within the single stanza considered as an isolated unit, but

---

[19] The same sort of satirical heightening of real language is to be found in the
mock Speech from the Throne (attributed to Marvell) which Members of Parliament found in their places on 13 Apr. 1675. In this speech, printed in *Andrew
Marvell, Selected Poetry and Prose*, ed. D. Davison, London 1952, pp. 209–12, Marvell
captures the very tones of Charles II's voice, just as Burns does those of the saints.
A similar talent is shown in Swift's *A Complete Collection of Genteel and Ingenious
Conversation* and in Dickens's treatment of the talk at the Veneerings' dinner-table
in *Our Mutual Friend*, to take only two examples. This type of irony, then, would
appear to belong as much to the English as to the Scottish literary tradition.

[20] Cp. Wittig, pp. 211–2.

whole stanzas and groups of stanzas balance each other, so that the contrast of larger masses is essential to the poem's structure. Thus the first five stanzas, which express Willie's idealised picture of himself, are negated by the next four, which describe his miserably petty amours, together with his hypocritical justification of them before the Deity. The tenth stanza mingles fanatical rage with elevated nobility, only to be followed, in the eleventh and twelfth, by an exhibition of small-minded, trivial jealousy. The thirteenth stanza is again tinged with some of the grandeur of the old beliefs, and is followed, in the fourteenth, by a demonstration of the ridiculous impotency displayed by their contemporary adherents. In the last two stanzas, these diverse elements come together in a conclusion that enhances the poem by its rhetorical justice. Holy Willie can see no distinction whatsoever between the divine purpose and his own material ends.

The tone of the poem varies from ordinary sarcasm to the most superbly dramatic irony. Thus Willie is quite blind to the implications of:

> At times I'm fash'd wi' fleshly lust;
> An' sometimes, too, in warldly trust,
> Vile self gets in,

or of:

> But, Lord, that Friday I was fou,
> When I cam near her,

when set beside the statement he is compelled to make about Gavin Hamilton's sins, which all but the Auld Lichts would regard as venial ones:

> He drinks, an' swears, an' plays at cartes,
> Yet has sae monie takin arts
> Wi' great and sma',
> Frae God's ain Priest the people's hearts
> He steals awa.

The reader, however, is at once aware of the comic significance of this contrast, and much of his amusement results from his ability to see through two pairs of eyes at one and the same time—Willie's and Burns's.

As in "Man was made to Mourn," and many other poems, Burns rings the changes on individual words which have been running in his mind, such as : "Lord," thirteen times ; "God," three times ; "chosen," three times ; "grace," three times ; "drink(ers)," three times ; "swear(ers)," three times ; "prayer," twice ; "bless," twice ; "people," twice ; "damned" or "damnation," twice ; "heart(s)," twice ; "flesh(ly)," three times. Sometimes, when a word is used only twice, the second sense is significantly different from the first ("the people's hearts" . . . "My vera heart and flesh are quakin" . . . "But for Thy people's sake destroy them.")

Critics of Shakespeare have, of recent years, pointed out that there are certain key concepts running through the plays ; and *King Lear*, for example, has been interpreted as an exploration of the conflict between various opposed but interpenetrating meanings of the word "nature."[21] It may be that, in its own way, "Holy Willie's Prayer" derives some of its explosive force from the coming together of different connotations of "flesh," "people" (the Elect ; *all* local inhabitants), and some of the other words I have mentioned. Burns's favourite phrases are interwoven in an almost symphonic fashion, and the last stanza harks back to the first. "Holy Willie's Prayer" begins by mentioning "glory" and "gifts an' grace" ; it ends by stressing "glory" and "grace an' gear." The resolution of the poem is therefore circular ; but when we return to these initial concepts in the last stanza they have—as a result of all that has been said since they were first mentioned—an ironical significance which they possess in no other context.

"Holy Willie's Prayer" is a perfect work of art. It is impossible to find fault with its content or its form ; and it is quite beyond the power of any critic to bring out all its excellences. One has to go beyond the confines of English literature,[22]

---

[21] Cp. J. F. Danby, *Shakespeare's Doctrine of Nature : a Study of King Lear*, London 1949, *passim*.

[22] English (as distinct from Scottish) literature also has its satirical portraits of canting hypocrites and nonconformist enthusiasts who fail to live up to their precepts. The Puritan was a figure of fun as early as Elizabethan times (cp. Malvolio in *Twelfth Night* ; Tribulation Wholesome and Ananias in *The Alchemist*) but it was not until after the Restoration that the ridicule of Puritanism reached really savage proportions. Incidentally, as Dr W. J. Cameron has pointed out to me, the burlesque prayer was a favourite device of *English* political satire in the

and to a much larger work—Molière's *Tartuffe*—to find its equal as an indictment of hypocrisy.

"The Twa Herds" and "Holy Willie's Prayer" were at first circulated orally and in manuscript, and during the months before 31 Jul. 1786, when the Kilmarnock edition was published, they gained a local celebrity which made Burns seem like a semi-official propagandist of the Moderate party in Church affairs. He was now the equal, perhaps even the hero, of liberal lawyers like Gavin Hamilton and Robert Aiken; and he was able to mix on friendly terms with New Licht clergymen such as the Rev. John M'Math of Tarbolton. But in the epistle "To William Simpson of Ochiltree" (May 1785),[23] whose postscript sets forth the difference between Auld and New Licht parties in terms of a spirited allegory, Burns specifically disclaims any intention of becoming the tool of a faction. Poets should be above the details of ephemeral theological squabbles, for their main business is elsewhere:

seventeenth-century. There are points in common between Burns's anti-Calvinist satires and the attacks on sectaries by such writers as Samuel Butler (in *Hudibras*) and Dryden in *Absalom and Achitophel* (esp. i, ll. 520–2, 529–32). Fairchild, i. 45–8, ii. 14–49, 119–30 and *passim*, quotes from many minor English poets and versifiers between 1700 and 1780 who show an attitude towards Nonconformism and Wesleyanism rather reminiscent of Burns's view of the Auld Lichts. In particular, Fairchild draws attention (i. 47–8) to Edward Ward's *Hudibras Redivivus* (1705–7), which contains a mock sermon with these lines:

> O sanctify this Congregation;
> Scatter their Seed throughout the Nation,
> And cleanse their wicked Souls within,
> From all the filthy Dregs of Sin;
> Wash from them all their Blots and Stains,
> As Housewives do their Pots and Pans:
> O stretch their Consciences I pray;
> O stretch 'em largely every way,
> That by that means they may embrace
> A greater Portion of thy Grace;
> Which well improv'd by Pray'r and Fasting,
> May make them Saints for Everlasting!
>> This he repeated o'er again,
>> And all the People cry'd, *Amen*.

That Nonconformists and Wesleyans were apt to be loose-living was a commonplace of this sort of *English* religious satire in the early eighteenth century; so, too, was the idea that there was something essentially comic about their style of preaching. The poem was originally published in a pamphlet, with a title-page which reads: "The | Prayer |of |Holy Willie, | a canting, hypocritical, Kirk Elder. | With quotations from the Presbyterian Eloquence. | . . . M DCC LXXXIX."

[23] i. 167 (383).

> Sae, ye observe that a' this clatter
> Is naething but a 'moonshine matter';
> But tho' dull prose-folk Latin splatter
>   In logic tulzie,
> I hope we Bardies ken some better
>   Than mind sic brulzie.

Some four months later, on 17 Sep. 1785, Burns penned an epistle "To the Rev. John M'Math" himself,[24] rejecting the Olympian detachment of the postscript to the epistle "To William Simpson." The Auld Licht party are withered, desiccated—the enemies of life; what can a generous red-blooded man do but scorn their antics?

> But I gae mad at their grimaces,
> Their sighin, cantin, grace-proud faces,
> Their three-mile prayers an' hauf-mile graces,
>   Their raxin conscience,
> Whase greed, revenge, an' pride disgraces
>   Waur nor their nonsense.

The whole tone of this epistle implies that Burns was no infidel even in 1785, when writing the ecclesiastical satires. True, he says:

> But twenty times I rather would be
>   An atheist clean
> Than under gospel colors hid be
>   Just for a screen.

An honest atheist is preferable to a religious hypocrite, but as he makes clear in the eleventh stanza ("All hail, Religion!...") and in the fourteenth ("O Ayr!..."), Burns thought of himself as a servant of true religion, identified with that "candid lib'ral band . . . Of public teachers" to which M'Math belonged. The position of the epistle to M'Math is an extremely dangerous one for any writer to take up, for it is suspiciously like the first stage of the process which so often turns a sincere man into a party hack.

Fortunately Burns was too inconsistent—and too great—to remain within such narrow bounds, and his next religious satire, "The Ordination,"[25] is less narrowly partisan than one would expect from the epistle to M'Math. When, early in 1785,

---

[24] II. 76 (357).   [25] I. 210 (397). For phonetics, see below, p. 355.

a Moderate clergyman called Multrie died in Kilmarnock, the
patron appointed as his successor McKinlay, a young man of
the opposite faction. The Auld Lichts were jubilant; the
devotees of common sense were much cast down. Before
McKinlay was actually inducted, Burns framed an imaginative
preview of his ordination. As in all his best satires, he slips into
the imputed point of view of those to whom he is opposed, and
personification (always a favourite mode of poetical thought
with him) is more daringly extended than in almost any other
work of his:

> Now auld Kilmarnock, cock thy tail,
> An' toss thy horns fu' canty;
> Nae mair thou'lt rowte out-owre the dale,
> Because thy pasture's scanty;
> For lapfu's large o' gospel kail
> Shall fill thy crib in plenty,
> An' runts o' grace, the pick an' wale,
> No gien by way o' dainty,
>   But ilka day. . . .
>
> See, see auld Orthodoxy's faes
> She's swingein thro' the city!
> Hark, how the nine-tail'd cat she plays!
> I vow it's unco pretty:
> There, Learning, with his Greekish face,
> Grunts out some Latin ditty;
> And Common-Sense is gaun, she says,
> To mak to Jamie Beattie
>   Her plaint this day.
>
> But there's Morality himsel,
> Embracing all opinions;
> Hear, how he gies the tither yell
> Between his twa companions!
> See, how she peels the skin an' fell,
> As ane were peelin onions!
> Now there, they're packèd aff to hell,
> An' banish'd our dominions,
>   Henceforth this day.

"The Ordination" is one of the finest and freshest things
Burns ever did. The first of the three stanzas just quoted may

be taken as typical of the way his mind worked when at its fullest stretch; as John Speirs has pointed out, the single phrase "gospel kail" is startling in its novelty, for the traditional concept of God's word as our spiritual food has become altogether transformed by the concrete associations of "kail."[26] It is as if these two words alone have generated a tremendous flash illuminating the whole of the surrounding scene: Kilmarnock compared to a half-famished cow (and, by implication, all its people to cattle) that charges over the fields because it has been starved on the meagre grass of passionless reason rather than filled to repletion on the solider winter-feed of orthodoxy. "Gospel kail," "runts o' grace": the parochial oafishness of these narrow-minded brutes could not be more witheringly expressed. The Burns of this poem is the man described by W. P. Ker as being not of the people but far above them,[27] for the world of "The Ordination" is put at such a distance that even the New Licht adherents are observed from the outside, and seen to be as limited—and almost as laughable—as their diehard enemies. In the twelfth stanza ("But there's Morality . . .") the Auld Licht contempt for mere legality is rendered in another homely image, linked to "gospel kail" by the associations of the kitchen—Morality peels off the skin of argument in successive layers "As ane were peelin onions"; the reader feels that Burns, in this poem at any rate, finds both antagonists rather funny. Something of the detached delight of an aloof but not altogether unsympathetic observer has entered into his vision, and the very fact of his dealing with a mass of people, a crowd of human beings pushing and jostling and feeling and hating, rather than with a single cosmic hypocrite, generates a geniality that persists even when he despises. In the very last stanza, however, there is a note of grim terror as he hints at the savage glee of a mob that could as easily be pushed into a lynching mood:

> Come, bring the tither mutchkin in,
> And here's—for a conclusion—

---

[26] Cp. John Speirs, *The Scots Literary Tradition*, henceforth cited as Speirs, London 1940, p. 130. In the 1787 Edinburgh Edition, "gospel kail" "runts," and "grace" are all italicised.

[27] W. P. Ker, "Robert Burns," in *On Modern Literature*, edd. T. S. Spencer and J. Sutherland, London 1955, p. 56.

To ev'ry New Light mother's son,
  From this time forth, confusion!
If mair they deave us wi' their din
  Or patronage intrusion,
We'll light a spunk, and, ev'ry skin,
  We'll run them aff in fusion,
          Like oil some day.

One of the elements in "The Ordination" is an impressionistically presented *genre* picture in which comedy and satire are one, emerging despite, and indeed *through*, the allegorical framework, and suggesting comparison with both "Halloween" and "The Holy Fair."[28]

"The Address to the Unco Guid, or the Rigidly Righteous,"[29] probably written at about the same time, is a much more personal poem than "The Ordination." It centres in the opposition between "Natural Instinct," identified with the poet and all erring lads and lasses, and the "Old Men (and Women) of the Tribe"—doubtless to be equated with the Auld Licht High-fliers of the surrounding poems. But all trace of the local and the contingent has been eliminated, so that the work reiterates the timeless plea of a young and passionate man to his intolerant elders:

Think, when your castigated pulse
  Gies now and then a wallop,
What ragings must his veins convulse,
  That still eternal gallop!
Wi' wind and tide fair i' your tail,
  Right on ye scud your sea-way;
But in the teeth o' baith to sail,
  It maks an unco lee-way. . . .

[28] In "The Ordination" Burns is making use of a modification of a traditional Scottish metre which older vernacular poets employed in works describing popular amusements (see H. & H., i. 328 ff.; Angellier, ii. 45–51; Wittig, p. 114). To describe the ordination of a clergyman in stanzas with orgiastic associations was in itself a satirical thrust. In the last two stanzas Burns increases the irony by substituting "some day" for the conventional "this day" of the final line. It is interesting that, as Mr R. L. C. Lorimer has pointed out to me, one of the stories that Barbour took (probably) from Douglas family oral tradition and versified, ends with the line: "Thusgat yschit Thrillwall *that day*" (*The Bruce*, ed. W. M. Mackenzie, London 1909, vi. 450). Does this mean that the stanza goes back at least as far as Scottish (prose) oral tradition of the fourteenth century?

[29] i. 217 (402).

Ye high, exalted, virtuous dames,
    Tied up in godly laces,
Before ye gie poor Frailty names,
    Suppose a change o' cases :
A dear-lov'd lad, convenience snug,
    A treach'rous inclination—
But, let me whisper i' your lug,
    Ye're aiblins nae temptation.[30]

The "Address to the Unco Guid" supplies one of the connexions between the ecclesiastical satires and the rest of Burns's poetry. The "unco guid" are the Holy Willies of this world, and also the profit-hunters of the epistles, whose life (and tongues) are "like a weel-gaun mill," and who—irony of ironies— would regard the pains of Hell as less to be feared than the waste of money which debauchery entails :

O, would they stay to calculate
    Th' eternal consequences,
Or—your more dreaded hell to state—
    Damnation of expenses !

Calvinist austerity, rigid righteousness, mechanical living, fear of the instincts, "miserliness" : all are seen as aspects of the same thing. The antinomies of "animal life" and control which the "Dialogue between Father and Son" had resolved into "inner regularity and order" are partly manifest in the social world as a struggle between two different sets of people, but they are also to be found inside the individual man as he painfully tries to place "nature in the order that its creator designed it."[31]

The final stanza expresses the theory which must have been

[30] This sixth stanza perhaps contains a reminiscence of Thomson, "Summer," ll. 1296–9 :

A delicate refinement, known to few,
Perplexed his breast and urged him to retire :
But love forbade. Ye prudes in virtue, say
Say, ye severest, what would you have done?

Cp. *Life and Works of Robert Burns*, ed. P. Hately Waddell, henceforth cited as Hately Waddell, Glasgow 1867, p. 99. And st. vii, l. 4, "To step aside is human," together with the underlying idea of st. viii, clearly stems from Pope, *Essay on Criticism*, l. 525 : "To err is human, to forgive, divine."

[31] Cp. above, pp. 40–1.

continually at the back of Burns's mind as he wrote the ecclesiastical satires—that salvation depends entirely on the quality of men's lives as judged by God alone :

> Who made the heart, 'tis He alone
>   Decidedly can try us :
> He knows each chord, its various tone,
>   Each spring, its various bias :
> Then at the balance let's be mute,
>   We never can adjust it ;
> What's done we partly may compute,
>   But know not what's resisted.[32]

And as befits the expression of a theory in that century of Scottish philosophers, it is couched in pure Scots-English ; characteristically, Burns moves from fairly broad Scots, as in the third stanza, into the more rarefied—but still thoroughly natural—diction of the conclusion, which unites the concepts of eighteenth-century sentiment ("who made the heart"), the rhythms of the Metrical Psalms (the first line of the stanza), a metaphor from his favourite art of music, the mechanist's governing image of the clock, and a reference to modern cost-accounting and double-entry book-keeping.[33]

In "The Holy Fair"[34] the opposition between instinct and rational control is projected on to the outer world, appearing first in the allegorical figures whom the poet meets "upon a simmer Sunday morn"—Superstition and Hypocrisy in "manteeles o' dolefu' black," and Fun, gaily clad in the latest fashion. The same antithesis is also manifest in the two sorts of people who come to listen to the communion sermons : sober ministers and orthodox laity versus bright crowds of sensual peasants. On the one hand there are the death-desiring clergy, Auld Licht and New strangely united in spite of all their mutual hostility ;

---

[32] A lighter gloss on the same theory is provided by a version of "For a' that" in *The Merry Muses of Caledonia*, henceforth cited as *The Merry Muses*, edd. J. Barke, S. G. Smith, and J. De Lancey Ferguson, Auk Society, Edinburgh 1959 : see below, p. 297.

[33] To trace the sources of this stanza in any detail would mean ranging widely over eighteenth-century literature, in verse and prose. Is there, perhaps, a fusion of Hume's "Mechanism of the Passions" with the idea of God as the Great Artificer ?

[34] l. 36 (328).

on the other, the life-worshipping, "swankie," fornicating lads and easy-going lasses of the countryside.

The main body of the poem is a realistic treatment of what went on at the "Occasion," "Great Work," or "Sacred Solemnity," as it was variously called—the Holy Communion which several parishes were accustomed to celebrate together. At these "Holy Fairs" a village of 500 souls would perhaps find its population swollen to upwards of 2,000. The Communion itself took place sometimes inside the church, sometimes outside in the open air ; but always a "tent" or movable (wooden) pulpit was set up outside, from which a number of the local ministers would preach in turn. The Occasions often lasted for as long as a week.

> There were two services and sermons on Thursday, two, or even three, on Saturday ; and the long communion services of Sunday, with the "action sermon" preceding the Supper, were concluded by another sermon at night, to be succeeded by the Monday services. . . . The communion services on Sunday in those days began usually at nine o'clock in the morning and continued till night, when a sermon wound up the laborious day. With 2000 communicants there would be thirty tables, each to be addressed by ministers in turn before the elements were handed round.[35]

These mass ceremonies always took place in the summer months, the Mauchline one on the second Sunday of August. How large was the assembly described by Burns can be gathered from the estimates in the records of the Kirk Session that 1350 persons took communion in 1784, 1242 in 1785, and "about fourteen hundred" in 1786. It must be remembered that the number of communicants was necessarily only a fraction (though in all probability a large fraction) of those actually present, since the tables were "fenced" before the actual celebration, and all "unclean and unworthy persons" forbidden to take part ; many more than twelve hundred people must, therefore, have been in and around Mauchline Kirkyard that August Sunday in 1785.[36]

However solemn they may have been in the days of persecution when the Covenanters had perforce to meet in the open,

[35] Graham, ii. 36–43.   [36] Chambers, i. 268, n.

by the middle of the eighteenth century these Holy Fairs often exhibited what H. G. Graham calls "ugly features."[37] An important document here is a *Letter from a Blacksmith to the Ministers and Elders of the Church of Scotland, in which the Manner of Publick Worship in that Church is considered, its Inconveniences and Defects pointed out, and Methods of removing them honestly proposed,* published (strangely enough) in London in 1759. The blacksmith's account of the goings-on at these Occasions is so like Burns's that some have suggested it as a possible prose source for "The Holy Fair":

> In Scotland, they run from kirk to kirk, and flock to see a sacrament, and make the same use of it that the papists do of their pilgrimages and processions; that is, indulge themselves in drunkenness, folly, and idleness. . . . At the time of the administration of the Lord's Supper upon the Thursday, Saturday, and Monday, we have preaching in the fields near the church. At first, you find a great number of men and women lying together upon the grass; here they are sleeping and snoring, some with their faces towards heaven, others with their faces turned downwards, or covered with their bonnets; there you find a knot of young fellows and girls making assignations to go home together in the evening, or to meet in some ale-house; in another place you see a pious circle sitting round an ale-barrel, many of which stand ready upon carts for the refreshment of the saints. . . in this sacred assembly there is an odd mixture of religion, sleep, drinking, courtship, and a confusion of sexes, ages, and characters. When you get a little nearer the speaker, so as to be within the reach of the sound, though not of the sense of the words, for that can only reach a small circle, you will find some weeping and others laughing, some pressing to get nearer the tent or tub in which the parson is sweating, bawling, jumping, and beating the desk; others fainting with the stifling heat, or wrestling to extricate themselves from the crowd: one seems very devout and serious, and the next moment is scolding and cursing his neighbour for squeezing or treading on him; in an instant after, his countenance is composed to the religious gloom, and he is groaning, sighing, and weeping for his sins: in a word, there is such an absurd mixture of the serious and comic, that were we convened for any other purpose than that of worshipping the God and Governor of Nature, the scene would exceed all *power of face.*[38]

[37] Graham, II, 46.   [38] Quoted in Chambers, I, 268–9.

However much "The Holy Fair" may have been suggested by the blacksmith's account, or by Fergusson's "Leith Races" (a description of mass jollification employing the same stanzaic form, in which the allegorised figure of Mirth addresses the poet just as Fun does in "The Holy Fair),[39] the fact remains that its vividness derives from actual observation of the Mauchline Occasion, which Burns must certainly have attended. The poem exhibits to a still further degree that detachment from the events described which one can sense behind all the dramatically presented mob emotion of "The Ordination." But the populace are not observed in any spirit of detestation; only the clergy are despised, though not nearly so violently as in more nakedly partisan poems. If he is aloof, as befits the "makar," the creator of it all, Burns is also delighted with what he beholds—he sees that it is good, with something of the same *joie de vivre* that impels the majority of the communicants:

> Here farmers gash, in ridin graith,
>   Gaed hoddin by their cotters;
> There swankies young, in braw braid-claith,
>   Are springin owre the gutters.
> The lasses, skelpin barefit, thrang,
>   In silks an' scarlets glitter;
> Wi' sweet-milk cheese, in monie a whang,
>   An' farls, bak'd wi' butter,
>   Fu' crump that day.

[39] The plan of the poem bears a general resemblance to those of the "Christ's Kirk on the Green," "Peeblis to the Play," Fergusson's "Hallow-fair" and "Leith Races," and Mayne's "Siller Gun"—all works dealing with popular festivals and all exhibiting a strong family likeness. In both "Leith Races" and "The Holy Fair" the poet is directed to go to an amusement by an allegorical personage, Mirth or Fun; in neither case did he have any idea of doing so at first. In both works allegory is left behind as soon as the poet reaches the scene of revelry. But Fergusson has only the one personified figure, that of Mirth; in Burns, Fun is accompanied by her two sisters, Superstition and Hypocrisy, who may, according to Ritter, have been suggested by Formalist and Hypocrisy in *The Pilgrim's Progress*. In Burns's poem there are many detailed echoes of "Leith Races" as well as of Fergusson's other poems, "Hallow-fair" and "Braid Claith"; and phrases occur which can be paralleled in Ballantyne's "Vertue and Vyce" (known to Burns from the version printed in Allan Ramsay's *Ever Green*), Ramsay's *Gentle Shepherd* and "Tale of Two Bonnets," Shakespeare's *Hamlet*, and the Bible. Burns draws on two traditions for the language of the poem—vernacular realism, and Biblical English as employed by Presbyterian preachers in Scotland. The use which he makes of these traditions is explosive, to say the least. Cp. Hately Waddell, p. 90; Angellier, II. 45–82; and Ritter, pp. 133–5.

This is the poetry of sense-perception—of motion, sound (*e.g.* the jangling of harness and cantering of horses echoed in the first two lines of the stanza, and, in the fifth, the slip-slop of naked feet on hard ground, reflected in "skelpin barefit"), vision (*e.g.* the combination of action and colour in the fifth and sixth lines), and, finally, taste. The stanza is so startlingly sensuous that it makes one wonder what Keats might have written had his sights and sounds and tastes and smells been those of peasant life.

Saints and sinners are sharply divided, but they are so used to one another that they provide a richly humorous spectacle of peaceful coexistence :

> Here some are thinkin on their sins,
>> An' some upo' their claes ;
> Ane curses feet that fyl'd his shins,
>> Anither sighs an' prays :
> On this hand sits a chosen swatch,
>> Wi' screw'd-up, grace-proud faces ;
> On that a set o' chaps, at watch,
>> Thrang winkin on the lasses
>>> To chairs that day.

The lover composes himself "sweetly" on his chair. His arm slips gradually round his mistress's neck until his hand rests upon her breast, while Mr Moodie of Riccarton (one of the main contestants in "The Twa Herds") pours out the vials of his wrath upon the multitude :

> Hear how he clears the points o' Faith
>> Wi' rattlin and thumpin !
> Now meekly calm, now wild in wrath,
>> He's stampin, an' he's jumpin !
> His lengthen'd chin, his turn'd-up snout,
>> His eldritch squeel an' gestures,
> O how they fire the heart devout—
>> Like cantharidian plaisters
>>> On sic a day.

"Cantharidian plaisters" is another of those lightning flashes which shoot through an entire poem, a galvanic unity of opposites : cantharides, or "Spanish fly," is a blistering agent if taken externally, an aphrodisiac if swallowed, so that the very use of the term establishes a connexion between the Hell-fire sermons of the body of the poem and the "houghma-gandie" of the conclusion. All the time Moodie pounds out his terrible homilies on Hell and damnation, the congregation slumbers peacefully, but as soon as Smith begins preaching reason and moderation, "There's peace an' rest nae langer."

There is yet another bond of union between the godly and the ungodly—love of strong drink. Burns's method is to shock us by bringing together images and words which we would not normally associate with one another; it is the "gospel kail" process on a larger scale. Far from distorting reality, the technique merely serves to reveal its inner truth, for what Burns does is to bring out into the light of day connexions actually existing in the scene before him" :

> Smith opens out his cauld harangues,
>   On practice and on morals ;
> An' aff the godly pour in thrangs,
>   To gie the jars an' barrels
>   A lift that day.

In this passage the point of view has shifted from that of the godly themselves (when he calls Smith's sermons "cauld," Burns is employing the very word the orthodox themselves would use) to that of the all-seeing omniscient Bard, so that when, in the next stanza, he returns to the phraseology of some Auld Licht stalwart, the effect is a curiously paradoxical one. We feel that *both* Smith and Moodie are being surveyed from a great height, and with amusement :

> What signifies his barren shine,
>   Of moral pow'rs an' reason ?
> His English style, an' gesture fine
>   Are a' clean out o' season.
> Like Socrates or Antonine,
>   Or some auld pagan heathen,
> The moral man he does define,
>   But ne'er a word o' faith in
>   That's right that day.

Two other preachers, William Peebles of Newton-on-Ayr

and "Wee Miller" of Kilmaurs are pilloried next—Peebles for the "meek an' mim" way he views the Word of God, and Miller for conscious dissimulation. Secretly, Burns says, Miller holds with the new doctrines but preaches the old ones because he "wants [*i.e.* lacks] a manse." The roving eye now shifts to the inn, full of ale-cup commentators and lads and lasses stirring their toddy or "forming assignations" in corners, only to return to the preaching-tent when Black Russell takes the rostrum. "The Lord's ain trumpet," Burns called him; many years later a correspondent of Chambers's described him as "the most tremendous man I ever saw. . . . His voice was like thunder, and his sentiments were such as must have shocked any class of hearers in the least more refined than those whom he usually addressed."[40]

In this particular sermon his subject is Hell, which he describes so loudly and so eloquently that

> The half-asleep start up wi' fear,
>   An' think they hear it roarin;
> When presently it does appear,
>   'Twas but some neebor snorin
>   Asleep that day.

The poem ends with further brief but distanced sketches of the people in holiday mood, executed in a spirit of tolerance and love. In the final stanza the two opposing sides of village life are once more set down side by side; by this time, after all the festive noise and bustle in which they have so strangely intermingled, they have become parallel and almost complementary. Burns on his rural Olympus can appreciate them both simultaneously, by means of something that can only be called wit. It is at once more humorous and less subtle than the wit of a Pope or a Donne, but it is still worthy of the term : a characteristically Burnsian quality bearing the poet's own personal stamp as surely as, say, "Insnar'd with Flowers, I fall on Grass," does that of Andrew Marvell. Burns's wit is like Marvell's in at least one important respect ; it endeavours to unite dissimilars, even if only temporarily :

[40] Chambers, I. 275.

How monie hearts this day converts
　　O' sinners and o' lasses!
Their hearts o' stane, gin night, are gane
　　As saft as onie flesh is:
There's some are fou o' love divine;
　　There's some are fou o' brandy;
An' monie jobs that day begin,
　　May end in houghmagandie
　　　　Some ither day.

David Daiches has pointed out that in this concluding stanza the choice of theological terms to describe the softening of the girls' hearts daringly reverses "an old tradition in religious poetry—the practice of using secular love terms to denote divine love. . . . Burns starts from the coldly theological and moves rapidly down to the physical and the earthy"[41]—a descent which Donne also made, though in a rather different way. In that last and greatest surprise of all, the rhyme of "brandy" with "houghmagandie," the opposites cease to balance and the scales tip until they kick the beam. That pagan, unspiritual love whose source and only dwelling is the body achieves total dominance, like the final crash of chords at the end of a symphony. Burns in "The Holy Fair" can love both sorts of people, sinners and "unco guid," because he can see them all as human and therefore comic: but Houghmagandie and the Life Force are in the end stronger and better than either the White Christ of the morality-men or the Jehovah and Muckle Black Deil of the extreme Calvinists.[42] Miss Keith maintains that "The Holy Fair" is "the most subtly constructed of all Burns' poems,"[43] and from the context it is clear that she is thinking mainly of its alliterative and assonantal

[41] Daiches, pp. 130–1.

[42] Folk-poetry recognised that life is in the last resort stronger than theory, and found irresistible comedy in a saint doing the act of darkness in broad daylight. Folk-humour of this kind is one element in "Holy Willie's Prayer." (Cp. above, p. 59). It is seen at its coarsest in some of the songs in *The Merry Muses*, e.g. "Errock Brae," p. 134, and "The Case of Conscience (I'll tell you a tale of a wife)," 37 ff., which show the clash between sex and Calvinism even more brutally than in Burns's acknowledged work. But it should not be forgotten that a similar humour is found in the English aristocratic anti-clerical satirist Charles Churchill, as well as in English anti-Puritan writings generally. See Fairchild, II. 35–41 and *passim*.

[43] C. Keith, p. 43.

qualities. The poem exhibits complete mastery of traditional poetic skills, employed for a dual purpose—to "make" a perfect work of art, in the sense which underlies the old Scots word "makar," or poet, and to perform what Ritter calls a cultural deed ("eine kulturelle That")[44] in the battle of ideas in Ayrshire. Indeed, the form and content of "The Holy Fair" are so indissolubly united that one cannot possibly take the sound-patterns as exhibiting what Dr Wittig calls "decoration on a small surface." In this poem, as is usual in Burns, rhyme, alliteration, and assonance are not added from the outside; they are not embroidery, but part of the poem's total meaning; they are not *on* the surface, but, rather they *are* the surface; and they reach down to the depths as well.[45]

There are three other poems in which Burns is concerned primarily with Kirk affairs—"The Calf,"[46] an impudent extempore on a text given out in church by the Rev. James Steven, dating from about September 1786; "A new Psalm for the Chapel of Kilmarnock,"[47] written much later, in April 1789; and "The Kirk's Alarm,"[48] written in July of the same year. "The Calf" is a spirited piece of essentially verbal tomfoolery; "The Kirk's Alarm" is mainly of local and historical interest, and is essentially an example of rather crude "flyting" or name-calling, which suggests that by 1789 Burns's heart was no longer in ecclesiastical satire. Only the "New Psalm" has something of the old solemnity of tone.

The great anti-Calvinist satires are pictures of the old Scotland from the point of view sometimes of the new rationalist outlook which had already been adopted by many of the gentry and the educated classes, sometimes of an imagination which can comprehend and transcend both Auld Lichts and New. Burns was not for long content to be the voice of a faction: "Holy Willie's Prayer," for example, derives its continued vitality from the high comedy which it distils from the rationalisations of a personality divided against itself, while both "The Ordination" and "The Holy Fair" are more than

---

[44] Ritter, p. 67. Though his statement referred originally to "Holy Willie's Prayer," it applies equally to "The Holy Fair."

[45] Wittig, p. 63; and for phonetic details, see Appendix I, § 4 (below, p. 356).   [46] I. 216 (401).   [47] II. 162 (391).   [48] II. 30 (324).

party polemics. If one ignores "The Calf" and "The Kirk's Alarm" as appendages important mainly as proving that Burns had by the end of 1786 lost interest in the *genre*, his ecclesiastical poems show a development from satire to humour and from partisanship to the acceptance of human beings as such—an attitude perfectly compatible with a certain personal isolation. "The Holy Fair" has something in common with "Halloween," but in some ways it also looks forward to "Tam o' Shanter"; it belongs to the sphere of comical realism as much as to satire. The further development of Kirk themes in Burns is associated with the half humorous, half emblematic figure of the Devil—a topic considered later.[49]

[49] Below, pp. 217–20.

IV

The first Epistles

O NE must not picture Burns even in the bitter years at Irvine and Lochlie as being exclusively dominated by gloom. There were books to explore and girls to love and human foibles to laugh away;[1] occasionally, too, the daily experiences of the farm might become the raw material of poetry, as in "The Death and Dying Words of Poor Mailie, the Author's only Pet Yowe : An unco Mournfu' Tale,"[2] which may well date from 1782, immediately after the disastrous flax-dressing experiment.[3] The poem belongs to a favourite Scottish *genre*, which has obvious affinities with a type of stall-ballad recounting the last words of some criminal or popular hero. The first modern example in vernacular verse is a piece of Hamilton of Gilbertfield's entitled "The Last Dying Words of Bonny Heck" (published in 1706), from which Allan Ramsay drew the inspiration of "Lucky Spence's Last Advice" and "The Last Speech of a Wretched Miser"; but because the last words on this occasion are not those of a bawd or an innkeeper but of a sheep, Burns's poem harks back to "Bonny Heck" itself, which was written about a dog, with the features common to the old beast fable so beloved of La Fontaine and John Gay—not to speak of Robert Henryson, the fifteenth-century Dunfermline schoolmaster who was, perhaps, the greatest of all Scottish poets.[4]

"Poor Mailie" is a delightfully comic treatment of many of the themes expressed elsewhere by Burns in mournful and elegiac numbers, but here objectified as animal attitudes and character types. The reader is able to recapture Burns's

---

[1] Cp. the autobiographical letter [to Moore], in *Letters*, I. 111–13.

[2] I. 53 (343).

[3] Cp. W. A. Craigie, *A Primer of Burns*, henceforth cited as Craigie, London 1896, p. 62.

[4] Such is the assessment of Henryson made by the latest European scholar to examine Scottish literature. Cp. Wittig, p. 52.

original delight at mastering himself and his society—an emotion which, if it does not help him to laugh away his own predicament, at least puts him in touch with a comic response to problems which, for all their surface irrelevancy, may well be at bottom similar to his own.

The first twelve lines set the scene with some remarkably vivid details—the tethered ewe tangled in her rope and groaning out her last message on earth to Hughoc, the half-witted labourer. The incident is particularly striking because of the lively associations aroused by the Scots words, such as the twisting action of "warsl'd," so inadequately translated as "floundered," in the line :

> An' owre she warsl'd in the ditch.

Again, Hughoc's aimless moonstruck straw-chewing vacancy is perfectly conveyed by only two words, "doytin by," which the English rendering "doddering past" somehow fails to catch. Mailie instructs Hughoc to report her dying words to her dear Master—Burns—and while Hughoc stands motionless she pours out a complaint in which, it is clear, the poet is playfully criticising himself :

> "Tell him, if e'er again he keep
> As muckle gear as buy a sheep—
> O, bid him never tie them mair,
> Wi' wicked strings o' hemp or hair !
> But ca' them out to park or hill,
> An' let them wander at their will. . . ."

There is indeed a delicious irony in this injunction to a master who was himself so often irked by the "wicked strings" of social restriction ; and it is perhaps also significant that release from restraint is linked with an increase of worldly goods, with the formation of capital. If Burns lets his flock loose he will grow rich :

> "So may his flock increase, an' grow
> To scores o' lambs, an' packs o' woo' ! . . ."

Modern readers may not immediately realise that Poor Mailie is doing nothing less than urging her master to adopt a new agricultural system—namely to give up the traditional tethering of stock on the stubble and to take up sheep-rearing on a larger scale, perhaps on enclosed fields. Though on upland farms, as a recent local historian informs us, "the indigenous blackfaced sheep maintained their sway," there was "a prejudice against keeping sheep in enclosed fields" in Ayrshire as a whole. "Eventually sheep on the lowland farms were restricted to a few 'pet sheep'—tame specimens of imported breeds kept to supply the farmer's wife with wool."[5] But Lochlie was an upland farm and sheep-breeding on the hill would have been, economically speaking, a step forward.[6] Release from restraint, the gathering of capital, new methods of production : Mailie is indeed asking her master to advance !

Still further *nuances* can be detected in this apparently artless little poem. Mailie, the apostle of freedom, is at the same time (as befits a matron) a believer in the sexual decencies. She wants her master to bring up her lambs to be honest and upright sheep, brimful of common sense and observant of decorum. The little "yowie," the daughter-sheep, must not be restricted, but at the same time she must not abuse the liberty given her ; she must associate only with respectable rams from the lower middle class and keep away from all undisciplined anarchists. The last adjuration of all is a precept of common-sense morality which is typically Burnsian, and derives from the Sermon on the Mount, and from Leviticus (xix.17–18) :

> Mind to be kind to ane anither.

Though Mailie is unmistakably a sheep, she is also a human being ; and the comedy springs in part from the reader's discovery of matronly characteristics under her sedate and comfortable fleece.

But perhaps in "Poor Mailie" there is yet another source of humour—the traditional identification of a parson's congregation with a flock of sheep. There is, naturally enough, no crude and obvious parallelism, no deliberate preaching of a

---

[5] Strawhorn, p. 157.

[6] That Mailie was not one of the native black-faced breed is proved by the last stanza of the companion piece, "Poor Mailie's Elegy," l. 56 (344) : "She was nae get o' moorlan tips . . . | For her forbears were brought in ships, | Frae 'yont the Tweed. . . ." To pasture the descendants of such a specially-imported English ewe on the hill would be revolutionary in the Ayrshire of the time.

religious message; but it seems probable that Burns had at the back of his mind the idea that if only the shepherd offered greater freedom to his flock, both the number of the faithful and their material prosperity (always a major preoccupation of Calvinists) would increase.

There is thus considerably more than a hint of New Licht doctrine in the poem. When writing it, Burns must have been conscious of these various "levels" of meaning only as comedy; but the fact remains that "Poor Mailie" derives much of its appeal from the humorous juxtaposition of liberty and coercion, "Love thy neighbour" and orthodox Calvinism. One thinks immediately of

> Freedom and whisky gang thegither . . .

and of:

> Courts for cowards were erected,
> Churches built to please the priest![7]

Liberty was for him a creative concept. In his view, it was the essential basis of true order, whereas repression produced only a forced outward conformity that was in reality the reverse of true harmony. Burns always regarded freedom as being closely connected with the continuance of Scotland as a nation; and in a later poem he visualised Liberty as a "Highland filly"[8]—interestingly enough, again in a humorous work. Burns often made poems out of various aspects of Liberty—personal (including both sexual and intellectual aspects), economic, social, ecclesiastical, political, and international; but he always saw freedom concretely, in relation to Scotland's problems and to the paradoxical psychology of her people.

In "Poor Mailie," Burns very lightly, and without the slightest suggestion of tub-thumping, puts his finger on some of Scotland's most fundamental religious, moral, psychological and educational problems. Mailie's advice to Burns bears some resemblance to the doctrines of Rousseau, as well as to those of the closely associated British "sentimental school." In Rousseau's view, as expounded in *Émile*, the child's education

---

[7] These two quotations are from "The Author's Earnest Cry and Prayer," and from the final chorus of "The Jolly Beggars." Cp. below, pp. 144, 153.

[8] In "On Glenriddell's Fox Breaking his Chain." See below, p. 242.

should in its earliest years be merely negative, concerned with "preserving the heart from vice and the spirit from error." And though there is no evidence that Burns knew Rousseau's works at this time, it is interesting that Mailie's advice to her master should correspond so closely to concepts expounded in *Émile*.

The "toop-lamb" was to be given positive instruction, when he was old enough to profit by it :

> An' no to rin an' wear his cloots,
> Like other menseless, graceless brutes.

In Rousseau's scheme, however, when the child reaches the age of fifteen or so, the teacher is exhorted in these terms :

> Let him know that man is by nature good, let him feel it, let him judge his neighbour by himself; but let him see how men are depraved and perverted by society.[9]

No doubt the "toop-lamb" would see how other sheep were depraved ; but he was also to be told, in unmistakable terms, what sort of conduct to avoid. Thus Burns's opinions, in this poem at least, are Rousseauistic only up to a point ; they are in reality much more akin to the eight chapters in *Pamela*[10] which deal with Locke's *Thoughts concerning Education*, or even to Locke's treatise itself, with its emphasis on positive moral precepts rather than on emotion. Nevertheless there can be little doubt that Burns would, in another context, have agreed with Annesley in Henry Mackenzie's novel, *The Man of the World* :

> It was chiefly in this manner of instilling sentiments . . . by leading insensibly to the practice of virtue, rather than by downright precept, that Annesley proceeded with his children ; for it was his maxim that the heart must feel as well as the judgement be convinced, before the principles we mean to teach can be of habitual service.[11]

In "Poor Mailie," Burns makes humorous use of educational

[9] Rousseau, *Émile*, BK. IV (Everyman edn., p. 198).
[10] Richardson, *Pamela*, VOL. III, Letters XCI–VII.
[11] Quoted in H. W. Thompson, *A Scottish Man of Feeling: Some account of Henry Mackenzie, Esq. of Edinburgh and of the Golden Age of Burns and Scott*, henceforth cited as H. W. Thompson, London and N.Y. 1931, p. 137.

ideas that are half-way between Locke and Rousseau. The exact flavour of his compromise is peculiarly Scottish ; but the philosophies which influenced him were not Scottish but European in their scope—yet another indication that it is not enough to judge Burns in terms of the Scottish tradition alone.

The eighteen months or so between the beginning of 1785 and May 1786 were a period of rapid development and achievement. They saw Robert's passionate spell of practical farming at Mossgiel ; the birth of his first illegitimate child ; the most dramatic incidents in the Armour affair ; the courting of Highland Mary ; a whole series of Church squabbles in which the poet intervened with his pen ; and the production not only of most of the pieces in the Kilmarnock volume, but of some major works not printed until much later.

"Dear-bought Bess" was born to Elizabeth Paton, a servant in the Burns household, on 22 May 1785.[12] For her Robert wrote "A Poet's Welcome to his Love-begotten Daughter : The first Instance that entitled him to the Venerable Appellation of Father"[13]—a fine poem, full of pride, tenderness, and defiance of convention. "To John Rankine : In Reply to an Announcement,"[14] written shortly before this, had metaphorically announced Bess Paton's condition in two stanzas which ended on a characteristically jubilant note :

> But now a rumour's like to rise—
> A whaup's i' the nest.

The "Epistle to John Rankine, enclosing some Poems,"[15] the earliest of Burns's verse epistles, was also a response to the same affair. It is a light, confident, even impudent poem exhibiting many traits characteristic of the mature Burns. Rankine's personality is indicated by a few bold strokes only, so that the reader feels he has known this crude hard-drinking old sinner all the years of his life ; and in the third and fourth stanzas essentially the same method is employed as in "Holy Willie's Prayer." The trick consists in the apparent acceptance of the real or imputed ideas of those attacked, which here takes

---

[12] Snyder, pp. 118–9. [13] II. 37 (334).
[14] II. 70 (355). Rankine was tenant of Adamhill, a farm near Lochlie.
[15] I. 176 (384).

the form of a despairing, almost whining appeal to Rankine
to spare Hypocrisy :

> Hypocrisy, in mercy spare it !
> That holy robe, O, dinna tear it !
> Spare't for their sakes, wha aften wear it—
> The lads in black ;
> But your curst wit, when it comes near it,
> Rives 't aff their back.
>
> Think, wicked sinner, wha ye're skaithing :
> It's just the Blue-gown badge an' claithing
> O' saunts ; tak that, ye lea'e them naething
> To ken them by
> Frae onie unregenerate heathen,
> Like you or I.[16]

It is only in the seventh stanza that the main subject appears
—an account of Burns's dealings with Elizabeth Paton in a
comic allegory of guns and partridges and poaching.[17] In the
tenth, he swears that in revenge for having to make public confession before the Holy Willies, he'll make havoc next year on
all the girls in sight :

> But, by my gun, o' guns the wale,
> An' by my pouther an' my hail,
> An' by my hen, an' by her tail,
> I vow an' swear !
> The game shall pay, owre moor an' dale,
> For this, niest year !

This is the humour of the lads of the village : rough, full of
energy and pride in physical prowess, but not to be taken too
seriously. It is an example of Burns making real poetry out of
the commonest bawdy material.

[16] There is an interesting ironical turn at the end of the sixth stanza : "I'd
better gaen an' sair't the King | At Bunker's Hill." Burns, as we know from "A
Fragment : When Guilford Good," i. 246 (411), was opposed to the British
foreign policy of his day. No course would have been more suicidal than enlist-
ment for service in America, since it would have represented the ultimate in
reckless despair ; it would have meant risking his life, for spite or devilment, in a
cause he knew to be wrong. Burns is, in this sixth stanza, expressing what has since
become the ordinary working-class attitude to patriotism and soldiering—and not
in Scotland only.

[17] Burns also uses the same "allegory" in "The Bonie Moor-hen," iv. 20 (89).

The ideas and emotions out of which the best pieces in the Kilmarnock Edition were made can be traced in a series of poems less disciplined and more informal than his set pieces— the epistles to "Davie," J. Lapraik, William Simpson, John Goldie, and James Smith.

The first "Epistle to Davie [David Sillar], a Brother Poet,"[18] written in January 1785,[19] is concerned with the contrast between riches and poverty which underlies "Man was made to Mourn," as well as with another subject—the Rousseauistic glorification of "the heart."[20] Beginning with a firm and brisk impression of winter, the poem soon moves to those "great-folk" who are well-housed and comfortable in winter. Burns feels, however, that it is very wrong of him to envy the rich—a sentiment that rather takes the edge off his criticism of their "cursed pride." In the second stanza he introduces one of his major preoccupations, the possibility of beggary, and decides —like many a member of the class of agricultural labourers into which the Burnses were always afraid of falling—that the prospect is less fearsome when treated philosophically :

> But Davie, lad, ne'er fash your head,
>> Tho' we hae little gear ;
> We're fit to win our daily bread,
>> As lang's we're hale and fier :
>> 'Mair spier na, nor fear na,'
>>> Auld age ne'er mind a feg ;
>> The last o't, the warst o't,
>>> Is only but to beg.

[18] I. 117 (365).   [19] I. 369, *med.*

[20] Rousseauism came to Burns through Henry Mackenzie, Shenstone, and the eighteenth-century cult of sentiment. The ideas behind this poem—and many other works of Burns—represent concepts common to both Rousseau and Anglo-Scottish sentimentalism. For this whole question, see H. W. Thompson, pp. 98–106 and *passim*. In the "Epistle to Davie" there are distinct parallels to passages in Goldsmith's "The Traveller" and "The Deserted Village" ; Thomson's "Summer," "The Castle of Indolence," and *Agamemnon* ; Isaac Bickerstaffe's *Love in a Village* ; Young's "Ocean" ; Sterne's *Sentimental Journey* ; Cowper's "The Task" ; Shenstone's ninth Elegy and "Love and Honour" ; and Pope's "Eloisa to Abelard"—all by English or Anglo-Scottish writers. Naturally, there are also echoes of Scottish poets—of Ramsay's "The Poet's Wish" ; William Hamilton's "Second Epistle to Allan Ramsay" ; Fergusson's "Against Repining at Fortune" (the diction here is English, however), and "The Farmer's Ingle" : but the interesting thing is that there should be so much Englishry behind the poem. Cp. Ritter, pp. 61–6, for detailed exposition of the parallels.

When utterly destitute, Burns and Sillar have nowhere to sleep except in kilns or deserted barns—

> Nae mair then, we'll care then,
> Nae farther can we fa'.

He imagines Davie and himself enjoying an equality of perfect comradeship as "commoners of air," taking pleasure in landscapes of 'sweeping vales" and "foaming floods," complete with daisies and blackbirds. In spring-time on the hillsides they will set words to traditional tunes, proud and free in their mendicancy like the beggars of W. B. Yeats :[21]

> It's no in titles nor in rank :
> It's no in wealth like Lon'on Bank,
>   To purchase peace and rest.
> It's no in makin muckle, mair ;
> It's no in books, it's no in lear,
>   To make us truly blest :
> If happiness hae not her seat
>   An' centre in the breast,
> We may be wise, or rich, or great,
>   But never can be blest !
>   Nae treasures nor pleasures
>   Could make us happy lang ;
>   The heart ay's the part ay
>   That makes us right or wrang.

[21] Esp. the "Crazy Jane" and "Old Tom" songs, in *Collected Poems*, London 1950, pp. 290–307. Burns's attitude to beggary is both old and new. As J. D. Ferguson has pointed out, "the tradition of the blue-gowns, or licensed beggars, still persisted in rural Scotland," and Burns "seriously thought" of ending his life as a sort of Edie Ochiltree (Ferguson, p. 188)—that is, as a privileged mendicant of a type that was already on the way out. There are many seventeenth and eighteenth-century precedents for the Burnsian outlook, and even for specific turns of expression, e.g. Samuel Butler, *Hudibras*, i. iii, 877 ("I am not now in fortune's power ; | He that is down can sink no lower") ; Bunyan, *The Pilgrim's Progress*, Everyman edn., p. 285 ("He that is down needs fear no fall") ; and James Thomson, "To the Rev. Patrick Murdoch", l. 1 ("Thus safely low, my friend, thou canst not fall"). All these quotations (like Burns's lines) must go back ultimately to the Latin tag "Qui iacet in terra, non habet unde cadat" ; but there are at the same time some new features in Burns's outlook. It is the lower middle-class man who cannot bear to think of going on the dole, or of sinking into the group below his own, while it is the traditional "proletarian" of Marxist analysis who—in the nineteenth century, at any rate—took little thought for the morrow. Burns, in this mood, faintly foreshadows a characteristic of later working-class psychology ; but on other occasions he is as "canny" as any peasant proprietor or street-corner grocer.

The Puritan "inner light" has after many vicissitudes become with Burns the "heart" of an eighteenth-century rustic Man of Feeling.[22]

In the sixth stanza Burns comes back to the contrast with which he began, between the labouring poor and the idle rich. It is confidently asserted that men who "drudge and drive thro' wet and dry" are just as happy as those who live in palaces and mansions :

> Think ye, are we less blest than they,
> Wha scarcely tent us in their way,
>   As hardly worth their while ?
> Alas ! how oft, in haughty mood,
>   God's creatures they oppress !
> Or else, neglecting a' that's guid,
>   They riot in excess !

Burns's solution of this class conflict, which fills him with such detestation of the aristocracy, is not a social one, but something personal and private—the cultivation of a contented state of mind, "making the best of a bad job." The epistle begins to deteriorate from this point. Surely these lines from the eighth stanza are as nauseating as any adjuration of "the lads in black," and come perilously close to "All is for the best in the best of all possible worlds" :

> And, even should misfortunes come,
> I here wha sit hae met wi' some,
>   An's thankfu' for them yet,
> They gie the wit of age to youth ;
>   They let us ken oursel ;
> They make us see the naked truth,
>   The real guid and ill. . . .

In this eighth stanza Burns asserts that inner happiness (the positive Good of the poem) can be realised only in love and friendship—or as we would say today, in personal relation-

---

[22] Cp. Fairchild, i. 545–6. Fairchild regards the evolution from "inner light" to the sentimentalist's "heart" as typical for the English trading classes during the seventeenth and eighteenth centuries. If this is true, it follows that there is a strong "bourgeois" side to the work. I do not know whether any of Burns's Russian commentators have noticed this.

ships—and in the ninth stanza he even depicts his feelings for Jean Armour as an escape from the woes of daily life :

> When heart-corroding care and grief
> Deprive my soul of rest,
> Her dear idea brings relief
> And solace to my breast.

If poetically the tenth stanza is not much superior to the ninth, yet intellectually it is one of the key passages in the epistle. One might paraphrase it, cockney-fashion, as "It's bein' so tender as keeps me goin' " :

> All hail ! ye tender feelings dear !
> The smile of love, the friendly tear,
> The sympathetic glow !

Burns is in this poem taking himself seriously as a Man of Feeling, having apparently forgotten the self-criticism of such moods as the following :

> Beware a tongue that's smoothly hung,
> A heart that warmly seems to feel !
> That feeling heart but acts a part—
> 'Tis rakish art in Rob Mossgiel.[23]

Yet the thought is one he returned to again and again, in various guises—that love is the only thing that makes life worth living for the poor. In slightly more robust form it is the ground and foundation of that well-known lyric "Green grow the Rashes, O,"[24] while the same idea (this time quite unashamedly equated with four-lettered words) is a recurrent theme of all the "cloaciniad" verse in *The Merry Muses of Caledonia* :

> And why shouldna poor folk mowe, mowe, mowe,
> And why shouldna poor folk mowe :
> The great folk hae siller, & houses & lands,
> Poor bodies hae naething but mowe.[25]

Thus if the eighth, ninth and tenth stanzas of the "Epistle to Davie" appear a trifle mawkish to modern readers, it is important to realise that they express but one variant—a refined and somewhat tenuous one, it is true—of a concept which

---

[23] "O, leave Novèls " iv. 11 (84). [24] i. 251 (414).
[25] "When Princes & Prelates," in *Letters*, ii. 250–1.

would surely have met with the approval of D. H. Lawrence. In part, it is a gospel of "Joy through Sex" that Burns is preaching here—not simply the sexual act itself (which receives its tributes in the *The Merry Muses*), but all the emotions and sentiments which grow out of its soil. The other "positive" in the poem is friendship; and these two values of the heart are held to be sufficient to compensate for the exploitation of man by man. Was it because Burns knew in his heart of hearts that these "positives" are not in themselves enough to offset the real ills of life that the poem remained an interesting but imperfect experiment clogged by abstract monstrosities of diction like "sympathetic glow" and "tenebrific scene"? Perhaps Burns flew to the pompous-sounding English words because he did not really believe what he was saying.[26]

The first "Epistle to J. Lapraik, An Old Scottish Bard, April 1, 1785,"[27] has none of these verbal infelicities. Written in the traditional "Standard Habbie" measure, so eminently suited to poetic gossip and conversational topics, it is the very perfection of occasional verse. On Fasten-e'en, the evening before Lent, Burns had attended a traditional "rockin" or small social gathering where women spun on the distaff or wove stockings while each member of the company sang a song in turn. One piece in particular pleased Burns—

[26] When judged in terms of the kind of statement it is making, the "Epistle to Davie" exhibits a fusion of English and Scottish influences; and the glorification of the "heart" already discussed on p. 84 (n. 20) is based on ideas which, however popular they were in Edinburgh, came to Scotland from England and France. But considered as poetry, the work does not achieve a real synthesis of Scots and Scots-English. One reason for the failure is surely that this is the least conversational, the least "familiar," of all the Burns epistles. On the whole, it lacks spontaneity—perhaps because of the form, which must have forced Burns to work hard at the piece. The metre is a modification of a traditional stanza, used by Montgomerie in *The Cherrie and the Slae* (1597), which was reprinted in Watson's *Choice Collection* (1706–11) and in Ramsay's *Ever Green* (1724), and thus made familiar to the eighteenth century. Ramsay himself used it in works of his own composition, and Burns took it over from him, with certain modifications of his own. A typical example is found in the "Epistle to Davie," st. vi, ll. 7–10 ("Alas how oft . . . in excess"), where moral indignation has caused Burns to slip unconsciously into the intonation of the Scottish Metrical Psalms, so that we seem to hear the very accents of the Covenanters themselves. In this poem, too, Burns gives rein to his habit of repeating important words, but with much less success than usual. Such recurring words as "rhyme, happy (happiness), heart, pleasures, love(r), breast, friend(ly), blest," are set against "great, rich(es), care, fortune."

[27] I. 155 (380). For phonetics, see below, pp. 356–7.

Thought I, 'Can this be Pope, or Steele,
      Or Beattie's wark?'
They tald me 'twas an odd kind chiel
      About Muirkirk.

It was Lapraik's "When I upon thy Bosom Lean," which happens to bear an extraordinary resemblance to a song published in Ruddiman's *Weekly Magazine* for 11 Oct. 1773, under the *nom-de-plume* of "Happy Husband": a circumstance which has led many editors to brand Lapraik as a plagiarist. But there is no evidence for this whatsoever; Lapraik himself may have been "Happy Husband." Burns longed to make the acquaintance of the man who could compose such a song and was, he felt, a kindred spirit. He sent him a verse epistle suggesting a meeting at Mauchline Races or Mauchline Fair —or, at the very least, that Lapraik should write him a few lines in reply.

The "Epistle to J. Lapraik" is an important document because it is in some respects Burns's poetic manifesto, proclaiming the superiority of inspiration over the learned "Jargon o' your Schools,"[28] and the relevance (to Burns at least) of the vernacular tradition:

Gie me ae spark o' Nature's fire,
That's a' the learning I desire;
Then, tho' I drudge thro' dub an' mire
      At pleugh or cart,
My Muse, tho' hamely in attire,
      May touch the heart.

O for a spunk o' Allan's glee,
Or Fergusson's, the bauld an' slee,
Or bright Lapraik's, my friend to be,
      If I can hit it!
That would be lear eneugh for me,
      If I could get it.[29]

[28] Cp. Pomfret (+ 1703), quoted by Ritter, p. 69 : "What's all the noisy jargon of the schools, | But idle nonsense of laborious fools ?"

[29] The *general* part of this theoretical statement appears to be of English origin, though its particular application is Scottish.

Cp. Sterne, *Tristram Shandy*, BK III, ch. 12 : "Great Apollo! if thou art in a giving humour—give me,—I ask no more, but one stroke of native humour, with a single spark of thy own fire along with it—and send Mercury, with the rules and

Nevertheless, it should never be forgotten that this often-quoted statement expresses Burns in only one mood. In the very same poem in which the credo occurs, in a stanza already cited (Stanza IV), he mentions the greatest English poet of the century, and finds it not in the least incongruous to praise Lapraik by saying he thought that Pope, or else Beattie—a Scotsman who usually wrote in English—had composed "When I upon thy Bosom lean." What he implies in this epistle is simply that creative imitation of vernacular verse is the way for him (indeed, it is perhaps only one of several possible ways), and that Scots poetry is a worthy kind in its own right, though not to the exclusion of others which might, for all we know, be superior to anything in the northern tongue. The famous condemnation of the classically-educated pedants who go into college as "stirks" and come out "asses," and the claim that he himself has "to learning nae pretence," but relies entirely on inspiration—

> Whene'er my Muse does on me glance,
> I jingle at her . . .

—all this is suspiciously like the disguise adopted in the prefaces to the Kilmarnock and Edinburgh Editions. But as a corrective to the self-portrait in these verses, one should remember the "Elegy on the Death of Robert Ruisseaux,"[30] where he appears as a voracious reader, pleased above all else when praised for his learning :

> Tho' he was bred to kintra-wark,
> And counted was baith wight and stark,
> Yet that was never Robin's mark
>   To mak a man ;
> But tell him, he was learned and clark,
>   Ye roos'd him then !

This Robert, too, is something of a *persona*, ironically ridiculing

compasses, if he can be spared, with my compliments to—no matter." Burns's Nature was, however, not Augustan Nature ; it was quite a different concept from Boileau's, or Pope's or Shaftesbury's. To them, Nature was objective, and more or less equated with external reality ; but to Burns, in this passage, Nature was subjective, the equivalent of "genius" or "originality." Cp. Ritter, p. 70, and B. Willey, *The Eighteenth Century Background*, London 1940, pp. 1–26 and *passim*.
    [30] II. 216 (412).

his own pretensions to learning; but both pictures—the Child
of Nature and the Eager Student—have their share of truth,
for each reflects a characteristic mood.[31]

The "Epistle to J. Lapraik" contains one of the most
thorough-going condemnations of money-grubbing and selfish
calculation in the whole of Burns:

> Awa ye selfish, warly race,
> Wha think that havins, sense, an' grace,
> Ev'n love an' friendship, should give place
>   To Catch-the-Plack!
> I dinna like to see your face,
>   Nor hear your crack.
>
> But ye whom social pleasure charms,
> Whose hearts the tide of kindness warms,
> Who hold your being on the terms,
>   'Each aid the others,'
> Come to my bowl, come to my arms,
>   My friends, my brothers!

Exactly as in the first "Epistle to Davie," money-economy and
the values of humanity are irreconcilable opposites; but in
this poem the antithesis is much more completely realised,
without abstraction and without sentimentality. Those who
chase after the yellow dirt subordinate everything—brains,
reason and the generous feelings—to a frenzied pursuit of
wealth. They live separate and alone; they abstain from consumption (and therefore from pleasure) in order to save. Real
men are the direct contrary of such caricatures of humanity;
they co-operate with one another. Individualism is the supreme
evil, and mutual aid the greatest good[32]—surely a tremendous
advance on the "tender feelings" of the "Epistle to Davie."

---

[31] David Sillar (quoted in C. & W., 1. 68–9) has left the following record of
Burns as he knew him in 1781 and the years immediately following: "Some book
(especially one of those mentioned in his letter to Mr Murdoch) he always carried,
and read when not otherwise employed. It was likewise his custom to read at table.
In one of my visits to Lochlea . . . he was so intent on reading, I think *Tristram
Shandy*, that his spoon falling out of his hand, made him exclaim, in a tone scarcely
imitable, 'Alas, poor Yorick!'"

[32] Ritter traces Burns's precise expression of these ideas in sts. xx, xxi, to Shenstone, Elegy IX (ll. 41 ff.), and "Economy" (i, ll. 223–7; ii, ll. 65–6, and *passim*);
to Thomson's "Spring" (ll. 874 ff.); and to Rule X of the Tarbolton Bachelors'

Even in this epistle, with its frank and unqualified homage to Ramsay and Fergusson, Burns modulates into something which on the printed page is indistinguishable from Standard English. The change of diction takes place right at the climax of the poem, in the twenty-first stanza; but the reader does not feel that the transition to "social pleasure" and the "tide of kindness" is in the least discordant. When one considers the whole context of the poem, it is evident that Burns can scarcely have regarded the passage as essentially un-Scottish: rather, as spoken by a Scot it is related to the early vernacular of the stanzas beginning

What's a' your jargon o' your Schools . . .

as, in music, one key is to another.

The "Second Epistle to J. Lapraik"[33] contains, in the sixth and seventh stanzas, one of the most astonishingly spontaneous outbursts in the whole of Burns:

Sae I gat paper in a blink,
An' down gaed stumpie in the ink:
Quoth I: 'Before I sleep a wink,
    I vow I'll close it:
An' if ye winna mak it clink,
    By Jove, I'll prose it!'

Sae I've begun to scrawl, but whether
In rhyme, or prose, or baith thegither,

Club, in which young Burns was himself the leading light: "Every man proper for a member of this society must have a frank, honest, open heart; above anything dirty or mean; and must be a professed lover of one or more of the female sex. No haughty, self-conceited person, who looks upon himself as superior to the rest of the club, and especially no mean-spirited, worldly mortal, whose only will is to heap up money, shall upon any pretence whatever be admitted. In short, the proper person for this society is a cheerful, honest-hearted lad, who, if he has a friend that is true, and a mistress that is kind, and as much wealth as genteelly to make both ends meet, is just as happy as this world can make him." (Ritter, p. 70; C. & W., i. 67). The positive values of the first "Epistle to Lapraik" appear to be identical with those of Freemasonry, which was—significantly enough—at one and the same time a Scottish and a European movement. See L. Staines, "Robert Burns and his Masonic Poems," and W. Hunter, "Burns as a Mason," in *British Masonic Miscellany*, ed. G. M. Martin, Dundee n.d., VOL. XIV, pp. 20–31, 50–90; and Fairchild, 1. 278–9, 338, 356, 458–9, 515, for other Freemason poets of the eighteenth century. All praised the social virtues, "sympathy," and mutual aid; and many were Scots.

[33] 1. 161 (382).

> Or some hotch-potch that's rightly neither,
> Let time mak proof;
> But I shall scribble down some blether
> Just clean aff-loof.

Here Burns transcends both Scots and English tradition in order to make a statement that is above all personal—one man speaking to another in his own individual voice, with little thought of models.[34]

Written only three weeks after the first, in content the "Second Epistle" strikes a completely new note. Fortune is still there in the background, but she is no longer all-powerful, as in "Man was made to Mourn":

> Ne'er mind how Fortune waft an' warp;
> She's but a bitch.

Though ultimate beggary is still a possibility, the dancing lines are radiant with a light-hearted comedy that takes away all terror from the prospect. The rich are no longer an undifferentiated mass, but particularised as two separate groups, the town merchants, and the country landlords, whom Burns specifically terms "feudal":

> Do ye envý the city gent,
> Behint a kist to lie an' sklent;
> Or purse-proud, big wi' cent. per cent.
> An' muckle wame,
> In some bit brugh to represent
> A bailie's name?
>
> Or is't the paughty feudal thane,
> Wi' ruffl'd sark an' glancing cane,
> Wha thinks himsel nae sheep-shank bane,
> But lordly stalks;
> While caps an' bonnets aff are taen,
> As by he walks?

Three weeks before, positive value had resided in sociability

---

[34] But even the "spontaneous" st. vii—so personal in tone, and so particular in its application—has some connexion with the thought of previous (English!) poets. Cp. Ritter, p. 72, who quotes Charles Churchill, "The Candidate," ll. 727-8: "Thoughts all so dull, so pliant in their growth, | They're verse, they're prose, they're neither, and they're both."

and co-operation; now (and this constitutes the innovation)
it resides in a kind of individualism, which is however rather
different from the individualism of calculating utilitarians soul-
lessly planning their own advantage. The "Second Epistle to
Lapraik" presses the claims of the free man, glorying in "wit
an' sense," and, emancipated from the bonds of custom,
turned adrift to fend for himself in a hostile Scotland. There
is nothing to prevent this new and genuine individual from co-
operating with others; he too is "social"—but he is a person
first, a friend and reveller second. Whatever is of worth in
this kind of man would be destroyed if either the "city gent"
or the "feudal thane" were according to nature; but, mercifully, it is the rich who are twisted and distorted, while men
like Burns and Lapraik are after nature's stamp:

> Were this the charter of our state,
> 'On pain o' hell be rich an' great,'
> Damnation then would be our fate,
>   Beyond remead;
> But, thanks to heaven, that's no the gate
>   We learn our creed.

> For thus the royal mandate ran,
> When first the human race began:
> 'The social, friendly, honest man,
>   Whate'er he be,
> 'Tis he fulfils great Nature's plan,
>   And none but he.'

In the sixteenth and seventeenth stanzas the isolated Individual, uncircumscribed, free as air, who can yet join together
with others in "social glee," is identified with the archetypal
figure of the Artist in a passage which makes amusing play
with the doctrines of reincarnation. The poem ends with a
hilarious vision of pie-in-the-sky for Lapraik and Burns,
while all the moneyed classes are reduced to bestial shapes.
Everything is bathed in a warm humorous glow—and yet the
irreconcilable opposition between Art and Money, which was
to take on almost tragic form in the nineteenth century, is
already prefigured in the ending.

From the fourteenth stanza onwards, as he nears the end

of the epistle, Burns once more modulates into Scots-English, without, however, leaving the vernacular completely behind ; he retains the liberty to use words like "remead," or Scots "gate," or "neivefu'." I cannot agree that the final stanzas are greatly inferior to most of the earlier ones—that is, if the magnificent sixth and seventh stanzas are left entirely out of consideration. One has only to look at the texture of the verse to realise that Burns's mastery of sound-patterns has not deserted him in Anglo-Scots :

> Tho' here they scrape, an' squeeze, an' growl,
> Their worthless neivefu' of a soul
> May in some future carcase howl,
>   The forest's fright ;
> Or in some day-detesting owl
>   May shun the light.

We are entitled to condemn the poem's ending only if we are prepared to reject all the English poetry of the mid-eighteenth century. If Burns thought that the translation of himself and Lapraik

> To reach their native, kindred skies,
> And sing their pleasures, hopes an' joys,
>   In some mild sphere

was the only possible artistic conclusion for the work, then he had no alternative but to employ Anglo-Scots ; by itself, the vernacular did not have the resources to deal with such an abstract idea.

Like the first "Epistle to Lapraik," the epistle "To William Simpson of Ochiltree, May 1785,"[35] contains some lines which suggest that Burns was dreaming of publication nearly a year before he circulated his proposals for the Kilmarnock Edition. Simpson had written in praise of Burns's verse, to which he replied :

> My senses wad be in a creel,
> Should I but dare a hope to speel,
> Wi' Allan, or wi' Gilbertfield,
>   The braes o' fame ;

[35] I. 167 (383).

Or Fergusson, the writer-chiel,
A deathless name.[36]

These lines exhibit, perhaps, the assumed modesty of a conventional disclaimer; one cannot reject the idea of becoming famous without at least having considered it as a possibility, and this in Burns's case surely implied a printed volume. As in the first "Epistle to Lapraik" he is anxious to place himself in the vernacular tradition, which (he now claims) the upper classes have tried to strangle; for that is surely the implication of his statement that a tenth of what the Edinburgh gentry were accustomed to waste at cards would have been sufficient to keep Fergusson from destitution. Verse-writing in Scots has, for Burns, an essentially cathartic function—"It gies me ease," and is therefore a supremely natural activity. In the sixth, seventh, eighth and ninth stanzas, he relates his local patriotism to this general Lowland Scots tradition by stating his intention of making the rivers of Ayrshire as well-known as Forth and Tay, Yarrow and Tweed, so often mentioned in vernacular poetry; but he enumerates the streams of Ayrshire in the wider context of the whole of Western culture, indeed of the whole known world, as revealed by geographical exploration. Irwin, Lugar, Ayr and Doon are part of a complex which includes "Illissus, Tiber, Thames an' Seine," New Holland and the remotest seas:

Or whare wild-meeting oceans boil
Besouth Magellan.[37]

[36] Interestingly enough, Fergusson had made the same sort of statement before Burns, in his "Answer to Mr J. S.'s Epistle," st. v. The subject is his Muse:

But she maun e'en be glad to jook,
An' play *teet-bo* frae nook to nook,
Or blush as gin she had the yook
Upon her skin,
Whan *Ramsay*, or whan *Pennicuik*
Their lilts begin.

[37] Cp. R. B.'s *Commonplace Book*, Aug. 1785, p. 36, where the same ambition is stated in prose; and Fergusson, "Hame Content," ll. 75–82:

The ARNO and the TIBUR lang
Hae run fell clear in Roman sang;
But, save the reverence of schools!
They're baith but lifeless dowy pools.
Dought they compare wi' bonny Tweed,
As clear as only lammer-bead?
Or are their shores mair sweet and gay
Than Fortha's haughs or banks o' Tay?

In the tenth stanza the poem moves from a level which is both local and international to one which is national and patriotic, by way of allusion to William Wallace, who often triumphed over the English on "Coila's plains an' fells." At this point, in the eleventh stanza, there occurs one of the most vivid and startling images in the whole of Burns, presented by means of a compound adjective:

> Oft have our fearless fathers strode
>   By Wallace' side,
> Still pressing onward, *red-wat-shod,*
>   Or glorious dy'd!

The next development is a return to the locality in order to describe its natural scenery, as a prelude to the introduction of something wider than either country or nation—Nature herself. The twelfth and thirteenth stanzas are as fine as any descriptive poetry written during the century:

> O, sweet are Coila's haughs an' woods,
> When lintwhites chant amang the buds,
> And jinkin hares, in amorous whids,
>   Their loves enjoy;
> While thro' the braes the cushat croods
>   With wailfu' cry!
>
> Ev'n winter bleak has charms to me,
> When winds rave thro' the naked tree;
> Or frosts on hills of Ochiltree
>   Are hoary gray;
> Or blinding drifts wild-furious flee,
>   Dark'ning the day![38]

The transition to Nature in general is made through the intermediary of the Man of Feeling. Nature has charms for "feeling, pensive hearts," and a poet ought to wander by himself, letting

[38] St. xii appears to contain a reminiscence of Montgomerie, *The Cherrie and the Slae,* as reproduced in Watson's *Choice Collection,* I. 72 ("The cushat crowds . . . | I saw . . . the hare, | In hidlings hirpling here and there" : but cp. *The Cherrie and the Slae,* ed. H. Harvey Wood, London 1937, pp. 29–30, where the text differs considerably from Watson's) ; and cp. Gavin Douglas, *En.,* Prol. XII, l. 237 ("The cowschet crowdis and pyrkis on the rys").

The love of winter expressed in st. xiii is similar to Burns's own "Winter: A Dirge" (see above, p. 13), and to Thomson's *Seasons.* "Autumn," ll. 1302 ff., 1327 ff.; cp. Ritter, pp. 73–5.

his emotions well up within him till they issue forth in "a heart-felt sang." The isolated individual of the "Second Epistle to Lapraik" is now viewed from another angle, in a mood which is far removed from even the joys of convivial drinking or friendly argument. Burns praises pensive pondering and the abjuration of rational thought, the sort of self-indulgent daydreaming condemned by Dr Johnson in the famous chapter on the dangerous prevalence of imagination in *Rasselas*.[39] In complete contrast to Johnson, Burns here considers such sensuous mind-wandering to be an essential part of the poetical character. Nature contemplated in this way, has now become the antidote to Mammon, as Art fulfilled the same function in the "Second Epistle to Lapraik":

> The warly race may drudge an' drive,
> Hog-shouther, jundie, stretch, an' strive;
> Let me fair Nature's face descrive,
>   And I, wi' pleasure,
> Shall let the busy, grumbling hive
>   Bum owre their treasure.

It is a fine stanza, with its images of jostling animals and buzzing hoarding bees—the real conclusion of the poem. The next two stanzas are simply an easy fade-out, while the Postscript, with its fable of the Auld and New Lichts, serves to heighten still further the informality of the piece.

Each of the epistles so far examined counterpoises some positive value to the mechanical utilitarianism of philistine hucksters and canting hypocrites. The epistle "To John Goldie, August 1785,"[40] which belongs rather with the ecclesiastical satires, sets the fellowship of the alehouse above that of the Church; a similar praise of alcohol is at the centre of the third epistle "To J. Lapraik":[41]

> But let the kirk-folk ring their bells!
> Let's sing about our noble sel's:
> We'll cry nae jads frae heathen hills
>   To help or roose us,
> But browster wives an' whisky stills—
>   They are the Muses!

[39] Ch. xliv.   [40] Above, p. 50.   [41] II. 73 (357).

Though the second epistle "To Davie"[42] is in some ways a dis-
appointing performance—the second stanza in particular is
almost as sickly-sentimental and falsely rustic as the productions
of the nineteenth-century Kailyard school—it provides contemporary evidence of the tremendous energy expended by
Burns (both in living and in writing) during his great creative
period :

> For me, I'm on Parnassus' brink,
> Rivin the words to gar them clink ;
> Whyles daez't wi' love, whyles daez't wi' drink
> Wi' jads or Masons,
> An' whyles, but ay owre late I think,
> Braw sober lessons.

In the following stanzas he holds fast once more to the con-
venient myth of the thoughtless, improvident "Bardie clan"
who are constitutionally incapable of behaving like ordinary
mortals, and again (as at the end of that far more successful
work, the "Second Epistle to Lapraik") he sees in poetry the
one sure buckler in a hostile world. Even in a bad poem the
same preoccupations recur, as they do in the rather bathetic
conclusion, with its hint of the beggar theme at the very end :

> Haud to the Muse, my dainty Davie :
> The warl' may play you monie a shavie,
> But for the Muse, she'll never leave ye,
> Tho' e'er sae puir ;
> Na, even tho' limpin wi' the spavie
> Frae door to door !

The "Epistle to James Smith"[43] is generally preferred to
the other verse epistles. It is certainly a remarkable work, over-
flowing with effortless spontaneity and bubbling humour.
Written a little earlier than April 1786, just before Burns had
definitely decided to bring out an edition, it shows him once
again in the role of the completely uneducated poet :

> Something cries, "Hoolie !
> I red you, honest man, tak tent !
> Ye'll shaw your folly. . . ."

---

[42] II. 81 (358).   [43] I. 59 (347).

How can such a man as he possibly hope for immortality when so many literate poets have faded from remembrance after their brief day of glory? Surely it would be safer to eschew print altogether, and remain simply an unknown bard who rhymes for fun. In the twelfth stanza, the ills of life, inevitable suffering and death, even the cosy retirement enjoyed by profiteers in their old age—all are viewed through a golden haze of humour and well-being:

> This life, sae far 's I understand,
> Is a' enchanted fairy-land,
> Where Pleasure is the magic-wand,
>   That, wielded right,
> Maks hours like minutes, hand in hand,
>   Dance by fu' light.[44]

Not that he is utterly oblivious of Time's chariot. As with Marvell, "To his Coy Mistress," the injunction is to

> . . . tear our Pleasures with rough strife,
> Thorough the Iron gates of life.

In an equally vigorous image, Burns puts it in his own way:

> Then top and maintop crowd the sail,
>   Heave Care o'er-side!
> And large, before Enjoyment's gale,
>   Let's tak the tide.

He wants nothing from life except the opportunity to make poetry: the varied positives of the earlier epistles now give way to a single positive, an idea which unites poetry and "real, sterling wit." The worshippers of Mammon are now *identified* with the "unco guid," the main target of the ecclesiastical satires. Holly Willie and Cent.-per-Cent. are fundamentally one and the same:

---

[44] Ritter (p. 121) thinks that Burns's st. xii contains verbal echoes from Shenstone's Elegy XI, st. i:

> Ah me, my Friend! it will not, will not last,
> This fairy scene, that cheats our youthful eyes;
> The charm dissolves; th' aërial music's past:
> The banquet ceases, and the vision flies.

But Burns's mood is utterly different from that of the anaemic Shenstone.

O ye douce folk that live by rule,
Grave, tideless-blooded, calm an' cool,
Compar'd wi' you—O fool ! fool ! fool !
    How much unlike !
Your hearts are just a standing pool,
    Your lives a dyke ![45]

Nae hair-brained, sentimental traces
In your unletter'd, nameless faces !
In *arioso* trills and graces
    Ye never stray,
But *gravissimo*, solemn basses
    Ye hum away.

Ye are sae grave, nae doubt ye're wise ;
Nae ferly tho' ye do despise
The hairum-scairum, ram-stam boys,
    The rattling squad :
I see ye upward cast your eyes—
    Ye ken the road !

I suppose the modern equivalents of the "rattling squad" are the juvenile delinquents, teddy-boys, rock-and-roll fiends, and all rebels with or without a cause. Translated into these terms, the "Epistle to James Smith" states that the iconoclastic young (not the angry young men of the middle classes, but those who make the street and the milk-bar their *rendez-vous*) represent Life and Libido and the Horn of Plenty, while the ordinary suburbanite worshipper of the god in the garage stands for death, debility, and the crucifixion of essential humanity. It is an opposition of this sort which lies at the heart of the "Epistle to James Smith," and indeed at the centre of Burns's own soul. On the one hand, the peasantry's old, half-pagan lust for life, survivals of which take on somewhat distorted shapes in twentieth-century dormitory towns ; on the other, puritanism, rationality, calculation, and control. During these two momentous years especially, Burns himself was one of the "hairum-scairum, ram-stam boys." But he was also the

[45] Ritter (p. 123) notes a remarkable parallel to the last two lines of this stanza in a poem that he ascribes to Charles Churchill, namely "The Poetry Professors," ll. 75 f. : "[Fellows] | Whose lives are like a stagnant pool, | Muddy and placid, dull and cool." The poem was printed in *The North Briton*, Nos. xxii and xxiii, 1762-3 ; 3 vols., 1763.

man who preached Common-sense, whose favourite quotation
was :

on reason build resolve,
(That column of true majesty in man) . . .[46]

This other side of Burns—Burns the Champion of Society,
paying his tribute to all the established virtues like any com-
pany-director, executive or racing reporter after a spree—is
exhibited in the last of the early epistles, the "Epistle to a
Young Friend"[47] of May 1786, composed at the very height of
the Armour crisis, when he was also (so it would seem) deeply
involved with Mary Campbell.[48] He advises his young friend
to keep to the path of conventional virtue :

> The sacred lowe o' weel-plac'd love,
>   Luxuriantly indulge it ;
> But never tempt th' illicit rove,
>   Tho' naething should divulge it :
> I waive the quantum o' the sin,
>   The hazard of concealing ;
> But, och ! it hardens a' within,
>   And petrifies the feeling !

Amusingly enough, the young man is given a homily on the
value of thrift—provided that he does not use his savings to
lord it ostentatiously over others :

> To catch Dame Fortune's golden smile,
>   Assiduous wait upon her ;
> And gather gear by ev'ry wile
>   That's justify'd by honor :
> Not for to hide it in a hedge,
>   Nor for a train-attendant ;
> But for the glorious privilege
>   Of being independent.

This is indeed the morality of small farmers and petty traders ![49]

[46] To [Mrs Maclehose], 19 Jan. 1788, and to other correspondents, in *Letters* i.
166, and *passim*. The quotation is from Young's *Night Thoughts*, Night i, 30–1.
[47] i. 140 (376).   [48] Cp. Snyder, pp. 143–5.
[49] In so far as there is any single literary source for the poem, it is probably
Polonius's advice to Laertes in *Hamlet*, i. iii. For parallels with Young's *Night
Thoughts* (which still further underline Burns's debt to 18th-cent. English writers),
see Appendix II § 2 (below, p. 364) ; and for further remarks on the sources, see
Ritter, pp. 146–8.

Established ethics, the maxims which his own father taught him, are of inestimable value in life; the only trouble with them is that they are so difficult to put into practice:

> And may ye better reck the rede,
> Than ever did th' adviser!

Into this *pot-pourri* of all the bourgeois virtues—complete with

> An atheist-laugh's a poor exchange
> For Deity offended!

—Burns intrudes the concept of personal honour, perhaps in the last resort derived from clan morality. Most significantly, he sets it side by side with the Calvinists' fear of Hell, so that the one doctrine appears as the negation of the other:

> The fear o' Hell's a hangman's whip
> To haud the wretch in order;
> But where ye feel your honour grip,
> Let that ay be your border. . . .[50]

A good way of appreciating the variety of Burns's moods is to place the "Epistle to James Smith" side-by-side with the "Epistle to a Young Friend." The latter is as much a fruit of experience as the former; it has taken some of its colouring from the remorseful mood of the fifth stanza of "Despondency, an Ode":[51]

> O enviable early days,
> When dancing thoughtless pleasure's maze,
> To care, to guilt unknown!
> How ill exchang'd for riper times,
> To feel the follies or the crimes
> Of others, or my own!

The man who takes the tide before "enjoyment's gale" is liable to find that his fairyland turns into a desert because his actions have caused suffering to others; as Burns remarks at the end of the second stanza of the ode the life of ordinary mortals striving for wordly success may have its compensations after all:

---

[50] Ritter notes that the idea contained in Burns's lines "The fear o' Hell's . . . order" appears in Burton, *Anatomy of Melancholy*, III. 4. i. 2 (Everyman edn., VOL. II, p. 340): ". . . the fear of some divine and supreme powers keeps men in obedience." This concept was of course perfectly familiar to Hume, and to many 18th-cent. deists. [51] I. 127 (372).

You, bustling and justling,
    Forget each grief and pain ;
I, listless yet restless,
    Find ev'ry prospect vain.

However, it would be wrong to represent this last position
as final ; like the others, it is the reflexion of a mood. The self-
dramatisations of the epistles express a mind in motion, giving
itself over at different times to *conflicting* principles and feelings ;
they mirror that mind as it grappled with a complex world. In
order to body it forth, Burns had to be, in himself, and not
simply in play, both Calvinist and anti-Calvinist, both fornicator and champion of chastity, both Jacobite and Jacobin,
both local and national, both British and European, both
anarchist and sober calculator, both philistine and anti-
philistine. He had to write in both Braid Scots and Scots-
English and in a blend of the two, being at one and the same
time a man of the old homely Scotland of village communities,
a forerunner of the Scotland of capitalist farmers employing
wage-labour and the new agricultural implements, and a poet
who shared—even before he went to Edinburgh—something
of the Anglo-Scottish culture of the capital. The occasional
and informal nature of the epistle was ideal for the expression
of a plethora of moods together with the transitions between
them ; consequently, Burns's experiments with the *genre* contain much of his finest work.

At the beginning of 1786, a fortnight or so before the
master-mason James Armour refused to have him for a son-
in-law, Burns began to arrange for the publication of a volume
of verse ; his first step was to issue "proposals" to the public.
According to his brother, his motive was entirely practical—
to get the wherewithal to pay his passage to Jamaica and
"provide him more liberally in necessaries" for the voyage.
Gilbert also insisted that the scheme was not in the first place
of Robert's own making, but was that of his friend and landlord, Gavin Hamilton.[52] But there is reason to believe that the
idea of publication had crossed his mind at least a year before ;
as we have seen,[53] a stanza in the "Epistle to William Simpson"
certainly implies as much. The first reference to the "pro-

[52] Gilbert Burns to Mrs Dunlop, in Currie, i. 78.   [53] Above, pp. 95–6.

posals" in the correspondence precedes any mention of Jamaica, apparently by several days ;[54] and neither in the letters, nor in the preface to the Kilmarnock Edition itself, nor in the poetical "Dedication to Gavin Hamilton, Esq.,"[55] does Burns say that the volume was primarily Hamilton's idea.

The Kilmarnock Edition was the first shot in a campaign which saved the Burnses from becoming agricultural labourers —the natural fate of small farmers without capital in the 1780s. After their father's near bankruptcy and death in February 1784, the family moved to the 118-acre farm of Mossgiel, near Mauchline. They were able to do so because of the legal fiction that the older children had been employees of their father (he had, in point of fact, paid them wages) and were therefore his creditors. This device enabled them to salvage enough from the estate to make a fresh start.[56]

After the rent of £90 was paid, the farm would barely produce a ploughman's wage of £7 a year for Robert and Gilbert, together with smaller amounts for the younger members of the family.[57] In order to succeed, the Burnses needed enough capital to buy lime, carts, improved seed-grain, and a herd of the new Ayrshire cattle; above all, they needed money with which to pay wages, for the land could not be improved without drainage and enclosure (there is some evidence that Mossgiel was unenclosed) ; and these were impossible without additional labour. Finally, the brothers would never feel really secure without some reserve against a bad season or a possible fall in agricultural prices.[58]

At first, Robert responded to the challenge of Mossgiel with something of the Napoleonic energy of the great improvers :

> I entered on this farm with a full resolution, "Come, go to, I will be wise !"—I read farming books ; I calculated crops ; I attended markets ; and in short, in spite of "The devil, the world and the flesh," I believe I would have been a wise man ;

[54] To [Robt. Aiken], 3 Apr. 1786, and to [John Arnot, Apr. 1786], in *Letters*, I. 24, 30.
[55] I. 147 (378).
[56] Chambers, I. 82–3 ; Gilbert Burns to Mrs Dunlop, in Currie, I. 75–6.
[57] Gilbert Burns to Mrs Dunlop, in Currie, I. 89.
[58] Cp. Strawhorn, pp. 153–7.

but the first year from unfortunately buying in bad seed, the
second from a late harvest, we lost half of both our crops : this
overset all my wisdom, and I returned "Like the dog to his vomit,
and the sow that was washed to her wallowing in the mire.—"[59]

The "vomit" was of course that indissoluble unity "Love
and Poesy" ; and a remarkably sustaining diet it proved in the
end to be. For the years between 1784 and 1786 saw the composition of the majority of the pieces in the Kilmarnock volume,
together with many fine poems which were not published till
later ; and the Kilmarnock Edition led to the more profitable
Edinburgh editions, which gave the Burnses sufficient ready
cash to save them from complete disaster.[60] In later years
Robert lent Gilbert £180 of this money, which was enough to
tide him over at Mossgiel until 1798. Two years later Gilbert
became the manager of a modern capitalist farm, and in 1804
the factor of Lady Blantyre's estates in East Lothian,[61] the
very centre of what Cobbett later termed the "steam-engine
farm" district[62]—a career which would have been impossible
without the initial impetus of Robert's loan. The poet himself
had £300 to see him through the years at Ellisland, so that his
literary success was a stroke of luck for himself, his mother
(whom Gilbert looked after), his brother, his sisters, and even
for Jean Armour.

Nevertheless, there is no evidence, apart from Gilbert's
statement that Robert's main aim was to earn his fare to the
West Indies, that money was anything more than a secondary
consideration with him when the proposals were issued. In the
autobiographical letter to Dr Moore (which, as Professor
Ferguson points out,[63] "has better withstood the probings—not
infrequently hostile—of subsequent research" than almost any
other autobiography in the language), he presents his decision
not as any sudden whim, any desperate response to an acute
crisis in his personal affairs, but as a deliberate act which had
been preceded by the most prolonged self-examination and
self-criticism :

[59] Autobiographical letter to Moore, in *Letters*, I. 113.
[60] Chambers, II. 248–9, 253.   [61] See *Letters*, II. 342.
[62] W. Cobbett, *Tour in Scotland*, London 1833, p. 104.
[63] In *Letters*, I. xxxiii.

I can truly say that pauvre Inconnu as I then was, I had pretty nearly as high an idea of myself and my works as I have at this moment. . . . To know myself had been all along my constant study.—I weighed myself alone; I balanced myself with others; I watched every means of information how much ground I occupied both as a Man and as a Poet: I studied assiduously Nature's DESIGN where she seem'd to have intended the various LIGHTS and SHADES in my character.—I was pretty sure my Poems would meet with some applause; but at the worst, the roar of the Atlantic would deafen the voice of Censure, and the novelty of west-Indian scenes make me forget Neglect.[64]

The preface to the volume also implies that it was a craving for fame that drove him on; he speaks of "that dearest wish of every poetic bosom—to be distinguished."[65] The careful deliberation with which Burns conducted his literary campaign is as remarkable as the eddying confusion of his personal life during these same months. Yet the calm and the storm were secretly connected. The love of fame was simply an aspect of his desire to dominate, perhaps to escape from, the locality that had so brutally tried to thwart his powers; and his second motive, the financial one, operated in the same direction. A negro-driving immigrant with £30 a year to start with but the prospect of more to come, or the author of a poetical bestseller—either way, he could thumb his nose at the rigidly righteous; either way, he would be better able to find capital for himself and the other members of his family.[66]

On 31 July, right in the middle of an extraordinary personal crisis well known to all readers of the biographies of Burns,[67] and exactly a week before his final appearance on the "stool of repentance" in Mauchline parish church to profess contrition for the sin of fornication with Jean Armour,[68] the famous volume was published. On 3 September he wrote to John Richmond, "Armour has just now brought me a fine boy and a girl at one throw.—God bless them poor little dears."[69]

---

[64] *Letters*, I. 114.
[65] I. 3. All quotations from the preface are given with spelling and punctuation as in H. & H.
[66] Cp. Snyder, p. 125.   [67] Cp. Snyder, pp. 118–46.
[68] Edgar, *Old Church Life in Scotland*, quoted in C. & W., I. 367.
[69] To J. Richmond, 3 Sept. 1786, as quoted in Daiches, p. 100.

Only a month earlier Jean's father had tried to have him arrested until he could find security for a capital sum large enough to provide her with alimony for many years, and Robert had to go into hiding, "wandering from one friend's house to another, and like a true son of the Gospel" with " 'nowhere to lay my head'." But now he had nothing to fear from old Armour and the "pack of the law," since—presumably as a result of the immediate success of his book—"some of the first Gentlemen in the county have offered to befriend me." Emigration, one imagines, now seemed increasingly chimerical and unreal, though he did not give up the project at once; more and more he came to feel that the furrow he had to plough was in Scotland and not in some island in the sun without tradition or nationhood. By 27 September he was writing to Richmond: "I am going perhaps to. try a second edition of my book.—If I do, it will detain me a little longer in the country; if not, I shall be gone as soon as harvest is over."[70] Some time later, when it had become clear that the printer would not risk a second edition unless he were paid for the paper in advance, Robert was still in a turmoil—though the wish to stay was beginning to come uppermost. He wrote of—

—the pang of disappointment, the sting of pride, with some wandering stabs of remorse, which never fail to settle on my vitals like vultures, when attention is not called away by the calls of society, or the vagaries of the Muse. Even in the hour of social mirth, my gaiety is the madness of an intoxicated criminal under the hands of the executioner. All these reasons urge me to go abroad, and to all these reasons I have only one answer—the feelings of a father. This, in the present mood I am in, overbalances everything that can be laid in the scale against it.[71]

Never, perhaps, had one slender book done so much for its author in so short a time. Before it came out, he was the local scapegoat, abominated by the "unco guid" because of his heresy and his "rakish art." Three months later he was dining with his first lord;[72] six months later he was known by name and reputation, not merely in Scotland, but all over the

[70] To Richmond 30 Jul., 1 and 27 Sep. 1786, in *Letters*, I. 35, 40, 44.
[71] To [R. Aiken, "about 8 Oct." 1786], in *Letters*, I. 47.
[72] Chambers, I. 328–30.

British Isles. Burns's is the most breathless of all the many success-stories in the history of Scotland. It was a triumphant guerilla foray against a harsh and frowning world, a victory for genius over mediocrity, produced by a strange mixture of uncontrolled passion and shrewd practical common-sense.[73]

The volume contained most of those poems so far written by Burns which would please aristocratic and sentimental readers, plus some of the milder satires and realistic pieces; that is to say, it let great folks hear what he or his advisers wanted them to hear. It had few lyrics, because many of the *literati* would not treat Scottish songs seriously; and—even though it excluded "Holy Willie's Prayer" and "The Ordination"[74]—"A Dream," and "The Holy Fair" must have caused considerable offence to the ultra-respectable. Whether by accident or design, its contents follow an emotional pattern, with the comical and "manners-painting" works at the beginning and the more sombre and "pathetic" poems near the middle and at the end. The preface is in itself a remarkable document, at once a sober statement of Burns's artistic intentions and a cunningly-constructed appeal to the upper-class

[73] Reviews of the Kilmarnock Edition appeared in *The Edinburgh Magazine, or Literary Miscellany*, IV (Oct. 1786); *The Lounger*, No 97 (Dec. 1786); *The Monthly Review*, London, LXXV (Dec. 1786); *The New Annual Register* (for 1786), London, VII (1787); *The English Review*, London, IX (1787); *The Critical Review*, London, First Series, LXIII (May 1787); and *The New Town and Country Magazine*, (Aug. 1787). All these, except the one in *The Critical Review*, are reprinted in whole or in part in J. D. Ross, *The Story of the Kilmarnock Burns*, Stirling 1933, pp. 25 ff. Cp. Hans Hecht, *Robert Burns*, henceforth cited as Hecht, 2nd (revised) edn., London 1950, pp. 92–4. A. M. Kinghorn ("Burns and his Early Critics," in *The Burns Chronicle*, 1954, pp. 4–5) puts the case for Burns the literary tactician as follows: "The only reason why the poet achieved fame in 1786 was because he was sufficiently endowed with the qualities of diplomacy to pave his own way to success as a poet in Scots by providing the literati with examples of the kind of poetry which they could openly appreciate." The immediate effect of the Kilmarnock Edition in providing Burns with a fairly large audience in England as well as in Scotland has been brought out by J. W. Egerer, "Burns and 'Guid Black Prent'," in *The Age of Johnson: Essays presented to C. B. Tinker*, New Haven 1949, pp. 269–79.

[74] Other poems, already composed, that Burns did not publish in the Kilmarnock Edition were "Adam Armour's Prayer," "Address of Beelzebub," "The Court of Equity," "Death and Dr Hornbook," "To John Goldie," "To the Rev. John M'Math," "The Jolly Beggars," "Mary Morison," "Second Epistle to Davie," "Third Epistle to J. Lapraik," and "The Twa Herds." "The Ordination" and "Death and Dr Hornbook" were, however, included in the Edinburgh Edition (1787).

cult of Innate Genius, Original Composition, and the Noble Savage—in this case, the Noble Peasant :

> The following trifles are not the production of the Poet, who, with all the advantages of learned art, and perhaps amid the elegances and idlenesses of upper life, looks down for a rural theme, with an eye to Theocrites [*sic*] or Virgil. . . . Unacquainted with the necessary requisites for commencing Poet by rule, he sings the sentiments and manners, he felt and saw in himself and his rustic compeers around him, in his and their native language. . . . He begs his readers, particularly the Learned and the Polite, who may honour him with a perusal, that they will make every allowance for Education and Circumstances of Life.

Yet there is nothing insincere in such an approach to his public. The preface is in its own way a subdued yet powerful poetical manifesto, comparable in seriousness with the longer and very different preface to the *Lyrical Ballads*. Professor Dewar has rightly seen in it "quiet hints that his experience perhaps brought something new for readers of poetry in his time."[75] Burns does not claim to be anything other than he is ; all he says is perfectly true ; there is no false window-dressing. It is merely that he achieves the miracle of being tactful and firm at one and the same time :

> It is an observation of that celebrated Poet [Shenstone] whose divine Elegies do honor to our language, our nation, and our species—that "Humility has depressed many a genius to a hermit, but never raised one to fame." If any Critic catches at the word *genius*, the Author tells him, once for all, that he certainly looks upon himself as possesst of some poetical abilities, otherwise his publishing in the manner he has done, would be a manoeuvre below the worst character which, he hopes, his worst enemy will ever give him.

To be at one and the same time respectful and challenging towards his potential public was surely the most effective means of letting great folks hear what he had to say—or rather, what he chose to let them know of his vision at that date.

[75] R. Dewar, "Burns and the Burns Tradition," in *Scottish Poetry: A Critical Survey*, ed. J. Kinsley, London 1955, p. 191.

V

Poet of the Parish

MANY poems of Burns's first period embody the experience of a rural community in a way that has rarely been equalled in English. Ever since neolithic times, the settled village has been, next to the family, the most fundamental unit of society; it has survived war and pestilence, flood and famine, the fall of empires and the decline of civilisations. An art which successfully reflects the way of life of such a community will tend to have a universality broader and more general, though not necessarily deeper, than that of any other sort; it will tend to mirror, not what the best or the cleverest men have seen and felt, but what the overwhelming majority of our species have met with during, let us say, the last five thousand years. There is nothing more international than nationality, nothing more all-embracing than locality.

Nevertheless, a writer like Burns is faced with certain pitfalls; in his rendering of the life of the parish, he will often be tempted to be too narrowly particular, too minutely realistic, too restricted to the vernacular, too faithful to the customs and idiosyncrasies of his district. If he wishes to reach a larger audeince than the men of his own place and time, he must concentrate on those aspects of the village which have the largest relevance; he must paint the streaks of the tulip without destroying the general form and shape of the flower. The moon that rises over Cumnock hills must still be recognisably the moon that shines over Fujiyama or the Urals.

Burns's development as a poet was from his immediate surroundings outwards towards the nation and finally to all mankind, but this movement was never simple and gradual; it never followed a straight line. One might have expected him to reproduce universal emotions in those poems, early or late, where his aim was to "transcribe the various feelings, the loves, the griefs, the hopes, the fears, in his own breast."[1] All too often, in poems of this sort, the result comes perilously close to mawkishness and bathos. Conversely, one might have expected his descriptions of the "sentiments and manners" of his "rustic compeers" to be of documentary interest only; instead of that, they often transcend parochial mediocrity and acquire a solidity that seems independent of time and place. But on other occasions Burns is unable to make the necessary leap from the particular to the general.

In the course of a letter to Mrs Dunlop dated 21 Aug. 1788,[2] Burns calls to mind a fragment of one of his "manners-painting" poems which is of extraordinary importance to the critic because it presents in concentrated form the raw material of the whole *genre*. In Aug. 1785 Robert had been in love with Betsy Miller, one of the Mauchline belles; her brother had recently married a sister of "Sandy Bell, who made a Jamaica fortune," and the "braw" Betsy began to put on airs because of her new sister-in-law's wealth—£500. The result was a comic burlesque, entitled "A Mauchline Wedding" :[3]

> When Eighty-five was seven months auld,
>   And wearing thro' the aught,
> When rotting rains and Boreas bauld
>   Gied farmer-folks a faught;
> Ae morning quondam Mason Will,
>   Now Merchant Master Miller,
> Gaed down to meet wi' Nansie Bell
>   And her Jamaica siller,
>   To wed, that day.

In the second verse there occurs a detail that seems even more narrowly confined than the mention of Cumnock, which John Ruskin thought so limiting;[4] it is a hill with the name of Blacksideen :

---

[1] Preface to the Kilmarnock Edition, i. 1–3.
[2] *Letters*, i. 248–9.
[3] "A Mauchline Wedding," ii. 42 (338). Though I have here adopted some of the readings in the version given in *Letters*, ed. Ferguson, i. 248–9, I have in general retained the conventions followed by H. & H.
[4] Ruskin, "Fiction, Fair and Foul," in *On the Old Road*, 3 vols., London 1899, ii. 84.

The rising sun o'er Blacksideen
  Was just appearing fairly,
When Nell and Bess get up to dress
  Seven lang half-hours o'er early!
Now presses clink, and drawers jink,
  For linens and for laces:
But modest Muses only *think*
  What ladies' underdress is,
      On sic a day!

By now we have moved away from Blacksideen to a region common to Burns and the author of *The Rape of the Lock:* the target is female affectation and pride in dress. As befits the humbler sphere that Burns is describing, the texture of his verse is coarser than Pope's, and the scene is freed from any suggestion of prurience by the presence of a typically Burnsian delight in human character:

But we'll suppose the stays are lac'd,
  And bonie bosom steekit;
Tho', thro' the lawn—but guess the rest!
  An angel scarce durst keek it.
Then stockins fine, o' silken twine,
  Wi' cannie care are drawn up;
An' garten'd tight, whare mortal wight—

—As I never wrote it down, my recollection does not entirely serve me.

The fourth stanza is surely as good as many of those in his published poems:

But now the gown wi' rustling sound
  Its silken pomp displays;
Sure there's no sin in being vain
  O' siccan bonie claes!
Sae jimp the waist, the tail sae vast—
  Trouth, they were bonie birdies!
O Mither Eve, ye wad been grave
  To see their ample hurdies
      Sae large that day!

In the first couplet Burns expresses the movement of silk as surely as ever Herrick conveyed the liquefaction of Julia's clothes, while in the second the point of view of the two girls is ironically assumed in order the more fully to display their naïve delight in their new finery; it is, of course, Burns's favourite trick when he writes satire. Like most Scots girls, Nell and Bess have been brought up to distrust the vanity of dress, so that in reproducing their very turn of expression the couplet mirrors also a conflict at the very centre of their minds. By the equation of "burd," a girl, with "bird," a flying feathered creature (the conflict of homonyms had probably long existed in Scotland), the stanza ends with the comedy of the bird-hizzies strutting like Papagenas across the Mauchline scene, and scandalising the common mother of us all with the shameless violation of Eve's state of nature provided by their enormous behinds.

The fragment ends in a flurry of colour and movement as Nell, Bessy and their father enter the post-chaise that will take them to the ceremony:

> Then Sandy, wi's red jacket braw,   {driver of the
>   Comes whip-jee-woa! about,   {post-chaise [R.B.]
> And in he gets the bonie twa—
>   Lord, send them safely out!
> And auld John Trot wi' sober phiz,   M—'s father [R.B.]
>   As braid and braw's a Bailie,
> His shouthers and his Sunday's giz
>   Wi' powther and wi' ulzie
>   Weel smear'd that day. . . .

Burns explains that the poem was never finished because his quarrel with Bess ended before he had time to write another line; if it had been completed, it might have become as lively a rendering of a lower-class marriage as Suckling's "Ballad upon a Wedding." This fragment was never intended for publication but was probably meant to be recited before a small number of Mauchline lads who knew the Miller family; and though Burns was certainly rhyming "for fun" here, he still had the taste of a particular group in view. As soon as he puts pen to paper he moves away from Mason Will and Black-sideen to the *universale in re*, the "concrete universal" that is to say, to those characteristics that Nell and Bess have in common with all clothes-conscious young women, and John Trot with all pompous fathers; despite the quarrel with Bess which set him writing, he produced a distanced but not unsympathetic presentation of the people concerned. If this is satire, it has a far more tolerant appreciation of the essential humanity of its victims than Swift's, Dryden's, or even Pope's, and it lacks the element of condescension to one's class-inferiors which mars Suckling's poem.

"The Court of Equity"[5] may have been written for the same audience as that for which "A Mauchline Wedding" was intended: the "ram-stam billies" Smith ("the slee'st, pawkie thief"), Richmond and Hunter. Together with "Poet Burns" they were the *élite* of Mauchline's "fornicator loons," chosen by the rank and file to form a Court of Equity:

> To take beneath our strict protection,
> The stays-unlacing quondam maiden,
> With GROWING life and anguish laden,
> Who by the Scoundrel is deny'd
> Who led her thoughtless steps aside.

Clockie Brown the watchmaker and Sandy Dow the Coachman are indicted because they have been so dishonourable as to

> refuse assistance
> To those whom [they have] given existence,

and are summoned to appear before the Court in the Whitefoord Arms on the fourth of June next. If Brown does not then acknowledge his crime and face up to his responsibilities he will be tied naked to the village pump while the girl he has ruined does what she likes with him for at least three hours. The poem ends with a parody of legal language; but in spite of this, and the euphemisms for certain actions and parts of the body derived from the watchmaker's trade, the verse does not attain the distinction of the fragment on William Miller's wedding. "The Court of Equity" is local bawdry and nothing more; it does not rise beyond the level of moderately competent light verse.

"The Auld Farmer's New-Year Morning ·Salutation to his Auld Mare, Maggie, on giving her the accustomed Ripp of

---

[5] I have used the text printed as an appendix in Catherine Carswell, *The Life of Robert Burns*, London 1930, pp. 457–62.

Corn to Hansel in the New-Year,"[6] provides yet another
example of Burns's manners-painting strain. It has often been
considered as a poem of essentially the same sort as "To a
Mouse,"[7] important primarily as exhibiting Robert's sympathy
with the lower animals;[8] and its language has been widely
praised. Miss Keith, for instance, says that it "shares with
'Halloween' . . . the honour of having the finest Lallans Burns
ever wrote," and that no poem "has more verbs to the square
inch—and all of them verbs of motion."[9] It seems to me, however, that the Scots of "The Auld Farmer's Salutation" is
often a matter of the individual word, so that in spite of the
sound and movement of lines like

> How thou wad prance, an' snore, an' skriegh,
>   An' tak the road !

or

> Thou never lap, an' sten't, an' breastit,
>   Then stood to blaw,

the vernacular is not so creatively employed as in "Death and
Doctor Hornbook,"[10] where Scottishness is more consistently
bound up with phrasing and idiom.

It is not Burns who speaks in "The Auld Farmer's Salutation," but a character whom he has projected, and the poem
is primarily a naturalistic sketch whose source is a gently
humorous and pathetic appreciation of personality and mood.
The life of man and beast has been a shared struggle on the
road and in the fields, from which the main values to emerge
are independence, companionship and sheer survival against
odds :

> Monie a sair darg we twa hae wrought,
> An' wi' the weary warl' fought !
> An' monie an anxious day I thought
>   We wad be beat !
> Yet here to crazy age we're brought,
>   Wi' something yet.

The horse, man's comrade in the life-long battle against
nature, is perhaps intended as a symbol of friendship ; if so, I

---

[6] I. 100 (360).   [7] Below, pp. 164–8.   [8] *E.g.*, by C. & W., III. 74.
[9] C. Keith, pp. 54–5.   [10] Below, pp. 117–22.

cannot feel that the symbolism is as vivid, or as moving, as it might have been.

In "The Auld Farmer's Salutation" the poet gets so completely inside his subject's brain at a unique moment of time that his very success constitutes an artistic limitation—largely because the farmer does not see the full meaning of his life. Although his situation obviously implies a criticism of society, the old man only hints at his sufferings : "monie a sair darg" and "monie an anxious day." Like most Scots (and many Englishmen and Americans) he is shy of giving expression to his deepest emotions ; but his understatement is so extreme as to form a real barrier to the non-Scottish reader. One feels that the farmer does not want to understand *why* his life has been such a hard one ; all he can do is to endure. "The Auld Farmer's Salutation" is photography, not painting ; it is documentary, not art of the most highly creative or imaginative kind. At the level of dramatic empathy which does not go beyond the limits of a single occasion it is a fine poem ; but— in my view at least—it does not rise above the local and the particular as the greatest of Burns's works certainly do. From the standpoint of literary history, however, the poem's novelty resides mainly in its particularity. In the Great Britain of 1786, to report a humble person's mind as completely as Burns does here was in itself an act with tremendous possibilities for the future, pointing forward to Wordsworth and the Lyrical Ballads.

"The Auld Farmer's Salutation" is generally ascribed to January 1786. Almost exactly a year before that date, Burns had written the best of all his purely local poems—"Death and Doctor Hornbook : A True Story."[11] Even in Scotland, where education has long been idolised, teachers have never been well paid ; and the Tarbolton schoolmaster's pittance was so meagre that he had been forced to open a little grocer's shop in order to make ends meet. Gilbert Burns tells us that "having accidentally fallen in with some medical books, and become most hobby-horsically attached to the study of medicine, he had added the sale of a few medicines to his little trade. He had got a shop-bill printed, at the bottom of which, overlooking

[11] I. 191 (391) ; Chambers, I. 108-9.

his own incapacity, he had advertised that 'Advice would be given in common disorders at the shop gratis'."[12] Robert used this situation as the occasion for a work which converts the ridicule of self-importance and pretence into pure comedy of the most fantastic and unrealistic sort. His humour consists in inflating his victim to superhuman proportions in order simultaneously to deflate him; Hornbook is larger than the real dominie, John Wilson, just as Holy Willie is larger than the real William Fisher. Such exaggeration is, of course, found elsewhere in Scottish poems and novels; but that it is a specifically Scottish characteristic may well be doubted, for it occurs in most of the great comic creations of European literature. One finds it, with individual modifications, in writers as different from each other as Rabelais, Shakespeare, Ben Jonson, Molière, Dickens and Joyce.

As Miss Christina Keith has pointed out, "Death and Doctor Hornbook" looks forward to "Tam o' Shanter," both in landscape and in narrative skill.[13] In the very first verse the point of view of the poem is established as a datum from which the work can proceed; it is in fact a poetic construct, a selection from the attitudes of the real Burns which becomes a framework around which he organises his piece. Some books, says Burns, are lies from beginning to end, some lies have never been written down, and

> Ev'n ministers, they hae been kend,
> In holy rapture,
> A rousing whid at times to vend,
> And nail't wi' Scripture.

Unlike these, the story we are going to hear

> Is just as true 's the Deil's in hell
> Or Dublin city.

This statement superficially resembles the well-known device by which writers like Defoe or Swift palm off their own inventions as the relations of actual voyagers or as the memoirs of somebody who actually lived through the Great Plague, but in reality it is more complex than that; there is an underlying audacity which implies that the Deil is *not* in Hell, or even in

---

[12] Chambers, *loc. cit.*   [13] C. Keith, p. 68.

Dublin—but that he is just as much a fabrication as the story whose truth Burns vouches for so loudly. The stanza is a triumph of ambiguity in some Empsonian sense.[14]

Miss Keith rightly praises the rhythmic effects of the third stanza, with its precise reflection of the staggering, erratic gait of a drunken man on his way home :

> I stacher'd whyles, but yet took tent ay
> To free the ditches ;
> An' hillocks, stanes, an' bushes, kend ay
> Frae ghaists an' witches.[15]

But the effect is as much the result of diction as of sound-values : it is the amount he "kens" that is important, his tipsy confidence in his ability to distinguish between the natural and supernatural worlds.

Inebriation is the ideal preliminary for an encounter with the unseen ; and sure enough, as he is approaching Tarbolton Mill, three hundred yards or so to the east of the village, he meets with *"Something"*—a supernatural figure called "Death," although in actual fact it incorporates some of the traditional attributes of Time, such as the beard and the scythe :

> Its stature seem'd lang Scotch ells twa ;
> The queerest shape that e'er I saw,
> For fient a wame it had ava ;
> And then its shanks,
> They were as thin, as sharp an' sma'
> As cheeks o' branks.

Death is seen through friendly eyes, as is Satan in the "Address to the Deil." He is as concrete as Coila in "The Vision." The effect is that everything is localised, and the whole universe, including Death, has shrunk to kailyard dimensions—this in spite of the tallness of Burns's allegorical personage. The poet and Death sit down to "have a crack" ; and Death is full of complaints about Doctor Hornbook, who peddles certain infallible specifics with strange Latin names, like *"sal-marinum* o' the seas," the *"farina* of beans an' pease," *"aqua-fontis"* [*sic*], *"urinus spiritus* of capons" :

---

[14] Here I am elaborating a hint in Daiches, p. 201.
[15] C. Keith, p. 69.

'Or mite-horn shavings, filings, scrapings,
         Distill'd *per se* ;
   Sal-alkali o' midge-tail clippings,
         And monie mae.'[16]

When the poet comments that this will ruin the local grave-
digger, Death groans out an "eldritch laugh" at such *naïveté*.
The trouble is that for every person that Hornbook saves from
natural death, he kills a score with his physic, thus cheating
Death of his lawful prey. Just as Death is about to tell Burns
of a scheme he has to get his own back on Hornbook, the church
clock strikes "some wee short hour ayont the twal," and the
two have to part :

         I took the way that pleas'd mysel,
                 And sae did Death.

   In "Death and Doctor Hornbook" Burns succeeded in con-
verting an apparent limitation into a source of positive strength.
The comedy arises from the grotesque belittling of universals
like death and human folly, which transmutes satire into
fantasy ;[17] in order to make Death (or Death-Time) into a

   [16] Interestingly enough, in the Fraser MS, David Hume exhibits the same sort
of humour that Burns shows here. Fraser was probably a Catholic, and Hume, as
part of a practical joke, addressed "To THE RIGHT HONBLE the LORD-CHIEF-
JUSTICE REASON, | and the HONBLE the JUDGES, DISCRETION, PRUDENCE, | RESERVE,
and DELIBERATION, | THE PETITION of | THE PATIENTS of WESTMINSTER against |
JAMES FRASER, apothecary," in which he satirised a political and religious controversy in medical jargon, *e.g.* "That the said James Fraser & his Associates now
finding that this *Catholicon* does not agree with the Constitution of the said Dame,
prescribe to her large DOZES [sic] of *Phillipiacum, Cottontium* & *Vandeputiana*, in
order to alter her Constitution & prepare her Body for the Reception of the said
Catholicon." In another clause of Hume's mock-petition, there is a rather
Burnsian play with the notion of apothecaries killing off their patients : "That
your Petitioners verily believe, that not many more have dy'd from amongst them,
under the Administration of the said James Fraser, than actually dye, by the
Course of Nature, in Places where Physic is not at all known or practic'd : Which
will scarcely be credited in this sceptical & unbelieving Age." See Hume, *Letters*,
II. 340–2. A possible source, which Burns may have seen, is Paul Whitehead's
"Death and the Doctor : To Dr. Schomberg of Bath," in *Scots Magazine*, XXXVII
(Jan. 1775), p. 43. See A. H. MacLaine, "A Source for Burns's 'Death and Doctor
Hornbook'," in *Burns Chronicle*, 1955, pp. 1–2.
   [17] Wittig (pp. 71, 174) sees in this somewhat gruesome fantasy an abiding
characteristic of Scottish literature. He finds a similar grotesquerie in Dunbar, in
the vernacular Scottish Gaelic poetry of the seventeenth and eighteenth centuries,
and in Burns's immediate predecessor, Robert Fergusson. There is more than a
trace of this quality in Smollett.

comic figure, Burns had to parochialise him through the intermediary of the raciest and most intimate conversation that it
was possible for him to create. Dialogue here is not primarily
a matter of choosing individual words, as it tends to be in "The
Auld Farmer's New Year Morning Salutation"; it is rather
an affair of idiom. Perhaps nowhere else in Burns do we get
so close to the actual give-and-take of village conversation.
To the seven examples noted by Miss Keith[18] one might add
another seven—or a score, for the whole poem is a synthesis of
colloquial, racy and semi-proverbial expressions:

> At length, says I : 'Friend, whare ye gaun?
>   Will ye go back?'

> 'Come, gie's your hand, an' say we're gree't. . . .'

> 'Sax thousand years are near-hand fled
> Sin' I was to the butching bred. . . .'

> 'Fient haet o't wad hae pierc'd the heart
> Of a kail-runt.'

> 'Just shit in a kail-blade an' send it,
>   As soon 's he smells 't,
> Baith their disease and what will mend it,
>   At once he tells 't.'

> 'Waes me for Johnie Ged's Hole now. . . .
> Nae doubt they'll rive it wi' the plew :
>   They'll ruin Johnie!'

The extraordinary skill with which Burns fits the dialogue into
his metre is something new—not only in Burns, but in Scots
poetry. Here he has achieved complete fusion between a
traditional stanzaic form and living conversation. Of English
poets, only Swift, Pope, Prior, Byron, and T. S. Eliot have
achieved a comparable excellence, though there are fore-
shadowings amongst the poets of the Restoration period. Unlike these English conversational poets, who are concerned
primarily with the speech of the upper classes, Burns weds
his form to a selection of the language of the people themselves,
and in doing so shows unique skill.

I cannot agree with Dr Daiches that the main interest of

[18] C. Keith, p. 70.

"Death and Doctor Hornbook" lies in its technical perfection, that its satire can be dismissed as "rather crude," or that it is "an amusing squib at best."[19] On the contrary, here are both poetry and comedy of a high order, as well as a highly creative use of all the resources of spoken Scots.

One of the last of Burns's purely parochial poems is "Tam Samson's Elegy,"[20] written in the interval between the publication of the Kilmarnock volume and his departure for Edinburgh.[21] Samson was a noted sportsman, especially fond of curling and shooting; and the poem is a linguistic *tour-de-force* in which the technical terms of these occupations are pressed into the service of the mock-elegy in order to describe the old man's imagined death. In the sixth and seventh stanzas, the traditional elegiac theme of "all Nature mourns" is transformed into its exact opposite:

> Now safe the stately sawmont sail,
> And trouts bedropp'd wi' crimson hail,
> And eels, weel-kend for souple tail,
>   And geds for greed,
> Since, dark in Death's fish-creel, we wail
>   Tam Samson dead!
>
> Rejoice, ye birring paitricks a';
> Ye cootie moorcocks, crousely craw;
> Ye maukins, cock your fud fu' braw
>   Withouten dread;
> Your mortal fae is now awa:
>   Tam Samson's dead!

There are lines as good as any Burns wrote—

> The Brethren o' the mystic level
> May hing their head in woefu' bevel. . . .
>
> Or up the rink like Jehu roar. . . .
>
> 'Lord, five!' he cry'd, an' owre did stagger. . . .

—and there emerges a clear impression of yet another of the "social, honest men" whom Robert loved. Tam Samson is completely alive—an unforgettable member of the gallery of

---

[19] Daiches, pp. 200, 205.   [20] I. 220 (402).   [21] C. & W., IV. 574.

Burnsian characters. He is worthy simply because he exists, a congeries of minute particulars; yet at the same time he is the Universal Sportsman. To find his like we have to go to Scott's Dandie Dinmont, or the novels of Surtees, or Sassoon's *Diary of a Foxhunting Man*, or the idyllic figure of "Uncle" in Tolstoy's *War and Peace*.

There is nothing obscurely parochial about the "sentiments and manners" underlying "The Auld Farmer's Salutation," however bare and restrained they may appear in the telling; nor does one need to know the exact meaning of such technicalities in the vocabulary of curling as "wick a bore" in order to appreciate the warmth and simple honesty of Tam Samson. It is quite otherwise with "Halloween."[22] The customs and habits in which it centres were so unfamiliar to at any rate the more sophisticated of his fellow-countrymen that Burns had himself to append a series of explanatory notes—an itemised account of the superstitions of the natives—in order that the poem should be understood by contemporary readers.

Most Scottish and American critics share the view of critics like W. E. Henley[23] and John Speirs[24] that Burns is the last and finest flower of an old vernacular tradition before it withered into inevitable decay. If they are right, then "Halloween" should be among the very best things Burns ever did. Its language is pure vernacular Scots, its subject a series of rustic *genre* pictures: homely, vigorous and concrete, full of a pulsating, joyous movement, and free from any taint of the abstract or the rhetorical. And yet, considered as a whole, the poem fails to please. Burns is always at his best when he connects local themes and personalities with the abiding interests of the nation and the universal preoccupations of mankind. Here, for once, he fails: and he fails because, for all its movement and activity, the poem does not *develop*. It revolves upon a single spot; and, furthermore, it seems to narrow in smaller and smaller gyrations. It is true that in the second stanza there is an attempt to unite a local scene with the heroes and symbols of nationhood:

[22] I. 88 (356).
[23] "Essay on Burns," in H. & H., IV. 270–3. Cp. also Angellier, II. 401, quoted above, p. xi, n.I. [24] Speirs, pp. 126–8.

> Amang the bonie winding banks,
> Where Doon rins, wimplin, clear;
> Where Bruce ance ruled the martial ranks,
> An' shook his Carrick spear. . . .

Bruce was at one and the same time an Ayrshire man and a leader of national resistance, and the mention of his name is surely intended to remind us that the "merry, friendly, country-folks" of the poem belong to a nation as well as to a parish. But the placing of the stanza is unfortunate; it comes so early that we soon forget it in our contemplation of the rustic high-jinks that follow. Though there is none of Jonson's intellectual wit, the comedy of "Halloween" is Jonsonian rather than Shakespearian. The characters are both objectified and framed, and their frantic animal gaiety seems to explode in miniature, as if seen through the wrong end of a telescope. Take the eighth stanza, in which a young girl puts two nuts in the fire to foretell the outcome of her courtship:

> Jean slips in twa, wi' tentie e'e;
> Wha 'twas, she wadna tell;
> But this is *Jock*, an' this is *me*,
> She says in to hersel:
> He bleez'd owre her, an' she owre him,
> As they wad never mair part;
> Till fuff! he started up the lum,
> And Jean had e'en a sair heart
> To see't that night.

This is one of the vividest stanzas in the poem: but the distorted accentuation of "máir part" and "sáir heart," forced on Burns by his metre, serves to dehumanise the emotions and subordinate them to the rhythm of an unending Bacchanalian dance. It is instructive to compare Burns's treatment of Jean in this stanza with his attitude in the seventh and eighth stanzas of the later dramatic lyric "Tam Glen."[25]

In "Tam Glen," Burns's sole concern is to transmute into poetry the loving and delighted recognition of character; in "Halloween," there are elements of superciliousness, of conscious superiority, and even of thinly disguised cruelty. Peasant and small-town humour is often of the sort which re-

[25] III. 85 (363). See below, p. 306.

joices in the misfortunes and discomfiture of others, but the admission does not thereby turn "Halloween" into a great comic poem. In "Halloween" there is altogether too much whimsical rusticity disporting itself for the amusement of such educated readers as have the patience to look up the glossary. Here, for example, is fighting Jamie Fleck, who sows hempseed, drags a dung-fork behind him as a harrow, and calls out the traditional charm :

> . . .'Hemp-seed I saw thee,
> An' her that is to be my lass
> Come after me, an' draw thee
> As fast this night.'

In spite of his boast that he does not believe in such old wives' tales :

> He whistl'd up *Lord Lenox' March*,
> To keep his courage cheery ;
> Altho' his hair began to arch,
> He was sae fley'd an' eerie ;
> Till presently he hears a squeak,
> An' then a grane an' gruntle ;
> He by his shouther gae a keek,
> An' tumbl'd wi' a wintle
> Out-owre that night.[26]

> He roar'd a horrid murder-shout,
> In dreadfu' desperation !
> An' young an' auld come rinnin out,
> An' hear the sad narration :
> He swoor 'twas hilchin Jean M'Craw,
> Or crouchie Merran Humphie—
> Till stop ! she trotted thro' them a' ;
> An' wha was it but grumphie
> Asteer that night ?

[26] Ritter (p. 81) points out the similarity between ll. 1–2 and Blair, *The Grave*, l. 59 : "Whistling aloud to bear his courage up." In so Scottish a poem as "Halloween" there are naturally many verbal echoes from earlier pieces in the Scottish tradition ; and Ritter (pp. 77–81) finds some fairly precise verbal correspondences with John Mayne's "Hallowe'en," which was published in Ruddiman's *Weekly Magazine*, Nov. 1780, and some parallels with Fergusson's "Hallow-fair" and "The Farmer's Ingle."

The commotion of all this is superb, and the passage reads like a rehearsal for the sixth, seventh and eighth stanzas of the "Address to the Deil" ;[27] but in spite of these undoubted merits it is marred by its tone. However much he may try, the modern reader cannot altogether share in mean guffaws at the physical defects of the helpless and the deformed ; he is unable to appreciate these lines to the full, just as he feels considerable embarrassment when reading a more fantastic exercise in the comedy of cruel flyting, the lyric "Willie Wastle" :[28]

> She's bow-hough'd, she's hem-shin'd,
>   Ae limpin leg a hand-breed shorter ;
> She's twisted right, she's twisted left,
>   To balance fair in ilka quarter ;
> She has a hump upon her breast,
>   The twin o' that upon her shouther :
> Sic a wife as Willie had,
>   I wad na gie a button for her.

The worst stanzas of "Halloween" are the fifteenth and sixteenth, containing the grandmother's reminiscences, where it almost seems as if we are expected to laugh at senility ; and the best are the twenty-fourth, twenty-fifth and twenty-sixth, which describe the amorous and sensual widow :

> A wanton widow Leezie was,
>   As cantie as a kittlin ;
> But och ! that night, amang the shaws,
>   She gat a fearfu' settlin !
> She thro' the whins, an' by the cairn,
>   An' owre the hill gaed scrievin ;
> Whare three lairds' lands met at a burn,
>   To dip her left sark-sleeve in
>   Was bent that night.

[27] I. 47 (335). Especially the lines :

> Or, rustlin, thro' the boortrees comin,
>   Wi' heavy groan. . . .

> Ye, like a rash-buss, stood in sight,
>   Wi' waving sugh.

> When wi' an eldritch, stoor 'quaick, quaick,'
>   Amang the springs,
> Awa ye squatter'd like a drake,
>   On whistling wings.

[28] III. 125 (388). Cp. below, p. 323.

Whyles owre a linn the burnie plays,
    As thro' the glen it wimpl't;
Whyles round a rocky scaur it strays,
    Whyles in a wiel it dimpl't;
Whyles glitter'd to the nightly rays,
    Wi' bickerin, dancin dazzle;
Whyles cookit underneath the braes,
    Below the spreading hazel
            Unseen that night.[29]

Amang the brachens, on the brae,
    Between her an' the moon,
The Deil, or else an outler quey,
    Gat up an' gae a croon:
Poor Leezie's heart maist lap the hool;[30]
    Near lav'rock-height she jumpit,
But mist a fit, an' in the pool
    Out-owre the lugs she plumpit,
            Wi' a plunge that night.

And they owe their brilliance almost entirely to their onomatopoeic quality, so all-pervasive as to evoke—not sounds merely,
as in

x   ç   ʃ
But och! that night amang the shaws,

which reflects the very "sough" of the wind in the trees—but
sights, moods, and—above all—human *character*.

The reader, if he has been responding actively to the poem,
creates for himself a picture of the widow's whole personality
and appearance: small, dark, vivacious, playful and exquisitely
silly. His heart jumps with hers, and he can almost feel the
bitter chill of the water as it fills her ears. He laughs; but
there is no malice or cruelty in his reaction, because the ducking
does not endanger life or limb or even beauty. It is the middle
stanza of the three just quoted that lifts the whole incident to

[29] Ritter (p. 81) finds in this stanza reminiscences of Thomson, "Summer,"
ll. 481–4, and "Spring," ll. 404–6, 646–9; of Milton, *Comus*, ll. 115 f; of Gay,
"Rural Sports," l. 62; of Pinkerton, "Bothwell Bank"; and of Montgomerie,
The Cherrie and the Slae, vi. 8 ff. It is clear that English, as well as Scottish tradition,
has made some contribution to "Halloween."

[30] Cp. Ramsay, *The Gentle Shepherd*, v. i, l. 40: "My Heart out of its Hool was
like to lowp."

the level of poetry, gaining an extra dimension from the
reader's recollection of the opening stanza of the whole poem :

> Upon that night, when fairies light
> On Cassilis Downans dance,
> Or owre the lays, in splendid blaze,
> On sprightly coursers prance ;
> Or for Colean the rout is taen,
> Beneath the moon's pale beams ;[31]
> There, up the Cove, to stray and rove,
> Amang the rocks and streams
>   To sport that night:

The stream which the widow seeks is white, cool and
dazzling like the fairies, and dances as lightly as they ; it is as
"cantie"—and even as treacherous, despite its apparent placid-
ity, as Leezie herself. Then, as so often with Burns, the poem
ends suddenly and abruptly, like some country dances, in a
rather perfunctory description of "social glee." It is all over,
Burns's longest flight in relatively uncontaminated vernacular
Scots ; and it is nearly as unsatisfactory as such purely "English" poems of his as those addressed to Robert Graham of
Fintry.[32] True, Burns here secures effects that are more impressive than anything in either of the poems to Graham : a
breathless, never-ending motion reminiscent of "Christ's Kirk
on the Green," Dunbar's "Dance of the Sevin Deidly Synnis,"
or that anonymous folk-ballad which is known to all Scotsmen
and many Englishmen and Americans—"The Ball of Kirriemuir." But the very merits of "Halloween" are also its defects.
It is all particulars, and lacks that saving infusion of the
general, uniting and giving significance to details and minutiae,
which is essential if a poem, or a scholarly treatise, or a scientific
dissertation, is to achieve the highest excellence. "Halloween,"
it is true, is not entirely without a tincture of philosophy. In its
Rousseauistic preference for the natural and in its criticism of
"art" (*i.e.*, civilisation), the poem is in intention similar to
"The Cotter's Saturday Night," but the reader would never
guess this for himself if it were not for the epigraph :

[31] Cp. Pope, "The Rape of the Lock," II, l. 81 : "Some less refin'd, beneath
the moon's pale light."
[32] I. 271 (427) ; II. 119 (371).

> Yes ! let the rich deride, the proud disdain,
> The simple pleasures of the lowly train :
> To me more dear, congenial to my heart,
> One native charm, than all the gloss of art.
>
> GOLDSMITH.

If it was part of Burns's purpose to illustrate this sentiment, his actual achievement was quite different. There is a detachment, a withdrawnness about the humour which would seem to make "Halloween" the perfect *exemplum* of W. P. Ker's judgment on the poet :

> But one must note that he does not 'render' or interpret the life of rural Scotland simply as one of the people. He stands apart. His is not the voice of the people, but the voice of a judge to whom the people are more or less indifferent, who is far above them, and who sees them as small creatures moved by slight and trivial motives.[33]

This is borne out by Burns's own lofty comment in his preface to the poem :

> The passion of prying into futurity makes a striking part of the history of human nature in its rude state, in all ages and nations ; and it may be some entertainment to a philosophic mind, if any such should honour the author with a perusal, to see the remains of it among the more unenlightened in our own.[34]

Precisely because in "Halloween" Burns has applied the tones and attitudes of a certain type of satire to ordinary everyday life, he is less universal, more embarrassingly parochial, and less truly national than in any other of his longer poems.[35] The consequence is that "Halloween" is today read almost exclusively by Burns scholars, while, despite the sneers of pro-

---

[33] Ker, *On Modern Literature*, p. 56.   [34] Quoted in H. & H., I. 356–7.

[35] This is not the view Wallace expresses in C. & W., IV. 478 : "Fergusson's 'Hallowfair' deals merely with the external, with the oddities and amusing features of popular activity as displayed in the scene it pictures. In 'Hallowe'en' Burns deals with the heart of the people and the weird beliefs still lingering in the darker recesses of their minds ; and the impression left is not that of mere condescending amusement, but of sympathy with the side of human nature to which we are introduced." But the "gudame" of Fergusson's "The Farmer's Ingle," sts. vii–ix, is far more sympathetically conceived than the "graunie" of Burns's "Halloween."

fessional critics, "The Cotter's Saturday Night" finds a welcome among quite ordinary readers throughout the world.

Like everything else that Burns wrote, "The Jolly Beggars, A Cantata,"[36] was influenced by literary tradition—by the burlesque cantatas so popular in the eighteenth century, where the trick consists in using recitatives to link songs set to popular tunes; by Gay's *Beggar's Opera*; and by innumerable stall-ballads and chapbooks celebrating the happy lives of beggars and tinkers and vagabonds of all sorts. Typical of this whole class of popular literature is the English song, "A Beggar, a Beggar, a Beggar I'll be" (1660), with its amusing use of the thieves' slang of the time:

> A Craver my Father, a Maunder my Mother,
> A Filer my Sister, a Filcher my Brother. . .
> In White wheaten Straw when their Bellies were full,
> There was I begot between Tinker and Trull.
> And therefore a Beggar, a Beggar I'll be,
> For none leads a Life more jocund than he.

The beginnings of this convention have been traced (at least in English) to the sixteenth century, but (as Miss Keith points out) its sources go much further back, to Old French and the medieval Latin lyrics.[37] The first vernacular examples in Scotland were "The Gaberlunzie Man" and "The Jolly Beggar," two songs traditionally attributed to King James V (*regn.* 1513–42). Now the sixteenth century was an age of agrarian crisis and of "sturdy rogues and vagabonds," displaced peasants and monks, many of whom were forced into a wandering life in town or country. Their very existence was a denial of the values and conventions of village communities and corporate towns; they were, surely, lower-class picaroons, the popular counterparts of those upper-class adventurers who were the originals of the heroes of the sixteenth-century Spanish novel. As Dr Kettle has pointed out, in another connexion:

> The best illustration in English literature of the social pheno-
> menon which gave rise to the picaresque novel is the Falstaff
> section of *Henry IV*. (Poins would have made an admirable

[36] II. 1 (291).   [37] C. Keith, p. 83.

picaresque hero with his vitality and resource and lack of morals.) Falstaff and his cronies are of varying social origin; but they are all the rejects of feudalism, and they belong to the Elizabethan rather than to the fifteenth-century world. In another sense they do not 'belong' to any society at all. They are without roots. They have no fixed abode. They live on their wits. They have no morals except the good new rule of each for himself and the devil take the hindmost. And they mock every sanctity of the feudal world—chivalry, honour, filial piety, allegiance, even kingship.[38]

In the country districts and the slum areas of towns like London and Bristol there were ragged equivalents of Pistol and Poins—the innumerable "rufflers, whipjacks, hookers, priggers of prancers, palliards, walking morts" and "kinchin coves" of Elizabethan rogue literature. It seems hardly accidental that the two great periods of agrarian change in British history, when society appears to have produced more than its usual quota of lawless vagabonds, footpads and prostitutes, were also ages in which the lower orders brought into being a large number of ballads and songs celebrating the prowess of the delinquent and the maladjusted. This is perhaps the place to recollect Dr Daiches's remark[39] that "The Jolly Beggars" appeals "to humanity's 'unofficial self' (to employ the useful phrase coined by George Orwell) to a degree extremely rare in literature" : a comment which applies not only to Burns's cantata, but holds good, to a lesser extent, of all the beggar songs of the eighteenth century. Labourers and small farmers struggling to remain in the state into which it had pleased the Lord to call them inevitably dreamed their dreams of irresponsible freedom, in which beggary and crime seemed preferable to the eternal struggle to make ends meet. "Acclaimed in chaps and broadsides for his love of liberty and his disdain of the proprieties," the Jovial Beggar had become, even before Burns got hold of him, something of a "popular Ideal" ;[40] and it is as such an archetype that he appears in "The Merry Beggars," one of the immediate precursors of Robert's work :

---

[38] A. Kettle, *An Introduction to the English Novel*, London 1951, I. 24.
[39] P. 231.
[40] H. & H., II. 296 *ad init.*

Whoe'er would be merry and free,
    Let him list and from us he may learn ;
In palaces who shall you see
    Half so happy as we in a barn ?[41]

Burns took this wish-fulfilment fantasy of the masses,
corresponding almost exactly to the educated profligate's
obsession with the symbolic figure of Macheath,[42] and made it
into a great lyrical dramatic poem.

Nae mair then, we'll care then,
    Nae farther can we fa',

he had written in the "Epistle to Davie" when contemplating
the possibility of destitution ; "The Jolly Beggars" extracts the
last ounce of meaning from such a situation, using it to frame
a root-and-branch criticism of organised community life and
morality from a point of view as extreme in its own way as those
sometimes found in Byron and Shelley. The world of "The
Jolly Beggars" is in opposition not simply to the aristocracy or
the citizen class or the "unco guid," but to every kind of social
stability and institutional cohesion ; yet, paradoxically enough,
it is at the same time a grotesque parody of the real world of
catch-as-catch-can, and even to a certain extent of the very
special individualism which, as we have seen, is expressed in
the "Second Epistle to Lapraik." It is also Burns's version of
the Superman and his noblest tribute to instinct and libido.
Over twenty years ago, Christopher Caudwell characterised as
the supreme illusion of modern times the idea that man is most
free when he is liberated from social restraint, when he is
allowed to live according to some inner primeval urge, or
secret prompting of the blood ; and he traced the development

---

[41] Quoted in Chambers, I. 183, n. It appeared in *The Charmer*, 2 vols., 1751. The
beggar literature has been listed exhaustively by H. & H., *loc. cit.*, and by Ritter,
pp. 84–90.
[42] The Macheath "ideal" runs through, *e.g.*, Boswell's *London Journal*. It may
also have inspired Deacon Brodie. At his trial, one of his accomplices gave evidence
that before setting out to burgle the Excise Office, Brodie "took a pistol from his
pocket, and repeated the verse of a song of Macheath's from a play—words like
'We'll turn our lead to gold,' or such like" ; and, according to a contemporary
account, "on the Tuesday before his execution . . . he began singing, with the
greatest cheerfulness, from the *Beggar's Opera*—' 'Tis woman that seduces all
mankind'." (Roughead, pp. 133, 213, 274).

of this concept from Marlowe through Rousseau to Freud and D. H. Lawrence.[43] Burns in this cantata gives vent to his own special variant of primitivism, and it is one which—in spite of Matthew Arnold—*does* constitute a genuine "criticism of life."

I do not think that Miss Keith is altogether right when she compares "The Jolly Beggars" with the literary world of the *Vie de Bohème*: "To Burns' beggars, as to Mürger, life is but that—noise and song and Bohemia."[44] The beggars' circle is more anarchistic than even the life of declassed students in a nineteenth-century Paris garret; and the poem is much more corrosive of accepted values than, say, the paintings of Toulouse-Lautrec. "Nothing," says Miss Keith, "—neither drink nor lust—can unite this pack,"[45] thereby putting her finger on one of the main qualities of the work. Though the beggars are a group, they have no abiding mutual loyalty, since their coming-together is altogether fortuitous. But because they burn with the flame of vitality, because the Life Force works in them still, they are the embodiment of a positive value. The competition of merchants and lairds is pettifogging and therefore evil, but the rivalry of wolves and tigers is good; are they not vigorous, earthy, and free from hypocrisy, and are not these qualities to be commended above the deceptions of civilised life? No doubt this is Burns's own special version of pastoral, and no doubt it is possible to see the concept of the Noble Savage behind it all; but the really important thing, the essential point of difference from other expressions of the Rousseauistic myth, is that Burns neither arcadianises nor sentimentalises his ragged crew.[46] They are that they are; in "The Jolly Beggars," existence and essence are one.

The cantata effectively demolishes the presuppositions of eighteenth-century society, and it does so partly by its special

---

[43] C. Caudwell, *Illusion and Reality*, London 1937, pp. 70 ff.; *Studies in a Dying Culture*, London 1938, pp. 69–72.

[44] C. Keith, pp. 90–1. [45] C. Keith, *loc. cit.*

[46] This is of great importance for the establishment of what is *new* in Burns. In this respect, he quite transcends the English and Anglo-Scottish "sentimental school" of writers, great though their influence upon him was. No doubt it was what he had learnt from the old vernacular tradition, as it came down to him through Watson and Ramsay and Fergusson, that enabled him to do this; but it is clear that Burns's best work was produced by the coming together of two traditions, rather than by the victory of the Scottish one over the English.

union of narrative and song, partly by the interpenetration of colloquial and literary diction, and partly by the humour of incongruity.[47] In the first *Recitativo*, the movement of the first stanza is from the cold inhuman natural scene to the warmth of alehouse fellowship. The next stanza telescopes ideas ("usquebae" and "blankets") and presents two extremely vivid images :

> Wi' usquebae an' blankets warm,
> She blinket on her sodger.
> An' ay he gies the tozie drab
> The tither skelpin kiss,
> While she held up her greedy gab
> Just like an aumous dish :
> Ilk smack still did crack still,
> Like onie cadger's whup. . . .

"Aumous dish" conveys the picture of a sordid receptacle bringing physical desire and voracious meanness into a strange and unexpected relationship; at the same time, the sound of the cadger's whip carries a slight undertone of sadism.

In the soldier's song ("I am a son of Mars. . . .") the element of surprise is provided not only by headlong pace of the verse—"with an effect," as Miss Keith claims,[48] "almost as daemonic as that of Catullus' *Attis* (the fastest thing in literature)"—but also by the detailed working-out of the stock expression "soldier's trade." In the second stanza the military life, essentially a career of legalised murder, is explicitly compared to that of an ordinary petty artisan. The first stage of

---

[47] Wittig (p. 211) notes that "The Jolly Beggars" is "the fullest symposium of the Scottish tradition. There is no other compilation in which we find such a wealth of old motifs, songs, tunes, Scottish metres, and echoes of the Makars, brought freshly to life in a congenial form." These motifs, metres, etc., unite with Scottish diction (often colloquial) to undermine the values and beliefs of the "unco guid." In addition to the *Christis-Kirk* and *Cherrie-and-the-Slae* stanzas and "Standard Habbie" (the Burns stanza), the Recitativos employ common measure, tail-rhyme, the 8-line stanza, and *a a, a b : c c, c b* with internal rhyme—all national forms. But the vocabulary of some of the songs is Anglo-Scottish rather than vernacular Scots, and certain of the tunes appear to be of English origin. Cp. *The Songs of Robert Burns*, ed. J. C. Dick, henceforth cited as Dick, London 1903, pp. 445-7. Thus the work as a whole exhibits both conflict and fusion of Scottish and English elements—in form (the very idea of a burlesque cantata is surely English), in diction, and in melody ; but both traditions are strictly subservient to Burns's artistic purpose.   [48] P. 85.

the soldier's career was of course that of apprenticeship, during which he took part in the storming of the "heights of Abram," under General Wolfe's leadership, at Quebec in 1759. Next came the journeyman period, the great event here being the reduction of El Moro, "the castle defending the harbour of Santiago de Cuba," which he had helped to storm in 1762. Twenty years later, in 1782, he took part in the destruction of the French floating batteries in front of Gibraltar, where he "left for witness an arm and a limb," and so was forced to retire from business :

> Yet let my country need me, with Eliott to head me
> I'd clatter on my stumps at the sound of the drum.

George Augustus Eliott, his old commander, was very much the contemporary Montgomery or Rokossovsky ; so that if, as Miss Keith asserts,[49] the Jolly Beggars are obsessed by self, then the soldier's obsession takes the form of proclaiming an intense personal loyalty to his hero.

The second *Recitativo*[50] is remarkable for its accommodation of Scottish idiom and eighteenth-century poetic diction, its fusion of what Boswell called the "sarcastical Scotch humour"[51] with the mock heroic comedy one finds in Fielding or Smollett or Pope :

> He ended ; and the kebars sheuk
>   Aboon the chorus roar ;
> While frighted rattons backward leuk,
>   An' seek the benmost bore :
> A fairy fiddler frae the neuk,
>   He skirl'd out *Encore* !
> But up arose the martial chuck,
>   An' laid the loud uproar :—

This is real "tone poetry," full of the rich music of alliteration and vowel patterns to which Christina Keith has drawn attention.[52] Equally important is the parody of classical epic contained in "He ended," which echoes the mock-Miltonic

---

[49] P. 91.   [50] H. & H., II. 4.   [51] *Boswell in Holland*, p. 378.
[52] *E.g.*, on p. 85. A detailed technical analysis of the alliteration in Burns's cantata (in both recitatives and songs) would give results similar to those already derived from "Man was made to Mourn" and "Holy Willie's Prayer." See below, pp. 352-3 and 354-5.

"Ane sat" of the first *Recitativo*[53] and the stupendous impudence
of "martial chuck," illuminating all the paradoxes of eighteenth
century society. The term "chuck" ought by rights to describe
an ordinary wife or maiden, but Burns applies it to a soldier's
drab who has had hundreds of men in her career and he
qualifies it with a high-sounding adjective from the language
of patriots and men of letters. The result is an intuitive and
instantaneous comparison of the low with the great, not
necessarily to the detriment of the low—and perhaps also the
drawing of certain parallels between officers' ladies and
privates' whores.

The chuck's song ("I once was a maid . . .") is the direct
negation of its source or one of its sources—a piece printed by
Allan Ramsay, which goes no further than a village nin-
compoop's Cinderella-dream :

> My soger laddie's over the sea
> And he will bring gold and money to me ;
> And when he comes hame, he'll make me a lady ;
> My blessing gang wi' my soger laddie.[54]

Burns's song, as Dr Daiches points out, "lists the sexual career
of the singer in a manner which does not so much flout or
attack ordinary social conventions as ignore them, as though
in the world of real, elemental living they did not exist."[55] At
the same time it carries forward the ironical interplay of contrasting concepts and kinds of language which is at the very
centre of the cantata :

> The sword I forsook for the sake of the church ;
> He riskèd the soul, and I ventur'd the body. . . .

> Full soon I grew sick of my sanctified sot . . .

> From the gilded spontoon to the fife I was ready. . . .

> But the Peace it reduc'd me to beg in despair. . . .

Balance, antithesis, the juxtaposition of grotesquely contrasting images are present also in the third *Recitativo*,[56] which
describes the self-centred "guzzling" of a tinker wench and a

---

[53] H. & H., ii. 1 *ad fin.*   [54] H. & H., ii. 300 ; Dick, p. 446.
[55] Daiches, p. 220.   [56] H. & H., ii. 6.

Merry-Andrew or professional fool. It is difficult to see why Miss Keith thinks the fool's song inferior—"Burns in a hurry, perhaps? Or Burns not caring? Or Burns on purpose, as he was writing for a fool?"[57] The tune goes back at least as far as the sixteenth century and, though apparently of English origin, it was well known in Scotland.[58] Its rhythms make possible those phrases in the fifth and sixth stanzas which anticipate the political and social anarchism of the conclusion:

> Poor Andrew that tumbles for sport
> Let naebody name wi' a jeer:
> There's even, I'm tauld, i' the Court
> A tumbler ca'd the Premier.
>
> Observ'd ye yon reverend lad
> Mak faces to tickle the mob?
> He rails at our mountebank squad—
> It's rivalship just i' the job!

The last line of the sixth stanza, which seems so harsh and incompetent to Miss Keith, surely reflects in its very lumbersomeness the clumsy falling and sparring of both fool and Prime Minister, as well as a certain drunken incoherence which may well be common to both. If the greatest achievement of "The Jolly Beggars" is the establishment of ironical correspondence between high and low life (which Fielding had already attempted in *Jonathan Wild*), then Merry-Andrew's song may well be regarded as the kernel of the whole work— and "It's rivalship just i' the job," almost because of its ugliness, as a highly successful line. The final couplet of the lyric stresses the "de'il tak' the hindmost" outlook of the beggars:

> The chiel that's a fool for himsel,
> Guid Lord! he's far dafter than I.

The emphasis now shifts[59] to the purely personal level; a sturdy woman, perhaps mature rather than elderly, and weeping drunk, sings a lament for her "braw John Highlandman," using a melody which may well go back to medieval times. Social criticism manages to creep in even here, for the "carlin" is given the following comment on the relativity of political morality:

[57] C. Keith, p. 87.   [58] Dick, p. 446.   [59] H. & H., II. 8.

The lalland laws he held in scorn,
But he still was faithfu' to his clan. . . .

Miss Keith finds the diction of this poem "odd. 'The ladies' hearts he did trepan' . . . and 'Adown my cheeks the pearls ran'. 'Pearls' indeed!'"[60] Here, however, "trepan" is probably not the surgical verb, but "trepan" meaning "to trap, ensnare, or beguile," from "trapan," an obsolete word for a decoy; the Highlandman seized hold of the ladies' hearts as skilfully as he captured game or cattle.

As for the other line to which Miss Keith takes exception, its full meaning is apparent only when the whole stanza is quoted:

They banish'd him beyond the sea,
But ere the bud was on the tree,
Adown my cheek the pearls ran,
Embracing my John Highlandman.

The second line gives us a stock image of popular song, while the third derives something from the "pearly tears" of teatable convention; and the lines are, one feels, placed side by side in order that the greatest possible amount of energy should be generated by their opposition. At the same time, "ere the bud was on the tree" carries two tremendous implications—firstly, that John's banishment was, in fact, winter for the singer, and, secondly, that it was not spring but the Highlandman's return that ended winter for her. And when one realises that oblique comment on a class-ridden society runs through "The Jolly Beggars" like a musical *motif*, "Adown my cheeks the pearls ran" becomes invested with a magnificent irony. Not only does "pearls" give a singularly bright and definite image of the tears on her cheeks, but the line carries the added social implication—"This woman of the people is just as capable of pure emotion as any refined young lady."

It is exactly the same with the carlin's final quatrain:

And now a widow I must mourn
The pleasures that will ne'er return;
No comfort but a hearty can
When I think on John Highlandman.

[60] C. Keith, p. 87.

This repeats the *frisson* of the previous stanza : it is at one and the same time a parody of drawing-room mawkishness, and a statement that hard-drinking robber-women can feel as deeply for "The pleasures that will ne'er return" as can society's great lovers. The lyric becomes almost overpowering when sung ; the tune, as printed in *The Caledonian Pocket Companion*,[61] is a very wild one, capable of expressing joy and sorrow by turns. There is thus additional tension between the essentially lawless nature of the melody, and the occasional conventional phrases. This serves to annihilate the conventions themselves, so that we are shocked into the realisation that "society is all but rude" when placed beside the widow's love and grief.

At this point[62] the Highland woman catches the eye of a "pigmy scraper on a fiddle" (the "fairy fiddler" of the second *Recitativo*), who thereupon sings her a love song, after an introductory stanza blending classical allusion, Italian musical terms, and the language of the people :

> Wi' hand on hainch and upward e'e,
> He croon'd his gamut, one, two, three,
> Then in an *arioso* key
> The wee Apollo
> Set off wi' *allegretto* glee
> His *giga* solo. . . .[63]

Like much eighteenth-century verse, the fiddler's song is dependent on allusion—from the recollection of Marlowe in the first stanza ("An' go wi' me an' be my dear"), to the associations of the last line of the chorus—"Whistle owre the lave o't," derived from the popular tune of that name.[64] Like all the rest of these raffish tatterdemalions, the Fiddler mixes the aristocratic (or middle-class) language of gallantry with common speech :

---

[61] Reprinted by Dick, p. 224.
[62] Fifth *Recitativo*; H. & H., II. 10.
[63] Cp. Ramsay, "Elegy on Patie Birnie," ix., ll. 4–6, cited by Ritter, p. 89 : "On which *Apollo*, | With meikle Pleasure play'd himsel | Baith Jig and Solo." This type of linguistic humour seems to appeal to the Scottish mind ; at least, there are many precedents in the vernacular tradition, from Dunbar onwards.

[64] H. & H., II. 303–04. It is clear from the old song, as printed by Herd (1769), that the line refers to the loss of a maidenhead.

But bless me wi' your heav'n o' charms,
And while I kittle hair on thairms'
Hunger, cauld, an' a' sic harms
May whistle owre the lave o't.

Here we have the same humorous conflict between two sorts
of diction that runs throughout the whole cantata, together
with an attitude to a tramp's life which we have noted in other
early poems.

A tough-looking tinker also has his eye on the widow; and
when, in the sixth *Recitativo*,[65] the two men quarrel, their duel
becomes a bizarre distortion of an aristocratic fight about a
woman:

Her charms had struck a sturdy caird
As weel as poor gut-scraper;
He taks the fiddler by the beard,
An' draws a roosty rapier;
He swoor by a' was swearing worth
To speet him like a pliver,
Unless he would from that time forth
Relinquish her for ever.

"Her charms . . . Relinquish her for ever"—here, too, the polite
clichés are boldly contrasted with the violence of the surrounding vernacular. Once again, the point seems to be that these
people have the same emotions as their "betters." The fiddler
is forced to yield up his doxy, sniggering away in his sleeve as,
in his turn, the tinker fits a song to a tune with suggestive
associations. What he does is to invite the widow to desert the
violinist for his own superior person.

In the next *Recitativo*[66] the parody of the language of
gallantry becomes more exquisite than anywhere else in the
work, in lines which might almost be regarded as a laboratory
specimen of Burns's favourite trick of shocking his reader by
the sudden putting-together of unexpected visual images and
idioms drawn from violently opposed "levels of usage":

The caird prevail'd: th' unblushing fair
In his embraces sunk,
Partly wi' love o'ercome sae sair,
An' partly she was drunk.

[65] H. & H., II. 12.   [66] H. & H., II. 14.

Despite Sir Violino's eminently civilised and prudent decision to hand the widow over to the tinker, he still manages to "rake her fore and aft" behind the hencoop, whereupon her real lord and master, a lame ballad-singer or bard who has all the time been of the company, rises up like a madman—not to assault the fiddler, but to offer him the Highland woman as a gift.[67] The fate of the dull-witted tinker is not stated—perhaps he is lying dead drunk in the yard, or clouting a metaphorical cauldron somewhere else. This is the grand reversal and comical *peripeteia* of the whole work, constituting a deliberate assault upon the reader's conventional morality. The ballad-singer, it is clear, does not regard women jealously. He can afford to be generous, for it is not as though the Highland woman were his only love; he has in fact two others—the "Deborahs" of the eighth *Recitativo*.[68]

Miss Keith,[69] in her analysis, appears to think that the fiddler is to be identified with the ballad-singer. The evidence is all against this extraordinary suggestion: but the ragged bard is perhaps a projection of one side of Burns's nature. Sir Herbert Grierson has noticed, in some of the songs in "The Jolly Beggars," an "inferior swaggering note in the tradition of Durfey's *Pills to Purge Melancholy*";[70] the same point could be made in another way by saying that the effect of the swaggering is to present the idealised images of his characters. Only in the case of the fiddler—a much more sensitive person than the

---

[67] That is the meaning of the somewhat obscure allusion "An' shor'd them 'Dainty Davie' | O' boot that night." Dainty Davie (the Rev. David Williamson, d. 1702, aged 79), was a Covenanting minister who often visited the house of Lady Cherrytree, near Edinburgh. One day in 1674 Capt. Creichton and his troopers came to search the house. According to Capt. Creichton (quoted in H. & H., ii. 312), "the lady, well knowing our errand, put Williamson to bed to her daughter, disguised in a woman's night-dress. . . . when the daughter raised herself a little in the bed to let the troopers see her, they did not discover him, and so went off disappointed. But the young lady proved with child, and Williamson, to take off the scandal, married her in some time after." Just as Lady Cherrytree presented her daughter to Dainty Davie, so, on catching his doxy "in the act", the ballad-singer hands her over to the fiddler. Like so much else in "The Jolly Beggars," these lines carry the implication that the respectable are not (always) so different from the disreputable as they seem. Dick (p. 474) dismisses the whole Cherrytree–Williamson story as an unauthenticated "chestnut," and claims that both the tune and its title go back beyond 1674.

[68] H. & H., ii. 17.   [69] P. 88.   [70] Quoted in Daiches, p. 218.

others—do we catch a glimpse of any inner subjective life. This peculiarity of the cantata enables the bard to swagger too ; quite clearly the "wight of Homer's craft" is a creation of Robert's, but at the same time he bears a definite resemblance to the real Burns.[71] I suggest that the connexion is one of caricature—a deliberate guying of one of Burns's favourite poses, that of the Child of Nature :

> I never drank the Muses' stank,
>   Castalia's burn, an' a' that ;
> But there it streams, an' richly reams—
>   My Helicon I ca' that.[72]

The Helicon in question is of course strong drink. The bard is free ; and freedom consists in doing exactly what one wants to do :

> Great love I bear to a' the fair,
>   Their humble slave an a' that ;
> But lordly will, I hold it still
>   A mortal sin to thraw that.[73]

At this particular moment he is enjoying the "raptures sweet" of "mutual love" with his "twa Deborahs" :

[71] He is also a rather extreme development of quite a common 18th-cent. idea, the result of the antiquarian revival and the growing popularity of ballads, that Homer, the supreme master of epic, was nothing more than a blind ballad-singer. ("Her lord, a wight of Homer's craft," *Recit.* 6, H. & H., ii. 14). Cp. (?) Ambrose Philips, *Introduction* to *Collection of Old Ballads*, London 1723, p. iii, and Allan Ramsay's line, "Auld Homer sang for's daily bread" (*Works*, 1877, i. 250), both quoted in Ritter, pp. 90–1. Thus this part of the social criticism of "The Jolly Beggars" can be traced to English as well as to Scottish sources.

[72] To place together terms of classical mythology and vernacular words was another favourite trick of Scottish vernacular poets. H. & H., ii. 313 derive "Helicon" from Montgomerie's "fontaine Helicon" in *The Cherrie and the Slae*, but Ritter draws attention (p. 91) to the third stanza of Fergusson, "The King's Birth-day in Edinburgh" :

> O *Muse*, be kind, and dinna fash us
> To flee awa' beyont Parnassus,
> Nor seek for *Helicon* to wash us,
>   That heath'nish spring ;
> Wi' Highland whisky scour our hawses,
>   And gar us sing.

Fergusson, like Burns, associates Helicon with whisky.

[73] Miss Keith has noted, p. 88, the similarity to Gargantua's famous motto, "Fais Ce Que Vouldras."

But for how lang the flie may stang,
Let inclination law that!

In these stanzas, as Dr Daiches has noted, "the entire Petrarchan tradition of love poetry is implicitly dismissed."[74] Odd
phrases from the ritual of upper-class lovers have appeared
from time to time in the course of the work, and been subjected
to ironical criticism : now, the whole convention is swept away
in a single Lawrencian gesture. The bard's song treats of the
same subject as "Green grow the Rashes, O," but without the
latter's sentimentality, yet in its context it has much the effect
that the "blackguard letter" to Ainslie of 3 Mar. 1788[75] has in
the correspondence—the contemptuous rejection of artificial
love, the assertion of the claims of vigorous physical passion,
and the identification of sexual prowess with the "lower orders."
In "The Jolly Beggars," joy through sex is shown in the very
rejects of rural society. One is reminded of the following entry
from the First Commonplace Book dated March 1784 :

I have often coveted the acquaintance of that part of mankind
commonly known by the ordinary phrase of Blackguards, sometimes farther than was consistent with the safety of my character ; those who by thoughtless Prodigality, or headstrong
Passions have been driven to ruin :—though disgraced by
follies, nay sometimes "Stain'd with guilt, and crimson'd o'er
with crimes ;" I have yet found among them, in not a few
instances, some of the noblest Virtues, Magnanimity Generosity, disinterested friendship and even modesty, in the highest
perfection.[76]

There is a quality allied to modesty in the "poor gut-scraper,"
despite the fact that he "snirtles in his sleeve" ; and when the
"Bard, of no regard" allows the fiddler to have one of his train
of dependent females, he, too, is displaying a parody of magnanimity and generosity, as the world understands them.

Finally, the Bard proposes his toast :

But clear your decks, an' here's the Sex !
I like the jads for a' that.

---

[74] Daiches, p. 228.   [75] *Letters*, I. 199–200.
[76] R. B.'s *Commonplace Book*, pp. 7–8.

But now[77] the whole ragged crew demand as an encore a ballad from his stock, and rising between his two remaining doxies, he obliges with a song to the air *Jolly Mortals fill your Glasses*. The grand finale and ultimate synthesis of the whole work is sung in Scots-English to an English tune,[78] as befits what is essentially a statement of principle; for abstract thought, Burns always went to English as spoken in Scotland. Miss Keith cavils at what she thinks is the intrusion of Burns's personality:

> Does the sober bed of marriage
> Witness brighter scenes of love?

Dr Daiches, on the contrary, does not find "the occasional generalisations in standard English diction" at all jarring; they "add a fitting note of solemnity, as though this is a profession of faith."[79] I feel that we must accept his judgment, with the qualification that "faith" is altogether too solemn a word for this poem. The underlying pattern of humour persists to the very end, despite the absence of Scots in the final stanzas. It is there in the pompous "variorum" and prim "decorum" of the fifth stanza, just as much as in the vigorous plebeian abandon of the sixth and final stanza:

> Here's to budgets, bags, and wallets!
> Here's to all the wandering train!
> Here's our ragged brats and callets!
> One and all, cry out, Amen!

W. P. Ker once wrote that "the politics of Burns are not, in 1786, affected by the great things coming on."[80] This is certainly untrue of "The Jolly Beggars"; the work was composed at least four years before the summoning of the States General, yet what could be more French-sounding than the chorus?:

> A fig for those by law protected!
> Liberty's a glorious feast,
> Courts for cowards were erected,
> Churches built to please the priest!

---

[77] H. & H., ii. 17.   [78] H. & H., ii. 304; Dick, p. 447.
[79] C. Keith, p. 89; Daiches, p. 230.
[80] W. P. Ker, "The Politics of Burns" in *Collected Essays*, ed. C. Whibley, 2 vols., London 1925, i. 130.

The slight element of artificiality in the diction should not blind us to what is new in the work. In "See the Smoking Bowl before us" Burns is saying something that is in no way incompatible with Blake's Songs of Experience, and indeed the total meaning of the cantata—which, as Dr Daiches says,[81] "is greater than the sum of the meaning of the various songs" —arises from the same sort of perception as "The Little Vagabond" or "The Garden of Love":

> Dear mother, dear mother, the Church is cold,
> But the Ale-house is healthy and pleasant and warm. . . .

> . . . And priests in black gowns were walking their rounds,
> And binding with briars my joys and desires.

Such unpleasant figures as "the lads in black" have been utterly banished from "The Jolly Beggars," except as "noises off," unreal memories of an ancient dream. The poem is full of the spirit of affirmation which Blake was later to put into the allegorical figure of Los; its motto could well be "Damn braces—bless relaxes" (in both senses of that pregnant aphorism) or "Energy is Eternal Delight."

"The Jolly Beggars" pushes parochialism to the level of the utmost universality. Beginning with the actual observation of a scene in a village inn (so Burns's friend Richmond assures us),[82] it concentrates in dramatic form the essence of "ram-stam," of all that is best in the early epistles. It takes its origin from that world of "Scotch drink" and "Scotch manners" which Matthew Arnold thought so unlovely; how then was Arnold compelled to call it a "puissant and splendid production"? "In the world of *The Jolly Beggars*," he says, "there is more than hideousness and squalor, there is bestiality; yet the piece is a superb poetic success. It has a breadth, truth, and power which make the famous scene in Auerbach's Cellar, of Goethe's *Faust*, seem artificial and tame beside it, and which are only matched by Shakespeare and Aristophanes."[83] The reason, I think, lies in this: the parochial unloveliness of "The Jolly

---

[81] P. 229.   [82] Chambers, I. 182–3.
[83] M. Arnold, "The Study of Poetry," in *Essays in Criticism*, Second Series, ed. Littlewood, London 1954, pp. 26, 30–1.

Beggars" is made to mirror a general European squalor and a general European energy of which Rousseau and Blake, each in his own way, were also aware—and at the same time to express the quintessence of a popular dream with a very long history behind it. "The Jolly Beggars" is the other side of the medal to "Man was made to Mourn." It is the poetry of lasting human values as they appear in times of agrarian revolution, and the flower of all the beggar literature of both Scotland and England.

VI

Poet of Scotland

THE time has now come to examine a group of Burns's poems which exhibit a fusion of the particular and the general of a rather different kind from the unity displayed in the "Jolly Beggars" cantata. I am referring to the political poems completed before the end of 1786, in which the general is represented by the nation—that is, by Scotland or by Great Britain considered as a whole. In these works the particular is sometimes the local, sometimes the personal ; and their peculiar effect derives from the close juxtaposition of Parliament and parish pump, of Court and ale-cup commentators. The ruling class is deprived of its glamour by the simple expedient of making the affairs of national and international politics as petty as the backyard squabblings of farmers and country ministers. This is, of course, the method I have already shown to be at work in "The Twa Herds." It is the mental habit revealed by the single phrase "gospel kail" extended to the proportions of an entire genre and becoming in the process a much more trenchant criticism of life than the Socratic morality which Matthew Arnold saw as the essence of Burns's philosophy.[1]

The earliest and by far the most daring of these works is the fragmentary ballad on the American War, "When Guilford good,"[2] which was printed in the Edinburgh Edition of 1787 though it may have been written as early as 1784.[3] The statesmen of the time are sometimes referred to by subsidiary titles or the names of obscure estates ; thus Lord North becomes "Guilford good" and Lord George Germain appears as "Sackville." Such deviousness was, as W. P. Ker noted,[4] "one

---

[1] M. Arnold, "The Study of Poetry," in *Essays in Criticism*, Second Series, ed. Littlewood, London 1954, p. 28.
[2] I. 246 (411).   [3] C. & W., II. 63.
[4] "The Politics of Burns," in Ker, *Essays*, I. 138. Burns's handling of this traditional popular metre, found previously in such songs as "Gillicrankie" [*sic*]

of the conventions of that sort of lyrical satire," although it is not allowed to dominate the poem. To have disguised Rocking-ham, Burgoyne, Dundas and Fox beyond all recognition would have destroyed the poem's character as a political comedy that could be enjoyed by ordinary people.

Here is how, in the first stanza, Burns handles the Boston Tea Party and the beginnings of the American Revolution:

> When Guilford good our pilot stood,
>   An' did our hellim thraw, man;
> Ae night, at tea, began a plea,
>   Within Americà, man:
> Then up they gat the maskin-pat,
>   And in the sea did jaw, man;
> An' did nae less, in full Congress,
>   Than quite refuse our law, man.

In the seventh stanza, Fox's short-lived political victory in 1783 and the collapse of his ministry after the defeat of his famous India Bill[5] are described with equal contempt, this time in terms of a game of cards:

> Then clubs an' hearts were Charlie's cartes:
>   He swept the stakes awa', man,
> Till the diamond's ace, of Indian race,
>   Led him a sair *faux pas*, man. . . .

In the fifth stanza, when "Charlie" Fox speaks against North's *régime* he loosens his "tinkler jaw" almost as if he were one of the Jolly Beggars; in the ninth, both he and North are likened to homely golfers, and "Willie" Pitt to their ball. British

---

and Adam Skirving's "Tranent Muir," differs from other examples of the form in that Burns always has an internal rhyme in ll. 1, 3, 5, and 7, and always ends ll. 2, 4, 6, 8 with the sounds "aw, man", as Ritter points out (p. 54). The pattern of the original "Gillicrankie" (1689) is not nearly so strict. Cp. the third stanza:

> The solemn League and Covenant
>   Came whigging up the hills, man,
> Thought Highland trews durst not refuse
>   For to subscribe their bills then.
> In WILLIE's name they thought nae ane
>   Durst stop their course at a' man,
> But hur nane sell, wi' mony a knock,
>   Cryd, Furich-Whiggs awa', man.

[5] Cp. C. & W., II. 65 n.

generalship is treated with the utmost derision, while West-minster political combinations are likened to the moves in a childish game that farmers and ploughmen, poor, voteless creatures though they may be, just cannot take seriously.

In "Scotch Drink"[6] Burns parodies his own nationalism as well as Fergusson's "Caller Water," his immediate source and model.[7] Burns begins by hailing Scotch Drink as his Muse. Barley is superior to other grains, or to such legumes as "pease an' beans." As food it merely supports life ; as drink, it comforts both rich and poor, especially the latter—at harvest-home, in the smithy, at births, and when neighbours go to law. It is an ironical presupposition of Burns's argument that, simply because it is Scotch, whisky is necessarily superior to other drinks ; from which it follows, ineluctably, that those Scots who hanker after brandy or "bitter dearthfu' wines" from foreign parts are guilty of treason.[8] John Barleycorn helps every village activity to function smoothly ; it is, in the sixth stanza, the Scottish opium of the people, annihilating the tribulations of all classes, "learned or lewèd" :

> Thou clears the head o' doited Lear,
> Thou cheers the heart o' drooping Care ;
> Thou strings the nerves o' Labour sair,
>   At 's weary toil ;
> Thou ev'n brightens dark Despair
>   Wi' gloomy smile.

The unity of local and national is realised at the comic level. Whisky is the drink of all Scotland for the very reason that it oils what are essentially parochial concerns, and the reader is made to feel that the killjoy and the prohibitionist are enemies of the nation as well as of good cheer. This is achieved by placing the seventeenth verse immediately after a stanza beginning "Ye Scots, wha wish auld Scotland well . . ." :

---

[6] I. 19 (322).

[7] Cp. H. & H., I. 322. The poem belongs to a *genre* which is as much English as Scottish ; behind "Caller Water" there lie such poems as Beaumont's "Praise of Sack," and the "Ballad on Ale" attributed to Gay. Cp. Ritter, pp. 112–3.

[8] This sort of protectionism was becoming out of date in Burns's day, and had been ridiculed by Hume even before Adam Smith wrote *The Wealth of Nations*. Cp. *David Hume : Writings on Economics*, ed. E. Rotwein, Edinburgh 1955, *passim*.

May gravels round his blather wrench,
An' gouts torment him, inch by inch,
Wha twists his gruntle wi' a glunch
     O' sour disdain,
Out owre a glass o' whisky-punch
     Wi' honest men !

"The Author's Earnest Cry and Prayer to the Scotch
Representatives in the House of Commons"[9] is a humorous
poem directed against the government's interference with the
liberties of whisky-drinkers and producers. Late in 1785 the
Scottish liquor-trade began an agitation against the excise
laws, which were then so strictly enforced as to drive many
distillers from business. Since it was widely believed that the
London trade was behind the sudden severity of the Excise
officers, the cause of John Barleycorn could once again be
presented as that of the whole nation. Burns tells us that this
poem "was wrote before the Act anent the Scotch Distilleries,
of Session 1786,"[10] which abolished duties on "low wines,"
spirits, and other liquors, and imposed a yearly tax calculated
according to the capacity of the stills. "The Author's Earnest
Cry" can have had absolutely no political effect.[11] Burns
simply used the situation to make yet another poem which
turns criticism of the powers that be into an ironical comedy
that is enjoyable for its own sake.

The first verse "humbly" conveys "a simple Bardie's
prayers" to the representatives of his country—Irish Lords,
some of whom occupied Scottish seats in parliament at a time
when the "eldest sons of Scottish peers were ineligible" for
election,[12] and native born knights and squires who "doucely"
(that is quietly, modestly, perhaps even tamely) "manage our
affairs." The humility and *naïveté* are deeply ironical, and the
mockery of the second stanza is alone sufficient to establish the
poet's equality, perhaps even his superiority, to all the other
people mentioned in the poem, including the great Pitt himself,
whom Burns deliberately reduces in size by referring to him,
in the twenty-first stanza, as "yon guid bluid of auld Bocon-

[9] 1. 26 (324).   [10] H. & H., 1. 324.
[11] Cp. C. & W., 1. 276–7.   [12] H. & H., 1. 324.

nock's," after a Cornish estate which had belonged to his grandfather.[13]

Pitt, in 1786, was only twenty-seven, and in the fourth stanza Burns urges the Scottish M.P.s to stand up boldly and announce their grievances to "yon Premier youth," the implication being that they were in the habit of speaking far too gently to the rich and powerful. And since most of those who had "the chief direction" would in point of fact be Englishmen, such timidity amounted in practice to a betrayal of Scotland; that, I think, is one of the undertones of:

> The muckle deevil blaw you south,
> If ye dissemble !

In the fifth and sixth stanzas the topic of political corruption is introduced, ever so delicately:

> Does onie great man glunch an' gloom?
> Speak out, an' never fash your thumb !
> Let posts an' pensions sink or soom
>   Wi' them wha grant 'em :
> If honestly they canna come,
>   Far better want 'em.

> In gath'rin votes you were na slack;
> Now stand as tightly by your tack :
> Ne'er claw your lug, an' fidge your back,
>   An' hum an' haw;
> But raise your arm, an' tell your crack
>   Before them a'.

Then follows one of those vivid semi-allegorical pictures in which Burns excels. In the seventh, eighth and ninth stanzas, he bids the M.P.s "paint Scotland greetin owre her thrissle," her pint-measure "as toom's a whissle," while wicked excise-men break up her stills and smugglers and podgy vintners pick her pocket. Is there, he asks in the ninth stanza, a single Scot whose blood does not boil to see his "poor auld mither's pot" thus smashed in pieces

> An' plunder'd o' her hindmost groat,
>   By gallows knaves?

[13] C. & W., I. 281 n.; W. P. Ker, *On Modern Literature*, p. 50.

For the rest of the poem—that is, until the Postscript, the pattern alternates between an ironical appeal addressed to the Scottish statesmen, and a further development of the allegorical presentation of the nation itself. Significantly enough, many of the politicians are Ayrshire figures—sometimes, the very same men whom he treats seriously in "The Vision" :

> But could I like Montgomeries fight,
>   Or gab like Boswell . . .
>
> Thee, aith-detesting, chaste Kilkerran . . .
>
> Thee sodger Hugh, my watchman stented,
> If Bardies e'er are represented ;
> I ken if that your sword were wanted,
>   Ye'd lend your hand ;
> But when there's ought to say anent it,
>   Ye're at a stand.[14]

"Sodger Hugh" was Montgomerie of Coilsfield ; and since this reference to his lack of parliamentary eloquence was felt to be too contemptuous, the stanza last quoted was marked "To be expunged" and was never printed in Burns's lifetime.[15]

In the course of the poem "auld Scotland" develops from a weeping "carlin" into a militant fighter liable to take direct action if her constitutional representatives fail her :

> An' Lord ! if ance they pit her till't,
> Her tartan petticoat she'll kilt,
> An' durk an' pistol at her belt,
>   She'll tak the streets,
> An' rin her whittle to the hilt,
>   I' the first she meets !
>
> For God-sake, sirs ! then speak her fair,
> An' straik her cannie wi' the hair,
> An' to the Muckle House repair,
>   Wi' instant speed,
> An' strive, wi' a' your wit an' lear,
>   To get remead. . . .

---

[14] Sts. x, xiii, xv.
[15] C. & W., I. 280 n ; H. & H., I. 326.

Auld Scotland has a raucle tongue ;
She's just a devil wi' a rung ;
An' if she promise auld or young
    To tak their part,
Tho' by the neck she should be strung,
    She'll no desert.[16]

The Postscript is remarkable for its contrasting attitudes
and the complexity of its irony. The threat of direct action has
subtly receded, but the keynote is still violence—the military
élan of loyal soldiers fortified by whisky. Yet in the twenty-
ninth stanza it is surely impossible to miss the tone of contempt
in the reference to the Hanoverian monarch, which gains added
point by being contrasted with the pathos of the soldier's death :

But bring a Scotsman frae his hill,
Clap in his cheek a Highland gill,
Say, such is royal George's will,
    An' there's the foe !
He has nae thought but how to kill
    Twa at a blow.

Nae cauld, faint-hearted doubtings tease him ;
Death comes, wi' fearless eye he sees him ;
Wi' bluidy han' a welcome gies him ;
    An' when he fa's,
His latest draught o' breathin lea'es him
    In faint huzzas.

Finally, it is important to notice the ambiguity of the conclusion, with its humorous blending of two of the values which
play so large a part in the poems written up to 1786 :

Freedom and whisky gang thegither,
    Tak aff your dram ![17]

The reader inevitably asks—what kind of Freedom ? Freedom
from "royal George," or from the "unco guid"? National
freedom, or freedom for the individual to do what he likes ?
The probability is that Burns means not one but all of these

---

[16] Sts. xviii, xix, xxiii.

[17] Ritter (p. 112) points out the similarity to the following lines from Gay's
(?) "Ballad on Ale" : "O blest potation ! still by thee, | And thy companion
Liberty, | Do health and mirth prevail." Once more, there is an English parallel
for a typically Burnsian idea.

things, and that the ambivalence of the ending is an intentional part of the poem's comic effect.

An analysis of the early political poems tends to make one question W. P. Ker's assertion[18] that Burns was in no sense a revolutionary writer before the seventeen-nineties. To make "Guilford good" and "Auld Boconnock" subjects of parish commentary and vernacular raillery reduces them to the level of the "friendly, social, honest man"—the grocer, the farmer and the freemason. Again, the threat of violence implicit in stanzas xiii–xxiii of "The Author's Earnest Cry" should not be ignored in any attempt to trace the development of Burns's social opinions; taken in conjunction with the Postscript to the same poem, and the equally two-faced savagery of the eighth stanza of the "Address to a Haggis,"[19] it seems to indicate that Burns was hardly a complete stranger to revolutionary emotions in the year of the Kilmarnock edition :

> But mark the Rustic, haggis-fed,
> The trembling earth resounds his tread,
> Clap in his walie nieve a blade,
>   He'll make it whissle ;
> An' legs, an' arms, an' heads will sned
>   Like taps o' thrissle.

Though this may simply refer to the valour of loyal troops, as in the Postscript to "The Author's Earnest Cry," it is also conceivable that it looks forward to a peasant war in Britain. I suggest that here, too, the issue is left deliberately uncertain, and that revolution is envisaged as at any rate a social possibility.

It is a tempting speculation that if "The Poet's Rambles on the Banks of the Ayr" had survived, Burns would be as well known today for his satire on the aristocracy as for his merciless criticism of the Auld Licht clergy. The piece is said to have been longer than any of his published works and to have constituted a ribald and scurrilous attack upon the solid families whose properties adjoined that river.[20] But even without "The Poet's Rambles" Burns left a sufficiently large body of non-

---

[18] *Essays*, I. 128 ff.   [19] I. 237 (407) ; below, pp. 236–7.
[20] See Joseph Train, "The Train MS," in *Robert Burns, his Associates and Contemporaries*, ed. R. T. Fitzhugh, N. Carolina 1943, henceforth cited as *R. B., his Associates*, p. 60. It is, of course, possible that Burns wrote no such poem.

ecclesiastical satire to be worth consideration on its own merits. Affectation, the traditional target of writers like Juvenal or Molière or Pope, is an object of scorn in some of the predominantly local poems analysed in the previous chapter, and it forms the theme of a delightful little satiric gem—"To a Louse, on seeing one on a Lady's Bonnet at Church."[21]

Behind this poem there lies the concept of a snobbish barrier between rich and poor, and in, for example, the third stanza, the comedy consists in the fact that it is the loathsome, creeping louse that bridges the gap as surely as it is Death and the graveyard Worm who are the levellers of an earlier tradition:

> Swith! in some beggar's hauffet squattle:
> There ye may creep, and sprawl, and sprattle,
> Wi' ither kindred, jumping cattle,
>   In shoals and nations;
> Whare horn nor bane ne'er daur unsettle
>   Your thick plantations.

That so low a creature should be able to climb so high is, in the fourth stanza, a matter for horrified amusement, besides carrying certain undoubtedly symbolic associations:

> Now haud you there! ye're out o' sight,
> Below the fatt'rils, snug an' tight;
> Na, faith ye yet! ye'll no be right,
>   Till ye've got on it—
> The vera tapmost, tow'ring height
>   O' Miss's bonnet.

The first four lines of the eighth and last stanza, which extract a general truth from this concrete situation, have become proverbial throughout the English-speaking world, but perhaps because of their implicit criticism of sanctimoniousness the two concluding lines are seldom quoted:

> O wad some Power the giftie gie us
> To see oursels as ithers see us!
> It wad frae monie a blunder free us,
>   An' foolish notion:
> What airs in dress an' gait wad lea'e us,
>   An' ev'n devotion!

[21] I. 152 (379). For a fuller analysis of the poem, see J. Speirs, "Burns and English Literature," in *The Pelican Guide to English Literature*, VOL. V (1957), pp. 95–6.

The piece entitled "Extempore to Gavin Hamilton: Stanzas on Naething"[22] gives vent to a mood that is really rather uncommon in Burns, although it has been the predominant one with many satirists throughout the history of literature. They are thus important in determining what Burns's satire was not; the fact that he so seldom proclaims the worthlessness of all endeavour marks him off from writers like Nashe and Swift and Wyndham Lewis. As a rule, Burns believed in the vanity of some, but not of all, human wishes; consequently, the conventional nihilism of these stanzas is rather an exception in Burns's total output. The poem is redeemed by a delightful little comment on his evening with a "feminine Whig" which is worth a place in any collection of "The Pleasures of Burns":

> Last night with a feminine Whig—
> A poet she couldna put faith in!
> But soon we grew lovingly big,
> I taught her, her terrors were—naething.
>
> Her Whigship was wonderful pleased,
> But charmingly tickled wi' ae thing;
> Her fingers I lovingly squeezed,
> And kissed her, and promised her—naething.

"A Dream,"[23] which deals with the Royal Family in exactly the same way as Pitt and North are treated in "When Guilford good" and "The Author's Earnest Cry," was set off by Thomas Warton's "Ode XVII for His Majesty's Birthday, June 4th 1786." Burns's own account of the matter is that "On reading in the public papers the Laureate's Ode with the other parade of June 4th, 1786, the Author was no sooner dropt asleep, than he imagined himself transported to the Birth-day Levee."[24] Most of Warton's ode is concerned with the statement that the Greek poets Alcaeus, Pindar and Theocritus sang the praises of just kings. George III is by definition a just king; therefore it is only natural for his laureate to wish for "a strain of these sublimer bards" in order to do justice to so glorious a sovereign:

[22] II. 93 (362).   [23] I. 68 (348).   [24] Cp. H. & H., I. 68.

> The bards of Greece might best adorn,
> With seemly song, the Monarch's natal morn;
> Who, thron'd in the magnificence of peace,
> Rivals their richest regal theme :
> Who rules a people like their own,
> In arms, in polish'd arts supreme;
> Who bids his Britain vie with Greece.

It is only necessary to place the second stanza of Burns's poem beside this nonsense to realise what dynamite vernacular Scots could really be :

> I see ye're complimented thrang,
> By monie a lord an' lady;
> *God Save the King*'s a cuckoo sang
> That's unco easy said ay :
> The poets, too, a venal gang,
> Wi' rhymes weel-turn'd an' ready,
> Wad gar you trow ye ne'er do wrang,
> But ay unerring steady,
> On sic a day.

But, says Burns, in the fourth stanza :

> . . . facts are chiels that winna ding,
> And downa be disputed. . . .

and the truth is that since the American colonies gained their independence, His Majesty's dominions have been reduced by two thirds. The very homeliness of the image in which, in this same stanza, he reminds George of those unfortunate events is enough to strip the Birthday Levee of all its adventitious lustre :

> Your royal nest, beneath your wing,
> Is e'en right reft and clouted,
> And now the third part o' the string,
> An' less, will gang about it
> Than did ae day.

Furthermore, the King, at one period not precisely specified, has entrusted the government

> To chaps wha in a barn or byre
> Wad better fill'd their station,
> Than courts yon day.

Now that peace has come, the country is crippled by taxation; yet if in spite of all appearances to the contrary the government should be smitten by a fit of economy, pray God it be not at the Navy's expense. In the eighth stanza, the first section of Burns's poem ends with an impudent and summary leave-taking in which the hope is expressed that parliamentary reform (a project to which the King was of course obstinately opposed) may be accomplished during the present reign :

> Adieu, my Liege ! may Freedom geck
> Beneath your high protection ;
> An' may ye rax Corruption's neck,
> And gie her for dissection !

In the second section of the poem Burns seems to have been inspired by that part of Warton's ode in which the Laureate mentions Theocritus' praise of Berenice :

> Pattern fair of female fame,
> Softening with domestic life
> Imperial splendor's dazzling rays,
> The queen, the mother, and the wife !

In the tenth stanza, Burns turns to the doings of George's queen and the other members of the Royal Family, in a spirit that is the very negation of Warton's :

> For you, young Potentate o' Wales,
> I tell your Highness fairly,
> Down Pleasure's stream, wi' swelling sails,
> I'm tauld ye're driving rarely ;
> But some day ye may gnaw your nails,
> An' curse your folly sairly,
> That e'er ye brak Diana's pales,
> Or rattl'd dice wi' Charlie
> By night or day.

In the twelfth stanza, he pours the greatest contempt upon the King's second son, the Duke of York and Albany, who had been elected Bishop of Osnaburg at the mature age of one,[25] and in the next he seizes delightedly upon the love-affairs of the young prince who was to become the future King William

[25] H. & H., I. 349.

IV. Since this young man had become a captain of the Navy on
10 Apr. 1786,[26] the nautical imagery is peculiarly appropriate :

> Young, royal Tarry-breeks, I learn,
> Ye've lately come athwart her—
> A glorious galley, stem an' stern
> Weel rigg'd for Venus' barter ;
> But first hang out that she'll discern
> Your hymeneal charter ;
> Then heave aboard your grapple-airn,
> An', large upon her quarter,
> Come full that day.

After appealing to the young princesses to be good as well as
"braw" (this adjective means something intermediate between
"beautiful" and "elaborately dressed"), and wishing them
"lads a-plenty," Burns ends with a somewhat ominous blessing
upon the whole Royal Family. Although they are fussed and
fondled now, they may quite conceivably endure bitter mis-
fortune in the future ; they are, in fact, just like those satiated
persons who pick listlessly at their food, only to scrape the very
bottom of the dish when assailed by real hunger. As with some
of the other works examined in this chapter, the ending is left
deliberately vague : Burns does not explain whether he is
thinking of the return of the Stuarts, or of the institution of a
republic. "A Dream" has often been considered a Jacobite
effusion, but its mood seems to be that of a romantic Jacobite
nationalism in the process of turning into something politically
radical and uncompromising—the sort of attitude which, seven
years after the Kilmarnock Edition, would be termed Jacobini-
cal.[27] It is closer to "Courts for cowards were erected" than to

---

[26] *Ibid.*

[27] Burns's predecessors, Ramsay and Fergusson, were both ardent nationalists,
of a somewhat romantic cast. In "The Vision," st. xv, for example, Ramsay
appears to look forward to a second Scottish War of Independence—the bloodier
the better. But in "The Ghaists : A Kirk-yard Eclogue" (ll.57–78), Fergusson's
nationalism becomes fused with social radicalism in a manner which anticipates
Burns's own :

> Black be the day that e'er to England's ground
> Scotland was eikit by the UNION's bond. . . .
> They raise provisions as the stents they raise,
> Yoke hard the poor, and lat the rich chiels be . . . .
> Whan they are doom'd to keep a lasting Lent,
> Starving for England's weel at *three per cent.*

the sentimental worship of Bonnie Prince Charlie; its author, one feels, is already well on the way to the position underlying the toast he is said to have proposed in his Dumfries years— *"Here's the last verse of the last chapter of the last* BOOK OF KINGS.*"*[28]

If "A Dream" is perilously close to being an attack upon royalty as such, then the "Address of Beelzebub"[29] is the most outspoken of all Burns's anti-aristocratic works to have come down to us. This poem arose in response to newspaper accounts of a meeting of the Highland Society in London on 23 May 1786, "for the encouragement of the fisheries in the Highlands, &c."[30] The only background information necessary for a full appreciation of the poem is the knowledge that many crofters of the Western Highlands and Islands were compelled by economic hardship to emigrate to Canada and elsewhere during the second half of the eighteenth century. Such traditional Malthusian checks on population as war and pestilence had ceased to operate during the previous fifty years. The crushing of the Jacobite rebellion of 1745 brought inter-clan warfare to a stop, while even family feuds and cattle-raids had become things of the past. Vaccination against smallpox, which came to the Gaelic West in the seventeen-sixties, removed yet another barrier to natural increase, but the improvement in the means of subsistence represented by potato-farming and the use of kelp to manure the crops was not in the long run sufficient to feed all these new mouths. Indeed, the introduction of the potato was itself a prime cause of the increase of population in the Highlands and Islands.[31]

Thus the primary cause of Highland emigration was the pressure of population upon the remains of the old Celtic system of cultivation. One contemporary observer, writing in 1785, summed up the situation admirably: "There is no doubt that one-tenth part of the present inhabitants would be

[28] C. & W., III. 379.

[29] II. 154 (388). "The Address of Beelzebub" was not published till Feb. 1818; "A Dream" is therefore the only one of these two poems to have been at all widely known in Burns's lifetime, since it appeared in the Kilmarnock Edition. Burns insisted on retaining the original version of "A Dream" in the 1787 Edition, in flat disregard of thóse timorous and loyalist advisers who wished him to tone it down.

[30] C. & W., I. 347.

[31] R. N. Salaman, *The History and Social Influence of the Potato*, Cambridge 1949, pp. 346 ff.

sufficient to perform all the operations there, were their industry properly exerted."[32] This is an opinion echoed by many other eighteenth-century commentators, and confirmed by modern historical research. The gentlemen of the Highland Society were undoubtedly concerned at the diminishing number of their tenants—a decline which they themselves, or their fathers before them, had done much to aggravate by racking the crofters' rents. At the meeting which sparked off Burns's poem, "three thousand pounds were immediately subscribed by eleven gentlemen present," in order to set various schemes of improvement afoot. In the words of the *Edinburgh Advertiser* for 30 May 1786:

> The Earl of Breadalbane informed the meeting that five hundred persons had agreed to emigrate from the estates of M'Donald of Glengary; that they had subscribed money, purchased ships, &c., to carry their design into effect. The noblemen and gentlemen agreed to co-operate with government to frustrate their design; and to recommend to the principal noblemen and gentlemen in the Highlands to endeavour to prevent emigration, by improving the fisheries, agriculture, and manufactures, and particularly to enter into a subscription for that purpose.[33]

Burns does not appear to have been over-impressed by these long-term schemes for the establishment of a balanced economy. What interested him were the immediate sufferings of the Highlanders, in particular the news that "the noblemen and gentlemen" intended to "co-operate with government" in order to keep their tenants on the land. The note of indignation is apparent even in the wording of the epigraph:

> To the Right Honorable the Earl of Breadalbane, President of the Right Honorable the Highland Society, which met on the 23rd of May last, at the *Shakespeare*, Covent Garden, to concert ways and means to frustrate the designs of five hundred Highlanders who . . . were so audacious as to attempt an escape from their lawful lords and masters whose property they were, by emigrating . . . to the wilds of Canada, in search of that fantastic thing—Liberty.

[32] J. Anderson, *An Account of the Present State of the Hebrides and Western Coasts of Scotland*, 1785, quoted in Handley, *Scottish Farming in the Eighteenth Century*, p. 246.
[33] Quoted in C. & W., i. 347.

Among twentieth-century Scottish novelists such as Neil Gunn and "Fionn MacColla" it has become conventional to represent the typical Highland laird as a wicked oppressor who forced his clansmen to emigrate. But here is Burns criticising the aristocracy for doing the very opposite—for trying to *prevent* the flight from the glens and isles.

After the epigraph, there follows the most savage of all Burns's satires; interestingly enough, it too was written under the shadow of the American Revolution. What justifies the lairds' forcible restraint of their tenantry is the terrible possibility that they might follow the example of the colonists :

> Then up amang thae lakes and seas,
> They'll mak what rules and laws they please. . . .[34]

If that were to happen, they might produce their own revolutionary leaders, men as daring as Hancock, Franklin, Washington, or Montgomerie. Once rid of such wise and experienced leaders as North and Sackville, the rabble might even "to Patrician rights aspire"—no land-owner could ever contemplate such a happening with equanimity. The sonorous list of these great American names adds an extra dimension to the poem, which is still further enriched by the delicious irony of the four succeeding lines :

> An' whare will ye get Howes and Clintons
> To bring them to a right repentance?
> To cowe the rebel generation,
> An' save the honor o' the nation?[35]

The point is, of course, that Howe and Clinton, for all their gallantry, did not in the end defeat the rebels;[36] consequently, they cannot have saved the honour of the nation, except in so far as they fought bravely. The Highland gentry would be even less capable of defeating their migrated tenants than the British government had been some five to ten years previously, for they would lack even such partially successful generals as those who defeated Washington at White Plains and Brandywine, or secured the capture of Charleston—perhaps, indeed, the lairds are now so degenerate that they can no longer

[34] H. & H., ii. 155 *ad init.*   [35] *Op cit.*, p. 155 *med.*   [36] C. & W., i. 348 nn.

produce good military leaders. It follows that the suppression of their former "property" would bring them even less glory than the British got from the American Revolution.

There are few lines in English poetry which express so violent a hatred of a ruling class as the next four, in which Beelzebub apostrophises Breadalbane as follows:

> They, an' be damn'd! what right hae they
> To meat or sleep or light o' day,
> Far less to riches, pow'r, or freedom,
> But what your lordship likes to gie them?

Turning to Glengarry, Beelzebub urges the Highland lairds to be even more ruthless towards their tenants than they are at present. To rob them and impound their goods is not enough to cow their stubborn spirit; nothing less than punitive expeditions will suffice:

> But smash them! crush them a' to spails,
> An' rot the dyvors i' the jails!
> The young dogs, swinge them to the labour:
> Let wark an' hunger mak them sober!
> The hizzies, if they're aughtlins fawsont,
> Let them in Drury Lane be lesson'd!
> An' if the wives an' dirty brats
> Come thiggin at your doors an' yetts,
> Flaffin wi' duds an' grey wi' beas',
> Frightin awa your deuks an' geese,
> Get out a horsewhip or a jowler,
> The langest thong, the fiercest growler,
> An' gar the tatter'd gypsies pack
> Wi' a' their bastards on their back![37]

If Glengarry fulfils this advice, he will deserve one of the best places in Hell, where, indeed, Beelzebub longs to meet him;

---

[37] H. & H., II. 156 *ad init.* The mood is similar to ll. 57–78 of Fergusson's "The Ghaists: A Kirk-yard Eclogue"; and there is a verbal reminiscence of the passage in Burns's poem. Fergusson's ll. 75–6 read: "How maun their weyms wi' sairest *hunger* slack, | Their *duds* in targets *flaff* upo' their *back*." (My italics). Burns's satire seems fiercer and more national than Fergusson's however—perhaps because Fergusson uses the heroic couplet, whereas Burns uses octosyllabics—a metre which "had become classical in Scotland through Barbour's *Bruce*" (H. & H., I. 319). Octosyllabics are as natural to vernacular Scots as they are to English; but—and this in spite of Ramsay's *Gentle Shepherd*—decasyllabic couplets do not seem to come nearly so easily to the Scottish poet.

he will be given the innermost corner next the fire, cheek-by-jowl with the great tyrants of history :

> 'Tween Herod's hip an' Polycrate,
> Or (if you on your station tarrow)
> Between Almagro and Pizarro. . . .

The "Address of Beelzebub," then, is yet another poem of the years 1784–6 which looks forward to the mood of the early seventeen-nineties. It may not be politically or historically accurate; it may do less than justice to the Highland Society; but in its championship of freedom from constraint and its passionate hatred of control by landlords it is as near to the French spirit as anything else produced by Burns at this period.

In their reaction against the sentimental side of Burns, some twentieth-century critics appear to have done less than justice to "To A Mouse, on Turning her up in her Nest with the Plough, November 1785."[38] Professors Ferguson and Fitzhugh, for example, both consider "To a Mouse" and "To a Mountain Daisy"[39] as poems of essentially the same sort, and would claim, in the words of the last-named writer, that both pieces "reek with over charged benevolence and carefully calculated appeals to our tender feelings."[40] Such a judgment overlooks the difference in quality between the two works. The daisy poem is artificial, second-rate, perhaps even insincere, whereas "To a Mouse" is charged with a genuine and intense emotion.

Though the exact source of this emotion has not always been consciously recognised, I believe that every sensitive reader of the past one hundred and seventy years has been intuitively aware of it. "To a Mouse" is linked by subtle and tenuous threads to the preoccupations of the first epistles, and to such poems as "Man was made to Mourn," as well as to the hatred of economic exploitation which fills the "Address of Beelzebub" ; it, too, can only be fully understood in the context of the Scottish Agrarian Revolution.

---

[38] I. 115 (365).   [39] I. 136 (375).
[40] Ferguson, *Pride and Passion*, N.Y. 1939, p. 307; *R. B., his Associates*, ed. Fitzhugh, p. 14. But cp. Wittig, pp. 203–4, where the two poems are discriminated much as they are here.

In the very first words of the opening stanza [41] we hear a strong, mournful, meditative voice expressing all that is involved in knowing a commonplace animal; in coming face to face with it, suddenly and brutally, the poet grasps its essential "mousiness" as never before or since. Burns sees the mouse as she really is : the outer and inner nature of the beast, her "inscape," as Hopkins would have called it. His intuitive act of vision comprehends first the size, the extreme smallness of the mouse; next, the texture of its outer covering; and finally, its crouching position. Burns proceeds from sight to touch (or rather to a perception of what it would be like to stroke the animal—it would be "sleekit") ; then he moves back to sight again. Complete knowledge is attained when the animal's "tim'rous" emotional state, the "panic" in its breast, are deduced from their external signs. The mouse is no isolated thing-in-itself divorced from its surroundings; on the contrary, it exists only in relation to a total situation of which the weather, the coulter, the poet's own emotions, and society itself are all integral parts.

As Dr Daiches has noted (contrary to the opinion of many other commentators), the modulation into Scots-English in the second stanza does not jar our sensibilities to any extent, but is fundamental to the poem in that it expresses a movement from the particular to the general and explains every implication of the mouse's state in such a way that all can understand it.[42] As a practical farmer Burns knows very well that the abstract ideas he is invoking are in a strictly literal sense untrue; he is quite aware that "Nature's social union"[43] embraces the relationships of hunter and hunted, of parasite and host. But he uses the concept of "social union" as a tool, in order to convey

[41] Ritter (p. 83), traces the structure of this line to Matthew Prior's rendering of Hadrian's "animula, vagula, blandula", viz. "Poor little, pretty, fluttering thing." Prior's line was adapted by Matthew Green in his song "The Sparrow and the Diamond" (x. 1) ; by Fielding, in his poem "Written Extempore"; and by (?) Oldys in the song "Busy, curious, thirsty fly." Thus the English neo-classic tradition has made its own peculiar contribution to one of the best-known lines in the whole of Scottish vernacular poetry, without in the least detracting from its pithiness, its concreteness—or its Scottishness.

[42] Daiches, p. 165.

[43] Ritter (p. 83) finds in this phrase an echo of Goldsmith's "The Traveller", l. 340 : ". . . breaks the social tie."

166 Poet of Scotland

his sense of the pathos involved in man's relationship to the animals he destroys. The breaking of bonds in the second stanza reminds one of what Erich Fromm has termed the "primary bonds" that link primitive society to nature and the civilised child to his family; indeed, it would appear that the poet's breach of social union illustrates one aspect of the conflict between man and Nature. Human beings, organised in an agricultural economy, are separate from the rest of creation and opposed to it for the very reason that they use animals and plants in a conscious and relatively planned way, in contrast to the blind adjustments of pre-human ecology. That is the truth behind the apparent falsehood of "social union" and "ill opinion," and it explains why the stanza does not grate on us any more than, say, Wordsworth's "Intimations of Immortality from Recollections of early Childhood" does, though we all know that the myth on which it is based is not literally true. The lines

> At me, thy poor, earth-born companion
> An' fellow mortal![44]

are full of Burns's passionate sense of what men and animals still have in common—there is unity as well as opposition between them. Both are transient products of common clay; both are the slaves of death, and slaves of forces much greater than themselves.

In the fourth, fifth and sixth stanzas, Burns describes the mouse's real plight with the greatest possible concreteness, and at the same time unobtrusively humanises her, so that we pity her as we would pity our own mother if we saw her deprived of her home and unable to find another, either because of natural disaster or social oppression. The mouse becomes more than any animal; she is a symbol of the peasant, or rather of the "poor peasant," condition. On a careful reading of the fifth stanza, the lines

> Till crash! the cruel coulter past
> Out thro' thy cell

---

[44] Cp. Young (1802 edn., vol. III, p. 341, as quoted by Ritter, *loc. cit.*) : "What art thou? Thou poor, feeble, earth-born mortal!"

affect us with all the terror of Blake's "dark Satanic mills."
The coulter is in reality Burns's equivalent of the mills—part
of the metaphorical plough of social change that breaks down
the houses of both Lowland and Highland cotters. This is not
to claim that the poem is allegorical in any crude or literal
sense. The mouse does not "stand for" the mother of "The
Cotter's Saturday Night" or the Highland "hizzies" whom
Beelzebub thought should be "lesson'd" in Drury Lane, but
she belongs to the same world as these others and gains an
extra dimension from emotions whose intensity arises from
the depth and power of Burns's own contemplation of human
wretchedness and exploitation.

In the two final stanzas this parallelism is first widened,
then narrowed. In the second-last, it is expounded until the
mouse's plight becomes identical, not just with that of a poor
peasant-woman, but with that of the entire human race :

> But Mousie, thou art no thy lane,
> In proving foresight may be vain :
> The best-laid schemes o' mice an' men
>   Gang aft agley,[45]
> An' lea'e us nought but grief an' pain,
>   For promis'd joy !

But in the last stanza, the scene contracts, and the comparison
is made, not with mankind in general, but with one man only
—Burns himself :

> Still thou art blest, compared wi' me !
> The present only toucheth thee :
> But och ! I backward cast my e'e,
>   On prospects drear !
> An' forward, tho' I canna see,
>   I guess an' fear ![46]

---

[45] Cp. Blair, "The Grave," ll. 185–6 : "The best-concerted schemes men lay
for fame | Die fast away." Cp. also Mrs Barbauld, "The Mouse's Petition," last
stanza : "When destruction lurks unseen, | Which men, like mice, may share."

[46] Cp. Johnson, *Rasselas*, ch. ii, where the Prince of "Abissinia" [*sic*] addresses
the animals around him : "Ye, said he, are happy, and need not envy me that
walk thus among you, burthened with myself ; nor do I, ye gentle beings, envy
your felicity ; for it is not the felicity of man. I have many distresses from which
ye are free ; I fear pain when I do not feel it ; *I sometimes shrink at evils recollected,
and sometimes start at evils anticipated :* surely the equity of providence has ballanced
[*sic*] peculiar sufferings with peculiar enjoyments." (My italics).

Here the focus is once again on the differences between men and animals. What is specifically human, namely conscious-ness of past, present and future, breeds a more intense suffering than the outraged and frustrated instinct that lies behind an animal's pain. Furthermore, the lines depict a single man and a single mood, but that mood is put before us in such a way as to exclude such irrelevant particulars as the specific causes of Burns's grief and fears in November 1785. Nothing is left but the emotions common to similar situations in the lives of all other men and women at all periods of human history. The result is akin to the effect of the very greatest music; it is like the measured perfection of one of Beethoven's slow movements, for example. It is towards this supreme distillation of pure grief that the whole poem has been moving; the most indi-vidual yet at the same time the most universal expression of loss and destruction, of personal insecurity and anxiety, that it was possible for Burns to attain.

Detailed analysis of the kind attempted here enables us to qualify the views of such a critic as Mr George Bruce, who, comparing Burns with Henryson to Burns's disadvantage, maintains that he simply sees the mouse and nothing else, and that "his pity extends to the creature and returns to himself. . . . This is to speak as mere man, and it is, therefore, to make an appeal from the common human situation. The reduction of a situation to human proportions is typical."[47] On the con-trary, it can be said that Burns raises the mouse to man's level; and that, as Burns sees it, no level is worthier, more dignified, or more essentially and inherently noble than that of humanity. It is not primarily of himself that Burns is thinking, but of his own experience as representative of all mankind's.[48]

[47] G. Bruce, "Burns: A Comparative View," in *New Judgments Robert Burns*, henceforth cited as *New Judgments*, ed. W. Montgomerie, Glasgow 1947, pp. 19–20.

[48] I cannot agree with Ritter (p. 82) that "To A Mouse" owes much to my uncle Toby's address to the bluebottle in *Tristram Shandy*, BK. II, ch. xii. Doubtless memories of this passage, as of Thomson's description of the stricken birds and animals in "Winter," ll. 240 ff., contributed to the subtle alchemy of genius : but, as always, Burns's own observation and experience are primary. Ritter is on surer ground when he says that the "inner form" of the poem is indebted to Fergusson's "Ode to the Bee," "On Seeing a Butterfly in the Street," and "Ode to the Gowd-spink." Burns's treatment of the mouse is not *merely* a fusion of realism and eigh-teenth-century sentimentalism; it has affinities with something much older—Henryson's fifteenth-century respect for animals as animals. Cp. Wittig, pp. 40 ff.

Literary historians tend to classify "The Twa Dogs: A Tale,"[49] as a satire in the beast-fable convention so beloved by Gay and La Fontaine, and some of them see it as deriving from Cervantes' *Colloquy of the Dogs*, an English translation of which appeared in 1767.[50] It may well be that Burns was aware of Cervantes, but the two works resemble each other so little that one is tempted to believe he knew only the title of the Spanish dialogue—that would be sufficient to set him off. In the two hundred and thirty-eight lines of "The Twa Dogs" there are reminiscences of Gay, Thomson, Ramsay, Shenstone, Goldsmith, Fergusson, Swift ("On Rover, a Lady's Spaniel"), Milton (both *Lycidas* and *L'Allegro*), Shakespeare, Soame Jenyns, and several anonymous street ballads.[51] The reader is not at all conscious of these echoes, because in this poem, as in all his best works, Burns is no passive copyist but a creative artist fusing every scrap of tradition into a poetic whole that is qualitatively different from any extraneous elements which it may happen to have ingested. "The Twa Dogs" is primarily a statement, or a series of statements, about the effect that the division of society into classes has upon the quality of individual lives. Since it is as much a pastoral as a satire, there is some justification for treating it as belonging to an independent *genre*, and for recognising that it is related to "The Vision" and "The Cotter's Saturday Night" as well as to the "Address of Beelzebub."

That the central preoccupation of "The Twa Dogs" is not savagely satiric is seen when one compares it with Cervantes' *Colloquy*. The butchers of Seville, the shepherds who deceive their masters, the police in league with the criminals, the soldiers committing crimes in the villages they pass through, the witch, the gipsies, the Moriscos—all are what they are because of the original and primitive evil of their natures. The few good and gentle souls in the story are doomed to be cozened and oppressed by the wicked majority. Everywhere hypocrisy

---

[49] I. 9 (318).

[50] Ritter, p. 118. The full title was *A Dialogue between Scipio and Berganza, two Dogs, belonging to the City of Toledo, giving an Account of their Lives and Adventures, with their Reflections on the Lives, Humours and Employments of the Masters they lived with . . . now first translated from the Spanish original.*

[51] Cp. Ritter, pp. 114–21.

is rampant, and the noblest principles are used as a mask for
robbery and extortion :

> 'God help me !' I said to myself. 'Who can do anything about
> this evil? Who is in a position to make it known that the
> defenders are the offenders, that the sentinels sleep, the watch-
> man robs, and the guardians kill ?'[52]

Cervantes' pessimism is like the mood of Burns's extempore
"Stanzas on Naething"[53]—only the latter was a temporary
and rather conventional gesture, whereas the *Colloquy* is deeply
tinged with a bitterness which denies altogether the possibility
of social change. The only positive value in Cervantes' story
is its humour, a wry but entrancing mixture of disillusion and
compassion.

Burns's humour, in contrast, firmly but gently pulls down
the barriers of class with a gay plebeian assurance. For
Cervantes, the world is composed of a majority of rogues, and
the few honest men, who may turn up in any walk of life ; his
butts are the officials, the bureaucrats and the criminals (often
with all the power of the State behind them). For Burns,
social class is the dominant theme, and the jack-in-office is
tyrannical as much because of the system of absentee landlordism as because of the sin he has inherited from Adam :

> There's monie a creditable stock
> O' decent, honest, fawsont folk,
> Are riven out baith root an' branch,
> Some rascal's pridefu' greed to quench,
> Wha thinks to knit himsel the faster
> In favor wi' some gentle master,
> Wha, aiblins thrang a parliamentin',
> For Britain's guid his saul indentin'. . . .[54]

Luath, the poor man's dog, takes too optimistic a view of the
gentry, as befits the *naïveté* which Burns has bestowed upon
him. Caesar, the rich man's Newfoundland, has to correct
him in the course of his reply :

> For Britain's guid ! for her destruction !
> Wi' dissipation, feud an' faction.[55]

[52] Cervantes, *The Colloquy of the Dogs*, in *Three Exemplary Novels*, tr. S. Putnam, London 1952, p. 142.
[53] Above, p. 156.   [54] H. & H., I. 15 *ad init.*   [55] *Op. cit.*, p. 16 *ad init.*

One of the fundamental ideas of the poem is a variety of what economists call the Labour Theory of Value—the notion that the toil and sweat of the "lower orders" is the source of all wealth and luxury. The rich squander the surplus extorted from the poor on their criminal follies :

> Stake on a chance a farmer's stackyard,
> An' cheat like onie unhang'd blackguard.[56]

In spite of the comforts they appropriate to themselves, they are denied true happiness, which, paradoxically enough, is quite a common experience of those who exist just above the level of bare subsistence. The gloom of the early poems of agrarian depression is quite excluded, and the accent is all on the compensations of a rustic existence :

> When rural life, of ev'ry station,
> Unite in common recreation ;
> Love blinks, Wit slaps, an' social Mirth
> Forgets there's Care upo' the earth.[57]

Burns lets his light-hearted picture of the essential worth and decency of the common man arise out of the partial impressions of contrasted and limited views. Caesar is largely ignorant of "poor bodies," and Luath is woefully in the dark about the corruption of the leaders of society, so that it is only by the end of the dialogue that we are aware of the whole "truth." Many who do not like Burns's political philosophy will object that this is nothing more than a propagandist's trick ; they will feel that it is a fundamentally dishonest attempt to deceive the reader. Some such opinion as this seems to have lain at the back of Sir William Craigie's cautious comment :

> It was very natural that Burns should be a partial judge, and contrast the virtues of the one class with the vices of the other. ... No doubt "Master Caesar's" disclosures were more applicable then than now, but Burns's later experience of the nobility of his country must have gone far to make him doubt whether all his strictures were universally just.[58]

---

[56] *Op. cit.*, p. 18 *med.*   [57] *Op. cit.*, p. 14 *med.*
[58] Craigie, pp. 79–80.

But the last couplet allowed to Caesar specifically states :

> There's some exceptions, man an' woman ;
> But this is Gentry's life in common.[59]

Presumably the good qualities of aristocrats like Lord Daer, who treated Burns as an equal, did not obviate the conceited stupidity of others, such as Lord Buchan, who slipped into the rôle of a sentimental Mæcenas whenever he addressed the poet.[60] In any case, Lord Daer was a radical Whig whose political principles were almost identical with those espoused by Burns in the seventeen-nineties,[61] so that it was thoroughly in character that, as Burns states in his "Lines on Meeting with Lord Daer" :[62]

> The fient a pride, nae pride had he,
> Nor sauce, nor state, that I could see,
>   Mair than an honest ploughman !

Furthermore, "The Vision" is largely concerned with those aristocratic virtues which Craigie apparently thinks should have been given their proper place in "The Twa Dogs." As we shall see presently,[63] Burns there considered aristocratic leadership in relation to the life of the nation as a whole in a way that is not necessarily incompatible with an intense hatred of affectation and pride.

The central theme of "The Twa Dogs" is, then, the age-old pastoral claim that virtue is more likely to appear in a cot than in a palace, despite the miseries which the cotter may sometimes suffer ; but its assertion that peasants are by and large better men than the gentry is coloured by a knowledge of the realities of social oppression which writers of pastoral have not generally possessed. Showing, as it does, the influence of the contemporary cult of the natural man, the poem is remarkably consonant with European literary trends. Figaro's criticism of Almaviva and his class in Beaumarchais's *Mariage de Figaro*[64]

---

[59] H. & H., I. 18 *ad fin.*   [60] C. & W., II. 46–7, III. 277–8.
[61] For Lord Daer's activities as a "Friend of the People," see H. W. Meikle, *Scotland and the French Revolution*, henceforth cited as Meikle, Glasgow 1912, pp. 106–11. Daer had been in Paris at the beginning of the Revolution and was a member of the London Friends of the People and the London Corresponding Society.
[62] H. & H., II. 49 (340).   [63] Below, pp. 182–92.   [64] Act V, sc. iii.

is almost identical with the indictment that comes from the mouths of Caesar and Luath, and the tone is similarly light-hearted.[65] An interesting conclusion seems to follow from this parallel. If it is in any sense true, as the histories of literature claim, that Beaumarchais's plays reflect the cynicism of intelligent young people in the five or six years immediately preceding the French Revolution, then it would seem logical to suppose that "The Twa Dogs" is as much pre-Revolutionary as some other works of Burns are "pre-Romantic."

Is "The Twa Dogs" thinly-disguised propaganda, or is it art? To frame the question in this way is to create an unreal distinction between art and propaganda.

It implies, too, that all propaganda is necessarily false. But provided that the class, Church or party whose doctrines the artist is propagating is (and can genuinely be) made into a symbol of perennial value, the resulting work need not *necessarily* be of low quality just because it is tendentious. The convictions that Burns expresses in "The Twa Dogs" truly reflect the interests of rural democracy as conceived by small farmers and agricultural labourers in Scotland in the 1780s. In that sense at least the poem has its share of contingent and relative truth; it has, in other words, considerable documentary merit. That in itself is not sufficient to make it a great work of literature, but the fact remains that Burns can and does express, at the level of comedy and in a pleasing manner, the peasants' view of the aristocracy whom their labour supports. Thus, even if the view in question were objectively false, the poem would still have its portion of absolute aesthetic value. But the view in question is *not* objectively false. On the contrary, there is a sense in which it contains a measure of absolute as well as of relative truth. Perhaps independently of Rousseau, and of the Sentimental School, the Scottish small farmers and agricultural labourers of the 1780s had discovered what some men have to learn afresh in every generation—that it is quite ordinary people, the Heartfree of Fielding's *Jonathan Wild*, the

[65] Yet Caesar and Luath never cease to be dogs. Cp. Wittig, p. 40 ("Henryson's animals are closely observed, and they are real animals"); and p. 214 ("Luath and Caesar are first presented as animals, . . . and the way in which Burns . . . brings animal and human into a common focus is very reminiscent of Henryson").

simple souls of Dickens's novels, and the Holy Fools of Dostoevsky, who are the guardians of mankind's ethical insights. In many of his best poems Burns made use of this discovery, or rediscovery, of a commonplace—for perhaps the peasantry have always known it. Worn very lightly and with the greatest assurance, it forms the basis of the social criticism of "The Twa Dogs."

Chiefly because of its sentimental rhetoric and English diction, it has long been fashionable to despise "The Cotter's Saturday Night."[66] Yet there are signs—notably in the recent critical studies by David Daiches and Christina Keith[67]—that the poem is once more coming into favour. "The Cotter" arises out of attitudes and experiences similar to those which underlie the deservedly popular verse epistles. There is the same patriotism, the same depiction of wintry landscape, the same love of the poor and hatred of the "paughty feudal thane," the same assertion that money-grubbing is evil, and that love and friendship are the finest things in life. In the epistles, these attitudes are poured out in an apparently spontaneous and decidedly humorous helter-skelter, like the patter of a rustic Figaro—and we are all enchanted. But in "The Cotter," Burns's favourite measure is exchanged for the complicated Spenserian stanza[68] which he does not handle really well even in the best sections; and the content is expressed in the contemporary English manner—a style that has never been very popular with poetry-readers since the canonisation of Wordsworth and Keats in the nineteenth century. Scholars and critics of our own time have made the common reader aware of metaphysical poetry and even of Dryden and Pope, but to most of us the poetry of the later eighteenth century still seems repulsive. It takes an effort of the imagina-

---

[66] I. 106 (361).   [67] Daiches, pp. 150–62; C. Keith, pp. 37–40.

[68] As J. Logie Robertson ("Hugh Haliburton") long ago pointed out (*Furth in Field*, pp. 260 ff.), Burns "maintains the perfect form of the Spenserian stanza," *a b a b b c b c c*—as Shenstone did in "The Schoolmistress." But Fergusson, in "The Farmer's Ingle" (sometimes regarded as Burns's sole model for the poem), rhymes *a b a b c d c d d*. Since there is no evidence that Burns knew Spenser at first hand until Apr. 1787 (cp. *Letters*, I. 86), and since we know from other evidence that Burns was soaked in Shenstone, it would seem to follow that the Englishman Shenstone contributed as much to "The Cotter's Saturday Night" as the Scot Fergusson.

tion to think in terms which the late eighteenth century understood, just as it takes an effort of the imagination to enter into the spirit of medieval Byzantium or the mental state of the Trobriand Islanders. Nevertheless, the attempt has to be made if we are to appreciate "The Cotter's Saturday Night."

The opening stanza addressing Robert Aiken, to whom the poem is dedicated, may be an afterthought, as some have suggested;[69] but it is not out of place, and it asserts the overwhelming value of friendship in a world of artificialities and corruption. The second line, "No mercenary bard his homage pays," allows the opposition between friendship and money, never far from Burns's thoughts, to appear in faint outline, but only as subdued by friendship. The direct worth of honesty is asserted, together with a scorn of selfish ends—a euphemism, I think, for what Burns elsewhere termed "catch-the-plack." In ll. 4–5, friendship is associated with the singing of "simple Scottish lays"—not altogether an accurate description of what follows, for the poem itself mixes simple Scots with the occasionally rather abstract poetic diction of eighteenth century England.

The second stanza has been condemned because it is full of echoes from older poets.[70] These, however, are not evidence either of simple plagiarism or of servile imitation, but rather of the deliberate use of familiar associations in order to enrich the reader's perception by referring him to poems he already knows. As James Sutherland has pointed out,[71] the method was standard throughout the eighteenth century, and it had been used by Milton himself in the seventeenth century. We do not condemn it when it is employed by T. S. Eliot, perhaps because his references are to poets like Dante and Webster, who possessed a certain snob-appeal in the 1920s. It is therefore difficult to see why we should turn up our noses at Burns when he does the same sort of thing with Gray, Goldsmith, Shenstone, Beattie, Fergusson, Pope, Thomson, Gay, Milton, Thomas Warton, Rochester, Bickerstaffe, Collins, Young, Sterne, Churchill, Skinner ("Tullochgorum"), Hamil-

---

[69] Cp. Daiches, p. 154.
[70] They include Fergusson as well as the English neo-classic poets.
[71] *A Preface to Eighteenth-Century Poetry*, Oxford 1948, pp. 132–6.

ton of Bangour, and Shakespeare (there are apparent echoes of all of these in "The Cotter's Saturday Night").[72] The only difference is that since these writers wrote in Scots or English and were popular in the eighteenth century, the results of the method were probably accessible to a large number of Burns's contemporary readers, whereas there are few today who can appreciate Eliot without a tutor. This stanza (thanks in part to these reminiscences of earlier works) presents a very attractive *genre*-picture and conveys a distinctively Scottish impression with only a sprinkling of Scots.

In the third stanza, almost as in a documentary film, the scene shifts from the cottage to the family inside it. The language attains a particularly satisfactory fusion of English and Scots; thus "The lisping infant, prattling on his knee," though pure English, does not in the least conflict with the surrounding lines, in which a faint tincture of Scots is present. In the fourth stanza, the Cotter and his family are no longer mere silhouettes, but seen in depth, in their economic and social setting. The elder children are wage-labourers to neighbouring tenant-farmers, and even "their eldest hope, their Jenny, woman-grown," is herself in service and may have to eke out the housekeeping with her "sair-won penny-fee." From the beginning of the fifth stanza the synthesis of Braid Scots and Scots-English tends to be expressed as an almost regular alternation between them:

> The parents, partial, eye their hopeful years;
> Anticipation forward points the view;
> The mother, *wi'* her needle and her *sheers*,
> *Gars auld claes look amaist as weel's the new;*
> *The father mixes a' wi' admonition due.*

[72] Cp. Ritter, pp. 93–108. All these allusions and echoes (conscious or unconscious) are a consequence of the *social* nature of Burns's diction. He was never interested in creating a private language, but rather in making his own selection from words, phrases and idioms actually used by some men. The process involved in turning "Even now sagacious foresight points to show" (Shenstone, "The Schoolmistress," xxviii. 2) into "Anticipation forward points the view" ("The Cotter's Saturday Night," v. 6) is not so very dissimilar from that of turning Biblical and homely phraseology into "Holy Willie's Prayer"; or the idiom of the people into the dialogue of "Death and Doctor Hornbook" (see above, pp. 57, 121); or the echoes of a large number of popular songs into "A red, red Rose" (see below, pp. 238–9). In each case, the attitude to language is similar; in each case, the inheritance of the past is something to be used.

It is important to realise that the first two lines of this passage, as well as the last, have an intentionally humorous undertone : Burns eyes the couple quizzically but not unkindly, and he chooses the artificial expressions quite deliberately, so that there can be no doubt as to his attitude. The sudden transition to a solid and straightforward presentation of the mother is also, I think, intentional. Burns puts before us not simply a woman sewing, but a woman forced to sew by economic necessity, who yet loves to do so, in order that her husband and children should appear decent in the eyes of others. A whole life of quiet heroism and the values and the struggles of an entire class are crystallised in these two lines. Their vocabulary may not seem radically un-English ; the Scotticisms may appear a matter of orthography and pronunciation merely ; but there is present nevertheless a specific northernness of idiom and phrase which is just sufficient to convey the intended impression ; southern English, for example, would surely prefer "as well as new" to "as well as the new."

Oscillation between Scots and Scots-English continues in the more detailed account of the father's admonitions that follows in the sixth stanza : but even when he is at his most English, the father remains Scottish in phrase and choice of idiom ; and so does his daughter Jenny when she explains that her sweetheart is waiting outside the door. In the seventh stanza, the time has come for another excursion into Scots-English :

> The wily mother sees *the conscious flame*
> Sparkle in Jenny's e'e. . . .

This pleasantly artificial antithesis is an example of a kind of humour which we have already noticed in "The Jolly Beggars" :

> The caird prevail'd : th' unblushing fair
> In his embraces sunk,
> Partly wi' love o'ercome sae sair,
> An' partly she was drunk.

We can all recognise that the "Jolly Beggars" passage is funny because the contrast between the poetic diction and the action described is so grotesque, and also because we know that the whole poem is comic; and yet when we come upon the same thing in "The Cotter," we are tempted to speak of "artificiality" and "Burns's inability to write in English." Yet, to those who have ears to hear, the line quoted conveys a delighted smile at the scene, enjoyment of the contrast implied between love in a cottage and love in sentimental novels, together with humane and compassionate understanding of both mother and daughter. This is humour of quite a subtle and civilised sort, utterly different from the self-regarding cruelty of "Halloween." Almost immediately, and in keeping with the poem's logic, the Scottish end of the see-saw begins to rise; and the mother,

> With heart-struck anxious care, enquires his name,
> While Jenny hafflins is afraid to speak;
> Weel-pleas'd the mother hears, it's nae wild, worthless rake.

Here "hafflins" is the only word in the passage which is at all unfamiliar to the English reader; its position in the line and the phrasing of "It's nae, wild, worthless rake," are sufficient to give the scene an unmistakably Scottish tone which is never absent from it in any subsequent stanza; for, no matter how far into "English" Burns's modulations may carry him, the keys are all closely related—at any rate in the present poem— and we are always aware of the same speaking voice. Any reader who calls these three lines sentimental has failed to appreciate all their *nuances*—the mother's fussy anxiety, the convulsive catch of the girl's breath (conveyed by the placing of "hafflins" and the very sound of the word), the mother's relief, and the poet's slightly ironical but still sympathetic observation of her complacency. W. E. Henley complains that the poem lacks "realism."[73] One may well doubt whether it is possible to convey a more accurate representation of the exteriors of social life than Burns gives us in this stanza and the next. In the ninth stanza, however, the poem begins to sink. We are presented with general reflexions of an abstract nature suggested by the scene, exactly as in the second stanza of "To a Mouse." In "To a Mouse" the device succeeds; in "The Cotter," it fails miserably. It is as if Burns were aware

[73] Henley, "Robert Burns," in H. & H., IV. 276.

of what had been lacking in "Halloween," and had determined
to repair the deficiency, only to err in the other direction
altogether by producing nine lines of entirely unnecessary
comment.[74] The fourth and fifth lines are certainly among
Burns's worst. Here, at least, it would have been far better to
have left the picture to make its own impression on the reader.
But if with its "heart-felt raptures! bliss beyond compare!"
the ninth stanza comes perilously near to bathos, there can be
no doubt about the tenth. It is one of the most nauseating
ever published by a reputable poet. The mask of the conventional moralist has been altogether too deliberately assumed;
whatever sort of mask it is, it is not a creative one; and we are
all the time aware, behind the disguise, of a face that could
only too easily lend itself to the "rakish arts of Rob Mossgiel."
It is not our knowledge of the poet's life-history which makes
us distrust his pose here, so much as the hysterical rhodo-
montade which runs through the stanza:

> A wretch! a villain! lost to love and truth! . . .
> Curse on his perjur'd arts! dissembling, smooth! . . .
> Is there no pity, no relenting ruth,
> Points to the parents fondling o'er their child?
> Then paints the ruin'd maid, and their distraction wild?[75]

Mercifully, the poem rallies in the eleventh stanza to a
finely-drawn picture of the evening meal. The whole of this
stanza is shot through with vernacular Scots, except for the
first line; taken together with the twelfth stanza, in which
Scottish intonations are present, it affords a marked and
intentional contrast to all the subsequent verses, which are in
English—or, rather, in English as pronounced in Scotland.
Stanzas xii–xvi contain the real centre of the poem: the

[74] In themselves, ll. 7–9 are quite good: "'Tis when a youthful, loving, modest
pair, | In other's arms, breathe out the tender tale | Beneath the milk-white thorn
that scents the ev'ning gale." There are, of course, echoes of Shakespeare, *Henry
VI*, Pt. II, I. i. 254, "the milk-white rose"; of Milton, "L'Allegro," ll. 67–8, "And
every Shepherd tells his tale | Under the Hawthorn in the dale"; and of in-
numerable eighteenth-century descriptive poets who used the same phraseology.
[75] Hately Waddell (p. 101) sees a striking similarity between this stanza and
The Kingis Quair, st. cxii: "Fy on all such! fy on thaire doubilnesse! | Fy on
thaire lust, and bestly appetite! | Thaire wolfis hertis, in lambis likenesse," etc.
Ritter (p. 103) sees the immediate sources in Goldsmith, *The Deserted Village*,
ll. 325 ff., and Sterne, *A Sentimental Journey*, ch. xxxix.

description of family worship from which everything else radiates. All that has gone before—the realism, the humour, the Scottish words—exist only for this scene; and, with its noble Scots-English diction, it is worthy to be the kernel of a great poem. Just as in previous sections Burns has relied heavily on the reader's reminiscences of Milton, Goldsmith, Gray and others, so now he relies on the association of well-known Scriptural names—Abraham, Moses, Job, Isaiah, Christ and His Apostles. In this section he makes serious use of that layer of Scottish experience and vocabulary which he had treated satirically in "Holy Willie's Prayer."[76] I cannot agree with Sir William Craigie that the slighting references to Italian music in the thirteenth stanza are a blemish,[77] any more than "blind mouths" and "the two-handed engine at the door" are faults in *Lycidas*; and though, as poetry, the seventeenth stanza is of lesser quality than the description of the Bible-reading itself, I do not feel that the poem is materially weakened by its explicit statement that the "pompous strain" of institutional religion is inferior to "the language of the soul."

The real conclusion is the eighteenth stanza in which "the parent-pair" pay their "secret homage," praying that God will not only provide for the material needs of the family, "But, chiefly, in their hearts with Grace Divine preside." The last three stanzas form a rather pedestrian coda which affects us like the more ludicrous recitatives of certain early operas. Though one wishes that they were less clumsy, it is important to realise that they—or something like them—are essential to the work as Burns planned it. They are meant to achieve what the second stanza of "Halloween" fails to do because it occurs too early in the poem, namely to raise the local to the level of the national; therefore, they are an integral part of the poet's intention. But if that were all that is in the poem, if "The Cotter's Saturday Night" were only a national poem and nothing more, it would not be as good as—with all its faults—it is. Its most abiding qualities reside in the universality of the central episode, which irradiates even the rhetorical conclusion. The evolution of the poem is from a sombre beginning, with its portrayal of the weariness that is the aftermath of physical

---

[76] See above, pp. 52–61.   [77] Craigie, p. 77.

labour, to a concretely presented interior that merges imperceptibly into a transfiguration and sublimation of the worshipping father and his family. The alternation between Scots and Scots-English is essential to the inner movement of the work : the English lines and diction of the earlier sections look forward to the later heightening and ennobling of reality, while the complete change-over to Scots-English in the fourteenth stanza is the outward and visible sign of a leap from the lowly to the "human sublime." If one is willing to close one's ears to the central statement of "The Cotter," it is all too easy to magnify its faults and say with W. E. Henley that it is "of its essence sentimental and therefore pleasingly untrue."[78] But perhaps a juster verdict is that of the French critic, Angellier :

> Never has the existence of the poor been invested with so much
> dignity . . . [It is] a solemn homage to humble virtues. . . . It
> attains the summits of human dignity, where all social distinctions
> have fallen, where the soul alone appears, where what there is
> of the absolute in virtue bursts forth and shines and causes to melt
> around it, like vain things of wax, rank, riches and noble birth.[79]

[78] Henley, "Robert Burns," in H. & H., IV. 277. A recent Russian critic, A. E. Elistratova, in the first biographical study of the poet to be published in the Soviet Union (*Robert Burns*, Moscow 1957), is equally convinced of the poem's falsity. Her reasons are economic ones : "And that countryman—the cotter whom Burns depicted in the 'Saturday Night'—was an owner, although a small one ; he was 'on his own,' the master of a self-contained economic unit, and at the time of Burns no longer a typical figure in the Scottish village. Hence one cannot but feel that this represents a utopian, retrospective glance into the past" (p. 74). This judgment is in a way acute. The cotter had indeed ceased to be a typical figure in Burns's time, and the poem *is*, in one of its aspects (but only in one), an idealisation of a dying class. Although his psychology might well have been that of a small proprietor since he did, in fact, enjoy considerable security of tenure, Burns's patriarchal "sire" did not *own* his tiny patch of land ; he rendered various services (or even paid rent) for it. His children had to work for the neighbouring farmers as labourers or domestic servants, and he himself would almost certainly have laboured for wages at certain seasons of the year. He owned one cow, and probably such tools as the spades, mattocks and hoes mentioned in st. ii. From one point of view, indeed, the cotters were the ancestors of the "rural proletariat." Mrs Elistratova's strictures could more accurately be applied to the central figure of Fergusson's "The Farmer's Ingle," evidently not a cotter, but a tenant, who employed both male and female workers (though he treated them well), and owned "owsen" and "hawkies" (in the plural). In view of the system of Scottish agriculture, it is extremely unlikely that even Fergusson's "gudeman" *owned* his holding ; he, too, would pay rent for it. The distinction between tenants and cotfolk is carefully drawn in "The Twa Dogs" and "The Holy Fair."

[79] Angellier, II. 222.

It is fashionable to sneer at such conceptions today, just as it was after the Restoration of Charles II. But the ethic of "The Cotter's Saturday Night" is not easily overthrown, nor can it be put down by the jibes of modern aestheticians. It is a morality with a long and honourable history behind it. King Lear on the heath was aware of its force, and it is present in the *Oresteia* of Aeschylus. Indeed, perhaps its noblest expression is a chorus in the *Agamemnon*:

> Δίκα δὲ λάμπει μὲν ἐν δυσκάπνοις δώμασιν,
> τὸν δ' ἐναίσιμον τίει βίον.
> τὰ χρυσόπαστ' ἐσθλὰ σὺν πίνῳ χερῶν
> παλιντρόποις ὄμμασι λι-
> ποῦσ', ὅσια προσέβαλε
> δύναμιν οὐ σέβουσα πλούτου παράσημον αἴνῳ·
> πᾶν δ' ἐπὶ τέρμα νωμᾷ.[80]

It is true that "The Cotter's Saturday Night" is no *King Lear* or *Agamemnon*; nevertheless, in spite of all its crudities, its clumsiness, its deplorable and sometimes unpardonable lapses, it gropes towards a sublimity of the same kind as theirs, and succeeds in conveying similar ethical insights in a non-tragic form.

It is almost as difficult for the modern reader of poetry, brought up on Eliot and Hopkins and Donne, to appreciate "The Vision"[81] at a first reading as it is for him to apprehend without special effort the full achievement of "The Cotter's Saturday Night." And yet the attempt is well worth while, for the work is evidence of Burns's ability to think poetically—not, it is true, in the actively reverberating symbols of the metaphysical school, but in images of a more passive and allegorical sort. W. P. Ker, one of the few critics to give "The Vision" its due, has pointed out that the sensibility exhibited in the poem has medieval affinities, and qualities that go back as far as Boethius.[82] This traditionalism does not prevent the content

---

[80] Aesch., *Ag.*, 772–80 : "And Righteousness is a shining in | the smoke of mean houses. | Her blessing is on the just man. | From high halls starred with gold by reeking hands | she turns back | with eyes that glance away to the simple in heart, | spurning the strength of gold | stamped false with flattery. | And all things she steers to fulfilment." (*Oresteia*, tr. R. Lattimore, Chicago 1953, p. 58).

[81] I. 74 (350).   [82] Ker, *On Modern Literature*, pp. 45–6.

of Burns's thinking from being surprisingly modern; the poem reveals an awareness of the causes of social change which many an historian might envy. Behind "The Vision" there is a rather special kind of self-knowledge, the exploration of the relationship between the poet and the nation to which he belongs. Like "The Cotter's Saturday Night," it moves from the particular to the general, from the local to the national, from the vernacular to eighteenth-century rhetoric; but Burns's handling of English is more successful than in "The Cotter," and there are few of those defects which make "The Cotter," for all its undoubted merits, a deeply-flawed poem.

"The Vision" is organised in two main sections or "Duans," the first of which sets the scene and describes the apparition of Coila, a rustic Muse, while the second reports her words and final disappearance. Since the centre of the poem purports to be a dream, Burns is compelled to depict his material surroundings as concretely as possible in order to render credible the ensuing supernatural event. The peculiarly vivid impressions of the first stanza are therefore necessary for what is to come. The winter sunset, the curlers stopping their noisy jollity on the ice, the starved hare loping towards the kitchen garden and leaving her prints on the snow—all are essential for Burns's purpose. The next four stanzas depict the poet's own personal situation, which is one of the determinants of the vision; they convey an overwhelming impression of melancholy and physical weariness. In the second stanza, twilight is described in a personification more direct than is usual for Burns:

> And when the day had clos'd his e'e,
> Far i' the west . . .

That, of course, is exactly what Burns himself should be doing, after long hours of wielding the flail. But, as often happens when the body is exhausted by physical labour, the poet's senses are acutely and nervously alive. At first it is the sense of sight which predominates. In the third stanza, he *eyes* the volleying smoke until, immediately afterwards, smell takes over ("reek . . . hoast-provoking smeek")—only to yield, in turn, to hearing as he suddenly becomes aware of the "restless rattons" above his head. Everything that he can see or hear or sense fits into the pattern of his brooding. In the fourth and fifth stanzas, he reflects that if he had not wasted his time

> . . . stringing blethers up in rhyme,
> For fools to sing,

he too might have been a commercial success; he is torn between poetry and the world, in a struggle which is the common experience of most of the artists of our present civilisation. Thus, even at his most personal, when he seems occupied solely with his own private and bardic concerns, Burns expresses the general and the typical, giving voice to a conflict not unknown in contemporary Britain, America and even Russia. He is just on the point of swearing to give up poetry altogether :

> When click ! the string the snick did draw ;
> And jee ! the door gaed to the wa' ;
> An' by my ingle-lowe I saw,
>   Now bleezin bright,
> A tight, outlandish hizzie, braw,
>   Come full in sight.
>
> Ye need na doubt, I held my whisht ;
> The infant aith, half-form'd, was crusht ;
> I glowr'd as eerie 's I'd been dusht,
>   In some wild glen ;
> When sweet, like modest Worth, she blusht,
>   And stepped ben.

As usual, Burns is working in a tradition; as usual, he is following literary sources—in particular, a work by Wollaston, dating from 1681, in which the Muse appears when the poet, in a mood of utter depression, is about to forswear the writing of poetry for ever :

> What indigested thought, or rash advice
> Has caused thee to apostatize
> Not my ill-usage, surely, made thee fly
> From thy apprenticeship in poetry.[83]

[83] The parallel in Wollaston was apparently first discovered by a writer in the *Gentleman's Magazine*, for Oct. 1852, quoted in C. & W., 1. 264–6, n. But visions of the Muse have been reported by poets from Hesiod onwards. Ritter (pp. 123 ff.) points out decided similarities between Burns's poem and Cowley's "The Com-

It was always Burns's method to "string his rustic lyre with emulating vigour" : and here, as was normal with him, he surpassed his models.

Burns treats his holly-decked Muse with a mixture of humour and courtesy that disarms us in advance. In the ninth stanza, just before his account of the Muse's features and symbolic accoutrements, he permits himself an introductory smile at his own expense :

> I took her for some Scottish Muse,
> By that same token ;
> And come to stop those reckless vows,
> Would soon been broken.

His Coila is a thoroughly Petrarchan lady whose flashing eyes "beam keen" with the courtly quality of "honor." She is dressed in bright tartan, and her bare legs are so perfectly moulded that those of the poet's own mistress could only equal, not surpass them : another flash of humour that serves to increase our belief in this creature of dream.

From the twelfth stanza onwards, Burns modulates into English poetic diction, but the poem does not deteriorate in quality. The stanzas describing the Muse are pervaded by a loveliness that is both natural and formal, and filled with a beauty utterly different from that of Romantic poetry. Coila's mantle has on it the physical features not of Ayrshire in isolation, but of Ayrshire seen in the larger context of the entire nation ; the Highlands and "the lordly Dome" of art are mentioned too, although local features are the most prominent. The rivers and towns of Burns's native county are set in a landscape alive with the figures of the local gentry—heroes who fought the English in the Scottish Wars of Independence

plaint." In Cowley's poem the Muse's dress (like Coila's) is described as covered with hieroglyphic pictures—an idea which presumably goes back to the shield of Achilles in Homer. The following lines of Cowley (II. 5–7) are also like Burns's sts. iv and vi : "Thou Prodigal ! who did'st so loosely waste | Of all thy youthful Years, the good Estate ; | Art thou return'd, here to repent too late ?" But, as Angellier notes, almost the same complaint was made by Villon (*Grand Testament*, xxvi). Did Cowley know Villon and Burns Cowley ? Or (a much more likely supposition) did all three poets have similar experiences ? Burns himself says that he took the "idea" of Coila from Alexander Ross's Muse, Scota ([To Mrs Dunlop], 7 Mar. 1788, in *Letters*, I. 205). But, as Ritter says (p. 125), Scota probably did no more than supply a hint for the name.

(1285–1371) and in later wars, together with Ayrshire notables of Burns's own century who had carried on this tradition of patriotism, or who, like Professor Dugald Stewart and his father, had served Scotland in the arts of peace. To regard these stanzas as flattery of the local nobility and nothing more would be to misunderstand Burns's intention completely. "The Vision" is the work, above all others, in which Burns shows himself most aware of the contemporary national renaissance : a movement which, in many spheres of life, from agricultural improvement to moral philosophy, was led by the most energetic and forward-looking of the landed gentry.

It might be argued that the outlook implied by these stanzas is in violent and absolute contradiction to the condemnation of aristocracy which informs "The Twa Dogs" and is implied in "The Cotter's Saturday Night" ; and some critics would no doubt explain the change by saying that Burns has simply adopted a different *persona* from his store of "creative masks." It seems to me, however, that the real explanation lies elsewhere. The position of the landed proprietors in late eighteenth-century Scotland was itself a confusing and contradictory one. The gentry who were compelled by economic difficulties to rack-rent their tenants and expose them to the brutal insults of stewards and factors were often the same men who in other branches of life were among the leaders of national revival. There were two sides to the landlords, and two sorts of men among them. In "The Twa Dogs," Burns's subjects are the sufferings of the poorer tenant farmers and the political and social corruption of those lairds who betray the nation by aping foreign ways. In "The Vision," Burns selects as being especially significant either those local worthies who are continuing in their own lives the old Scots military tradition of the thirteenth and fourteenth centuries, or those who are in fact among the intellectual leaders of the Scottish people : unjust lairds and parasites are not mentioned at all.[84]

There is a sense in which the landlords and the common people are opposed to one another, and a sense in which they are connected like root and flower. In the second part of this poem, Burns explores this other and more organic relationship

[84] Cp. H. & H., I. 354–5.

between the gentry and the mass of the people by means of a thoroughly English type of machinery, an "aërial band" of guardian spirits reminiscent of the sylphs in Pope's *Rape of the Lock*. These supernatural beings act under orders from the all-inspiring "Genius of this land," a masculine figure probably suggested by the "Warden" in Allan Ramsay's "Vision."[85] When W. E. Henley dismissed all this as intolerably sentimental and artificial,[86] he allowed his lack of sympathy with the eighteenth century to blind him to the significance of what Burns is really doing. In this Duan Burns asserts his right to be considered as part of a great and many-sided national movement. The leaders of this resurgence are the soldier, the liberal politician advocating parliamentary reform, the poet, and the hoary sage. Burns is well aware that Scottish poets and savants writing in English, men like Thomson and Beattie and Robertson and Smith, are all offshoots of the one renaissance; indeed, so convinced is he of their importance that he puts "the rustic bard, the laboring hind, | The artisan" into an inferior class. As individuals, they are no doubt equal to their social betters; but by simply mentioning them in this order, Burns achieves a peculiar effect of modesty and politeness very different from that conveyed by his more egalitarian writings.[87]

[85] In Drayton's *Poly-Olbion* (1612), I. 8–9, the *genius loci* is seen in process of being transformed into the tutelary spirit of a nation. Drayton addresses the "Genius" of Albion as "Thou *Genius* of the place (this most renowned *Ile* | Which livedst long before the All-earth-drowning Flood. . . ." Collins, in his "Ode, to a Lady on the Death of Colonel Ross" (ll. 1–3) personifies "Britannia's Genius" as a male being who "bends to Earth, | And mourns the fatal Day." Ramsay's "Warden," clad in "A various rainbow-colourt plaid," leads "A strampant and rampant | Ferss lyon in his hand," carrying a thistle in its paw and wearing a collar engraved with the motto "NEMO ME IMPUNE LACESS | —ET" [*sic*]. Scotland's Warden is accustomed to meeting with other beings in a region "far abufe the mune . . . Quhair evry Warden represents | Cleirly his nation's case." There are inferior supernatural beings to wait upon these various "Wardens"; but not (as in Burns) to do their business on earth. And cp. also Thomson, *Liberty*, III. 547 ("each good genius in my train"), and 550 ff., (where the King of Nature holds his court, including "tutelary gods, | Of cities, nations, empires, and of worlds").

[86] Henley, "Robert Burns," in H. & H., IV. 274.

[87] Mr R. L. C. Lorimer has suggested to me that it might be an amusing exercise for some modern Otto Ritter to find out how much of Burns's vision can ultimately be traced back to Plato's *Phaedrus*, and through what channels. According to Plato, the soul that "has seen most" in the upper world becomes "a philosopher, or artist, or some musical and loving nature"; the next, "a righteous king, or lordly warrior"; the third, "a politician, or economist, trader"; the

Closely associated with the rustic bard, and with those who actually produce the material means of subsistence, are some of Coila's kindred spirits, who teach the new methods of production :

> Some teach to meliorate the plain,
> With tillage-skill. . . .

Moreover (though this is implied by the arrangement of the stanzas and the succession of images, rather than stated directly), the continuity of life is essential for the existence of a nation. The idea of Scotland would be meaningless without people, and there would be no people unless men and women fell in love :

> Some hint the lover's harmless wile ;
> Some grace the maiden's artless smile ;
> Some soothe the laborer's weary toil
> For humble gains,
> And make his cottage-scenes beguile
> His cares and pains.

The order in which these various ranks and concepts is mentioned cannot, in my opinion, be fortuitous ; to suppose otherwise is to degrade Burns to a mere mechanical rhymester or "crambo-jingler." Those men who are traditionally and most obviously the leaders of a people are mentioned first—the landowners, the legislators, the thinkers and the writers ; all those whose task it is to guide the nation, or to adorn and interpret its thoughts and moods. Next come those who are to be described perhaps as its foundation, the men and women without whose labour there could be neither spiritual nor material values ; and they are mentioned in the same breath as the improvers of crops and the devisers of new machines. It is surely no accident that the lover and the maiden, so essential

fourth, "a lover of gymnastic, or a physician" ; the fifth, "a prophet or hiero-phant" ; the sixth, "a poet or some other imitative artist" ; the seventh, "an artisan or husbandman" ; the eighth, "a sophist or demagogue" ; the ninth, "a tyrant" (*Phaedr.* 248 D-E). The order followed in Burns's vision is : first, the soldier ; second "the patriot," or politician ; third, "the bard, or hoary sage" ; fourth, the "rustic bard" ; fifth, "the lab'ring hind" ; sixth, "the artisan." The ultimate origin of many Burnsian attitudes is classical—for example, some lines in "The Cotter's Saturday Night" go right back to Virgil's *Georgics* ; but, following Ritter, I have preferred to draw attention to the English and Scottish writers of the seventeenth and eighteenth centuries who were the proximate *media* by which classical ideas and verbal formulae reached Burns.

for the continuance of the race, appear in close juxtaposition to the agricultural workers, whose labour is in the last resort the source of the wealth of nations. It is the rustic lovers and the toil-worn Cotter of the "Saturday Night" all over again, with the difference that in "The Vision" they take their places in a poetic analysis and synthesis of a whole society and its inter-relations. As in "The Cotter's Saturday Night" and "The Twa Dogs," the labourer and the cotter toil for "humble gains" and endure "cares and pains." Now, however, they are seen as being not simply exploited and oppressed, but rather as part of an altogether more complex set of relationships—as being, in the words of John Davidson, "the dung that makes the roses sweet."[88]

The fact that the poem returns to the figure of the Bard, outlining his life-history in a miniature Poet's Progress *after* the mention of the lovers and the labourer, serves to connect Burns with everything that is most creative in the ordinary activities of men. The mere ordering of the stanzas links him with the essence and informing principle of all Scotland rather than with anything superfluous or merely ornamental. As the poem develops, the Bard is put into the context of something even more fundamental than human labour; in the fourteenth, fifteenth and sixteenth stanzas, he is seen as indissolubly connected with nature. The next topic mentioned is that of the poet's instincts, which, because of their proximity to a description of the natural scene, are made to seem like nature taken into himself. Our feeling that they are the same instincts as those of the lover and the maiden strengthens the association between the poet and the foundations of social life; and it is noteworthy that the instincts, like fancy, are divine:

> 'I saw thy pulse's maddening play,
> Wild-send thee Pleasure's devious way,
> Misled by Fancy's meteor-ray,
>   By passion driven;[89]
> But yet the light that led astray
>   Was light from Heaven.'

[88] Davidson, "The Testament of a Man Forbid," in *The Centuries' Poetry*, ed. D. K. Roberts, 5 vols., Harmondsworth 1938, iv. 168.

[89] Cp. Young, *Night Thoughts*, Night viii, 166: "... by gusts of passion driven."

The total effect of this group of stanzas (II. xiv–xviii) is to
achieve a unity of the personal and the elemental of the sort
which we associate with poets like Shakespeare and Yeats
rather than with those who confine themselves to literal statements and obvious meanings. That Burns, employing non-
symbolic conventions and a diction that is sometimes hackneyed,
can in this poem penetrate so deeply beneath the surface of
social life, is at once a tribute to his genius and a reminder that
good poetry can be written without reverberating imagery. It
is surely significant that even Burns found it necessary to
abandon his accustomed naturalism in order to reveal the
inner workings of his society. To write "The Vision," he had
to desert the everyday for the world of fantasy and dream.[90] In
spite of his conviction that a rustic bard must inevitably be
inferior to a Thomson, a Shenstone or a Gray, he knows that
his own lot is better than the courtier's or the millionaire's. In
the twenty-third stanza, Coila sums up the aim of a national
poet—indeed of any poet—as follows :

> 'To give my counsels all in one :
> Thy tuneful flame still careful fan ;
> Preserve the dignity of Man,
>   With soul erect ;
> And trust the Universal Plan
>   Will all protect.'[91]

There is therefore not the slightest conflict between Burns's
nationalism and the interests of the broadest humanism. His
is a patriotism compatible with internationalism, for it merges
with "the dignity of Man." The poem ends in a fine image of
sight, sound and motion :

> 'And wear thou *this*'—She solemn said,
> And bound the holly round my head :
> The polish'd leaves and berries red
>   Did rustling play ;

[90] Here Burns is very close indeed to the spirit of Thomas the Rhymer—
especially to the earliest version, "Thomas off Ersseldoune," for which see, e.g.,
F. J. Child, *The English and Scottish Ballads*, N.Y. 1957, I. 326 ff.

[91] Ritter (p. 131) thinks that "the Dignity of Man" comes from the following
title : Young, *The Centaur not fabulous. Letter VI: The Dignity of Man.* "The
Universal Plan" is pure Pope : cp. *Essay on Man*, I. 6, III. 1, IV. 35.

And, like a passing thought, she fled
In light away.

"The Vision" is one of Burns's highest achievements. Its
movement from a vernacular prelude to a rhetorical centre
and conclusion is highly successful, and in its use of English it
is superior to both "The Cotter's Saturday Night" and "Man
was made to Mourn." Although the language into which
Burns finally modulates inevitably appears to the Scot as if it
ought to be read with a Scottish accent, it is often, on the
printed page, indistinguishable from the poetic diction of much
mid-eighteenth century poetry. In his use of this convention,
Burns surpasses his masters—a remarkable feat, in view of
Coila's own statement:

> 'Thou canst not learn, nor can I show,
> To paint with Thomson's landscape glow;
> Or wake the bosom-melting throe
>   With Shenstone's art;
> Or pour, with Gray, the moving flow
>   Warm on the heart.'

The language of "The Vision" is successful because the poem
is written in "Standard Habbie," with all the vernacular and
national associations of that measure; had he employed heroic
couplets or neo-Spenserian stanzas, Burns would not have been
nearly so impressive. Again, the reader remembers the fine
Scots of the opening stanzas right to the end; "meliorate the
plain" and "embryotic trace | Of rustic bard" exist in the same
context as "the thresher's weary flingin-tree" and "heard the
restless rattons squeak | About the riggin"; both kinds of
language seem perfectly in place, both are related to Burns's
central experience. It is the extraordinarily vivid picture of
his Muse that makes the work seem such an impressive statement of a poet's relation to his country and its traditions:
surely, despite all literary sources and parallels, Burns must
actually have *seen* Coila standing before him. Towards the end
of "The Vision" the diction is not so much Scots English as
English English[92] revitalised by the form and by our memories

---

[92] It is surely significant that a very high proportion of the parallel passages
cited by Ritter (pp. 123 ff.) come from Thomson and Beattie—Scotsmen writing

of the poem's beginning; yet, in its cumulative effect, it is as poetry equal to all but the best of Burns's writing in Scots. "The Vision" is fashioned out of the same preoccupations and conflicts that underlie Burns's early lyrics and epistles— the war between poetry and prudence, the scorn of money-chasing, the challenge of ungovernable instincts (for example, he implies that he wrote poetry to soothe his passions),[93] the riddle of riches and poverty; but these topics are illuminated by an understanding of politics and history which he never surpasses elsewhere. It is the very summit of Burns's work as a national poet—symbolised, not only by Coila, but by "the Genius of this Land," a concept which perhaps shows him thinking along the same lines as an earlier Scot, Buchanan, with his *"ingenium praefervidum Scotorum."* "The Vision" displays an emotional and intellectual awareness of historical processes that can be paralleled among his contemporaries only in the work of William Blake. I should say that Blake is the greater poet—in some respects, though not in all; one would never go to Blake for "manners-painting strains." Only our twentieth-century respect for the irrational and the supra-rational makes us feel that the mystic is *bound* to be a better poet than the realist. In this one magnificent but little-read poem, Burns attains something of Blake's visionary insight, though by very different means.

in English. Again, Ramsay's English poem, "The Vision," has made a considerable contribution to Burns's. Thus, if Burns almost passes beyond "Scots English" into "English English" itself, his models are still predominantly Scottish. This may well be another reason why the poem is so successful: even at its most rhetorical, it never goes beyond the bounds of what it was natural for eighteenth-century Scotsmen to attempt.

[93] Duan II, st. xvii, l. 6.

VII

Conflict of Tongues

"THE BRIGS OF AYR"[1] is the first major poem examined in this book that was composed after the publication of the Kilmarnock edition. It shows Burns more completely in the grip of his legend than in any previous work. In some of the Kilmarnock poems, notably in the more rhetorical passages of "The Cotter's Saturday Night," Burns had yielded to the stereotyped preconceptions of an imagined audience; but now, even before his departure for Edinburgh, he was experimenting with heroic couplets—a measure in which he was never thoroughly at home. Not that everything he wrote under neo-classic influences was bad; I have already pointed out that much of his best work is shot through with English, a favourite pattern being the movement from a vernacular or "particular" beginning to an English or generalised conclusion. And we shall see later that some of the very best of the songs contain few distinctively Scottish words. Since this whole matter was settled by Sir Walter Scott a hundred and fifty years ago, it is difficult to understand why so many modern critics have persisted in denying any excellence to Burns's work in English. Writing in the *Quarterly Review* for February 1809, Scott argues that the poems composed entirely in English are poor stuff indeed, but that

. . . the sublimer passages of his 'Saturday Night,' 'Vision,' and other poems of celebrity, always swell into the language of classic English poetry. But although in these flights he naturally and almost unavoidably assumed the dialect of Milton and Shakespeare, he never seems to have been completely at his ease when he had not the power of descending at pleasure into that which was familiar to his ear, and to his habits. In the one case, his use of the English was voluntary, and for a short time; but when assumed as a primary and indispensable rule of com-

---

[1] H. & H., I. 200 (393). For phonetics, see below, p. 357.

position, the comparative penury of rhimes [*sic*], and the want of a thousand emphatic words which his habitual acquaintance with the Scottish supplied, rendered his expression confined and embarrassed.[2]

In "The Brigs of Ayr," Burns still had "the power of descending at pleasure into that which was familiar to his ear"—but the poem nevertheless does not exhibit the singleness and coherence of, say, "The Cotter's Saturday Night." It was suggested by Fergusson's "Mutual Complaint of Plainstanes and Causey," "The Ghaists: a Kirkyard Eclogue" and "A Drink Eclogue," and perhaps by Allan Ramsay's poem "The Twa Books," which contains the lines:

> For as auld-fashion'd as I look,
> May be I am the better Book.[3]

Burns's couplets sometimes turn into triplets, the third line being an alexandrine. Most critics complain of the extreme roughness of the versification, and certainly there are many redundant syllables; alexandrines occur apart from the triplets; and there is little variation in the placing of the caesura. But there are many good individual lines, in both Scots and English, such as, in English:

> His manly leg with garter-tangle bound . . .

in English, thinly disguised:

> And thack and rape secure the toil-won crap

and, the following line, in Scots:

> Potatoe bings are snuggèd up frae skaith . . .[4]

The reader should be conscious of the same speaking voice throughout, with the English passages pronounced in a distinctly Scottish way.

[2] [Sir Walter Scott], review of Cromek's *Reliques of Burns*, in *Quarterly Review*, (1809), 30.

[3] Cp. Ritter, pp. 151–4; H. & H., I. 394; Craigie, p. 87. H. & H. point out that the pentameter couplet was early naturalised in Scotland; it was used in Blind Harry's "Wallace" (*c.*1460); in "The Three Priests of Peebles" (*c.*1500); and in Gavin Douglas's translation of the *Aeneid* (1513). To Burns, however, the measure seems to have represented an essentially literary and "ambitious" mode. As Craigie says, "it is one that he is given to using in his later work, and its employment here, as well as the general style of the poem, may indicate that Burns was beginning to aim at different literary effects from those in which he had hitherto shown his strength." [4] H. & H., I. 209 *ad init.*; 201 *med.*

The work begins with a somewhat conventional dedication to his friend and patron John Ballantine, who was Dean of Guild in Ayr in 1786 and therefore one of those primarily responsible for municipal building.[5] Burns here puts forward the familiar idealised conception of his rôle as the inspired bard "nurst in the peasant's lowly shed,"[6] determined to be the reverse of servile to his benefactor. He would display simple, unaffected gratitude—and nothing more. In complete and violent contrast to the first twenty-four lines of conventional English diction, there follows[7] a more distinctly Scottish passage descriptive of the autumnal landscape, which contains, as Ritter points out,[8] more reminiscences of Thomson's *Seasons* than perhaps any other work of Burns. Commenting on one of these parallels, Hately Waddell wrote : ". . . it will be seen that Thomson's accumulated outline does not contain one twentieth part of the activity and vital force of Burns's picture."[9] This judgment can be extended to the other borrowings too.

Ayr, the market-town and local centre in which the poem is set, is placed in relation to its economic hinterland by means of Burns's description of the surrounding countryside, and the scene is further particularised by means of a fine picture of streets and foreshore at two o'clock in the morning :

> The drowsy Dungeon-Clock had number'd two,
> And Wallace Tower had sworn the fact was true ;
> The tide-swoln Firth, with sullen-sounding roar,
> Through the still night dash'd hoarse along the shore ;
> All else was hush'd as Nature's closèd e'e ;
> The silent moon shone high o'er tower and tree ;
> The chilly frost, beneath the silver beam,
> Crept, gently-crusting, o'er the glittering stream.[10]

[5] C. & W., i. 419 n.   [6] H. & H., i. 200 *ad fin.*
[7] *Op. cit.*, p. 201 *med.*   [8] Ritter, pp. 151–4.
[9] Hately Waddell, p. 93, quoted in Ritter, *loc. cit.* A few of the parallels in Thomson's *Seasons* are to be found in "Spring," ll. 314 ff. ; "Autumn," ll. 330 ff., 360 ff., 1172 ff., 1217 ff. ; "Winter," ll. 94 ff., 990 ff. Ritter also notes echoes of Pope's version of "The Merchant's Tale," ll. 620 ff. and 460 ff. ; of "Windsor Forest," l. 330 ; and "Rape of the Lock," iii. 55 ff. Burns's conclusion (H. & H., i. 209) is so reminiscent of *The Faerie Quene*, vii. vii. 28–31, that Ritter thinks Burns may have come across at least this part of Spenser *before* acquiring a volume in Apr. 1787. The Burns passage also resembles Ovid's *Metamorphoses* ii. 27 ff., which the poet could have come across in Addison's translation.
[10] H. & H., i. 202 *ad fin.*

The passage in which Burns now describes the spirits swishing through the air is in itself a highly satisfying combination of sights and sounds, as in

> The clanging sugh of whistling wings is heard. . . .[11]

No matter how traditional it may be, the imagery rarely sinks to the level of cliché or stereotype, and at its best it is as simple and effective as Chaucer's, as, for example :

> Swift as the gos drives on the wheeling hare. . . .[12]

As always, Burns feels compelled to introduce humorous qualifications into his picture of the supernatural. In "The Brigs of Ayr," these are of the self-deprecating sort, as befits the rôle he has assumed of the Bard in a Rational Society. Sometimes their peculiar mixture of arch inflation of mood and mock-modesty grates on the ear, as in the line :

> That bards are second-sighted is nae joke.[13]

Burns knows he is not really second-sighted and that Ballantine is aware of it too—but how cheap the line seems when set beside the real insight into social processes that underlies "The Vision," or the creative imagination of a William Blake !

"The Brigs of Ayr" marks an advance towards the poetical tolerance of views and attitudes which Burns normally opposed. In "The Holy Fair," as we have seen, Burns's satire envelops not only the Auld Lichts, but also the New, while positive value resides in the sheer life and exuberance of the crowd. In "The Brigs of Ayr," a gentler comic vision, itself owing much to English and Scots-English sentimentalism, enables the reader to sympathise with both the Auld and the New Brig, with both tradition and progress. The effect in its own way is not unlike T. S. Eliot's reconciliation of Cavalier and Puritan in *Little Gidding* :

> These men, and those who opposed them
> And those whom they opposed
> Accept the constitution of silence
> And are folded in a single party.[14]

---

[11] *Op. cit.*, i. 203 *ad init.*   [12] *Ibid.*
[13] *Op. cit.*, p. 203 *med.*   [14] III. 20–52.

The New Brig equates progress with the architecture of Robert Adam, whom the Town Council paid for a plan of the bridge, according to the Ayr Burgh accounts; and advancement is seen as identical with Reason, with anti-celibacy, with the mean between two extremes.[15] Reaction, on the other hand, is manifest in Gothic architecture, Roman Catholicism, the celibacy of nuns, and the Calvinist fanaticism of the later seventeenth century.

In reply the Auld Brig points out[16] that there is a great deal to be said for tradition too, and its criticism of the modern citizenry, of whom Ballantine was himself the representative, reads not unlike some of the shafts directed against the lairds in "The Twa Dogs":

> 'Nae langer rev'rend men, their country's glory,
> In plain braid Scots hold forth a plain, braid story;
> Nae langer thrifty citizens, an' douce,
> Meet owre a pint or in the council-house:
> But staumrel, corky-headed, graceless gentry,
> The herryment and ruin of the country;
> Men three-parts made by tailors and by barbers,
> Wha waste your weel-hain'd gear on damn'd New Brigs and
> harbours!'

It may even be an accident that Burns lets the New Brig have the last word. The bailies and ministers of religion of the past, it maintains, were far from being heroic figures. On the contrary, they were ignorant, stupid, and lacking in plain common sense. After this sudden and rather arbitrary support for the forces of social advance, Burns seems to tire of the poem, as Craigie notes:[17]

> What farther clish-ma-claver might been said,
> What bloody wars, if Sprites had blood to shed,
> No man can tell. . . .[18]

In lieu of a genuine reconciliation he produces from nowhere a fairy band dancing strathspeys and singing Scottish songs. There is quite a procession—the Genius of the Stream in front,

---

[15] H. & H., I. 203, 206.
[17] Craigie, p. 87.
[16] *Op. cit.*, p. 204 *ad init.*, pp. 205, 207.
[18] H. & H., I. p. 208, *ad init.*

followed by the allegorical figures of Female Beauty, Spring, Rural Joy, Summer, Plenty, Autumn, Winter, Hospitality, Courage, Benevolence, Learning, and Worth. With consummate tact, Burns associates the last four with some of the local gentry referred to in "The Vision," and he ends on a note of general harmony when "white-rob'd Peace" bequeaths to "rustic Agriculture" :

> The broken, iron instruments of death :
> At sight of whom our Sprites forgat their kindling wrath.

Though one must admit "The Brigs of Ayr" contains some very fine passages, such as the actual altercation between the two bridges, it is what Burns himself would have called "mixtie-maxtie," lacking in design and general proportion. It is interesting as demonstrating the increasing tolerance and breadth of Burns's ideas and as anticipating the general tenor of his later lines on "The Solemn League and Covenant" :[19]

> The Solemn League and Covenant
> Now brings a smile, now brings a tear.
> But sacred Freedom, too, was theirs :
> If thou'rt a slave, indulge thy sneer.

And, once more, it illustrates Burns's fondness for extravagant personification as a mode of poetic thought, and embodies an experiment with supernatural machinery that is as much a failure as "The Vision" is a success.

It is, of course, true that Burns's irruption into Edinburgh and his high-pressure Border and Highland tours involved him in considerable mental stress. He assumed a deliberate disguise in order to storm his way into high society at the same time as he was seriously tempted by the world of Hugh Blair, Dr Moore's letters, and Clarinda's sentimental eroticism. In politics, he was a strange mixture of Pittite and Jacobite ; in aesthetic sensibility, he did his best to cultivate the correct responses to noble, picturesque and romantic prospects ; in sexual matters, there was an almost complete cleavage between "spirit" and "body," except that "spirit" here would seem decidedly sensual to most Platonic lovers.[20] Mrs MacLehose

---

[19] ii. 258 (446).
[20] When Robert Anderson taxed him with being more learned than he pre-

represented "soul," while May Cameron and Jenny Clow took care of physical desire.[21] And in the all-important matter of language, the gulf between Scots and English gradually widened. In "The Brigs of Ayr," and even at times in "The Vision" itself, there are occasions when it approaches a complete dissociation of tongues. Moreover, so far as poetic ambition was concerned—and this is indicated, among other things, by the symbolic posturings of his tours—he desperately tried to be the *wrong* sort of National Bard. Already in Ayrshire he had become one type of Scottish laureate; later, in Dumfriesshire, he was to develop into another, the collector and refurbisher of his country's songs. But in Edinburgh and at intervals afterwards he tried to be the Orpheus of the New Town, and of all that the New Town represented—an ambition which for him meant intellectual suicide and spiritual death. Only a few songs dating from 1787–8, the first trickle of what was in later years to become a flood, are of supreme poetic merit. Some of these will be briefly considered later, along with the rest of his lyrical output.

In "A Winter Night"[22] the harmony that once existed between the Scots and English sides of Burns's consciousness appears temporarily destroyed, and yet the extraordinary thing is that the poem almost comes off, in spite of its artificiality. The first six stanzas, in the familiar Standard Habbie measure, make use of a fairly generous sprinkling of distinctively Scottish words and the third, in particular, is noteworthy for its moving and vivid picture of animals out in the storm:

tended to be, Burns frankly admitted the deception: "It was . . . a part of the machinery, as he called it, of his poetical character to pass for an illiterate plough-man who wrote from pure inspiration. When I pointed out some evident traces of poetical imitation in his verses, privately, he readily acknowledged his obligations, and even admitted the advantages he enjoyed in poetic composition from the *copia verborum*, the command of phraseology, which the knowledge and use of the English and Scottish dialects afforded him; but in company he would not suffer his pretensions to pure inspiration to be challenged, and it was seldom done where it might be supposed to affect the success of the subscription for his *Poems*." (R. Anderson to J. Currie, 28 Sep. 1799, printed in *Burns Chronicle*, 1925, p. 12).

[21] For the correspondence with Clarinda, see C. & W., II. 215 ff.; for May Cameron and Jenny Clow, see Snyder, p. 142 *et passim*, and J. De Lancey Ferguson, "Burns and Jenny Clow," in *Modern Language Notes*, XLVIII (1933), 168–72.

[22] I. 225 (404).

List'ning the doors an' winnocks rattle,
I thought me on the ourie cattle,
Or silly sheep, wha bide this brattle
      O' winter war,
And thro the drift, deep-lairing, sprattle
      Beneath a scaur.

At night, just as in "The Vision," "still-crowding thoughts" rose in his soul, and a slow and plaintive strain stole on his ear, taking the form of an English ode of the type written by Collins, Gray or Thomas Warton. Craigie says that "the ode proper is a paraphrase of Shakespeare's 'Blow, blow, thou winter wind,' with touches from *King Lear*, and its piled-up phrases are much less effective than the simple language of his model"; but Ritter maintains (quite rightly, I think) that it was influenced by Shakespeare only in a rather general way. There are detailed reminiscences and apparent echoes of various passages in Goldsmith, Thomson, Young and Blair.[23] In any case, it is a restatement of the themes of "Man was made to Mourn" and "To a Mouse"; there cannot be the slightest doubt that in "A Winter Night" animal suffering and human woes are regarded as misfortunes of essentially the same sort, and therefore as equally deserving of pity. Again, the extremely artificial and conventional diction of the second part is used to push the analysis of society in the same direction as in "The Vision." Burns indicates the social origin of crime (a common idea of the Enlightenment), and the economic reality behind the surface of eighteenth-century life, namely that it is

      . . . the simple, rustic hind,
      Whose toil upholds the glitt'ring show. . . .

This idea had already appeared in Scottish poetry in Fergusson's eclogue, "The Ghaists"—

      . . . lat the rich chiels be,
      Pamper'd at ease by ither's industry[24]

----

[23] Craigie, p. 88; Ritter, pp. 160–6. The introductory stanzas seem at first sight to be based on faint but unmistakable recollections of Gavin Douglas, *En.*, Prol. VII; but Ritter, who discusses the possibility (p. 161), is convinced that Burns did not know Douglas in 1786. But he did know him late in 1790, for the epigraph to "Tam o' Shanter" comes from Douglas.

[24] Ll. 71–2.

—which merely proves the continuity of radical thought, and
the fact that similar minds have similar insights, rather than
any plagiarism on Burns's part.

Burns's sensibility next expands to encompass

> . . . Maiden-Innocence a prey
> To love-pretending snares . . .[25]

in a passage similar to the tenth stanza of "The Cotter's
Saturday Night," though slightly more convincing to a modern
reader because its context of suffering extends throughout the
entire natural and social worlds. Burns enunciates the ethical
principle that

> the selfish aim,
> To bless himself alone,

is fundamentally evil, and at its most reprehensible when it
involves the sufferings of another, "beneath Love's noble
name." In the ode's last stanza, complete bathos is reached
with "chinky wall" and "drifty heap" and—

> Affliction's sons are brothers in distress;
> A brother to relieve, how exquisite the bliss![26]

That is the end of the ode, but there are two further stanzas to
complete the anti-climax; and these are so abysmally bad
that they jingle like a motto. Nor do the values they preach
justify the animal suffering with which the poem began:

> The heart benevolent and kind
> The most resembles God.[27]

If "A Winter Night" expresses set Burnsian attitudes in a
highly rhetorical manner, the "Address to Edinburgh"[28] fails
primarily because it is artistically insincere, and only in the
second place because of the lumbersome artificiality of its
diction. Indeed, the fourth stanza describing the women of
Edinburgh is quite a good example of conventional social
compliment, while, in the fifth, the treatment of the Castle is a
not unpleasing imitation of the contemporary pre-Romantic
style:

[25] H. & H., i. 228 *ad init.* [26] *Loc. cit., ad fin.*
[27] *Op. cit.*, p. 229 *med.*
[28] "Edina! Scotland's darling seat . . .": i. 239 (408).

There, watching high the least alarms,
Thy rough, rude fortress gleams afar ;
Like some bold vet'ran, grey in arms,
And mark'd with many a seamy scar. . . .

But it was perhaps no longer possible, as it had been in the
days of Dunbar's "London, thou art of townes *A per se*,"[29] to
commend a city's wealth and beauty without also revealing
something of the squalor of its "charter'd streets," as Blake
was shortly to do. In this address, Burns tries to flatter the
powers that be, to suppress all that he knows about "catch-the-
plack," and to combine a sentimental Jacobitism with practical
support of the Union, as in the sixth stanza :

Alas, how chang'd the times to come !
Their royal name low in the dust !
Their hapless race wild-wand'ring roam !
Tho' rigid Law cries out : ' 'Twas just !'

It is hardly surprising, therefore, that the poem is not an
artistic success.

Nor is it altogether unexpected to find that many of Burns's
compliments to the aristocracy sound utterly hollow and unreal today. This holds good not only of poems written entirely
in English, such as the "Verses intended to be written below a
Noble Earl's Picture,"[30] but also of some works written almost
wholly in Scots, like the epistle "To the Guidwife of Wauchope
House."[31] Not a single one of this entire group of poems is
worth reading today for its own sake, although some of them
have a limited importance for the historian of Burns's attitudes
inasmuch as they suggest certain conclusions about the development of his mind, or increase the force of others derived from
a perusal of the prose correspondence.

For example, the political poems of the Edinburgh period
and the years immediately following are predominantly
Jacobite and anti-Hanoverian. Burns's nationalism was never
more passionate than at this time ; but, under the influence of

---

[29] For the attribution, cp. esp. R. L. Mackie, *King James IV of Scotland*, Edinburgh 1958, pp. 95–6, 281–2.
[30] "Whose is that noble, dauntless brow ? . . .": II. 217 (412).
[31] II. 104 (364) ; below, pp. 206–7.

Holyrood house, the Castle and the persons and places he visited when on tour, it was considerably less democratic and more backward-looking than it was to become in the seventeen-nineties. As examples one may perhaps take the lines "On Seeing the Royal Palace at Stirling in Ruins"[32] or the "Birth-day Ode for 31st December 1787."[33] It is surely not without significance that, though Jacobite ideas produced some of the finest lines Burns ever penned, notably in the songs, they produced many others so appallingly bad that they can hardly be quoted without a blush, such as the second stanza of the "Address to Wm. Tytler, Esq., of Woodhouselee" :[34]

Tho' something like moisture conglobes in my eye—
Let no one misdeem me disloyal!
A poor friendless wand'rer may well claim a sigh—
Still more, if that wand'rer were royal.

Burns's motive in writing many of these thoroughly bad poems seems to have been the desire to please refined and educated women. In order to do this, he had to adopt, for the time being at least, the modes of feeling of a higher class than his own. The "Lament of Mary Queen of Scots, on the Approach of Spring"[35] is a perfect example of the sentimental *boudoir* poem : as soon as he composed it, he sent off copies to Mrs Dunlop and Mrs Graham of Fintry, and a few months later to Lady Winifred Constable and Mrs MacLehose[36]—a sure indication that he had their taste in mind when writing such lines as (in the first stanza) :

Now Nature hangs her mantle green
On every blooming tree. . . .

and (in the fifth) :

The weeping blood in woman's breast
Was never known to thee;
Nor th' balm that draps on wounds of woe
Frae woman's pitying e'e.

---

[32] Aug. 1787 : II. 244 (434).   [33] II. 157 (388).
[34] II. 107 (365).   [35] 1790 : I. 268 (425).
[36] R. B. [to Mrs Dunlop], 6 Jun. 1790, in *Letters*, II. 21 : "To you, and your young ladies, I particularly dedicate the following Scots Stanzas—Queen Mary's Lament." See also his letters to Mrs Graham of Fintry, Dr John Moore, Lady Constable, and Mrs Maclehose, in *Letters*, II. 25, 58, 73, and 101.

But when Burns was able to let his sense of humour play on refined concepts and forms, the result was sometimes as charming as the delightfully artificial and derivative "Clarinda, Mistress of my Soul,"[37] with its consistently worked-out image-pattern of sun, time, night, eyes, beams and planets. And if he were genuinely struck by the personality of a girl from a higher circle than his own, such as "Miss Cruickshank, a very young lady," he could produce lines as charming as the second stanza of "Beauteous Rosebud, young and gay."[38]

One ruling-class habit of mind which Burns resolutely tried to share was the cult of the picturesque. Not only did he make prose notes about "noble prospects" and "romantic ruins," but he wrote a surprising number of indifferent verses on similar topics, shot through with reminiscences of Thomson, Gray, Young, Beattie, Goldsmith and other popular eighteenth century writers.[39] "On Scaring some Water-Fowl in Loch Turit," "Verses written with a Pencil at Taymouth," "Castle Gordon" (a song), and the Scots-English "Humble Petition of Bruar Water"[40] are some of the best-known instances. Interestingly enough, Burns's indebtedness in his "high English" poems to neo-classic writers for particular lines and ideas is no greater than his reliance on Scottish or even English writers in those of his works in which Scots predominates. In both types of poem he uses his source-material in fundamentally the same way : the stock of inherited diction is, as it were, a quarry from which new buildings can be made at will. The chief difference is that in the best poems he really manages to emulate his models by pressing their phraseology into the service of his own individual conception of reality, while in his failures he falls far short of the originals.

His references to the picturesque have many images of "tumbling floods" and "hermits' mossy cell[s]," of "howling

---

[37] III. 39 (334).   [38] I. 292 (447). See below, p. 289.

[39] Ritter, pp. 172–9. For Burns's attempts to feel correctly about romantic scenery, see *Journal of the Border Tour*, in *R. B., his Associates*, ed. Fitzhugh, pp. 114–16; and *Journal of the Highland Tour*, in C. & W., II. 149–51. Ritter (pp. 172–3) points out that "Verses written with a Pencil at Taymouth" derive from Addison, "Letter from Italy," and Dyer, "Grongar Hill," at the same time as they look forward to Byron, *Childe Harold's Pilgrimage*, I. xv ff, xxx.

[40] I. 299 (450), 301 (451) ; II. 60 (349) ; I. 295 (449).

blasts whistling in rocky caves," of "groaning trees" that
"untimely shed their locks," of "leafless forests" and "hollow
caves." Though the result is mostly fustian, he is still able to
find a good line here and there. Taken as a whole, the neo-
classic poems of 1787 look forward to Burns's more successful
use of English diction and imagery in the Revolutionary era.
As such, they are not entirely retrograde; they have their
positive as well as their negative aspects. The satirical "Ode,
sacred to the Memory of Mrs Oswald of Auchencruive"[41] of
1789, a product of the Ellisland period, may be taken as
transitional in mood between the faintly servile English poems
of 1787, and the "Ode for General Washington's Birthday" [42]
of 1794. In spite of the rhetorical energy which it generates,
the ode on Mrs Oswald is really little more than a pompous
overflow of personal spleen. Burns does not quite succeed in
making the "wither'd beldam" into a symbol of upper-class
arrogance, while the final section—the "Epode"—is little
more than a refurbishing of the medieval "Erthe upon Erthe"
theme:

> And are they of no more avail,
> Ten thousand glittering pounds a-year?
> In other worlds can Mammon fail,
> Omnipotent as he is here?
> O bitter mockery of the pompous bier!
> While down the wretched vital part is driven!
> The cave-lodg'd beggar, with a conscience clear,
> Expires in rags, unknown, and goes to Heaven

From October 1786 to the end of his life—that is, throughout the period during which he turned out English and semi-
English odes and other poems he hoped would be pleasing to
refined taste—Burns went on writing in his earlier Scottish
strain. One example is that fine occasional poem the "Address
to the Toothache,"[43] which may have been written at any time
between the first Edinburgh visit and 1795. In addition, Burns
composed a number of late epistles and satires in something
approaching the old vein. The first of these, the epistle "To

[41] I. 260 (420).   [42] II. 171 (393).
[43] II. 51 (342). Some authorities have placed it as early as 1786, in the period
between the Kilmarnock Edition and the poet's departure for Edinburgh.

Major Logan,"[44] should perhaps have been considered earlier, since it is roughly contemporaneous with "Tam Samson's Elegy."[45] It is a fine instance of Burns's tendency, in a poem centred upon a particular person, to draw his imagery from the occupation or special interest of his protagonist. Since the great hobby of "thairm-inspirin, rattlin Willie" was fiddle-music, Burns expressed himself in the technical terms of that art, as in the fifth and seventh stanzas:

> May still your life from day to day,
> Nae *lente largo* in the play
> But *allegretto forte* gay,
>   Harmonious flow,
> A sweeping, kindling, bauld strathspey—
>   *Encore*! *Bravo*! . . .

> My hand-wal'd curse keep hard in chase
> The harpy, hoodock, purse-proud race,
> Wha count on poortith as disgrace!
>   Their tuneless hearts,
> May fireside discords jar a bass
>   To a' their parts!

Though poetically of little worth, the epistle "To the Guid-wife of Wauchope House"[46] is noteworthy as evincing Burns's desire to appear as the national bard in the Edinburgh years, and as adding some biographical details to his own account of poetic inspiration:

> But still the elements o' sang
> In formless jumble, right an' wrang,
> Wild floated in my brain;
> Till on that hairst I said before,
> My partner in the merry core,
> She rous'd the forming strain. . . .
>   I fir̀ed, inspir̀ed,
>   At ev'ry kindling keek,
>   But, bashing and dashing,
>   I fear̀ed ay to speak.

In the second stanza he claims that even in early adolescence his greatest desire was to do something for his native country:

[44] II. 99 (363).   [45] Above, p. 122–3.   [46] 1787: II. 104 (364).

> E'en then, a wish (I mind its pow'r),
> A wish that to my latest hour
> Shall strongly heave my breast,
> That I for poor auld Scotland's sake
> Some usefu' plan or book could make,
> Or sing a sang at least.

These lines, however, are insufficient to counteract the sentimentality and false *bonhomie* of the rest of the poem; indeed, they contain one faintly maudlin touch—"poor auld Scotland's sake"—that is all their own.

The epistle "To Hugh Parker,"[47] in octosyllabic couplets, presents a delightful picture of the interior at Ellisland, and another of his mare Jenny Geddes, while that "To James Tennant of Glenconner,"[48] in the same measure, shows him reacting against the disguises of the Edinburgh interlude. Though it is an imperfect and rather ill-balanced poem, it has some good lines on Adam Smith and Thomas Reid, two of Burns's favourite philosophers, that reveal him perfectly at home with the latest intellectual crazes:

> To common sense they now appeal—
> What wives and wabsters see and feel![49]

There follows a characteristic trick that looks back to 1785—a mock-assumption of orthodox Calvinism: Burns has become "sae cursed douse" that he sits in the kitchen, praying and pondering and reading Bunyan, Brown and Boston

> Till by an' by, if I haud on,
> I'll grunt a reàl gospel groan . . .
> Sae shortly you shall see me bright,
> A burning an' a shining light.[50]

In the next paragraph he returns to the mood of the "Epistle to a young Friend," assuming the morality of the typical Scottish philistine. Finally, he wishes Glenconner "ay eneugh o' needfu' clink"—enough, but not too much. The attitude to money is rather different from that of some earlier epistles; at bottom, it is surprisingly like the arguments "Centum per Centum" would use to justify his own cautious calculation. Of

---

[47] 1788: II. 116 (370).   [48] 1789: II. 124 (375).
[49] H. & H., II. 124 *ad fin.*   [50] *Op. cit.*, p. 125 *med.*

course, Burns is here being rhetorical in the traditional sense
of that word—he is suiting his discourse to its recipient, whose
values were nothing if not conventional; but the mood is
paralleled in purely personal verses like the song "I hae a
wife o' my ain,"[51] so that perhaps we are entitled to conclude
that after his Edinburgh visit he was at least as prone to express
middle-class and lower middle-class values as during the
Mauchline years.[52]

The "Epistle to Dr Blacklock,"[53] also dating from 1789,
is quite worthy of a place beside the verse epistles of four years
earlier—that is, if we leave out of account the bathetic final
stanza, in which Burns was tasteless enough to call his
correspondent "my guid auld cockie." There are two fine
stanzas—the second and third—on Robert Heron, devoted to
humorous fantasy rather than to the realistic depiction of
character, and a comic homily on economic necessity, the real
theme of the poem. In the seventh stanza, thoughts of his own
poverty give rise (five months after the summoning of the
States General in Paris) to a statement uniting the concepts of
fraternity and social equality—

> But why should ae man better fare,
> And a' men brithers?

but, in the eighth, he can see no way out except to follow
certain conventional adages:

> Come, firm Resolve, take thou the van,
> Thou stalk o' carl-hemp in man!
> And let us mind, faint heart ne'er wan
> A lady fair:
> Wha does the utmost that he can
> Will whyles do mair.

These traditional proverbs lead on quite naturally to a statement of Burns's own that has itself become proverbial. Taken
in isolation, or mouthed by red-faced businessmen at Burns
suppers, it sounds unbelievably complacent; but in its context
of somewhat pessimistic resignation, it is both moving and true:

[51] III. 109 (381). Below, p. 283.
[52] But there is some evidence for the view that the poem was written at Mossgiel; cp. C. & W., III. 76–8 nn.   [53] II. 128 (377).

To make a happy fireside clime
          To weans and wife,
That's the true pathos and sublime
          Of human life.

Yet it is divided by only a hair's breadth from the smug
materialism of the second half of the epistle "To Tennant."
The best of all these later epistles in Scots, that addressed
"To Colonel De Peyster,"[54] will be briefly discussed later; in
the meantime, it is only necessary to note that it contains two
fine stanzas which express yet another of Burns's many moods
—a strange marriage between his revolutionary speculations
("la carrière ouverte aux talents") and a much older outlook
that is strongly reminiscent of Dunbar :

          O, what a canty warld were it,
          Would pain and care and sickness spare it,
          And Fortune favor worth and merit
                    As they deserve,
          And ay a rowth—roast-beef and claret !—
                    Syne, wha wad starve ?

          Dame Life, tho' fiction out may trick her,
          And in paste gems and frippery deck her,
          Oh ! flickering, feeble, and unsicker
                    I've found her still :
          Ay wavering, like the willow-wicker,
                    'Tween good and ill ![55]

Turning to the later satires in Scottish measures, one finds
that neither the burlesque "Lament for the Absence of William
Creech, Publisher,"[56] nor "The Fête Champêtre"[57] (which is
semi-political, and, since it was meant to go to the tune of
Gillicrankie, is at least half a song) rises above the level of the
mediocre, except in the delightful reference to Boswell and
Johnson in the latter poem :

[54] II. 139 (380); below, pp. 219–20.
[55] Cp. Dunbar's "Lament for the Makaris," st. iv, ll. 1–3 : "No stait in erd
heir standis sickir; | As with the wynd wavis the wickir, | Wavis this warldis
vanite. . . ." This seems one of the few deliberate echoes of Dunbar in the whole
of Burns; he may have read the *Ever Green* version.
[56] II. 53 (344).   [57] II. 174 (394).

Or him wha led o'er Scotland a'
The meikle Ursa-Major. . . .[58]

And it is perhaps because it is set to the rhythms of that rollicking tune *Come rouse, Brother Sportsmen* that "The Kirk's Alarm"[59]
seems so much less subtle than the great ecclesiastical satires of
Burns's *annus mirabilis*—a fact immediately apparent whenever
one compares the handling of William Fisher in "Holy Willie's
Prayer" with the seventeenth stanza of "The Kirk's Alarm" :

Holy Will ! Holy Will !
There was wit i' your skull,
When ye pilfer'd the alms o' the poor :
The timmer is scant,
When ye're taen for a saunt
Wha should swing in a rape for an hour—
Holy Will !
Ye should swing in a rape for an hour.

The later Scottish epistles and satires[60] are on the whole
worse than similar pieces dating from before the end of 1786,
and few of them are greatly superior to the best English poems
of the same sort which Burns composed after 1787. By "best
English poems," I mean here a few passages in the two epistles
"To Robert Graham of Fintry," "New Year's Day, 1791," and
the epistle "From Esopus to Maria,"[61] written after the
quarrel with Mrs Riddell. The fact that much of his non-
lyrical work in Scots dating from this time was almost as
insipid as his English experiments is one more point against the
view that Burns *always* wrote badly in English and *always* well
in Scots. There is, surely, very little to choose between the
passages below :

[58] Cp. the remark attributed to Boswell's wife, to the effect that she had seen
many a bear led by a man, but never (until she saw Boswell and Johnson together)
a man led by a bear. [59] II. 30 (324).
[60] Excluding the Election Ballads, on which see below, pp.251–6.
[61] I. 271 (427) ; II. 119 (371), 64 (352), 66 (353). The second of these ("When
Nature her great master-piece design'd") is probably (H. & H., II. 372) the piece
referred to in Burns's letter of 16 Sept. 1788 to [Margaret Chalmers] (*Letters*, I. 258) :
"I very lately . . . wrote a poem, not in imitation, but in the manner of Pope's
Moral Epistles. It is only a short essay, just to try the strength of my Muse's
pinion in that way. . . . I have likewise been laying the foundation of some pretty
large Poetic works : how the superstructure will come on I leave to that great
maker and marrer of projects—TIME." The last sentence quoted throws a good
deal of light on the motivation of these "English English" works.

May bliss domestic smooth his private path;
Give energy to life; and soothe his latest breath,
With many a filial tear circling the bed of death![62]

And Auchenbay, I wish him joy;
If he's a parent, lass or boy,
May he be dad and Meg the mither
Just five-and-forty years thegither!
And no forgetting wabster Charlie,
I'm tauld he offers very fairly.[63]

The one is just as pedestrian, as lacking in any spark of true creative fire, as the other; and they may be taken as representative of the worst of which the later Burns was capable.

But there was one kind of English, the rhetoric of the Kirk and the language of the Metrical Psalms, that was usually able to inspire Burns to a high pitch of excellence. The best satire he wrote after 1787 was "A new Psalm for the Chapel of Kilmarnock,"[64] which links anti-Hanoverianism with anti-Calvinism. The single Scotticism of the last verse ("kens") seems perfectly natural—for the English of Presbyterian eloquence was just as truly national as the vernacular itself: consequently, it would be quite logical to classify "A New Psalm" as a Scottish poem. At this point the distinction between "Scots" and "English" as linguistic categories clearly has no validity. By and large, the English poems of 1787 and after reach out for a polite kind of universality which was the wrong kind for Burns; as we shall see in the next chapter, some of their falsity was taken over into the genuinely universal poetry of the songs and other works directly inspired by the French Revolution.

A distinctly elegiac strain runs through one group of Burns's later poems in both Scots and English. Although the purely English elegies, like those on the deaths of Lord President Dundas and Sir James Hunter Blair and "On the late Miss Burnet of Monboddo,"[65] do not deserve any sort of detailed examination, the vernacular "Elegy on Captain Matthew

---

[62] "To Robert Graham of Fintry, Esq.": H. & H., I. 274 *med.*
[63] "To James Tennant of Glenconner": H. & H., II. 125–6.
[64] 1789: II. 162 (391).   [65] II. 221 (414), 218 (413), 224 (417).

Henderson, a Gentleman who held the Patent for his Honours immediately from Almighty God!"[66] ought certainly to be rescued from the obscurity into which it appears to have fallen. After Capt. Henderson's death in the last few days of November 1788, Burns had "composed an elegiac Stanza or two," but something came in his way, forcing him to give up "the design of an Elegy to his memory." When he came across "the fragment . . . among some old waste papers" in the summer of 1790, he decided to finish it, which he did on 23 Jul. 1790.[67]

The work is worthy of being considered as one of the greatest elegies to have been produced in the British Isles. It begins as quite a conventional piece in a tradition which goes right back to antiquity and which Wordsworth describes to perfection in *The Excursion*:

> The Poets, in their elegies and songs
> Lamenting the departed, call the groves,
> They call upon the hills and streams to mourn,
> And senseless rocks; nor idly; for they speak,
> In these their invocations, with a voice
> Obedient to the strong creative power
> Of human passion.[68]

No doubt Burns got the idea from Milton's *Lycidas* and Fergusson's "Elegy on the Death of Scots Music," but he succeeds in introducing personal variations of his own, fusing his own direct observation of natural scenes with reminiscences of Thomson, Gray, Beattie, Collins, Pope and Pomfret.[69] The result is a very moving tribute to a typical representative of the Burnsian ideal of the Honest Man.

This is a lament for a real death; yet, as Ritter notes, it begins in the manner of the Scottish mock elegy with a grotèsque image of the Devil dragging Death to his smithy and spreading ˅ his "auld sides" over the anvil to be dried and cudgelled like stock-fish. Nature's self shall mourn Matthew:

[66] I. 262 (423).
[67] Burns to Robert Cleghorn, 23 Jul. 1790, in *Letters*, II. 31.
[68] Bk. I, ll. 475–81.
[69] Alexander Grosart maintained that the "Elegy on Captain Matthew Henderson" is merely "a magnificent expansion of [Fergusson's] 'Elegy on the Death of Scots Music'," esp. in the third stanza. But Ritter (pp. 213–6) notes the long history of the convention, and a large number of 18th-cent. parallels.

By wood and wild,
Where, haply, Pity strays forlorn,
Frae man exil'd.

Groves well known to the dove are asked to mourn him, and so too are a large number of individual plants and animals. The reader's poetic response is awakened sometimes by the associations formed by the naming of objects like the "eldritch tower," the "cowslip cup," or "clam'ring craiks," and sometimes, as in the sixth and eighth stanzas, by a particularised or metaphorical description :

At dawn, when every grassy blade
Droops with a diamond at his head ;
At ev'n, when beans their fragrance shed
I' th' rustling gale ;
Ye maukins, whiddin through the glade ;
Come join my wail ! . . .

Mourn, sooty coots, and speckled teals ;
Ye fisher herons, watching eels ;
Ye duck and drake, wi' airy wheels
Circling the lake ;
Ye bitterns, till the quagmire reels,
Rair for his sake !

In these stanzas a satisfying unity is established between visual impressions and that aural music whose interplay of vowels and consonants delights such critics as Dame Edith Sitwell and Miss Keith ;[70] sight and sound are one, as it were. In the twelfth, thirteenth and fourteenth stanzas, the personified seasons and the sun, moon and stars are asked to mourn Henderson ; in the fifteenth, he is apostrophised as "the man ! the brother !" and his death is classically and archetypally identified with the crossing of an "unknown river." Since all of Burns is in the background of this elegy, it is not in the least surprising that the last stanza should have political and moral undertones, drawing its main effect from the sharp dichotomy of the plebeian's simple "turf" and the elaborate graves of the upper classes :

[70] Judged purely by deployment of the musical values of vowels and consonants, the second stanza is magnificent. It is surely one of the most verbally melodious stanzas in British—perhaps in any—literature. See Appendix I, § 7, below, p. 358.

> Go to your sculptur'd tombs, ye Great,
> In a' the tinsel trash o' state !
> But by thy honest turf I'll wait,
>   Thou man of worth !
> And weep the ae best fellow's fate
>   E'er lay in earth !

The quiet rumination of Gray's *Elegy* has taken on a Scottish tinge and become imbued with the Honest Man's indignation against his aristocratic opponents. Even at his most traditional, and when writing an elegy, Burns could not avoid all trace of social criticism. It is only his very worst poems that are completely innocuous.

"The Epitaph," which concludes the elegy proper, is only superficially divided from the sixteen stanzas that precede it. In reality, it develops all the democratic implications of "thy honest turf" and "Thou man of worth" until it becomes like the second half of a diptych : taken together, the two parts constitute the complete poem. To some minds it may appear as if "The Epitaph" negates the Elegy itself, but I am sure that such an effect was far from Burns's intention—or from the result actually achieved. There is, for Burns, no unbridgeable gulf between, on the one hand—

> Mourn him, thou Sun, great source of light !
> Mourn, Empress of the silent night !
> And, you, ye twinkling starnies bright
>   My Matthew mourn !
> For through your orbs he's taen his flight,
>   Ne'er to return,

and, on the other, Matthew's real human qualities, his bravery, intelligence ("For Matthew was a bright man"—shining, like the Sun that is asked to mourn him), kindness, sensibility, truth, and humour : all these qualities taken together constitute greatness, and greatness is scarce indeed. Nature may justly lament him because, one feels, such a man, though poor, is himself according to Nature. But the "unco guid" are specifically banished from the scene : they, as always, are most definitely *not* according to Nature :

If onie whiggish, whingin sot,
To blame poor Matthew dare, man ;
May dool and sorrow be his lot !
For Matthew was a rare man.

When one regards the Elegy and the Epitaph as two parts of a single unity, one realises that (just like Yeats's "In Memory of Major Robert Gregory," which may itself owe something to Burns's poem) the work "combines the majesty of traditional elegy with the simplicity of personal conversation."[71]

Summing up, one might perhaps hazard the generalisation that the poems written between, say, 1786 and 1790 tend to exhibit a dissociation of language that is not found in earlier works like "The Cotter's Saturday Night" and "The Jolly Beggars." My contention can best be illustrated from a comparison of "The Vision" and "A Winter Night." In the first poem, everything is as Sir Walter said it was. English is a "flight" from Scottish soil, but Burns remains at his ease because he was careful to reserve "the power of descending at pleasure into that which was familiar to his ear, and to his habits." In "A Winter Night," however, the separation between the first and the second half is so absolute that one feels they almost belong to two entirely different poems—a Scottish descriptive lyric, and a neo-classic ode. Once embarked upon the ode, the poet has, as it were, gone into orbit and denied himself all chance of re-entry into his native atmosphere. It is tempting to deduce a parallel "dissociation of sensibility," though not exactly of the kind Mr Eliot was describing when he coined that famous phrase : on the one hand, the refined and "literary" emotions of the Edinburgh gentry, their women, and their men of letters—on the other, the simpler and more homespun feelings of the peasantry. I am,

---

[71] M. Witt, "The Making of an Elegy : Yeats's 'In Memory of Major Robert Gregory'," in *Modern Philology*, xlviii (1950), 116. Miss Witt points out that Oliver St. John Gogarty, in his "Elegy on the Arch-poet William Butler Yeats lately dead" (*Elbow Room*, N.Y. 1942), states that Yeats preferred Burns's "straight lines" on Matthew Henderson, "For Matthew was a queer man," to "Adonais," ("Shelley's cosmic sermon.") Since, as Miss Witt notes, Gogarty misquotes the lines as being on Matthew Grose, and not on Matthew Henderson, it is possible that his recollection is still further at fault, and that it was the poem as a whole, not simply "The Epitaph," to which Yeats was referring. What Yeats liked most about the poem was the "great voice" that he found there.

of course, postulating a barrier between two regions of Burns's mind which became much more difficult for him to cross after 1786 than it had previously been. But he did not stay long enough in Edinburgh for it to become absolutely impassable— the "Elegy on Captain Henderson" alone is evidence of that; while the greatest venture of all, the songs, enabled him to move from one side to the other almost at will.[72]

[72] Mr J. D. Scott ("The Clarinda Letters," in *New Judgments*, pp. 43–52) has given Burns's "dissociation of sensibility" a Lawrencian explanation—viz. that when Burns acknowledged Jean Armour as his wife and went to live with her at Ellisland, this represented a return to his own folk, and a rejection of middle-class sentimental brinkmanship which stopped short of the "right true end of love."

VIII

Maturity

FROM one point of view, poems like "The Kirk's Alarm" and the "Elegy on Captain Matthew Henderson," so different from the English poems of Burns's middle years, are simply throwbacks to an earlier style; from another, they are forerunners of a poem in which the two poetic traditions with which Burns was associated, the Scots and the English, are indissolubly united as rarely before or since. I am referring to "Tam o' Shanter,"[1] the work which he himself termed his "standard performance in the Poetical line."[2] It is at one and the same time a breathless narrative *tour de force* worthy of Chaucer himself; a comical-satirical treatment of the supernatural, half-way between Augustan contempt for old wives' tales and the romantic exploitation of the "other world" for specific literary purposes; an essay in symbolism; and an experiment in multiple tone. The Devil is almost as crucial to the poem as Tam himself; and, even at the risk of a certain violation of strict chronology, it is perhaps desirable to examine the part he plays elsewhere in Burns before considering him in relation to the total pattern of "Tam o' Shanter."

Burns's first major treatment of the Devil is in the "Address to the Deil."[3] It is preceded by a most revealing Miltonic epigraph—

O Prince! O Chief of many thronèd Pow'rs!
That led th' embattl'd seraphim to war . . .

—which suggests that the comedy of the "Address" lies in an interplay between the concept of a sublime and terrible Evil One and the familiar devil of a jocular peasantry, many of

---

[1] i. 278 (433) : first printed in *The Edinburgh Magazine* for Mar. 1791; *The Edinburgh Herald* for 18 Mar. 1791 ; and Grose's *Antiquities* (Apr. 1791), the work for which it was specially written. For details, see H. & H., i. 438–9.
[2] To Mrs Dunlop, 11 Apr. 1791, in *Letters*, ii. 68.   [3] 1785–6 : i. 47 (335).

whom were becoming somewhat sceptical of his objective existence. This folk-devil is transmuted into something not only rich and strange, but decidedly personal to the poet; and I think that Mr William Montgomerie is on the right track when he claims that Satan sometimes means for Burns what Blake implied by a wellknown passage in *The Marriage of Heaven and Hell*:

> The reason Milton wrote in fetters when he wrote of Angels and God, and at liberty when of Devils and Hell, is because he was a true Poet and of the Devil's party without knowing it.[4]

Mr Montgomerie draws attention to a humorous letter from Burns to James Dalrymple[5] in which there is a similar suggestion that poets are Satan's men :

> I suppose the devil is so elated at his success with you that he is determined by a coup de main to effect his purposes on you all at once, in making you a Poet. . . .

Montgomerie might also have quoted certain other prose references pointing in the same direction :

> Give me a spirit like my favorite hero, Milton's Satan. . . .[6]

> I have bought a pocket Milton, which I carry perpetually about with me, in order to study the sentiments—the dauntless magnanimity; the intrepid unyielding independance [*sic*]; the desperate daring, and noble defiance of hardship, in that great personage, Satan. . . .[7]

If there is some reason for supposing that Burns identified himself imaginatively with Satan, and if, further, he had an inkling of the truth of another aphorism of Blake's, that all deities (including, presumably, evil ones) reside in the human breast —a conclusion which would seem to follow from my earlier analysis of Burns's religion [8]—then a peculiar interest attaches to the much-quoted final stanza of the address :

[4] W. Montgomerie, "Tam o' Shanter," in *New Judgments*, pp. 79–83.
[5] Feb. [1787], in *Letters*, 1. 74.
[6] To James Smith, 11 Jun. 1787, in *Letters*, 1. 95.
[7] To [William Nicol], 18 Jun. 1787, in *Letters*, 1. 96–7.
[8] Above, pp. 43–8.

> But fare-you-weel, Auld Nickie-Ben!
> O, wad ye tak a thought an' men'!
> Ye aiblins might—I dinna ken—
>   Still hae a stake:
> I'm wae to think upo' yon den,
>   Ev'n for your sake!

Perhaps (as Mr Montgomerie suggests) it is not so much for the real "Auld Hornie" as for a part of his own nature that Burns demands forgiveness.

But in the fourth and fifth stanzas of the epistle "To Colonel De Peyster,"[9] written in 1796, within a few months of his death, Burns sees his diabolical emanation in quite the traditional way:

> Then that curst carmagnole, Auld Satan,
> Watches, like baudrons by a ratton,
> Our sinfu' saul to get a claut on
>   Wi' felon ire;
> Syne, whip! his tail ye'll ne'er cast saut on—
>   He's aff like fire.
>
> Ah Nick! Ah Nick! it is na fair,
> First showing us the tempting ware,
> Bright wines and bonie lasses rare,
>   To put us daft;
> Syne weave, unseen, thy spider snare
>   O' Hell's damned waft!

In order that this passage should not be taken as suggesting that Burns died a "true believer" after all,[10] it is necessary to give due weight to its irony and to set it beside an even later document, a letter written early in June 1796:

> No! if I must write, let it be Sedition, or Blasphemy, or something else that begins with a B, so that I may grin with the grin of iniquity, & rejoice with the rejoicing of an apostate Angel.
>   —"All good to me is lost;
>   Evil, be thou my good! . . ."[11]

Burns could, it should be noted, still swing over towards a savagely jocular recognition of a special bond between himself

---

[9] II. 139 (380).   [10] Cp. C. Keith, p. 112.
[11] To Maria Riddell, [? 1 Jun. 1796], in *Letters*, II. 323.

and Satan even after writing the last four lines of the epistle
"To Colonel De Peyster" :

> Abjuring a' intentions evil,
> I quat my pen :
> The Lord preserve us frae the Devil !
> Amen ! Amen !

Nevertheless, it seems reasonable to conclude that by the end
of Burns's life the Devil—the objective embodiment of much
of his own nature—had begun to take on some of the attributes
which it had possessed in his infancy. In "Tam o' Shanter,"
however, as Mr Montgomerie has recognised,[12] Satan represents the creative energy behind his own best work.

The poem originated in oral folk tradition of the sort
preserved in the three prose tales that Burns sent to Grose in
June 1790.[13] From the first of these, Burns takes the stormy
setting, "on such a night as the devil would chuse to take the
air in" ; the farm-body's "anxious look-out in approaching a
place so well known to be a favorite haunt of the devil and
the devil's friends and emissaries" ; the possibility that "he
had got courageously drunk at the smithy" ; and the detail of
"a kind of kettle or caldron, depending from the roof, over the
fire, simmering some heads of unchristened children, limbs of
executed malefactors, &c. for the business of the night."

From the second of these local traditional tales Burns took
an even larger number of features—the witches' dance itself;
"their old sooty blackguard master, who was keeping them all
alive with the power of his bagpipe" ; the fact that "one of
them happening unluckily to have a smock which was considerably too short to answer all the purpose of that piece of
dress, our farmer was so tickled that he involuntarily burst out
with a loud laugh, 'Weel luppen, Maggy wi' the short sark !' " ;
the night pursuit to the middle arch of the Doon bridge, and
the loss of the horse's tail. Even the final moral comes from the
second local story : "However, the unsightly, tailless condition
of the vigorous steed was to the last hours of the noble creature's
life, an awful warning to the Carrick farmers, not to stay too
late in Ayr markets."

[12] *New Judgments*, p. 81.   [13] *Letters*, II. 22–4; H. & H., I. 434–7.

"Tam o' Shanter" belongs to the well-known *genre* of the Wild Ride, of which Byron's "Mazeppa" is perhaps the next best example in British literature. Angellier points out that there exists another *comic* Wild Ride beside which it is natural to put our poem—Cowper's "John Gilpin." The comparison is greatly to Burns's advantage. Cowper's poem evinces a delightful humour, certainly—but it is the humour of an ordinary man, of a man of talent merely. "Tam o' Shanter," in its synthesis of rapid motion, high energy, pure comedy, imaginative fantasy, and a sense of the stubborn realities of everyday life that never departs altogether from the poem, is by contrast a work of genius, whose qualities are perfectly compatible with considerable borrowings from folk tradition, and the literatures of Scotland and England.[14]

The strain of realism that runs through the work derives, at the level of the superficial and the merely obvious, from Burns's own quizzical recognition that he, too—emancipated man of the eighteenth century though he was—could, in the appropriate circumstances, feel some of the terrors that afflict the superstitious and the simple-minded ; from personal knowledge of "Alloway's auld haunted kirk" and the warm interiors of inns ; and from vivid recollections of riding at all times and in all weathers as he pursued his excise duties during the Ellisland period.[15] At a deeper level still, as we shall shortly

[14] Cp. Angellier, II. 139. It is not quite clear whether Peter Hill the bookseller actually sent Burns the books he ordered on 18 Jul. 1788 (*Letters*, I. 236)—among which was Cowper's *Poems* ; but if they did come to hand, it follows that "John Gilpin" (first published in *The Public Advertiser*, 14 Nov. 1782) could quite easily have exercised some influence on "Tam o' Shanter." Ritter (p. 216, n.) thinks that Burns may have got the idea of writing a short narrative poem from La Fontaine, whose works he had been reading in 1790 : "Les Contes de Fontaine is in the way of my trade & I must give it another reading or two . . ." (To [Robert Graham *of Fintry*], 9 Dec. 1789, in *Letters*, I. 372.)

[15] Cp. R. B. [to Moore], 2 Aug. 1787, in *Letters*, I. 106 : "In my infant and boyish days too, I owed much to an old Maid of my Mother's, remarkable for her ignorance, credulity and superstition.—She had, I suppose, the largest collection in the county of tales and songs concerning devils, ghosts, fairies, brownies, witches, warlocks, spunkies, kelpies, elf-candles, deadlights, wraiths, apparitions, cantraips, giants, inchanted towers, dragons and other trumpery.—This cultivated the latent seeds of Poesy ; but had so strong an effect on my imagination, that to this hour, in my nocturnal rambles, I sometimes keep a sharp look-out in suspicious places ; and though nobody can be more sceptical in these matters than I, yet it often takes an effort of Philosophy to shake off these idle terrors." Cp. also R. B. to

see, the poem's overwhelming impression of reality is due to its
embodiment of *all* Burns's imaginative pre-occupations. In
"Tam o' Shanter" realism, fantasy, humour and symbolism
are skilfully intermingled in a work that is typical not only of
Burns, but of the Scottish mind; for it is—next to "The
Vision"—the most genuinely *national* of all his poems.

Now that these preliminaries are completed, it is possible
to begin a detailed analysis of the poem. The first paragraph
brings to life a bustling country town at the end of a busy
market day, and it does so largely by means of subtle onomatopoeic patterns. Although there is no mention of noise, we
are somehow aware of the various sounds of the evening : the
clatter of horse-shoes, the jangling of harness—"When chapman billies leave the street"[16]—and the press of many people.
The second couplet—

> As market-days are wearing late,
> An' folk begin to tak the gate . . .

—conveys the impression of horses' hoofs striking against
cobblestones no less surely than Mr T. S. Eliot's more direct
statement :

> Stone, bronze, stone, steel, stone, oakleaves, horses' heels
> Over the paving. . . .[17]

Almost at once, however, attention shifts to a group, a *"com-
pagnie*," drowning their cares in a tavern. There has been no
mention of a Night Ride, but—from "The mosses, waters,
slaps, and styles"—we now receive an auditory impression
which somehow suggests the motion of a rather wet homeward
journey. And at the end, as every "gudeman" well knows, the
roysterer must inevitably face the reproaches of a strong-willed
woman of the old school—the sort that is known as a "woman
of character."

Mrs Dunlop, 2 Oct. 1789, in *Letters*, I. 360: "Five days in the week, or four at
least, I must be on horseback, and very frequently ride thirty or forty miles ere I
return." There have been attempts to trace Tam, Souter Johnie, and the Witch
Nance back to real Ayrshire folk of Burns's day—which, if justified, would add
further point to the poem's illusion of reality. Cp. C. & W., III. 219, 222–3;
H. & H., I. 437.
   [16] Cp. Fergusson, "Hallow-Fair," l. 28 ("Here chapmen billies tak their
stand"); and for l. 2, cp. Blair, *The Grave*, l. 462 ("when drunkards meet");
Ritter, p. 218.   [17] "Triumphal March," ll. 1–2.

It is only at the beginning of the second paragraph that Tam himself is introduced, and it is significant that he is then apostrophised in mock-moralising tones. The first we hear of him is that experience has taught him a lesson—namely that time flies, and that when it does wives are apt to sit up late brooding over their grievances. The parenthetical couplet,

> (Auld Ayr, wham ne'er a town surpasses,
> For honest men and bonie lasses),[18]

is not merely a graceful compliment to the county town, but just such a tribute as any of Tam's boozing companions might have paid it—hearty, comfortable, and slightly maudlin. The couplet establishes a particular point of view as normal for the whole work—not Burns's own, but that of the "boys in the back room," the "Average Man." On one side of his nature—despite his concern with what Jeffrey termed the "dispensing power" of genius[19]—Burns, of course, was precisely the Average Man; and in "Tam o' Shanter" he speaks with several different voices. In telling the story, he assumes the voice and language of a narrator whose outlook is indistinguishable from that of Jock Tamson, the Scottish John Smith. But this is not the only voice; for whenever he directly apostrophises Tam, he adopts the voice of yet another of Tam's cronies, a shrewd, quizzical commentator whose ostensibly rather sententious utterances ironically reflect the outlook of common morality; and in those other passages in which he utters his own comments, he assumes the voice and manner of an educated Scots eighteenth-century poet and man of letters. Both as narrator and as commentator, Burns of course speaks Scots, and as man of letters, he speaks English: but since it is English as spoken in Scotland, it does not destroy the linguistic unity of the poem; indeed, as Dr Wittig remarks, Burns's use of "near-English of this type gives 'Tam o' Shanter' a touch of perfection."[20]

---

[18] H. & H., I. 279, *ad init.*

[19] [Francis Jeffrey], review of Cromek's *Reliques of Robert Burns*, in *The Edinburgh Review*, XIII (1809), 253.

[20] Wittig, p. 202. So far as I am aware, the concept of a crony narrator first appears in Daiches, p. 283 ff. For phonetic details, see below, pp. 358 ff.

At the beginning of the third paragraph, Burns rather sadly wags his finger, and assumes the voice of the commentator:

> O Tam, had'st thou but been sae wise,
> As taen thy ain wife Kate's advice![21]

Here we can almost see him winking, too. And then we are given a picture of both Tam and Kate that is as full of movement and noise as the market itself. We catch the very accent of her voice, the shrill torrent of her words; and at one and the same time we see Tam through her shrewish eyes, and in the glass of a rather ironical humour. It is in the last line of this paragraph[22] that Alloway Kirk is mentioned for the first time, and its introduction at this point is a piece of superb narrative technique, reminiscent of the first appearance of an all-important phrase in a musical work. Then, in the commentator's voice, there is more moralising:

> Ah! gentle dames, it gars me greet,
> To think how monie counsels sweet,
> How monie lengthen'd, sage advices
> The husband frae the wife despises![23]

Having established his dual point of view, and bathed the whole scene in the warm light of his irony, Burns moves on to a realistic interior *genre*-picture in his manners-painting strain, which, as Mr Montgomerie has noted, is also a part of the poem's underlying symbolic meaning. The drink, the warmth, the talk, the landlady's "secret favours"—*these* are the Pleasures that are "like poppies spread," obscurely connected with the Art and Energy and Music which are later associated with Satan and the witches' dance in the ruined church. In a very few lines indeed Burns gives us a masterly sketch of the garrulous and amorous drinkers, all the time half-conscious of the storm outside and its contrast with the cosy interior of the inn.[24]

The whole passage is charged with a delightful humour (*e.g.*, "And ay the ale was growing better"; "The landlord's

[21] H. & H., I. 279 *med.*   [22] *Op. cit.*, p. 279 *ad. fin.*   [23] *Op. cit.*, p. 280 *ad init.*
[24] Ritter (p. 218) notes the parallel with Thomson, "Winter," ll. 89 ff.: ". . . while the cottage hind | Hangs o'er the enlivening blaze, and taleful there | Recounts his simple frolic: much he talks, | And much he laughs, nor recks the storm that blows | Without, and rattles on his humble roof."

laugh was ready chorus"), and we are given a compressed poetry of human beings that is surely as good as anything in the *Canterbury Tales*. In the first couplet of the next paragraph—

> Care, mad to see a man sae happy,
> E'en drown'd himsel amang the nappy—[25]

the personification is done so deftly that we do not notice it very much, but pass on to the homely simile of the bees after a somewhat ruminative pause to take breath. The recurrence of these insects at a later stage in the poem suggests that Burns, too, has his image-patterns. Here they are perfectly in tune with Tam's alcoholic glow:

> As bees flee hame wi' lades o' treasure,
> The minutes wing'd their way wi' pleasure. . . .[26]

The later simile is of quite a different nature—a perfect reflexion of the poem's change of mood:

> As bees bizz out wi' angry fyke,
> When plundering herds assail their byke. . . .[27]

At the same time, the continuity of the imagery serves to reinforce the imaginative connexion (as well as the contrast) between the witches and pleasure—which is, incidentally, a key-word and therefore a key-concept in the poem. Before we leave the fifth and sixth paragraphs, there are two other features of the poem's symbolism that I should like to mention in passing—namely that the "sangs and clatter"[28] at once anticipate and counterpoint the later grotesque music and revelry of Satan and the "beldams," and that the "ingle, bleezing finely," looks forward to the bright lights of the orgy in Kirk-Alloway. There is room even for a trace of Burns's anti-royalism at this point—for in the couplet

> Kings may be blest but Tam was glorious,
> O'er a' the ills o' life victorious!

—does not the poet's choice of auxiliary verbs carry with it the suggestion that, in reality, monarchs *may* just as easily be

[25] H. & H., I. 280 *ad fin.*
[26] *Ibid.* Cp. Hamilton, *Wallace* (1722), p. 101 : "Let wing'd with pleasure the soft minutes flow" (Ritter, p. 219).
[27] H. & H., I. 286 *ad init.*   [28] *Op. cit.*, p. 280 *med.*

accurst ? In any case the reader feels that the Honest Man (here Tam) is far superior to such "trashtrie."

The passage beginning "But pleasures are like poppies spread"[29] has often been quoted as an instance of the insufficiency of Burns when writing in English.[30] It is said that the transition from Scottish diction is unnecessary, and that the sentimental truisms impede the narrative and alter the tone in a most disconcerting fashion. And even those who like the lines are not always disposed to rate them very highly in the scale of poetical excellence. Gerard Manley Hopkins, for example, thought them "the most strictly beautiful lines of his that I remember," but felt that Burns never came any nearer "pure beauty" than "the fresh picturesque expressed in fervent and flowing language."[31] All these criticisms seem to me to proceed from an incomplete understanding of the poem. Once it is realised that Burns, throughout, is speaking with several different voices, the Scots-English that he adopts at this point becomes simply a heightening and mellowing of the mood expressed in the couplet

> Auld Ayr, wham ne'er a town surpasses,
> For honest men and bonie lasses,

and serves, as Dr Wittig remarks, to "point a moral and adorn the tale." But it is necessary in order to provide an artistic transition to the darker but none the less comic matter of Tam's journey on horseback. The lines in question still carry some faint overtones of the moralistic commentator's voice, but by adopting a more sophisticated pose Burns transforms the commentator's sentiments into something that is both more wistful and more universal than the expressions that would naturally have sprung from the crony's lips. What many critics seem to have missed is that the lines have themselves a humorous air—not the Flemish or Hogarthian comedy found elsewhere in the poem, but a spirit reminiscent, perhaps, of

---

29 *Op. cit.*, p. 281 *ad init.*

30 But cp. Wittig, pp. 201–2. I cannot altogether agree with Dr Daiches when he remarks (p. 286) that here "Burns is seeking a form of expression which will set the sternness of objective fact against the warm, cosy and self-deluding view of the half-intoxicated Tam."

31 Hopkins, 22 Oct. 1879, in *Letters of Gerard Manley Hopkins to Robert Bridges*, ed. C. C. Abbott, London 1935, p. 95.

Sterne or Goldsmith. The gentle, melancholy smile which (if one is reading the poem aloud) here comes over one's face is that of a slightly tipsy man—part narrator and part Bard. There is surely little to complain of in the simile of the poppies or in that of the snow falling in the river, while the "borealis race" and the "evanishing" rainbow are connected with the dominant storm imagery, and act as a link in the poem's pattern of flickering light. Furthermore, for all their complexity of tone, these lines are connected with the underlying theme of the whole poem—the relationship between Pleasures (condemned *in toto* by Calvinism and in part by the business world) and the Devil of art and music, for whom "Energy is Eternal Delight."[32]

All at once, however, there is a dramatic change. The poet disappears altogether and we are left only with our sententious *homme moyen sensuel*, the jovial narrator:

Nae man can tether time or tide;
The hour approaches Tam maun ride. . . .

Then follows a remarkably vivid sensuous impression of a storm as it would seem to a man who has just emerged from a warm interior. The whole scene is dominated by gleams of light and the rolling of thunder; and in the passage beginning

Weel mounted on his gray mare Meg . . .[33]

[32] Ritter (p. 219) shows how Burns may have drawn on various parts of his reading when he wrote these well-known lines. Cp. Marlowe, *Hero and Leander*, 2 Sestiad ("Joy graven in sense *like snow in water wastes*"); William Browne, "Elegy," ed. Goodwin, II. 269 ("Th'art lost *forever*, as a drop of rain | *Fall'n in a river*"); Shakespeare, *Romeo and Juliet*, II. ii. 119-20 ("Too like the lightning, which doth cease to be | Ere one can say 'It lightens' "); Johnson, "Anningait and Ajut, A Greenland Tale," in Arthur Masson, *Collection of Prose and Verse*, Burns's school reading-book ("O life, frail and uncertain! . . . What art thou, deceitful pleasure! but a sudden blaze streaming from the north which plays a moment on the eye . . . and then vanishes for ever ?"). There is an even clearer recollection of the last of these passages in a later work of Burns's, "As I stood by yon roofless Tower," H. & H., III. 144 (406), st. iv. In establishing the "Scots-English" character of the passage beginning "But pleasures are like poppies spread," one should consider the possibility that contact clauses like "Or like the snow falls in the river" are commoner in the North than in the South. Again, "evanishing" sounds quite natural on Scottish lips: as Professor S. Musgrove has pointed out to me, the word was used by King James VI in *Basilicon Doron* (1603), p. 104, and elsewhere. Most of the earlier examples of "evanish" in the *N.E.D.* are from Scottish authors, and Allan Ramsay used it in *The Gentle Shepherd*.

[33] H. & H., I. 281 *med.* As Ritter notes (p. 220), this is ballad diction. Cp. "Chevy Chase": "Well mounted on a gallant steed."

Burns recaptures the movement of the horse and of Tam's swaying body as he holds on drunkenly to his bonnet, sometimes singing, sometimes prudently peering round to see if there are any "bogles" or other supernatural creatures as he draws closer to the tumbledown church. The element of the grotesque —full-bodied, grim and more than a trifle repulsive—is a most important constituent of the poem's humour, and its effect is heightened by our recollections, already evoked, of falling petals, snow melting in the river, and an evanescent auroral display. By the time that Tam has crossed the ford,[34] the mood almost (but not quite) becomes serious as he remembers the violent deeds associated with the various landmarks that he passes on the way, obscurely establishing a connexion with the symbolic level I have already referred to. The whole landscape is like the *décor* of a fantastic ballet—a clump of birch trees; a great stone like the standing stones that play so large a part in Mitchell's *Scots Quair*[35] and the Glastonbury novels of John Cowper Powys; whins that recall the old Lyke Wake Dirge ("The whinnets sall prick thee to the bare bane"); a cairn of stones; and a thorn-tree above a well. Although the reader may not be willing to accept a psychological explanation which would equate standing stones and walls with male and female genitalia, or the rivers as symbols for the continuity of life, as "archetypes of the collective unconscious," he will find it hard to deny the scene's imaginative power. Normally peaceful and silent, it is overwhelmed by the roar of the swollen river and the creaking and crashing of trees in the gale. The whole sky is given over to lightning; Kirk-Alloway seems positively ablaze; and over everything there rise the tremen-

[34] H. & H., I. 282 *med.* Ritter (p. 220) notes the likeness of one passage to Thomson, "Summer," ll. 1676 ff. ("But far about they wander from the grave | Of him whom his ungentle fortune urged | Against his own sad breast to lift the hand | Of impious violence"): and also to Ramsay *The Gentle Shepherd*, II. 3 ("When Wattie wandered ae night thro' the shaw, | And tint himsell amaist amang the *snaw*; | When *Mungo's mare* stood still, an' swat wi' fright" (my italics). For Burns's lines beginning "The doubling storm roars thro' the woods," cp. Dryden, "Ceyx and Alcyone; out of the eleventh book of Ovid's Metamorphoses," ll. 123–4 ("At once from East to West, from Pole to Pole, | The forky Lightnings flash, the roaring Thunders roul"); and Pope, *Odyssey*, XII. 486–7.

[35] J. Leslie Mitchell ("Lewis Grassic Gibbon"), *A Scots Quair*, London 1946, pp. 19 *et passim*.

dous sounds of infernal revelry, audible even above the storm. Since his *genre* demands that comedy should predominate, Burns cannot allow himself to continue in this strain for too long. Briefly, he apostrophises strong drink, and then reverts once more to the Average Man's point of view, with the aloof Bard still looking on and enjoying the sight:

> Inspiring bold John Barleycorn,
> What dangers thou canst make us scorn!
> Wi' tippeny, we fear nae evil;
> Wi' usquabae, we'll face the Devil!
> The swats sae ream'd in Tammie's noddle,
> Fair play, he car'd na deils a boddle.[36]

Gone are all the "prudent cares" that so recently inspired his timorous glowering round in case there were any bogles; now Tam is game for anything. Not even his gray mare's terror can dissuade him from coming closer. He sees "Warlocks and witches in a dance"[37]—warlocks and witches who are, incidentally, such good Scottish nationalists that they will not have anything to do with foreign music, above all with French music—a prejudice which appears elsewhere, in "The Cotter's Saturday Night" and "The Twa Dogs," and which Fergusson[38] had aired before Burns. Obviously, there is nothing newfangled or unpatriotic about Satan and his friends. It had long been traditional to associate the Devil with bagpipes,[39] with savage dancing, and with complete abandonment to instinctive enjoyment; and Mr Montgomerie writes:

> Auld Nick's place in the poem is significantly in the Kirk, though in opposition to it. He is a creature of the historical

[36] H. & H., i. 282 *ad fin.*   [37] *Op. cit.*, p. 283 *ad init.*
[38] In his "Elegy on the Death of Scots Music," st. ix.
[39] Thus some women burnt for sorcery at Bo'ness in 1679 were accused of meeting Satan "at the croce of Murestane, above Kinneil, where they all danced, and the Devill acted as piper"; elsewhere Satan, in the semblance of a "rough tanny-Dog," is said to have acted as piper at a dance in the Pentland Hills (Webster's *Tracts*, p. 97, and Sinclair, *Satan's invisible World discovered*, both quoted in J. G. Dalzell, *Musical Memoirs of Scotland*, Edinburgh 1849). In *The Darker Superstitions of Scotland* (Dublin 1834, p. 573), Dalzell also draws attention to a chapter in Olaus Magnus, *Gent. sept. hist.* (Rome 1555), with illustrations in which Satan is shown "officiating as a piper," which shows that the association of the Devil with the bagpipe was not confined to Scotland, and that it probably went back before the Reformation.

past, like his warlocks and witches, like the dead. . . . He is
part of the human personality suppressed by Calvinism, Burns
the poet and fornicator, the creator of music, the inspirer of
dancing (the Kirk for centuries discouraged dancing), summing
up in himself all the elements in the Scotsman that the Kirk,
unable to destroy them . . . has suppressed. He is "a touzie
tyke," the animal in us.[40]

If Mr Montgomerie is right here—and I think he is—it follows
that "Tam o' Shanter" draws heavily on those preoccupations
and levels of experience that underlie the first epistles, the anti-
Calvinist satires, and indeed all that is best in Burns's early
work; "Tam o' Shanter," too, has its origin in the universal
conflicts of reason and emotion, appearance and reality,
instinct and the will. Where "Tam o' Shanter" differs from
these earlier poems is in the additional depth which it derives
from the imagery.

Mr Montgomerie goes on to argue that the symbolism in
"Tam o' Shanter" extends to the one member of the "hellish
legion" who was at all personable:

So Nannie, the young witch [he continues] . . . is all the young
women that Burns himself has seduced. Burns' own desire is
reflected in Tam, and projected into the Devil himself: 'Even
Satan glowr'd, and fidg'd fu' fain.'[41]

But this is surely to make too explicit an identification between
a character in a narrative poem and persons whom its author
knew in real life, and to forget the various levels of tone and the
different points of view which are undoubtedly present in the
work. Tam is Tam, a creation of the author's viewed through
one or more pairs of spectacles, and not entirely, or even
mainly, a representation of the poet; and Nance is "dear,
deluding Woman," "Venus," and "the lasses" in general,
rather than the mere sum of Elizabeth Paton, Jean Armour,
Highland Mary, Jenny Clow, May Cameron, Anne Park, and
a few others.

It is, however, necessary to return to a detailed examination

---

[40] Montgomerie, *New Judgments*, p. 79, Cp. Ramsay, "The Monk and the
Miller's Wife. A Tale," l. 254 ("No like a Deel in Shape of Beast").
[41] Montgomerie, *op. cit.*, p. 80.

of the text. In describing the eldritch paraphernalia of the witches' orgy,[42] Burns repeats the grotesquerie of the passage beginning "By this time he was cross the ford." As Henley and Henderson point out,[43] the effectiveness of this section is almost entirely due to revision. Thus, instead of the four lines beginning "Coffins stood round . . . ,"[44] the first draft had a solitary couplet:

> The torches climb around the wa'
> Infernal fires, blue-bleezing a'.

After "Five scymitars wi' murder crusted,"[45] the first version had two lines, later deleted:

> Seven gallows pins; three hangman's whittles;
> A raw o' weel seal'd doctor's bottles.

And after the last couplet of the whole section—

> Wi' mair of horrible and awefu',
> Which even to name wad be unlawfu'. . . .[46]

—these four lines occurred in all the manuscripts, in Grose, and in the two periodicals in which the poem was printed in 1791:

> Three Lawyers' tongues, turned inside out,
> Wi' lies seamed like a beggar's clout;
> Three Priests' hearts, rotten black as muck,
> Lay stinking, vile, in every neuk.

They were omitted from the 1793 edition on the advice of Alexander Fraser Tytler, then Professor of Universal History at Edinburgh University. The effect of these progressive alterations is to strengthen the Romantic impressions of the scene and suppress any urge to be satirical in at least the conventional sense: doctors, lawyers and priests are, after all, among the stock figures of eighteenth-century social criticism. Nevertheless, there is irony here too, in the sarcastic inflexions

---

[42] H. & H., I. 283-4. This whole section undoubtedly owes something to reminiscences of the witch scenes in *Macbeth*.

[43] I. 440.   [44] *Op. cit.*, p. 283 *med.*   [45] *Op. cit.*, p. 283 *ad fin.*

[46] *Op. cit.*, p. 284 *ad init.* Ritter (p. 221), notes what appear to be two reminiscences of Ramsay, "Three Bonnets," Canto I ("Sae tho' the aith we took was awfu', | To keep it now appears unlawfu' | . . . She was a winsome wench and waly, | And could put on her claes fu' brawly"). For Burns's parallel to the second couplet, see H. & H., I. 284 *ad fin.*

which the reader inevitably puts into "heroic Tam" and into the line "Which even to name wad be unlawfu'."

In spite of the wealth of action stored up in verbs and epithets like "new-cutted," "crusted," and "mangled," and in the exquisitely expressive phrase "stack to the heft," this long "horror passage" is relatively slow-moving. Consequently, the tremendous motion of the next verse-paragraph bursts upon us with quite exceptional vividness :

> The piper loud and louder blew,
> The dancers quick and quicker flew,
> They reel'd, they set, they cross'd, they cleekit,
> Till ilka carlin swat and reekit,
> And coost her duddies to the wark,
> And linket at it in her sark ![47]

The effect is also in part due to the crossed alliterations and internal vowel rhymes in the second couplet, which vividly suggest the figures of a Scottish country dance.[48] And in the apostrophe "Now Tam, O Tam ! had thae been queans," the canny commentator, with his "breeks" that "ance were plush," is present more concretely than he has been for some time ; one can almost see him sagely wagging his finger at Tam.

It is quite important to notice that there is as much interplay between Scots and English in "Tam o' Shanter" as there is in "The Cotter's Saturday Night." To take one instance out of many, here are two earlier lines which, on the printed page at least, seem pure English :

> Till, by the heel and hand admonish'd,
> She ventur'd forward on the light. . . .[49]

They are embedded right in the middle of a passage in Scots where they do not seem in the least odd or unusual. And now, almost at the climax of the work, there occur :

> That night enlisted in the core . . .
> And kept the country-side in fear . . .
> In longitude tho' sorely scanty . . .
> And scarcely had he Maggie rallied,
> When out the hellish legion sallied.

[47] H. & H., i. 284 *med.*   [48] Cp. Wittig, p. 218.   [49] H. & H., i. 283 *ad init.*

As open pussie's mortal foes,
When, pop ! she starts before their nose ;
As eager runs the market-crowd,
When 'Catch the thief !' resounds aloud . . .[50]

As pronounced by a Scot, the first of these lines sounds perfectly
natural—but it would surely seem rather clumsy on English
lips. Again, the Latinity of the third line quoted is to my ear
much better suited to a Scottish than to an English pronunciation, while the simile beginning "As open pussie's mortal foes"
is in deliberate contrast to the preceding couplet :

As bees bizz out wi' angry fyke,
When plundering herds assail their byke. . . .

As always with Burns at his best, the motive for intermingling
Scots and Scots-English is primarily an artistic one ; it serves
to make the last couplet of the passage funny, as well as
menacing :

So Maggie runs, the witches follow,
Wi' monie an eldritch skriech and hollo.

At this point Burns achieves the effect of tremendous concentration of energy by combining all his voices in a great
choric and dramatic climax—the climax, indeed, of the whole
poem, in the paragraph beginning "Ah, Tam ! Ah, Tam !"[51]
These lines are superb in their evocation of motion. Their
effect rests on the dynamic alternation of Scots and Scots-
English, so evident in the last couplet of the paragraph, lines
which might well be regarded as typical of the language of
the entire poem :

The carlin claught her by the rump,
And left poor Maggie scarce a stump.

During the last sections of "Tam o' Shanter" Burns often
speaks with the commentator's voice, as in :

But wither'd beldams, auld and droll,
Rigwoodie hags wad spean a foal,
Louping and flinging on a crummock,
I wonder did na turn thy stomach !
But Tam *kend what was what fu' brawlie.* . . .[52]

[50] *Op. cit.*, pp. 285–6.   [51] *Op. cit.*, p. 286 *med.*   [52] *Op. cit.*, p. 284 *ad fin.*

The same shrewd tone can also be heard in the eye-witness commentary of

> Ah, Tam ! Ah, Tam ! thou'll get thy fairin !
> In hell they'll roast thee like a herrin !

and in the masculine cattiness of the two subsequent lines, with their wish-fulfilment implication of "Serve the shrew right !" :

> In vain thy Kate awaits thy comin !
> Kate soon will be a woefu' woman !

And it most definitely takes over in the conclusion, where the moral is stated :

> Now, wha this tale o' truth shall read,
> Ilk man, and mother's son, take heed :
> Whene'er to drink you are inclin'd,
> Or cutty sarks run in your mind,
> Think ! ye may buy the joys o'er dear :
> Remember Tam o' Shanter's mare.[53]

The commentator's Scots is thus, as Dr Wittig has put it, the "home key" of the whole poem.

Miss Keith thinks that in the last six lines we hear the voice of Burns himself :

> And yet—and yet—Robin was not his father's son for nothing. 'Think ! Remember !' ring out in sonorous warning in the concluding lines of the poem. 'Damnanda est voluptas', Calvin had written. 'Think ! Remember !' And Calvinism for Burns still has the last word.[54]

This, it seems to me, is to fall into what Mr C. S. Lewis calls the "personal heresy,"[55] that of mistaking the words of a character in a poem, drama or work of fiction for the definitive pronouncement of the author himself. Miss Keith seems to

---

[53] *Op. cit.*, p. 287.
[54] C. Keith, p. 103. Daiches (p. 292) aptly compares this warning note with the speech of the ghost in Hamlet, while recognising it as "a mock moral, a deliberately absurd oversimplification of the meaning of the tale to make it a warning against drinking and wenching."
[55] See C. S. Lewis and E. M. W. Tillyard, *The Personal Heresy*, London 1939, *passim*.

have overlooked the possibility that Burns may be speaking with several different voices; that the narrator may not in fact be Burns himself, but someone else, however shadowy; and that the total meaning may reside, not in the final lines, but in the interplay of the several points of view of which we become aware as we yield our attention to the full pleasure of the poem.

Carlyle's judgment on "Tam o' Shanter" is worth pondering, because it points forward in a curiously inverted fashion to a true assessment of the poem.

> It is not so much a poem [he wrote], as a piece of sparkling rhetoric; the heart and body of the story still lies hard and dead. He has not gone back, much less carried us back, into that dark, earnest, wondering age, when the tradition was believed, and when it took its rise; he does not attempt, by any new-modelling of his supernatural ware, to strike anew that deep mysterious chord of human nature, which once responded to such things; and which lives in us too, and will for ever live, though silent, or vibrating with far other notes, and to far different issues. . . . The piece does not properly cohere; the strange chasm which yawns in our incredulous imaginations between the Ayr public-house and the gate of Tophet, is nowhere bridged over, nay, the idea of such a bridge is laughed at; and thus the Tragedy of the adventure becomes a mere drunken phantasmagoria, painted on ale-vapours, and the Farce alone has any reality.[56]

An unsympathetic critic, obscurely aware of the presence of several points of view in a work of fiction, would naturally conclude that it lacks unity; but his very judgment would be an unconscious recognition of the complexity of the very piece he was condemning—which is exactly what Carlyle does here. Again, Carlyle was a doctrinaire Romantic quite out of touch with the hostility of the Enlightenment towards the supernatural. When he found Burns apparently laughing at the idea of a bridge between an Ayr public-house and the gate of Tophet, he gave up trying to understand what the poet was saying; never for one moment did he suspect that the "Hero's"

[56] [Carlyle], review of J. G. Lockhart, *Life of Burns*, in *Edinburgh Review*, XLVIII (1828), 285.

attitude was both broader and deeper than his own humour-
less obscurantism, or that it embraced more than one level of
discourse at the same time. Sir William Craigie, after a brief
discussion of Carlyle's view, concludes that "the humour is not
the only note, but is combined with a serious and impressive
strain"; in other words, he recognises the symbolism, but
without exploring it in detail.[57] "Tam o' Shanter," then, is
not quite so simple a poem as it appears on the surface; but
it can be enjoyed and loved quite apart from any such "deep
analysis" as is attempted here. No examination, however
minute, can take away from it the glory of being one of the
very best short narratives to have been produced in the British
Isles.

In his later years, Burns turned increasingly to political
poetry, and to song. The former is often given a false emphasis
by Burns's critics. Sometimes it is explained away as the jaun-
diced vapourings of a man who had come to hate those whom
fortune or society had favoured above himself,[58] sometimes its
true significance is distorted until it is subtly converted into an
apology for the *status quo*.[59]

Of all the many attempts to construct a Tory Burns, the
most intelligent is that of W. P. Ker, whose arguments should
be carefully pondered by all who are inclined to follow the
traditional conception of "Burns the democrat." I believe that
the conventional picture is broadly correct, though it needs to
be qualified in relation to Burns's shift of opinion from one
period of his life to another, and even between one poem and
the next. "The French Revolution counted for very little in
the poetry of Burns," says Ker, "for the good reason that in
1786 the French Revolution was not yet in sight, at any rate
from the horizon of Mauchline." The real politics of Burns
were Pittite—that is, orthodox, conservative and Unionist.
"He is not particularly good at Scottish history. His Scottish

[57] Craigie, p. 100.
[58] Cp. H. & H., notes to "Is there for honest Poverty ?", iii. 489 ff.; Fitzhugh,
in *R. B.,; His Associates*, pp. 6–7, and in "Burns' later years : Candid Notes by his
Friend John Syme" in *Studies in Philology*, xxxvii (1940), pp. 535–41.
[59] Cp. Alexander Smith, "The Life of Robert Burns," in *Complete Works of
Robert Burns, (Self-interpreting)*, ed. [G. Gebbie], 6 vols., Philadelphia 1886, reissued 1908 and 1909, henceforth cited as Gebbie, vi. 251-3.

politics are determined by Scotch drink." Finally, his involve-
ment with the French Revolution was slight, and "like Wordsworth, he turns to think of his own country when his country
is in danger."[60] The whole argument of the present study
tends to disprove or at least substantially to modify each of
these points.

In point of fact, the American Revolution and the Enlightenment, agrarian crisis and class conflict, were very much
in sight from the horizon of Mauchline in 1786. If these events
and processes are to be regarded as precursors and even as
causes of the revolutionary and reformist movements of the
seventeen-nineties (I am thinking of Scotland now, not of
France), then many of Burns's poems written before 1786 can
surely be regarded as a reflexion of the popular mood that
preceded the struggles of Thomas Muir[61] and the Friends of
the People. Far from being bad at Scottish history, Burns, as
I have tried to show in my analysis of "The Vision," was a man
who thoroughly understood the social processes of his own
time : that is to say, he had a good grasp of *contemporary* history.
Moreover, Burns's attitude to the war with France was shifting
and ambivalent ; it is by no means certain that the patriotic but
still radical mood of "Does haughty Gaul invasion threat?"[62]
would have been any more permanent than that which under-
lay his public declaration of "attachment to the Constitution
& . . . abhorrence of Riot"[63] two years earlier, in 1793. It is
surely significant that in his essay on "The Politics of Burns"
Ker devotes only one tenth of his space to the French Revolution[64]—and none at all to "As I stood by yon roofless Tower,"[65]

[60] W. P. Ker, "The Politics of Burns," in *Essays*, I. 128, 138, 146.

[61] Thomas Muir, the son of a Glasgow merchant, was educated at the Uni-
versities of Glasgow and Edinburgh. He became an advocate in 1787, and in
July 1792 one of the founders of the Edinburgh Friends of the People (a democratic association which had arisen under the stimulus of the French Revolution).
Sentenced in Sep. 1793 to transportation to Botany Bay for fourteen years, he
escaped from that settlement on 11 Feb. 1796 in an American ship specially sent
for that purpose, and after various adventures died in exile in France in January
1799. See H. W. Meikle, *Scotland and the French Revolution, passim*.

[62] III. 195 (441).

[63] See letter [to Graham *of Fintry*], 5 Jan. 1793, in *Letters*, II. 144.

[64] W. P. Ker, *loc. cit.*

[65] III. 144 (406) ; printed by Currie as "A Vision."

the "Ode for General Washington's Birthday"[66] or the question
of the authenticity of "The Tree of Liberty."[67]

Almost everything that Burns ever wrote was political, in
the broadest sense of that word. Even his refurbishing of
traditional love-songs can be subsumed under that head, for
he regarded their collection and arrangement as a patriotic—
that is, as a political—act.[68] The central core of all his thought
was his exploration of the Scottish predicament; he belonged
to a nation which had lost its independence but was at the
same time part of a larger state in whose successes he could
rejoice and in whose better government he was interested, so
that his patriotism was always of a peculiarly double sort. His
attachment to what, for want of a better word, must be termed
his "class"—that is, to the "lower orders," broadly conceived
—reinforced and buttressed his nationalism. Take, for example, Caledonia's lament in the ninth stanza of the "Elegy
on the Death of Sir James Hunter Blair,"[69]

"I saw my sons resume their ancient fire;
I saw fair Freedom's blossoms richly blow.
But ah! how hope is born but to expire!
Relentless fate has laid their guardian low. . . ."

This is nationalistic enough, and addressed to an upper-class
audience; yet it is rhetoric of the same kind as the minstrel's
apostrophe of Liberty in "As I stood by yon roofless Tower."
In the latter, Liberty is in part a social concept—freedom
from restraint; in the "Elegy," it is national freedom; but
quite clearly the two are connected.

The "Prologue spoken by Mr Woods on his Benefit Night,"[70]
also dating from 1787, contains further praise of the national
revival. There is one especially interesting passage making
explicit those conceptions which are allegorically conveyed in
"The Vision":

---

[66] II. 171 (393). In a letter to Mrs Dunlop, 25 Jun. 1794 (*Letters*, II. 246),
Burns sends her a "first sketch" of the stanza beginning "Thee, Caledonia . . . ,"
and says: "The subject is LIBERTY. . . . I design it as an irregular Ode for General
Washington's birthday."

[67] IV. 58 (107); below, pp. 246–51.

[68] Cp. his letter to Thomson, 16 Sep. 1792, in *Letters*, II. 122–3.

[69] II. 218 (413).   [70] II. 144 (381).

Hail, Caledonia, name for ever dear!
Before whose sons I'm honor'd to appear!
Where every science, every nobler art,
That can inform the mind or mend the heart,
Is known (as grateful nations oft have found),
Far as the rude barbarian marks the bound!
Philosophy, no idle pedant dream,
Here holds her search by heaven-taught Reason's beam;
Here History paints with elegance and force
The tide of Empire's fluctuating course;
Here *Douglas* forms wild Shakespeare into plan,
And Harley rouses all the God in man.[71]

We are, I think, entitled to use as evidence certain Jacobite
songs which Burns altered or touched up in the late seventeen-
eighties: they show that he was emotionally affected by them
to the extent of being able to enter into the spirit of the originals,
although it is extremely difficult—as always with the songs—to
say where tradition leaves off, and Burns (or one of his *personae*)
begins. "Such a Parcel of Rogues in a Nation"[72] is a song
about the historical challenge which was the ultimate cause of
the national revival—the situation caused by the Act of Union,
which stimulated the men of subsequent generations to try to
beat the English in the only sphere now open to them, the arts
of peace, even if it sometimes meant that they anglified themselves in the process.[73] It is "in character," for one must
imagine it as sung by an opponent of the Union; and it
shows Burns working in the spirit of his source-material to
produce an imaginative reconstruction of a patriot's feelings
in 1707:

> What force or guile could not subdue
> Thro' many warlike ages
> Is wrought now by a coward few
> For hireling traitor's wages.

---

[71] H. & H., II. 144–5. The Harley mentioned in the last line quoted is the hero
of Henry Mackenzie's novel *The Man of Feeling.*

[72] III. 127 (391).

[73] Cp. Hume's letter to Gilbert Elliot of Minto, 22 Sep. 1764 (*Letters*, ed.
Greig, I. 470), written under the stress of personal humiliation: "Am I, or are you,
an Englishman? Will they allow us to be so? Do they not treat with Derision
our Pretensions to that Name, and with Hatred our just Pretensions to surpass &
to govern them? I am a Citizen of the World. . . . ."

The English steel we could disdain,
Secure in valour's station ;
But English gold has been our bane—
Such a parcel of rogues in a nation !

"Ye Jacobites by Name"[74] might almost be the second half
of an eclogue of which "Such a Parcel of Rogues" is the first
part, because it ironically negates any political action that
might have been deduced from the latter poem. It is another
character-song, apparently sung by a Whig, on the subject of
political moralising—that is, on the elaboration of ideas to
justify material gains already won by force :

. . . What is Right, and what is Wrang,
          By the law ?
What is Right, and what is Wrang ?
A short sword and a lang,
A weak arm and a strang
          For to draw !

And in the next stanza, "heroic strife" against the existing
Establishment is simply another name for murder and parri-
cide, since civil war can never be regarded as a good. It
follows, therefore, that historical necessity forces us to be un-
heroic. It is nothing less than duty to betray our prince and
the "heroes" who revolt against the Hanoverians :

. . . Then let your schemes alone,
          In the State !
Then let your schemes alone,
Adore the rising sun,
And leave a man undone
          To his fate !

On the purely Jacobite level, this is a song about the bitterness
of defeat in a complicated political situation ; and it is characterised by that historical understanding which was so marked
a feature of Burns's genius—the knowledge that in eighteenth-
century Scotland the heroic no longer "paid off."

Here I wish to stress the point that Burns has a natural gift
for identifying himself with the men on both sides of a national

[74] III. 120 (386).

struggle, and also for standing back and observing the warring factions quite impersonally, and from a distance. That this "withdrawnness" was not peculiar to Burns but a part of the Scottish way of looking at things is suggested by the series of ballads composed on the Battle of Sheriffmuir, one of which Burns "condensed" from a composition of the Rev. John Barclay. Here are some lines from the sixth stanza of Burns's version, "The Battle of Sherramuir,"[75] which illustrate the aloofness I have been speaking of:

> "Now wad ye sing this double flight,
> Some fell for wrang, and some for right,
> But monie bade the world guid-night:
> Say, pell and mell, wi' muskets' knell
> How Tories fell, and Whigs to Hell
> Flew off in frighted bands, man!"

This particular trait is possibly an offshoot of eighteenth-century historicism, which advanced further in Scotland than perhaps in any other country in Europe.[76] It may also be due in no small measure to the fact that many Scots families had some members on either side of the dynastic struggle. Scottish Tories were less loyal to the Hanoverian *régime* than their English brethren, besides being better educated, and therefore better able to see both sides of the question.

"Liberty" is a key-concept with Burns, and he means different things by it at different times. Often it signifies anti-feudalism, simple absence of external coercion and control. This seems to be an implication, not only of the early epistles, but also of the second stanza of the later "Lines on Fergusson,"[77] the poet:

> O, why should truest Worth and Genius pine
> Beneath the iron grasp of Want and Woe,
> While titled knaves and idiot-greatness shine
> In all the splendour Fortune can bestow?

In the highly ironical fragment "On Glenriddell's Fox breaking

---

[75] III. 73 (356).
[76] *E.g.*, in the works of Lord Kames, John Millar, and the early Scottish political economists. For this point I am indebted to Dr R. L. Meek, of the University of Glasgow.   [77] II. 224 (416).

his Chain,"[78] Liberty is naturalised; but she is still somewhat
alien to the South and West, for she is Highland—and therefore, temperamental in the extreme. Incidentally, the following
lines are surely among the finest Burns ever wrote in English:

> Thou, Liberty, thou art my theme:
> Not such as idle poets dream,
> Who trick thee up a heathen goddess
> That a fantastic cap and rod has!
> Such stale conceits are poor and silly:
> I paint thee out a Highland filly,
> A sturdy, stubborn, handsome dapple,
> As sleek 's a mouse, as round 's an apple,[79]
> That, when thou pleasest, can do wonders,
> But when thy luckless rider blunders,
> Or if thy fancy should demur there,
> Wilt break thy neck ere thou go further.

If Liberty is here something of a comic figure, it simply goes to
show that Burns was so completely in command of himself that
he could laugh at the things he loved.

On other occasions, as in the "Ode for General Washington's Birthday," Liberty is something of a rhetorical abstraction; on yet others still, as in "Here's a Health to them that's
awa,"[80] it becomes an embodiment of the most urgent political
demands of the day:

> Here's freedom to them that wad read,
> Here's freedom to them that would write!
> There's nane ever fear'd that the truth should be heard
> But they whom the truth would indite!

"As I stood by yon roofless Tower"[81] reveals Liberty as
emblematic, the "sacred posy" on the bonnet of the "stern
and stalwart ghaist" of a minstrel of the olden time who be-
wails the political reaction which set in after the end of 1792.
In the eighth stanza of the version published by Currie in

[78] II. 168 (392).
[79] The elision of "a" in this line would not be possible in "English English,"
even for the sake of the metre. Hence this whole passage should perhaps be
termed "Scots English."
[80] IV. 35 (96).
[81] III. 144 (406). For "sacred posy," see H. & H., III. 407.

1800,[82] Burns implied that he did not dare to write down the minstrel's words for fear of persecution :

> He sang wi' joy his former day,
> He, weeping, wail'd his latter times :
> But what he said—it was nae play !—
> I winna ventur't in my rhymes.

I cannot agree with Craigie that this verse is bathetic ; on the contrary, I find it a peculiarly moving depiction of the feelings of a liberal during a period of political reaction. Milton must have felt very much like that after 1660, and so must many Americans during the reign of Senator McCarthy. The chorus has a message that can hardly be misunderstood :

> A lassie all alone was making her moan,
> Lamenting our lads beyond the sea :—
> 'In the bluidy wars they fa', and our honor's gane an' a',
> And broken-hearted we maun die.'

The American editor Gebbie, whom William Wallace followed in his improvement of Chambers' edition in 1897, was convinced that "As I stood by yon roofless Tower" was originally intended to prefix the stanzas now known as the "Ode on General Washington's Birthday," and that the latter was in fact the song that the minstrel sang.[83] Gebbie accordingly prints them as one, omitting the eighth stanza (beginning "He sang wi' joy his former day"), which he thinks Burns added to complete the fragment when he had decided, for reasons of prudence, to separate it from the "Ode." There is strong circumstantial evidence in favour of his hypothesis. For one thing, if these two poems are in reality but halves of a single work, then the relation between them must be exactly

[82] Currie, IV. 346–8 ; H. & H., st. vii. Currie's note on this work is of some interest : "This poem, an imperfect copy of which was printed in Johnson's Museum, is here given from the poet's MS with his last corrections. . . . Though this poem has a political bias, yet it may be presumed that no reader of taste, whatever his opinions may be, would forgive its being omitted. Our poet's prudence suppressed the song of *Libertie*, perhaps fortunately for his reputation." It is to be hoped that the Besterman papers, which include many MSS used by Currie in the preparation of his edition, and which are at present being edited by Prof. R. D. Thornton, may throw some light on whether the suppressed "Song of *Libertie*" was, in fact, the "Ode for General Washington's Birthday."

[83] Gebbie, VI. 3–12 ; C. & W., IV. 124. But it must be admitted that a formal ode was the very reverse of what Burns usually meant by a song in 1794.

the same as that which subsists between the two parts of "A Winter Night"; there, too, Burns describes a formal ode as a "plaintive strain" which stole over the poet in the evening. For another, the "Ode" contains two lines—

> Dark-quench'd as yonder sinking star,
> No more that glance lightens afar . . .[84]

—which cannot easily be explained except on the supposition that the poem was originally preceded by stanzas descriptive of a night scene. Nowhere else in the "Ode" as it stands is there any mention of darkness, but, with its moonbeam and its stars shooting along the sky, "As I stood by yon roofless Tower" would be the perfect prelude to it, and the two puzzling lines just quoted could then be explained by supposing that the minstrel's song took so long that it was almost morning when it finished. Finally, additional evidence is provided by the strong parallels in mood and idea between the two poems. If they were not originally intended as a single unit, then at the very least we must agree that they proceeded from similar trains of thought and were probably written very close to one another.

If Gebbie is correct, then it would seem at first sight that the main subject of this reconstituted unity is the American War of Independence, together with the associations aroused by the phrase "our honor's gane an' a' " in the chorus that he attached to the version of "As I stood by yon roofless Tower" that he sent to Johnson for inclusion in *The Scots Musical Museum*. What other unjust and inglorious war had Britain engaged in, apart from the struggle with the American Colonies? The answer, of course, is—the early stages of the contemporary war with France. Burns was always in the habit of linking the national and revolutionary struggles of different periods together in his mind. If, to quote his own words, "Scots wha hae" was influenced by "the glowing ideas of some other struggles of the same nature, *not quite so ancient,*"[85] and if Snyder is right in assuming that in *this* passage Burns was thinking of the French Revolution and the Scottish Reform

[84] H. & H., II. 173 *ad fin.*
[85] To Thomson, [*c.* 30 Aug. 1793], in *Letters*, II. 196.

Movement,[86] then it would seem highly plausible to suppose
that the war referred to in "As I stood by yon roofless Tower,"
and also the "tyrant's cause" which England is described as
espousing in the "Ode for General Washington's Birthday,"
are in fact the struggle with France:

> That hour accurst how did the fiends rejoice,
> And Hell thro' all her confines raise th' exulting voice!
> That hour which saw the generous English name
> Link't with such damnèd deeds of everlasting shame![87]

Thus the "sacred posy" on the minstrel's bonnet turns out
to be no mere rhetorical abstraction, but the summation of the
aspirations of the Americans, the French, and Scottish (and
English) political Reformers like Thomas Muir. In "Scots,
wha hae," the concept of nationalism (earlier often present in
a Jacobite form) is completely fused with that of freedom;
and in the fifth stanza of "Is there for honest Poverty?"[88] it has
been transcended in a blending of internationalism with the
revolutionary idea of fraternity:

> Then let us pray that come it may
> (As come it will for a' that)
> That Sense and Worth o'er a' the earth
> Shall bear the gree an' a' that!
> For a' that, an' a' that,
> It's comin yet for a' that,
> That man to man the world o'er
> Shall brithers be for a' that.[89]

[86] Snyder, p. 420.
[87] H. & H., II. 173 *ad init.* France had declared war on Britain on 1 Feb. 1793;
the "Ode for General Washington's Birthday" was written in June 1794. (See
R. B. to [Mrs Dunlop], 25 June 1794, in *Letters* II. 246). [88] III. 271 (489).
[89] Burns (to [Thomson, Jan. 1795], in *Letters*, II. 284) described "Is there for
honest Poverty?" as "two or three pretty good *prose* thoughts, inverted into
rhyme. . . ." As J. MacCunn points out (*Ethics of Citizenship*, Glasgow 1921, pp.
43–4), the prose thoughts are those of Tom Paine; for details, see Appendix II,
§ 3 (below, p. 365). At the trial of Deacon Brodie, John Clerk of Eldin, defending
the pannel George Smith, is alleged to have had the following passage-at-arms with
the Lord Advocate: "MR CLERK—Gentlemen, . . . this infernal witness was con-
victed of felony in England, and how dare he come here to be received as a witness
in this case? THE LORD ADVOCATE—He has, as I have shown you, received His
Majesty's free pardon. MR CLERK—Yes, I see; but . . . can His Majesty make a
tainted scoundrel an honest man? [Great applause in Court.] THE LORD JUSTICE-
CLERK—Macers, clear the Court if there is any more unruly din." According to

In another poem in the Scottish style that appears to have been composed in the early seventeen-nineties, "The Tree of Liberty,"[90] internationalism is seen as entailing complete and unreserved support for embattled France. If this work, which many editors consider to be apocryphal, is ever definitely proved to be by Burns, it will have to be recognised as the most extreme development of his political thought and emotions that we possess. Even if it were simply a forgery—the work of someone like Hogg, or of the mysterious Mr Duncan of Mosesfield who communicated the poem to Chambers in time for his edition of 1838[91]—it would still be a remarkable feat of imaginative projection back into the Messianic atmosphere of 1793-5. It is not markedly different in sentiment from "When Princes & Prelates"[92] or "You're welcome to Despots, Dumourier!"[93] which we know were undoubtedly produced by Burns; and it chimes in perfectly with his prose remarks about the execution of Louis XVI and Marie Antoinette, which so offended Mrs Dunlop.[94]

It has not, perhaps, been sufficiently realised by critics that the poem (whoever its author may have been) has undeniable documentary qualities. Trees of Liberty, "hung round with garlands of flowers, with emblems of freedom and various inscriptions"—the description is from the pen of Dr John

Roughead, this "is said" to have "reached the ears of Robert Burns," and later to have prompted him to write the famous lines "A prince can mak' a belted knicht, . . . | But an honest man's aboon his might. . . ." (see *Trial of Deacon Brodie*, ed. Roughead, pp. 60, 178). Chambers (iv. 129) points out that "The rank is but the guinea's stamp" is paralleled in Wycherley, *The Plain Dealer*: "I weigh the man, not his title; 'tis not the king's stamp can make the metal better or heavier. Your lord is a leaden shilling, which you bend every way, and debases the stamp he bears." H. & H. (iii. 490) note that the same idea also occurs in *Tristram Shandy*. The measure was traditional in popular bawdry (cp. *The Merry Muses*, pp. 69-70, and H. & H., ii. 304). Thus "Is there for honest Poverty?" owes something to the Augustan literary tradition, to European revolutionary doctrines, and to the old ribald rhymes of the Scottish countryside.   [90] iv. 58 (107).

[91] R. Chambers, *Life and Works of Robert Burns*, Edinburgh 1838, p. 86.

[92] For which see *Letters*, ii. 250 f.   [93] ii. 228 (419).

[94] To [Mrs Dunlop], 12 Jan. [1795], in *Letters*, ii. 281-2: "What is there in the delivering over a perjured Blockhead & an unprincipled Prostitute to the hands of the hangman, that it should arrest for a moment, attention, in an eventful hour, when, as my friend Roscoe in Liverpool gloriously expresses it— | 'When the welfare of Millions is hung in the scale | 'And the balance yet trembles with fate'!" The dating of this outburst is significant; "Is there for honest Poverty?" was written in the same month.

Moore, with whom Burns corresponded—were actually erected in Scottish towns during the height of the Reform agitation.[95] In November 1792, for example, the radicals of Perth set up such a tree at the Cross in honour of General Dumourier's entry into Brussels. At Dundee, in the same month, another was set up and decked with apples, a lantern, candles and the slogan "LIBERTY, EQUALITY AND NO SINECURES." Again, during the State trial of the democrat Margarot in Edinburgh, the accused was escorted by his friends "from the Black Bull Inn, in the Grassmarket, to the court room, bearing a Tree of Liberty, 'shaped like the letter M,' with a scroll inscribed, 'LIBERTY, VIRTUE, REASON, JUSTICE AND TRUTH'." And as late as 1797, when Burns had been dead for a year and one would have imagined that the majority of the people had swung round in support of the war, there were widespread demonstrations throughout Scotland against the Militia Act— that is, against the call-up of some six thousand young men aged between nineteen and twenty-three. In the course of this agitation, Trees of Liberty were erected at Galston and Dalry in Burns's native Ayrshire.[96] Thus during the Scottish Reform Movement of the seventeen-nineties the Tree of Liberty became almost as much a Scottish symbol as the kilt, the lion, the thistle or the holly.

Against Burns's authorship of the poem, one must set, firstly, the fact that the manuscript has not yet come to light, and, secondly, certain internal indications which cast doubt on its authenticity. These are mainly linguistic—there are many fewer Scots words than one would expect in a poem or song in the "Gillicrankie" measure,[97] and the writer speaks of "England" when he appears to mean Britain, a fault which Burns rarely committed. Although England is indeed mentioned in the "Ode for General Washington's Birthday," it is

---

[95] J. Moore, *A Journal of a Residence in France*, London 1793, II. 7.

[96] Meikle, *Scotland and the French Revolution*, pp. 96–8, 145, 179–82.

[97] In "When Guilford good our Pilot stood," Burns's early experiment in the "Gillicrankie" style (above, pp. 147–9,) ll. 2, 4, 6, 8 of each stanza end with the sound "aw, man." The fact that "The Tree of Liberty" does not follow the same rigid pattern is no argument against Burns's authorship. Such a rhyme-scheme would have been restrictive in so "international" a poem; besides, the original "Gillicrankie" is in this respect looser than "When Guilford good."

in a stanza that begins by apostrophising Alfred, who could never by any stretch of the imagination be described as King of Britain ; and when first named, the country is deliberately called "thy [*i.e.*, Alfred's] England," to distinguish it from Scotland, which is referred to in the next stanza as "Caledonia." To reinforce the argument, we have Burns's explicit statement in a letter to Mrs Dunlop—"Nothing can reconcile me to the common terms, 'English ambassador, English court,' &c. And I am out of all patience to see that equivocal character, Hastings, impeached by 'the Commons of England'."[98] On the face of it, then, it would seem that lines such as the following cannot be by Burns :

> . . . That sic a tree can not be found
> 'Twixt London and the Tweed, man.

> Syne let us pray, Auld England may
> Sure plant this far-famed tree, man. . . .

These considerations can, however, all be explained away by various processes of reasoning. One could assume that the manuscript apparently in the possession of Mr Duncan of Mosesfield in 1838 was not in Burns's handwriting, but had been copied from a Burnsian original, and that a certain amount of textual corruption had taken place during the transcription, involving among other things the toning-down of Scots passages. Or, alternatively, the author may deliberately have introduced the expressions "London and the Tweed" and "Auld England" in order to point a contrast with Scotland, as in the third and fourth stanzas of the "Ode for General Washington's Birthday."

Immediately before the first of the two references to England which I have just quoted, and in the same stanza, the poet writes :

> Let Britain boast her hardy oak,
> Her poplar, and her pine, man !

At this point, when he says Britain, he means Britain—a unified political whole with subsidiary parts ; he chooses the oak as the traditional symbol of England, and the pine as the

[98] To [Mrs Dunlop], 10 Apr. 1790, in *Letters*, ii. 18.

emblem of Scotland. It follows that when, six lines later, he speaks of "London and the Tweed," it *is* England—not Britain—that he has in mind.[99] The last couplet of the eighth stanza is thus ironically intended—a devastating subtlety which, as much as anything else in the poem, tells in favour of Burns's authorship. In cold prose, what the stanza means is this : "The Scots agree with the Americans, the French, and many people in Europe—it is only the English who are holding Britain back."[100]

Now Burns (or the unknown author) cannot possibly have been talking about freedom in the abstract. When one considers the probable date of the poem, one must surely agree that he is thinking of the whole contemporary movement of Corresponding Societies, Friends of the People, and the national conventions of such bodies. If Burns believed that the democratic movement was more advanced in Scotland than in England, and that Trees of Liberty, though they had been set up for a few days in Perth, Dundee, and perhaps elsewhere, had not yet made their appearance " 'twixt London and the Tweed," then the poem could be interpreted as—at least in part—a plea to the English to follow Scotland's example. And in that case, may not the poem originally have been written for dispatch to one of Burns's correspondents in England ?[101]

[99] I am indebted for this point to Dr James C. Corson of the University of Edinburgh.

[100] I am told that in Edinburgh today some people still sometimes say the same sort of thing about such issues as Cyprus : "We sympathise with the Cypriots because we resisted Edward I ; but that's something the English just can't understand." Similar sentiments were expressed about Spain in the late nineteen-thirties, and about India during the Second World War. Cp. the letter to Mrs Dunlop, 25 Jun. 1794 (*Letters*, II. 246) in which Burns sends her part of the "Ode for General Washington's Birthday" : "After having mentioned *the degeneracy of other kingdoms* [my italics] I come to Scotland thus— | Thee, Caledonia, thy wild heaths among, etc."

[101] In *Letters*, I. xlix, Professor Ferguson notes that Burns "wrote to Allan Masterton, William Roscoe, and other friends no letters to whom have been recovered." The poem was known to Allan Cunningham, but rejected by him "on internal evidence." Chambers (who was editorially far more scrupulous than Cunningham, as a rule) printed the poem in 1838, and subsequently ; Hately Waddell (1867 ; p. 437) states that "The poem is admitted to be in our Author's handwriting," and then concludes : "On the whole, although we do not doubt the genuineness of the authorship in this case, we frankly admit that it is by no means in Burns's own style." W. Scott Douglas, *The Works of Robert Burns*, 6 vols., Edinburgh 1877–9, did not print the poem, though he had included it in his

Irrespective of all questions of authenticity, Angellier's words still apply, with the phrase "the unknown author" substituted for "Burns" wherever his name occurs :

The bitterness already apparent in these stanzas is of a kind that one does not find in [Wordsworth and Coleridge]. The next stanza is still more savage. It is brutal—bantering and cruel at the same time—like a *sansculotte's* refrain. It is like an echo of "*Ça ira.*" It might even have been chanted by the mob on the way back from seeing the execution of Louis XVI :

> But vicious folk ay hate to see
> The works o' Virtue thrive, man ;
> The courtly vermin's bann'd the tree,
> And grat to see it thrive man !
> King Louis thought to cut it down,
> When it was unco sma', man ;
> For this the watchman crack'd his crown,
> Cut aff his head and a', man. . . .

. . . This is a genuine revolutionary song. Purely out of sympathy with the people, Burns was rendering much more closely [than any contemporary English poet] the accent of the common people impelled into a frenzy of suspicion, cruelty and impetuosity. Some kind of instinct had given him, quite spontaneously, that tone composed of a mixture of dynamic vulgarity, heroic defiance, and cynical mockery.[102]

Kilmarnock edition of 1876 ; and Gebbie (vi. 13) states that in 1876 the original MS was still in the possession of Mr James Duncan of Mosesfield. Angellier, writing in 1893, refers (ii. 205) to "the existence of the manuscript," but I have never seen any description of it or any account of the handwriting. H. & H. (iv. 107) say that "the MS has not been heard of since 1838," and intemperately assert that "we may charitably conclude that Burns neither made the trash nor copied it." Professor R. D. Thornton assures me that there is no reference to "The Tree of Liberty" in the Besterman papers ; and Professor Egerer, the most recent of Burns's bibliographers, has not been able to trace the MS. Russian critics and translators accept the genuineness of "The Tree of Liberty" without much question. It appears in the latest edition of Samuel Marshak's translations (Moscow, 1957, pp. 85 ff.), and is referred to in Mme R. Raït-Kovaleva's lengthy introduction to the same volume (pp. 28, 56), as well in M. Morozov, *Izbrannye statji i perevody*, Moscow 1954, p. 313. Burns's authorship of "The Tree of Liberty" is clearly assumed by Morozov in Marshak, p. 438 n. ; while Mme. A. E. Elistratova (*Robert Burns*, Moscow 1957, p. 129), omitting all mention of Scott Douglas's doubts or Henley and Henderson's "trash," roundly claims : "It is characteristic that in many editions of Burns's works 'The Tree of Liberty' was left out by cautious editors and publishers, although Burns's authorship was not even contested."
[102] Angellier, ii. 203, 205.

If Scott Douglas, Henley and Henderson and all the other editors who have rejected "The Tree of Liberty" are correct, then we must attribute all these excellences not to Burns, but to some talented literary criminal of the early nineteenth century, or some anonymous democrat of the seventeen-nineties who wrote nothing else of value which has been preserved.

There is still another form of Liberty celebrated by Burns—not the goddess in cap and bells, or the ideal of agrarian communism which seems to have inspired the poorest of the Scottish cotter-folk and landless agricultural labourers during the seventeen-nineties, but the rather prosaic and humdrum deity of the Whig opposition, whose mystic rites included a reform of Parliament, to be achieved by means of victory at the polls. Perhaps he saw that as the first step towards a fraternal commonwealth in Britain, or perhaps he was interested—like those whom Sir William Maxwell termed in 1792 "the discontented in a higher rank in life"—mainly in political freedom.[103] At any rate, from 1789 to 1795 he wrote a number of election ballads that are models of the sort of political satire found today in the verses of writers like "Sagittarius" and Reginald Reynolds.

The election squibs of 1789–90—the "Election Ballad for Westerha'," "The Five Carlins," and the "Election Ballad at Close of the Contest for Representing the Dumfries Burghs, 1790"—are mildly Pittite in tone, but not bitterly anti-Whig, since on many issues Burns was already leaning towards that party. In the "Election Ballad for Westerha'"[104] the leader of the Whig magnates in Scotland, the notorious Duke of Queensberry, is singled out for especial attack—a fact which is surely of a piece with Burns's treatment of the aristocracy throughout his career :

[103] Cp. James Mitchell, Kirriemuir, 29 Nov. 1792 : "An opinion got amongst the lowest class that a division of property should also take place, and that they would be equally free and equally rich." Cp. also Sir W. Maxwell to the Duke of Buccleuch, 19 Nov. 1792 : "Scots peasants understand nothing of parliamentary reform, equal representation, and other grievances of which the discontented in a higher rank of life complain, while they may be tempted to unite to try their strength and risk their necks in the hopes of bringing about a division of the landed property . . ." Both quoted in Meikle, *Scotland and the French Revolution*, p. 99 n. [104] II. 182 (397).

The day he stude his country's friend,
Or gied her faes a claw, Jamie,
Or frae puir man a blessin wan—
That day the Duke ne'er saw, Jamie.

And in a set of similar verses preserved in the Glenriddell MSS Burns again turns all his scorn against the Duke, one of whose country seats was Drumlanrig; he sees "Old Q" as the scion of a degenerate line :

Drumlanrig's towers hae tint the powers
That kept the lands in awe, man :
The eagle's dead, and in his stead
We've gotten a hoodie-craw, man. . . .

The lads about the banks o' Nith,
They trust his Grace for a', man :
But he'll sair them as he sair't his King,
Turn tail and rin awa, man.[105]

"The Five Carlins"[106] and the Dumfries "Election Ballad"[107] of 1790 are pleasingly mock-heroic, describing a contemporary election battle in terms of the epic conflicts of former times. The Dumfries "Election Ballad" has a decidedly uncommitted air, like the songs in the "Sherramuir" tradition. It ends, in the twenty-sixth and twenty-seventh stanzas, on a note which stresses the needs of Scotland as a whole, and the desirability of freeing the country from political corruption and oppression :

For your poor friend, the Bard, afar
He sees and hears the distant war,
A cool spectator purely :
So, when the storm the forest rends,
The robin in the hedge descends,
And, sober, chirps securely.[108]

Now, for my friends' and brethren's sakes,
And for my dear-lov'd Land o' Cakes,
I pray with holy fire :—

[105] H. & H., II. 398. The resemblance to the traditional "Gillicrankie" makes the sarcasm still more savage. See above, p. 147 n.
[106] II. 177 (395).   [107] II. 183 (399).
[108] I prefer "sober," which appears in the Glenriddell MS, to H. & H.'s "patient," the reading of the Fintry MSS and the Afton Lodge Book.

Lord, send a rough-shod troop o' Hell
O'er a' wad Scotland buy or sell,
To grind them in the mire !

Five years later Burns actively intervened in the election
for the Stewartry of Kirkcudbright, a neighbouring constituency
to Dumfries. On this occasion he was most definitely not on
the Tory side ; on the contrary, he was an impassioned Whig,
advocating the return of his friend and possible patron,
Patrick Heron of Kerroughtrie. The first of the Ballads on
Mr Heron's Election[109] shows Burns in 1795 interpreting the
French Revolutionary doctrines in terms of the general Whig
demands for Parliamentary Reform—a synthesis which is
evident in the elaborate use of quotations from his own "Is
there for honest Poverty ?" I do not mean to imply that Burns
expected his audience to be so familiar with it as to be able to
identify the echoes, but rather that his own song had so im-
pregnated his mind that cross-reference, as in the chorus of
the second, fourth and sixth stanzas, seemed the most natural
thing in the world to him :

> . . . For a' that, an' a' that,
> Here's Heron yet for a' that !
> The independent patriot,
> The honest man, and a' that !

> . . . For a' that, and a' that,
> Here's Heron yet for a' that !
> A Lord may be a lousy loun,
> Wi' ribban, star, and a' that.

> . . . For a' that, and a' that,
> Here's Heron yet for a' that !
> A House of Commons such as he,
> They wad be blest that saw that.

When it comes down to practical politics, the translation of
French ideals into British reality means nothing more nor less
than the election of a House of Commons composed of "honest
men" and "independent patriots."

"Ballad Second : The Election,"[110] the next of the set, is

[109] II. 191 (401).   [110] II. 193 (402).

devoted to a spirited blackguarding of leading Tory personalities in the constituency, and also to certain more or less genial remarks about the Whig stalwarts. "Ballad Third : John Bushby's Lamentation"[111] is his song of triumph over the defeated Tory candidate. "Ballad Fourth : The Trogger,"[112] a song to the tune of *Buy Broom Besoms*, is a piece of lyrical flyting seasoned with crude sarcasm. The satire here is emblematic, as in the seventh and eighth stanzas describing the local notables—the minister of Urr (who had written an epigram on Burns, "To Vaccerras") and Walter Sloan Lawrie ("Redcastle") :

> Here's armorial bearings
> Frae the manse o' Urr :
> The crest, a sour crab-apple
> Rotten at the core.

> Here is Satan's picture,
> Like a bizzard gled
> Pouncing poor Redcastle,
> Sprawlin like a taed.

All Burns's political opponents end in Clootie's keeping :

> Saw ye e'er sic troggin ?—
> If to buy ye're slack,
> Hornie's turnin chapman :
> He'll buy a' the pack !

The Burns election literature is important for three main reasons. It indicates the evolution of Burns's political views from the mild Toryism and left-wing Jacobitism of 1789–90 to the Whig partisanship of 1795 ; it reveals the continuity of that development, in spite of the apparent inconsistencies—for example, in the first of the Heron ballads one of the main ideas is that

> We are na to be bought and sold,
> Like nowte, and naigs, and a' that. . . .

—an exact parallel to the last stanzas of the supposedly Tory "Election Ballad for Westerha' " ; and, finally, it demonstrates that for Burns the abstract notion of liberty meant, at any rate

[111] ii. 197 (405). 　　　　　[112] ii. 201 (406).

towards the very end of his career, the reformist programme of the left-wing Whigs. Not only does the first Heron Ballad echo the Painite sentiment of "Is there for honest Poverty?"; it also carries the positive implications of these lines from the second, third and fourth stanzas of "Does haughty Gaul invasion threat?":[113]

> . . . For never but by British hands
> Maun British wrangs be righted!

> The kettle o' the Kirk and State,
> Perhaps a clout may fail in 't . . .

> . . . But while we sing *God save the King*,
> We'll ne'er forget the People!

It is not enough to say, with Angellier, that in writing "Does haughty Gaul Invasion threat?" Burns became a patriotic Briton overnight, anticipating—but suddenly and impulsively —the evolution which Wordsworth and Coleridge were later to undergo.[114] For Burns's political poetry exhibits consistency in its inconsistency, and shows continuity of development amid all its apparent twists and shifts of view.

Finally, the democratic poems of Burns's last period reveal that he was on the way to resolving the conflict of tongues which we examined in a previous chapter. There are, it is true, throw-backs to an earlier mode; but even "As I stood by yon roofless Tower" and the "Ode for General Washington's Birthday," if we can regard them as together constituting the lost "Ode to Liberty," are more successful than the two halves of "A Winter Night." On the whole, Burns's development was towards a new harmony of English and Scots, with complete mastery in each, the perfect example, of course, being "Tam o' Shanter." The English-type rhetoric that occurs in "Scots, wha hae" is not nearly so artificial as the rhetoric of the epistles to Graham of Fintry and the "Elegy on the Death of Sir James Hunter Blair";[115] as in the "English" passages of "The Vision" and "The Cotter's Saturday Night," it requires

---

[113] III. 195 (441).   [114] Angellier, II. 206–7.
[115] Above, p. 238.

only the slightest trace of Scots to make it truly national.[116] Again, in many parts of the Heron election ballads, the Scottishness resides in the intonation rather than in the vocabulary, so that one is reminded of the kind of effect that Mr W. S. Graham secures in works like "Baldy Bane." But in "Is there for honest Poverty?" the fusion of Scots and English is complete: such words and phrases as "cuif" and "Guid faith, he mauna fa' that!" exist cheek by jowl with "Their tinsel show" and "Tho' hundreds worship at his word." Here nationality and internationalism are one; the "*Marseillaise* of Equality" as Angellier called it,[117] has also been termed (and with justice) "the best known, and most important national song of our Author's—that is, of the language."[118]

---

[116] *E.g.*, the somewhat synthetic Scots of the title, or "Let us do, or die!" rhyming with "free," etc.

[117] Angellier, II. 216.   [118] Hately Waddell, p. 296.

IX

Maker of Songs

AFTER 1787, Burns's main creative activity was the writing of songs; and it is agreed on all sides that it was singing Edinburgh and the singing and fiddling Highlands that turned him into a song-writer. Even his best political pieces—the works produced under the stimulus of the French Revolution and the Reform movement at home—are songs first, and poems second; even "The Tree of Liberty" itself (if Burns is indeed the author)[1] is a revolutionary *song*. Given his early familiarity with the songs and dances of the countryside, and given his discovery that there were men and women in the capital who loved them and wished to preserve them—men like David Herd the antiquary[2] and James Johnson the engraver,[3] or young girls like Janet Cruikshank, the twelve-year-old daughter of the Classical Master at the Royal High School,[4] not to speak of the nameless young ladies and gentlemen who footed it night after night to the old measures in the fashionable Assemblies [5]—it was almost inevitable that Burns should turn to the allied pursuits of collecting folk-songs and setting his own words to traditional tunes. And once he had begun on this business, it was also inevitable that he should carry it out with all the passion that had gone into his poetry during the twelve months or so that culminated in the Kilmarnock Edition. It has not always been realised exactly how much energy went into the three hundred and fifty songs, or so, in which he had a hand; for what he did, by way of preparation, was nothing less than to familiarise himself with *all* that had been previously published on the subject—all the available collections of

[1] See above, pp. 246–51.
[2] For biographical details of Herd, see introduction to *Songs from David Herd's Manuscripts*, ed. Hans Hecht, Edinburgh and London 1904, pp. 30–65.
[3] For Johnson, see below, pp. 261.
[4] For Janet Cruikshank and her father, see *Letters*, ii. 346–7.
[5] Cp. Graham, i. 97–102.

Scottish songs, with and without music, and all the volumes of Scottish instrumental music without words.[6] The gathering and publishing of Scottish songs was one of the most important branches of the antiquarian movement of the eighteenth century; and on this subject, so closely bound up with the contemporary national revival, Burns became the greatest expert of them all.

One of the most delightful things about songs is that they do not take up much room on the page—less than the decasyllables of our epics and blank-verse drama, and less, far less, than prose. In countries with a strong tradition of puritanism there has always been a disposition to look down on them for that reason, and to regard song-writing as an essentially godless and frivolous pursuit. It is, therefore, not altogether surprising that there has been considerable disagreement about the importance of the lyrics in relation to the whole course of Burns's poetic development. Two main answers have been given to this last question during the hundred and sixty years since the poet's death.

The first of these holds that Burns's preoccupation with the lyric after 1787 was, on the whole, a bad thing; a conclusion which follows from the austere assumption that song-writing is only, at best, a marginal occupation. Thus, although Sir Walter Scott liked many of the songs, and although he was careful to say "Let no one suppose that we undervalue [them]," from what he says about them it· is clear that in practice he thought them less worthy than grander and more imposing literary kinds:

> . . . we cannot but deeply regret that so much of his time and talents should have been frittered away in compiling and composing for musical collections. . . . But the writing of a series of songs for large musical collections, degenerated into a slavish labour which no talents could support, led to negligence, and above all, diverted the poet from his grand plan of dramatic composition.[7]

[6] Cp. Burns to [Johnson, ? 1791], in *Letters*, II.75: "I was so lucky lately as to pick up an entire copy of Oswald's Scots Music, and I think I shall make glorious work out of it. I want much Anderson's Collection of strathspeys &c., *and then I think I will have all the music of the country.*" [My italics.]

[7] [Scott], review of Cromek's *Reliques*, in *Quarterly Review*, I. (1809), 30–2.

R. L. Stevenson was of the opinion that "during the remainder of his life"—that is to say, after 1786—Burns "rarely found courage for any more sustained effort than a song," and that "it is not the less typical of his loss of moral courage that he should have given up all larger ventures, nor the less melancholy that a man who first attacked literature with a hand that seemed capable of moving mountains, should have spent his later years in whittling cherry-stones" ;[8] and when, in his essay on "The Politics of Burns," W. P. Ker says that "Burns as a poet is to be judged by the work of those years"— that is, by the work of 1781-6—he implicitly dismisses the songs as intrinsically less important.[9] A corollary of this view is that Burns's poetry did not develop—or even, as Stevenson believed, that his work declined in quality towards the end of his life.

The other assessment of the place of the songs in Burns's literary career is that put forward as early as 1809 by Francis Jeffrey, when he prophesied that they would "transmit the name of Burns to all future generations."[10] Echoed and developed by Hazlitt,[11] Carlyle,[12] Tennyson,[13] Angellier,[14] Henley,[15] Wallace,[16] and many lesser commentators, this judgment has almost completely ousted the conception of Scott and Stevenson, although traces of it can sometimes be found in the comments of modern academic critics. An interesting variant of this second opinion is Professor Ferguson's contention that the true bent of Burns's genius was in the direction of lyrical composition, and that even the great satirical and comic poems of the Kilmarnock period were in a sense deviations from his real mission in life.[17]

The "majority view" has the advantage of drawing attention to the general and universal qualities in Burns's art while minimising the contingent, the temporary, and the ephemeral.

---

[8] R. L. Stevenson, "Some Aspects of Robert Burns," in *Familiar Studies of Men and Books*, London 1923, p. 46.   [9] W. P. Ker, in *Essays*, 1.146.

[10] [Jeffrey], review of Cromek's *Reliques*, in *Edinburgh Review*, xiii (1809), 263.

[11] "On Burns, and the Old English Ballads," in *Lectures on the English Poets*, in *Complete Works*, ed. Howe, 21 vols., London 1930–4, v. 139–40.

[12] In *Edinburgh Review*, xlviii (1828), 286–7.

[13] Cp. Hallam, Lord Tennyson, *Tennyson, A Memoir*, 2 vols., London 1924, I. 211, II. 201–2.

[14] II. 395–6.   [15] In H. & H., iv. 322–4.

[16] C. & W., iv. 499–501.   [17] In *Pride and Passion*, pp. 247–8.

Some of its implications are to be seen in the remarks of a Chinese specialist in English literature, Dr Wen-Yuan-Ning,[18] who said in a broadcast on 25 Jan. 1944 that Burns's treatment of common incidents and feelings reminded him very much of the poetry of his own country, "where the maximum effect of vastness and grandeur is conveyed through simple and common incidents; the shadow cast by bamboos on the wall, the flight of wild geese in autumn, or the sound of temple bells in the evening." Dr Wen claimed that if Burns could only be translated into Chinese, he would find a response in the heart of every Chinese peasant; and though it appears from the context that Dr Wen was thinking of the whole corpus of Burns's poetical output, (he specifically cites "To a Mouse" and "To a Mountain Daisy"), it is obvious that what he said is particularly applicable to the songs. For though a Chinese peasant could hardly understand "Holy Willie's Prayer," or "Tam o' Shanter," or even "The Cotter's Saturday Night," without knowing something about the alien ideas of Scottish religion, he would respond immediately to "O, Whistle an' I'll come to ye, my Lad" and "As I stood by yon roofless Tower."

This second and most widely held assessment of the Burns songs has still another point in its favour; it very naturally tends to stress the evolution of Burns's poetic consciousness, and to concentrate on the real differences between the earlier and later periods of Burns's art. We must, however, be careful to notice exactly how those changes came about. They did not take place simply and easily, but in a roundabout manner and after setbacks and recessions, and they happened as the result of the whole man's struggle to understand, and, if possible, to master, divided and distinguished worlds. At one time, Burns was attracted by the somewhat arid universality of Edinburgh neo-classicism; only when he had rejected and overcome it could he pass on to the supreme achievement of the best of the later songs and political pieces. And that rejection was itself made possible by one of the most vital movements in that same Edinburgh—the contemporary folk-song revival. Even so, traces of artificiality—of the desire to let great folks (and,

[18] B.B.C. Home Service, 25 Jan. 1944; *Burns Chronicle* (1945), pp. 6–7. Cp. below, p. 336.

especially, their wives and daughters) hear the drawing-room inanities to which they had become accustomed—spoil many of the later lyrics.

Burns's songs are, in the first instance, songs, not poems to be read or even orally recited, however effective many of them may be apart from the music. The conflict of opinion over their worth arises partly from failure to consider them in a musical context, and partly from an inability to realise that discussions of this type are meaningless if allowed to rotate round such absurd generalisations as that "Music is better than poetry," or *vice versa*. Obviously, the tone-deaf man, and the musical snob who despises folk-songs (especially those of his own country), are both unfitted to judge Burns's songs; equally, the English or American bookman who thinks that good verse ought to be primarily an affair of images and symbols will fight shy of much in the Kilmarnock volume, and in Burns's songs will seek much of what he has come to expect from other poetry. Since the present study is a work of criticism, it is bound to pay particular attention to the poetic values inherent in the songs—to pick out their literary qualities and leave the rest in shadow. But it must not ignore their musical content altogether; it must also say something (however briefly) of the lyrics as *songs*.

If it had not been for the musical editors James Johnson and George Thomson, the great songs might well have been fewer in number. Johnson was an engraver and music-seller who had just completed the first volume of his *Scots Musical Museum*, containing a hundred melodies, when Burns met him early in 1787. Burns became co-editor for the next three volumes, and the real driving-force behind the undertaking. A fifth volume was on the point of publication when the poet died in 1796, and vol. vi, the last, did not finally appear till 1803. Johnson's great service was that he published everything Burns cared to send him, without alteration or demur; that of Thomson, the editor of the *Select Collection of Original Scotish Airs*, consisted at least in part of an irritating propensity to amend or reject. By suggesting changes in both the words and music he received from Burns, he forced the poet into elaborating a theoretical justification for his lyric art; and this, it is reasonable to assume, in its turn helped on his creative activity.[1]

It is clear from the correspondence with Thomson that by the seventeen-nineties Burns knew quite well that he could not often make good songs in the southern literary tongue. On 16 Sep. 1792 he wrote:

Apropos, if you are for *English* verses, there is, on my part, an end of the matter.—Whether in the simplicity of *the Ballad*, or the pathos of *the Song*, I can only hope to please myself in being allowed at least a sprinkling of our native tongue. English verses, particularly the works of Scotsmen, that have merit, are certainly very eligible.—[2]

And again, on 26 Oct. 1792 :

But let me remark to you, in the sentiment & style of our Scotish airs, there is a pastoral simplicity, a something that one may call, the Doric style & dialect of vocal music, to which a dash of our native tongue & manners is particularly, nay peculiarly apposite.—[3]

On 26 Jan. 1793 he returned to the same topic :

If it were possible to procure songs of merit, I think it would be proper to have one set of Scots words to every air—& that the set of words to which the notes ought to be pricked.—There is a naïveté, a pastoral simplicity, in a slight intermixture of Scots words & phraseology, which is more in unison (at least to my taste, & I will add, to every genuine Caledonian taste,) with the simple pathos, or rustic sprightliness, of our native music, than any English verses whatever.—For instance, in my Auld Rob Morris, you propose instead of the word, "descriving," to sub-stitute the phrase "all telling", which would spoil the rusticity, the pastoral, of the stanza.[4]

The antiquarian movement and the cult of Scottish airs meant different things to different people. Thomson and Burns stood for two diametrically opposite conceptions of Scottish

---

[1] For biographical details of Johnson and Thomson, see *Letters*, II. 355–6, 373–4; for Johnson's *Scots Musical Museum*, see also Burns's letter to [Rev. John Skinner], 25 Oct. 1787, in *Letters*, I. 133–4; and for "theoretical justification," see esp. his letters to Thomson, 26 Jan. 1793, [Apr. 1793], 7 Apr. 1793, [Sep. 1793, and Sep. 1794], in *Letters*, II. 148–9, 161, 167, 200–01, 256.

[2] In *Letters*, II. 122.   [3] *Letters*, II. 126.   [4] *Letters*, II. 148–9.

song : Thomson, for Anglicised refinement—the "Scotch Airs" which Jane Austen's young ladies liked to play ; and Burns, for a passionate simplicity far removed from the culture of the tea-table and the pianoforte. The radical difference between their ideas is apparent in the following passage from a letter of Burns's which probably dates from Apr. 1793 :

> I have still several M.S.S. Scots airs by me, which I have pickt up, mostly from the singing of country lasses.—They please me vastly ; but your learned lugs would perhaps be displeased with the very feature for which I like them.—I call them Simple ; you would pronounce them Silly. . . . I send you likewise, to me a beautiful little air, which I had taken down from viva voce. On the other page, I will give you a Stanza or two of the Ballad to it.—
>
> There was a lass and she was fair[5]
>
> I know these Songs are not to have the luck to please you, else you might be welcome to them.[6]

Much earlier, in Sep. 1785, Burns had elaborated the first hint of the theory which lay behind these remarks ; and a most revolutionary concept it was :

> There is a certain irregularity in the old Scotch Songs, a re-dundancy of syllables with respect to that exactness of accent & measure that the English Poetry requires, but which glides in, most melodiously with the respective tunes to which they are set. For instance, the fine old Song of The Mill Mill O, to give it a plain prosaic reading it halts prodigiously out of measure ; on the other hand, the Song set to the same tune in Bremner's collection of Scotch Songs which begins "To Fanny fair could I impart &c." it is most exact measure, and yet, let them be both sung before a real Critic, one above the biasses of prejudice, but a thorough Judge of Nature,—how flat & spiritless will the last appear, how trite, and tamely methodical, compared with the wild-warbling cadence, the heart-moving melody of the first.—This particularly is the case with all those airs which end with a hypermetrical syllable.—There is a degree of wild irre-gularity in many of the compositions & Fragments which are daily sung to them by my compeers, the common people—a

---

[5] The whole ballad is printed in H. & H., iii. 281 (495).
[6] *Letters*, ii. 162–3.

certain happy arrangement of old Scotch syllables, & yet, very
frequently, nothing, not even *like* rhyme, or sameness of jingle
at the ends of the lines.—This has made me sometimes imagine
that perhaps, it might be possible for a Scotch Poet, with a nice,
judicious ear, to set compositions to many of our most favorite
airs, particularly that class of them mentioned above, independent of rhyme altogether.—[7]

To the Edinburgh *literati*, this would have seemed the height of
absurdity; and, as Professor Ferguson has pointed out,[8]
Coleridge's alleged invention of hypermetrical syllables in
"Christabel" is "timid conventionality" when set beside what
Burns advocates here.

Unfortunately, Burns often gave way—albeit reluctantly—
to Thomson's suggestions, and produced for him a number of
sentimental songs which were later beloved by many nineteenth-century readers and singers. That he himself despised
these monstrosities is suggested by an often-quoted passage of
19 Oct. 1794, where he vents his irritation at Thomson's desire
for "civilised" verses :

> These English Songs gravel me to death.—I have not that
> command of the language that I have of my native tongue.—
> In fact, I think my ideas are more barren in English than in
> Scotish.—I have been at "Duncan Gray," to dress it in English,
> but all that I can do is deplorably stupid.—For instance—
>
> Song—Tune, Duncan Gray—
>
> Let not woman e'er complain[9]

At the same time Burns was not averse to putting words to an
English tune, provided that it could be assimilated to Scottish
ideas and *motifs;* he had done so in his *annus mirabilis*, when
writing "The Jolly Beggars," and he was quite prepared to do
so again, in Nov. 1794 :

> There is a pretty English song, by Sheridan, in the Duenna, to
> the air [*Deil tak the Wars*] : which is out of sight superior to
> D'urfey.—It begins—
>
> "When sable night, each drooping plant restoring."

---

[7] *Commonplace Book*, pp. 37–8.   [8] In *Pride and Passion*, p. 243.
[9] In *Letters*, II. 268. For the song, see H. & H., III. 219 (455), where the first
line reads "Let not *women* e'er complain. . . ."

The air, if I understand the expression of it properly, is the very native language of Simplicity, Tenderness, & Love.—I have again gone over my song to the tune, as follows—

> Sleep'st thou, or wauk'st thou, fairest creature ;[10]

I could easily throw this into an English mould; but to my taste, in the simple & tender of the Pastoral song, a sprinkling of the old Scotish, has an inimitable effect.—[11]

The last comment is relevant only to Burns's practice as a song-writer in the seventeen-nineties, and should not be applied to the vernacular poetry of 1784–6. It refers to a type of lyric which resembles art-song rather than folk-song; and it demonstrates that Burns wrote pieces like "Sleep'st thou or wauk'st thou, fairest Creature" in the manner of a verse-craftsman creating his own poetic diction almost as he went along. Though it might be supposed that by "the old Scotish" Burns here meant even, on occasion, quite *archaic* Scots, "Sleep'st thou, or wauk'st thou" contains only such contemporary Scots words as "ilka," "wi'," and "frae." In this letter, at any rate, Burns seems to accept the widely propagated view that Scots was a dying language ;[12] and he comes out in favour of the Scots-English of the lyric, a style that fitted in admirably with the late eighteenth-century sentimental delight in simple rusticity. That Burns was, in songs of this type, quite consciously appealing to literary modes is suggested by his comment of Sep. 1793 that "a small sprinkling of Scoticisms, is no objection to an English reader."[13]

Because of Thomson's repeated endeavours to get Burns to "write genteel," it is not surprising that his contributions to Thomson's *Original Scotish Airs* were often a good deal more artificial than most of those he sent to the *Scots Musical Museum.*

Burns's favourite method of composition is well known. In almost every case, he first took a melody (usually a traditional one) and then fitted words to it. Here is the famous account of

---

[10] The whole is printed in H. & H., III. 280 (494).   [11] In *Letters*, II. 273.
[12] Cp. [Sir] W. A. Craigie, in *The Scottish Tongue: A Series of Lectures on the Vernacular Language of Lowland Scotland*, London 1924, p. 13 : "Prefixed to the poems of Andrew Shirrefs, published in 1790, there is a piece written in 1788 entitled 'An Address in Scotch, on the Decay of that Language'."
[13] In *Letters*, II. 199.

how he intended to find verses for the tune, *Laddie, lie near me* :

> Laddie, lie near me—must *lie by me*, for some time.—I do not know the air ; & untill I am compleat master of a tune, in my own singing, (such as it is) I never can compose for it.—My way is : I consider the poetic Sentiment, correspondent to my idea of the musical expression ; then chuse my theme ; begin one Stanza ; when that is composed, which is generally the most difficult part of the business, I walk out, sit down now & then, look out for objects in Nature around me that are in unison or harmony with the cogitations of my fancy & workings of my bosom ; humming every now & then the air with the verses I have framed : when I feel my Muse beginning to jade, I retire to the solitary fireside of my study, & there commit my effusions to paper ; swinging, at intervals, on the hind-legs of my elbow-chair, by way of calling forth my own critical strictures, as my pen goes on.—[14]

He often composed on horseback ; and I am sure that this is what happened when he made "I'll ay ca' in by yon Toun."[15] It was written for a tune that appears in Bremner's *Scots Reels* (1757) :[16] and rhythm, words and melody combine to render a lover's mood as he gallops joyously towards his sweetheart's farm :

> There's nane shall ken, there's nane can guess
>   What brings me back the gate again,
> But she, my fairest faithfu' lass,
>   And stow'nlins we sall meet again.

> She'll wander by the aiken tree,
>   When trystin time draws near again ;
> And when her lovely form I see,
>   O haith! she's doubly dear again.

> *Chorus*

> I'll ay ca' in by yon town
>   And by yon garden green again!
> I'll ay ca' in by yon town,
>   And see my bonie Jean again.

---

[14] To Thomson, [Sep. 1793], in *Letters*, ii. 200–1.
[15] iii. 166 (423).   [16] Dick, *Songs*, p. 383.

A tune; the open air; the rhythms of riding or walking; the influence of the fields, streams and bushes of the Lowland countryside; and, finally, conscious revision—all these went into the making of Burns's songs, which were thus as much the product of deliberate artistry as "Tam o' Shanter" itself.

A hundred and fifty years have passed since the songs were first divided into categories according to the amount of traditional material they contain.[17] The first of these categories comprises those to which Burns contributed nothing, or next to nothing—ballads like "Aften hae I play'd at the Cards and the Dice,"[18] which he set down after the manner of a modern folk-song collector, being apparently content simply to record the music and words, with the very minimum of alteration. A second category consists of pure folk-songs which he altered to a greater or lesser extent, with the idea of improving the original. "The Highland Widow's Lament"[19] may belong to this class, or to the former; the tune was contributed to Johnson's *Scots Musical Museum* by Burns from the communication of "a lady in the north of Scotland," and the refrain "Ochon, ochon, ochrie" is old—but, as with "Auld Lang Syne," we are not certain how much is original and how much is traditional.[20] Sometimes—and this is especially true of the songs he sent to Thomson—his motive was to substitute polite and innocuous verses for gross popular bawdry. A case in point is the revised version of "As I came o'er the Cairney Mount,"[21]—in Burns's own words, "an excellent but somewhat licentious song still sung to the tune [*The Highland Lassie*],"[22] which evidently is preserved in four stanzas in *The Merry Muses*. Sometimes the new version is far inferior to the folk source; as William Mont-

---

[17] Cp. [Scott], in *Quarterly Review*, I. (1809), 80; A. Keith, *Burns and Folk Song*, henceforth cited as A. Keith, Aberdeen 1922, p. 83; and J. C. Dick, *Notes on Scottish Song by Robert Burns*, henceforth cited as *Notes*, London 1908, intro., *passim*.

[18] Dick, *Songs*, pp. 330 (494); Johnson, *Scots Musical Museum*, henceforth cited as Johnson, v (1796), No. 462. A manuscript in Burns's handwriting is in the B.M.

[19] "O, I am come to the low countrie": III. 184 (436).

[20] H. & H., III. 436; Dick, *Songs*, p. 469.

[21] III. 171 (427).

[22] Dick, *Songs*, p. 473. The name of the tune is given as *The Highland Lassie*, which is also its title in Oswald, *Curious Collection of Scots Tunes*, 1740; but in McGibbon, *Scots Tunes*, 1742, it is called *The Highland Laddie*.

gomerie has pointed out, "The Birks of Aberfeldie"[23] is an example of such debasement, where a simple, artless original has been replaced by an effete and spiritless drawing-room piece.

Still a third class of songs are those where only the chorus and the original melody, or merely, perhaps, a single line or couplet, have been retained—sometimes for the very good reason that these fragments were all that Burns knew or could remember. The result might be one of three things—an entirely new creation, but still in the folk tradition, like "Wha is that at my Bower Door" ;[24] a literary incrustation upon that tradition, like "By Allan Stream" ;[25] or, finally, a more or less successful blend of these styles, like the second set of "Ca' the Yowes to the Knowes."[26] A fourth major group of Burns's songs consists of lyrics such as "A red, red Rose"[27]—which are predominantly mosaics of traditional phrases set to old tunes; there is also a fifth, which consists of lyrics whose words (apart from the inevitable echoes of previous poets) are wholly by Burns. Many of the songs included in this last group were written for dance-tunes which were purely instrumental, or which at any rate had lost such words as they had originally possessed. "Lassie wi' the lint-white Locks,"[28] intended for the reel-tune *Rothiemurchus Rant*, may be taken as typical of this last category ; another example is "Where are the Joys,"[29] which altogether suppresses the words of the original folk-song "Saw ye my Father?" and replaces them with personal but somewhat artificial verses.

Besides classifying the songs according to their manner of composition and use of traditional material, it is also possible to arrange them in relation to their subject-matter. One favourite division is into personal and impersonal pieces.[30] With few exceptions, the songs which arose directly out of the circumstances of the poet's own life are markedly inferior to the more impersonal songs, which appear to have been deliberately manufactured. Yet these exceptions are of great signi-

[23] Montgomerie, "Folk Poetry and Robert Burns," in *Burns Chronicle* (1950), pp. 21–9.　　　[24] III. 102 (375).　　　[25] III. 231 (462).
[26] "Hark, the mavis' e'ening sang . . .": III. 268 (488).
[27] III. 143 (402).　　[28] III. 259 (482).　　[29] III. 264 (486).
[30] Cp. Dick, *Songs*, where his first group of songs is headed "LOVE : PERSONAL," and his second "LOVE : GENERAL."

ficance. Inasmuch as they speak with the genuine voice of individual feeling, they seem to anticipate the direct emotions of the best Romantic poetry :

> . . . Tho' I were doom'd to wander on,
> Beyond the sea, beyond the sun,
> Till my last weary sand was run,
> Till then—and then—I'd love thee.[31]

> . . . Had we never lov'd sae kindly,
> Had we never lov'd sae blindly,
> Never met—or never parted—
> We had ne'er been broken-hearted.[32]

> O, wert thou in the cauld blast
> On yonder lea, on yonder lea,
> My plaidie to the angry airt,
> I'd shelter thee, I'd shelter thee.
> Or did Misfortune's bitter storms
> Around thee blaw, around thee blaw,
> Thy bield should be my bosom,
> To share it a', to share it a'![33]

More often, Burns's *personal* songs are of the type of "Anna thy Charms,"[34] "Sweet Afton,"[35] "Thou lingering Star"[36] and "Highland Mary" ,[37] to modern taste, these appear much worse as *poetry* than many of the songs put into the mouths of imagined persons. But when considered as a *song* the last of these appears perfectly wedded to its tune, *Katherine Ogle*. "Thou Lingering Star," however, is set to a sentimental melody composed by Lucy Johnson (later Mrs Oswald of Auchencruive) ;[38] both words and music are equally deplorable.

Some of the best of the songs usually classified as "personal" are only apparently so. Such a piece as "The Rantin Dog, the Daddie o't"[39] arose, it is true, in response to a situation in the poet's own life ; but it is the girl who speaks, not Burns, and

[31] From st. iii of "O, were I on Parnassus Hill," written for Mrs Burns : III. 59 (346) ; Dick, *Songs*, p. 377.
[32] St. iv of "Ae fond Kiss," written for Clarinda : III. 105 (379) ; Dick, *Songs*, p. 379.
[33] St. i of "O, wert thou in the Cauld Blast," written for Jessie Lewars, during Burns's last illness : IV. 43 (102) ; Dick, *Songs*, p. 369.
[34] I. 293 (447).   [35] III. 134 (394).   [36] III. 71 (355).
[37] "Ye banks and braes and streams around . . ." : III. 255 (480).
[38] Dick, *Songs*, p. 373.   [39] III. 70 (354).

the essence of the song resides in the delighted recognition of character :

> When I mount the creepie-chair,
> Wha will sit beside me there?
> Gie me Rob, I'll seek nae mair—
> The rantin dog, the daddie o't!
>
> Wha will crack to me my lane?
> Wha will mak me fidgin fain?
> Wha will kiss me o'er again?—
> The rantin dog, the daddie o't!

Here, and elsewhere, as in "Here's his Health in Water,"[40] the inspiration is essentially dramatic. But other love-songs of the kind usually termed "personal" seem to be the result of a method of composition that nineteenth-century critics have found it difficult to square with their conceptions of sincerity. Burns himself described the process in these terms :

> Whenever I want to be more than ordinary *in song* ; to be in some degree equal to your diviner airs ; do you imagine I fast & pray for the celestial emanation?—Tout au contraire! I have a glorious recipe, the very one that for his own use was invented by the Divinity of Healing & Poesy when erst he piped to the flocks of Admetus.—I put myself on a regimen of admiring a fine woman ; & in proportion to the adorability of her charms, in proportion you are delighted with my verses.[41]

To this class belong that highly-wrought song of artificial compliment "Saw ye bonie Lesley,"[42] written for Miss Lesley Baillie of Mayfield, Ayrshire, and the equally felicitous "Bonie wee Thing,"[43] composed in honour of Miss Deborah Duff-

---

[40] III. 177 (431). The form of this song is equally impersonal ; it is influenced by folk-ballads like "Wha will bake?" (Herd, *Ancient and Modern Scottish Songs, Heroic Ballads, Etc.* henceforth cited as *Scottish Songs*, 2 vols. Edinburgh 1776, I. 167) : "Wha will bake my bridal bride [*sic*], | And brew my bridal ale? | And wha will welcome my brisk bride | That I bring o'er the dale ?" And cp. a song worked over by Ramsay, "Where wad bonny Annie lie?" (Ramsay's *Tea-table Miscellany*, 2 vols., Glasgow 1871, I. 83) : "What if I shou'd wauking lie | When the hoboys are gawn by, | *Will ye tent me when I cry*, | My dear, I'm faint and iry ?" The line that I have italicised is, of course, the source of l. 2 of Burns, "The rantin Dog, the Daddie o't," for which see H. & H., III. 70 (354). Cp. Ritter, pp. 131–2.

[41] To [Thomson], 19 Oct. [1794], in *Letters*, II. 265.

[42] III. 224 (458).　　　　　[43] III. 103 (378).

Davies of Pembrokeshire, whom he had met in the company of his genteel friends, the Riddells. In the first of these, the tune is the soil from which has grown a lyric whose words are superior to the melody to which it is attached ;[44] today, it survives as poetry alone. The first two stanzas provide an excellent example of Burns's use of assonance, instead of strictly formal rhyme; it is what he advocates in his commonplace-book :

> O, saw ye bonie Lesley,
> As she gaed o'er the Border?
> She's gane, like Alexander,
> To spread her conquests farther !

> To see her is to love her,
> And love but her for ever ;
> For Nature made her what she is,
> And never made anither !

The second two show an elegant modulation from pure Scots-English to Scots-English with "a sprinkling of our native tongue" :

> Thou art a queen, fair Lesley—
> Thy subjects, we before thee!
> Thou art divine, fair Lesley—
> The hearts o' men adore thee.

> The Deil he could na skaith thee,
> Or aught that wad belang thee :
> He'd look into thy bonie face,
> And say :— 'I canna wrang thee !'

In this song, written to a casual acquaintance, a woman of higher social status, Burns creates an impression of great comeliness and charm of character, and makes us feel his own anguish at the knowledge that he could never possess her. As so often when he is writing really well, "The Deil" appears— and is negated by Lesley's beauty as, in the "Address to the Deil," the "Address to the Unco Guid," and "Tam o' Shanter,"

---

[44] Dick, *Songs*, p. 366. The tune that Burns had in mind probably was that of the "old ballad" beginning "My bonie Lizzy Baillie, I'll rowe ye in my plaidie . . ." Johnson, v (1796), No. 456. In Thomson's *Original Scotish Airs*, henceforth cited as Thomson, [1]. ii (1798), p. 33, "O saw ye bonie Lesley?" is set to *The Collier's bonie Lassie*. For phonetic details, see below, p. 361.

he is negated by humour or compassion. In the early poems and first epistles, positive value had resided in strong drink, or comradeship, or "generous love" ; now, it is inherent in Beauty. Though at a casual reading this song seems an exercise in the eighteenth-century manner, it is in reality forward-looking. For comparison, one has to go to Byron's "She walks in Beauty" and—even further—to Keats's awe-struck perception of Fanny Brawne.

When one considers "Bonie wee Thing," however, it is nothing less than criminal to ignore the music. In themselves, the words are remarkable enough, with their fusion of polite clichés ("look and languish," the abstractions "Wit and Grace and Love and Beauty," the hackneyed statement that the adored one is the "Goddess" of the poet's soul), and the finely contrived Scots of:

> Bonie wee thing, cannie wee thing,
>   Lovely wee thing, wert thou mine,
> I wad wear thee in my bosom
>   Lest my jewel it should tine.

These apparently disparate elements are united by the Scots accent of reader or singer into a beautifully simple and polished lyric poem. When sung to the traditional tune (recorded, in a primitive form, as early as 1627, in Straloch's Manuscript[45]) it conveys an almost agonised mingling of protective tenderness with the conviction of absolute unattainability. One is reminded again of Marvell—this time, of "The Definition of Love" :

> My Love is of a birth as rare
> As 'tis for object strange and high :
> It was begotten by despair
> Upon Impossibility.
>
> Magnanimous Despair alone
> Could show me so divine a thing,
> Where feeble Hope could ne'r have flown
> But vainly flapt its Tinsel Wing.

The emotion aroused by "Bonie wee Thing" is similar to that behind Marvell's more cerebral poem ; and, when sung, it

[45] Dick, *Songs*, p. 365.

emerges far more intensely, like a fact of the physical world. Some of the songs inspired by Burns's wife are in their own way as good as any of those written for refined ladies whom he could admire only from a distance. Nothing could surpass the tone of wondering delicacy (conveyed almost entirely by intonation when read and by melody when sung) in which he celebrates his early passion for Jean Armour.[46] The best of all the songs inspired by Jean Armour is the popular "Of a' the Airts,"[47] written to the rollicking *Miss Admiral Gordon's Strathspey*, which was composed by William Marshall, the Duke of Gordon's butler, in a thoroughly traditional mode. The tune is an elaboration of melodies of the type of *Alace! I lie my alon I'm lik to die auld*, in the Skene Manuscript (*c.*1630) ;[48] and, like that of "I'll ay ca' in by yon Toun," it calls up a vision of a journey on horseback to the beloved :

> There wild woods grow, and rivers row,
> And monie a hill between,
> But day and night my fancy's flight
> Is ever wi' my Jean.

Later, in "Louis, what reck I by Thee,"[49] he expressed the common experience of young husbands—the feeling that in the marriage bed they are superior to kings and princes :

> Louis, what reck I by thee,
> Or Geordie on his ocean?
> Dyvor beggar louns to me !
> I reign in Jeanie's bosom.
>
> Let her crown my love her law,
> And in her breast enthrone me,
> Kings and nations—swith awa !
> Reif randies, I disown ye !

---

[46] *E.g.*, in "The Mauchline Lady" : iv. 12 (84) ; Dick, *Songs*, p. 374 ; H. & H., ii. 212 (410). In assuming that this song was written for Jean Armour, I am following the traditional practice of editors and commentators. The rhythm of the folk-song "I had a Horse, and I had nae mair," was probably in Burns's mind when he wrote it. It is also in some degree similar to "Walking down the Highland Town," in D'Urfey, *Pills to Purge Melancholy*, 6 vols., London 1719–20, ii. 201 ; and to a song in *Spectator*, No. 470 ("My love was fickle once and changing, | Nor e'er would settle in my heart ; | From beauty still to beauty ranging, | In ev'ry place I found a dart . . .") Cp. Ritter, pp. 54–5.   [47] iii. 56 (345) ; *Songs*, p. 375.
[48] *Songs*, p. 376 ; W. Dauney, *Ancient Scottish Melodies*, Edinburgh 1838, p. 227.
[49] iii. 149 (410).

The tune identifies Burns as husband, not only with kings as symbols of power, but with the military might of their nation states; for, as Dick points out,[50] "the first two lines in the relative major key are the opening bars" of *The British Grenadiers*. Burns, rejoicing in vigorous married love, is stronger than armed monarchs; compared with the power and energy of the sexual relationship, their glory and their battles are as nothing.

The same mood can become attached to illicit love just as easily as to the married state, and in the postscript to "Yestreen I had a Pint o' Wine"[51] (the subject is Anne Park) Burns inflated it into a superb contempt for the laws of God and man :

> The Kirk an' State may join, and tell
> To do sic things I maunna :
> The Kirk an' State may gae to Hell,
> And I'll gae to my Anna.

In these last two songs, Burns dramatises himself; but they are the vehicles of a *persona* which bears a definite relationship to Burns's real character, not of a "creative mask." This also holds good of "There was a Lad,"[52] in which (rejoicing in his role of "fornicator loon"), Burns states that at his birth "The gossip keekit in his loof," and prophesied :

> 'But sure as three times three mak nine,
> I see by ilka score and line,
> This chap will dearly like our kin',
> So leeze me on thee, Robin !

> 'Guid faith,' quo' scho, 'I doubt you, stir,
> Ye gar the lassies lie aspar ;
> But twenty fauts ye may hae waur—
> So blessins on thee, Robin !

When sung—either to the tune with which it is usually printed, *O, an ye were dead, gudeman*, or to *Dainty Davie*, for which Burns intended it[53]—the chorus rants itself out in sparkling merriment and lilting dancing abandon. Thanks to the music, Robin's

---

[50] *Songs*, p. 377.   [51] IV. 25 (92).
[52] IV. 13 (85). The chorus, as H. & H. note, derives from an old song called "The Roving Lad with the Tartan Plaid."   [53] Dick, *Songs*, pp. 473-4.

peccadilloes have become a natural force, like sun glancing on thousands of leaping wavelets :

> Robin was a rovin boy,
> Rantin, rovin, rantin, rovin,
> Robin was a rovin boy,
> Rantin, rovin, Robin !

For all the magnificence of Burns's individual voice in the songs just discussed, it is surpassed by the achievements of his impersonal Muse. The truth is that Burns's songs are just as contradictory as the other flowers of his genius; and this applies not only to their attitudes, but also to their form. It is important to realise that all the twenty-three Scots song-books with music which Dick lists as having been printed before Burns began to publish were in fact heavily edited, and that practically all the eighteenth-century collections of Scottish songs without music (there were about thirty of these) were subjected to at least some degree of modernisation.[54] Long before Burns began to write, both Allan Ramsay and Robert Fergusson had tinkered with the words of traditional songs; consequently, when Burns became a maker and mender of verses for old ditties he was simply following in the footsteps of his predecessors, including so-called scholars and antiquarians. In one sense he was the preserver and transmitter of Scottish song to future generations; in another, the last of a long line of its more or less deliberate creators. So inseparably connected were these two activities of his that it is often his most apparently traditional songs that show the boldest and most striking innovations.[55]

As an example, let us take "My Love, she's but a Lassie yet" :[56]

> My love, she's but a lassie yet,
> My love, she's but a lassie yet !
> We'll let her stand a year or twa,
> She'll no be half sae saucy yet !

[54] Dick, *Songs*, pp. xxvii ff. Since in *Notes* pp. xx ff., Dick defines a Scots song-book much more narrowly, his totals are there correspondingly smaller.

[55] On what might be termed the "contradiction" between experience and tradition in Burns's songs, cp. the suggestive sentence in A. Keith, p. 82 : "Within himself he carried the passionate, primitive, animal nature out of which the traditional songs had sprung, and within himself also he enclosed that sense of the steadying, upward movement in humanity by which the unrestrained nature is transformed into beauty and sweetness." [56] III. 51 (341).

I rue the day I sought her, O!
I rue the day I sought her, O!
Wha gets her need na say he's woo'd,
But he may say he has bought her, O.

Come draw a drap o' the best o't yet,
Come draw a drap o' the best o't yet!
Gae seek for pleasure whare ye will,
But here I never missed it yet.

We're a' dry wi' drinkin o't,
We're a' dry wi' drinkin o't!
The minister kiss't the fiddler's wife—
He could na preach for thinkin o't!

One of Burns's most recent critics, Miss Keith, has complained that the song has no unity and that "its technique is clumsy, not to say elementary."[57] I do not think this judgment will stand up to a really searching analysis. The work is a dramatic lyric, made out of traditional elements that harmonise perfectly with three of Burns's deepest and most permanent preoccupations: the opposition between love and money, the supreme worth of good fellowship between men, and the quarrel between the Kirk and desire. As I see him, the protagonist of "My Love, she's but a Lassie yet" is sitting or standing in the inn, one of a closed masculine society of hearty drinkers. He has just made an unsuccessful foray into the alien world of husband-hunting girls, and found it a humiliating experience. All this he recounts to "the boys" in order to get the bad taste out of his mouth: a pert little minx has turned him down because of his poverty, but perhaps when she grows a little longer in the tooth she will be glad to take anyone that wears breeks. If she ever marries when in her present mood it will be for money and nothing else; she will be bought as a thing, not wooed like a real girl of flesh and blood.

The third stanza—"Come draw a drap o' the best o't yet" does not "strike off," as Miss Keith asserts,[58] "at a tangent"; on the contrary, it contains the central situation of the whole song—the rejected lover defiantly asserting to both publican and cronies that the pleasures of drink, being certain and

[57] C. Keith, p. 143.　　[58] *Op. cit.*, p. 142.

known, are far more satisfying than the company of flirts and flibbertigibbets. Miss Keith complains that the couplet which begins "Gae seek . . ." is ambiguous.[59] Of course it is; it is meant to be so. It is at one and the same time an imperative statement addressed to his fellow drinkers, and a sour-grapes remark directed at the girl. The song gains, rather than loses, from the fact that this line means two things simultaneously. The fourth stanza is not so irrelevant as it seems at first sight, nor does the fact that Burns found it ready to hand in Herd's *Scottish Songs* of 1776 detract from its supreme fitness.[60] The young man's mind is still running on weddings, even in the midst of an all-male company; weddings suggest ministers, who have been known to get drunk after such ceremonies and to do things which make public the discrepancy between their outward appearance and the secret desires of their hearts. Thus the song ends with a brief glance at the very conflict which underlies "Holy Willie's Prayer." "My Love she's but a Lassie yet" must stand here as our main specimen of Burns's art as a patcher of folk-songs. Out of isolated lines from other songs, and one entire verse apparently lifted from Herd, he has made a condensed comedy of small-town or rural life. Though the song is completely in character, the whole of Burns's own experience lies behind it; and so, too, do some of his favourite ideas. Here, as so often, Burns's values were precisely those of inherited Scottish folk-song; yet the total effect is of something fresh and novel, however old the parts from which it is made. Miss Keith has quite rightly described much of Burns's work as "impressionistic"; surely that is exactly the word to sum up "My Love, she's but a Lassie yet." When sung (to a tune

[59] *Ibid.*

[60] On the question of Burns's use of Herd, cp. A. Keith, p. 41 : "Certain songs or fragments, closely akin to lyrics by Burns, are in Herd's unpublished MS. [But this does not necessarily mean that he and Herd] were tapping the same flow." Obviously the same argument might be made to apply to Herd's published works. Even when fragments of the same folk-material are found in a song of Herd's and one of Burns's, we are not entitled to infer that Burns "stole" the lines from Herd ; for, quite independently of each other, both men may have borrowed from the same living popular tradition. As A. Keith remarks (pp. 40–1), it is strange that there is no allusion to Herd in Burns's correspondence (or in Dick's *Notes*), and that we do not possess a single letter from Burns to Herd. Burns *does* refer to other contemporary song-collectors, such as Ritson; but he knew Herd's printed works only by the printer's name, as the *Collections of Wotherspoon*.

originally entitled *Miss Farquharson's Reel* and published in Bremner's *Reels*, 1757),[61] it gains an extra dimension. The elements of the little drama are subordinated to the rhythms of the original dance, and we feel that "this is the way the world wags," in endless, light-hearted movement, and that passions and disappointments, as well as "mirth an' dancin'," have their place in the *perpetuum mobile*.

"A red, red Rose"[62] is yet another example of the perfection of the old achieving the shock and immediacy of the new. The tradition on which it leans is that of late eighteenth-century popular songs and chapbook literature, the equivalent of the "pop" or "hit" productions of a later age; and there is literally not a line or an image that cannot be traced back to some such "debased" source.[63] Burns's imagination and his ear gathered these inherited comparisons and metaphors together, altered them (however slightly), mysteriously purged them of all vulgarity—and created in the end one of the loveliest lyrics in the language. Miss Keith calls it "a masterpiece of technique . . . rather than of passion," and goes on to say that "it is by the superb blending of the varied 'units into one harmonious whole that the song achieves its beauty— carrying the passion over, if it does carry it, from the originals from which Burns patched it."[64] But it is surely possible for a relationship to subsist between "tradition" and "the individual talent" roughly analogous to that which normally holds between the writer and his native language. We have already gathered many instances of this on the purely linguistic plane. When Burns uses phrases like "Waes me for Johnie Ged's Hole now,"[65] or "She'll no be half sae saucy yet," he is not inventing them; he is letting his fine ear choose the best possible idioms for his purpose, words and phrases already created by the people and sanctified by decades of constant use. A poem—any poem— is, in this sense, an affair of "technique," and even the boldest innovators can rarely do more than use familiar words in strange contexts: the majority of the words in Catullus or Shakespeare or Yeats had already been used long before them

---

[61] Dick, *Songs*, p. 413.
[63] Cp. H. & H., III. 402–6.
[65] "Death and Doctor Hornbook," st. xxiii, l. 1; see above, p. 121.

[62] III. 143 (402).
[64] C. Keith, p. 154.

by countless writers and speakers. Even the basic units which underlie Dylan Thomas's homophone play, or which Gerard Manley Hopkins brings together to form novel compounds, are not *their* creations : "to and fro," "tender," "tram," "beam," and "truckle" had been current coinage for centuries before Hopkins arranged them into the pattern "Or to-fro tender trambeams truckle at the eye."[66] In a song like "A red, red Rose," Burns is doing much the same thing as poets have always done with single words, except that here he is dealing with set phrases—the proverbs of passion :

> O, my luve is like a red, red rose,
> That's newly sprung in June.
> O, my luve is like the melodie,
> That's sweetly play'd in tune.
>
> As fair art thou, my bonie lass,
> So deep in luve am I,
> And I will luve thee still, my dear,
> Till a' the seas gang dry.
>
> Till a' the seas gang dry, my dear,
> And the rocks melt wi' the sun !
> And I will luve thee still, my dear,
> While the sands o' life shall run.
>
> And fare thee weel, my only luve,
> And fare thee weel a while !
> And I will come again, my luve,
> Tho' it were ten thousand mile !

As an additional aid to the understanding of Burns's use of stock expressions in "A red, red Rose," it is interesting to turn to that very fine lyric of character "In Simmer, when the Hay was mawn."[67] The song takes the form of a dialogue between "Blythe Bessie in the milking shiel," who wants to marry for love, and "a dame in wrinkled eild" advising worldly wisdom and caution. Both speak in the clichés of their respective states, youth and age—especially of age, for everything the old woman says has the air of ancestral wisdom. Nowhere, except in "Death and Doctor Hornbook,"[68] has Burns come so close to

[66] Hopkins, "The Candle Indoors," l. 4.
[67] III. 117 (384). [68] Above, pp. 118–21.

the language actually used by people; and nowhere that I can recollect, except perhaps in the catechism section of Joyce's *Ulysses* or the nurse's remarks in *Romeo and Juliet*, have clichés been employed for such a triumphantly creative purpose as in the third, fourth and fifth stanzas of this song :

> 'It's ye hae wooers monie ane,
>   And lassie, ye're but young, ye ken !
> Then wait a wee, and cannie wale
>   A routhie butt, a routhie ben.
> There Johnie o' the Buskie-Glen,
>   Fu' is his barn, fu' is his byre.
> Tak this frae me, my bonie hen :
>   It's plenty beets the luver's fire !'

> 'For Johnie o' the Buskie-Glen,
>   I dinna care a single flie :
> He lo'es sae weel his craps and kye,
>   He has nae love to spare for me.
> But blythe's the blink o' Robie's e'e,
>   And weel I wat he lo'es me dear :
> Ae blink o' him I wad na gie
> For Buskie-Glen and a' his gear.'

> O thoughtless lassie, life's a faught !
>   The canniest gate, the strife is sair.
> But ay fu'-han't is fechtin best :
>   A hungry care's an unco care.
> But some will spend, and some will spare,
>   An' wilfu' folk maun hae their will.
> Syne as ye brew, my maiden fair,
>   Keep mind that ye maun drink the yill !'

In "A red, red Rose," traditional similes and comparisons perform, on the serious plane, much the same function as that of the proverbs in "In Simmer, when the Hay was mawn." But the rose, the melody, the drying seas and melting rocks and sands of the former song are not symbolic in the modern sense of that word; that is, they are not like the flower (Earthly Love), the worm (Corrupt Lust) and the storm of Blake's "Sick Rose." At the same time the reader feels they are not merely physical objects of the ordinary kind, but draw their evocative power from all the roses that young girls have ever

been compared to, and from age-old prophecies that some day
the seas will evaporate and the earth be consumed in some
enormous conflagration. It seems to me that we can speak of
"archetypal images" only if we are willing to define them as
the concentrated experiences and feelings of many generations,
organised by language and handed down over a long period
from father to son; and it is from socially-transmitted emotional patterns of this sort that Burns's song derives its peculiar
beauty. Another way of stating the same conclusion is to say
that "A red, red Rose" is a lyric of genius, made out of the
common inherited material of folk-song by an author whose
name we happen to know. Placed in the context of the whole
of European poetry it is thus an example of something that is
very old; but set beside the poetry of the eighteenth-century
polite world, or even against such examples of pre-Romanticism
as Burns's own "Cotter's Saturday Night," it seems startlingly
new because—"original" or no—it manages to convey deep
feeling without qualification or embroidery. In "A red, red
Rose" there is no incongruence between particular and universal. The reader—and still more so, the singer—experiences
what he has felt for a woman he has himself loved. He attaches
the beautiful words and still more beautiful tune to his own
image of her face and person; and he does so only because the
song generalises the emotions of countless lovers, high and low,
at all times and in all places. Here the distinction between
"personal" and "impersonal" becomes quite worthless:
Burns is *any* man in love with *any* woman, yet in the act of
artistic creation he is more truly and more intensely himself
than at any ordinary moment of daily life.

In addition to grouping Burns's songs according to the
amount of traditional matter they contain, the type of melody
for which they were written, and their relationship to the
events of the poet's life, one can also examine them under such
headings as, for example, Songs on Love itself, and on its
mutability; songs on Married Love, or on Lifelong Faithfulness; songs on such conventional themes as (*a*) a Lover's
Desire to be some object that the Beloved has touched, or (*b*) a
Lover's Address to a Plaintive Bird; Songs mingling Land-

scape with Sentiment; Songs dealing with Rustic Courtship, especially with Evening Walks or Meetings, or with the theme of the Night Visit; Songs of Gross Popular Drollery; Songs on the Comedy of Love and Marriage; Songs of Pure Passion, almost devoid of intellectual content, and approximating to the primitive emotional cry; Drinking Songs; Songs of Humorous Fantasy; Jacobite, Patriotic and Political Songs—and so forth. Categories of this sort cut across the divisions of "personal" and "impersonal," and the equally valid distinction between "dramatic" and "non-dramatic" lyrics.[1]

Burns's best-known song on the mutability of love, is the ever popular "Green grow the Rashes, O,"[2] where the tune (which goes back to an air in Straloch's MS (1627)—*A Dance: Green grow the Rashes*)[3] conveys both the idea of gaiety and of inevitable, almost cyclical change from lass to lass:

> For you sae douce, ye sneer at this;
> Ye're nought but senseless asses, O:
> The wisest man the warl' e'r saw,
> He dearly lov'd the lasses, O.

> Auld Nature swears, the lovely dears
> Her noblest work she classes, O:
> Her prentice han' she try'd on man,
> An' then she made the lasses, O.

> *Chorus*

> Green grow the rashes, O;
> Green grow the rashes, O;
> The sweetest hours that e'er I spend,
> Are spent among the lasses, O.[4]

---

[1] In the main, this classification follows Angellier, ii. 235–313; but "Songs of Humorous Fantasy" is, I think, my own category, while "Patriotic and Political" and "Jacobite" follow the division in Dick, *Songs*. For details of Angellier's classification, which is particularly thorough, see Appendix iii (below, pp. 366 ff.)

[2] i. 251 (414).   [3] Dick, *Songs*, p. 388.

[4] Ritter (pp. 49–52) finds additional sources and parallels to those noted in H. & H.—for example, similar sentiments occur in Sterne, *Tristram Shandy*, ch. i. And cp. "Dainty Davie," st. ii, ll. 3–4, in Herd, *Scottish Songs*, ii. 215 ("The sweetest kiss that e'er I got, | Was frae my dainty DAVIE"); Thomson, *The Castle of Indolence*, i. v, ll. 437 ff.; Goldsmith, *The Deserted Village*, l. 264. For the last stanza, Ritter, following C. & W., quotes an interesting passage from

The best songs on married love and lifelong faithfulness are "I hae a wife o' my ain,"[5] written for Jean Armour, which relates the mood of "Louis, what reck I by thee"[6] to the Burnsian conception of the independent man, and that splendid lyrical monologue, "John Anderson my Jo."[7] "I hae a wife o' my ain" is wholly different in mood from the sentiment of:

> Who hold your being on the terms,
> 'Each aid the others,'
> Come to my bowl, come to my arms,
> My friends, my brothers![8]

Now, Burns is the independent small farmer *par excellence*, beholden to no feudal superior or bureaucratic caste, and resentful of supervision and control, however paternally exercised; he is the small owner in love. Nowhere in literature, perhaps, is there a more succinct, more engaging, more sympathetically humorous presentation of a *petit bourgeois* attitude; and the humour is conveyed as much by the tune as by the words themselves:

> I hae a wife o' my ain,
> I'll partake wi' naebody:
> I'll take cuckold frae nane,
> I'll gie cuckold to naebody.

> I hae a penny to spend,
> There—thanks to naebody:
> I hae naething to lend,
> I'll borrow frae naebody.

Cupid's Whirligig, "a comedy in 5 acts . . . London 1607, attributed to Edward Sharpham": "Oh woman . . . since we were made before yee, should we not love and admire ye as the last and therefore most perfect work of Nature? *Man was made when Nature was but an apprentice; but Woman when she was a skilful mistress of her art*" [Ritter's italics]. This extract was printed in a fairly well-known book, *The British Muse: A Collection of Thoughts*, by Thomas Hayward, Gent., 3 vols., London 1738 (C. & W , I. 127). And in Hayward's volume, too, not long after the excerpt above, there occur the following lines, expressing a typically Burnsian sentiment: ". . . a fair woman, which is the | Ornament of heaven, the grace of earth, | The joy of life and the delight of all sense, | Ev'n the very *summum bonum* of man's life." Thus it would seem that even so "Scottish" a song as "Green grow the Rashes, O," has English, as well as Scots, sources, and is not a product of folk-tradition alone.

[5] III. 109 (381).   [6] Above, p. 273.   [7] III. 63 (349).
[8] St. xxi, ll. 3–6 of the epistle "To J. Lapraik": I. 155 (380).

By thus giving expression to what millions of lower-middle-class people have known, he makes us feel for and with them as *people*, so that we glory in their essential humanity just as in reading "The Jolly Beggars" we rejoice in our fellowship with vagabonds and social outcasts. In the third and fourth stanzas Burns links this kind of married love with some of his deepest-rooted political and social convictions :

> I am naebody's lord,
>   I'll be slave to naebody.
> I hae a guid braid sword,
>   I'll tak dunts frae naebody.

> I'll be merry and free,
>   I'll be sad for naebody.
> Naebody cares for me,
>   I care for naebody.

"John Anderson my Jo" is an example of Burns's transformation of a bawdy original, itself by no means utterly contemptible as a song, or even as a poem, and possessing a peculiar pathos of its own—the sadness and inevitability of man's declining sexual powers.[9] Burns's "respectable" version can only have been written in order to explore in words all the implications of the lovely tune, one of the most beautiful in the whole of Scottish folk-music.

It has sometimes been claimed as a defect of folk-song that its melodies are too simple, too repetitive to convey a diversity of emotions, or even any sort of developing theme or story. What it does best is to give us the same feeling over and over again ; it creates its effect by cumulative means.[10] Such an opinion is true largely of folk music as it has emerged from the hands of early collectors, or from late "folk singers" who have themselves been influenced by Grub Street, drawing room, or "Tin Pan Alley." It is most definitely not true of genuine Scottish folk music, Lowland or Highland. Folk-song *is* suited to the turns and twists of narrative : were not most of the

[9] Cp. esp. the second stanza, as printed in *The Merry Muses*, p. 114; and S. G. Smith, "Robert Burns and 'The Merry Muses of Caledonia'," in *Arena*, No. IV (1950), p. 23.

[10] B. H. Bronson, "Some Aspects of Music and Literature in the Eighteenth Century," henceforth cited as Bronson, in *Music & Literature in England in the Seventeenth and Eighteenth Centuries*, Los Angeles 1954, pp. 52–3.

Border ballads, as well as most of the traditional ballads of other parts of Europe, originally sung? And Scottish folk-song, more perhaps than that of any other European people, is characterised by what Professor B. H. Bronson has termed the "chameleon quality" of its tunes.[11] The same melody, with the slightest variations in rhythm or intonation, can make the transition from love to hate and from grave to gay; and for an example of such alternation, we need go no further than the "respectable" version of "John Anderson my Jo."

There are two eight-lined stanzas, dividing naturally into two halves. The first four lines of each stanza refer to the early years of marriage, the second four to the last; yet there are contrasts of mood within these divisions which should be brought out in the singing. In the first half of the first stanza, nostalgia is mingled with a deep tenderness as the wife recreates in her mind the image of her husband as he was in his prime. It is the poetry of *perception*—not the direct perception of an admired woman, as in "Bonie wee Thing," but the imaginative experience of seeing through the eyes of another, of penetrating another's memory. At the same time, the singer should convey the woman's *pride* in the husband of her youthful years:

> John Anderson my jo, John,
> When we were first acquent,
> Your locks were like the raven,
> Your bonie brow was brent. . . .

The second half of the first stanza emphasises the durability of married love; even on the verge of old age, John Anderson and his wife are still sweethearts, and she still feels the same deep tenderness for him:

> But now your brow is beld, John,
> Your locks are like the snaw,
> But blessings on your frosty pow,
> John Anderson my jo!

[11] *Op. cit.*, p. 54. Prof. Bronson continues: "The adaptability appears to be especially Scottish, and I suspect that part of the cause lies in the gapped scales so frequently appearing in the music of that country, so uncommon in English folk-music. These are natural bridges from mode to mode; and each pentatonic scale has latent reference to the heptatonic and two hexatonic scales, every one with its own special character and feeling." Angellier (II. 33–7) makes much the same point in less technical language. Cp. below, pp. 327, n. 3, and 328, n. 10.

When the singer comes to the first four lines of the second stanza, she should try, while still maintaining the noble elegiac flow of the melody, to communicate all the happy vigour of mature love :

> John Anderson my jo, John,
>   We clamb the hill thegither,
> And monie a cantie day, John,
>   We've had wi' ane anither. . . .

In its concatenation of vowels and consonants, "We clamb the hill thegither" suggests the struggles and difficulties of ordinary life, and should be taken somewhat slower than "And monie a cantie day, John . . ."; this contrast in tempo is absolutely essential in order to arouse in the listener the requisite feeling of remembered joy. But in the last four lines of the whole song resignation and pathos are mingled. The dissolution of the body, perhaps also of the soul, is certain—but it is both good and beautiful that a man and woman should love until death, and perhaps afterwards :

> Now we maun totter down, John,
>   And hand in hand we'll go,
> And sleep thegither at the foot,
>   John Anderson my jo ![12]

"Sleep thegither at the foot" suggests finality, calm, the peace that passeth all understanding—something much stronger and more enduring than the old "*Ubi sunt?*" theme, and at least as natural as Wordsworth's

> Rolled round in earth's diurnal course,
>   With rocks, and stones, and trees.[13]

But Burns's lines convey a state of immobility only—Wordsworth's a unity of rest and perpetual motion.

Thus, although the various parts of "John Anderson my

---

[12] Cp. Wither, "I lov'd a lass, a fair one," where, as noted by Ritter, pp. 206–7, the following lines occur : "Many a merry meeting | My love and I have had." Burns's line "But blessings on your frosty pow" seems to be a reminiscence of a line in "Lucky Nansy," a song in *The Tea-table Miscellany*, 1. 23 : "Leez me on thy snawy pow, | Lucky Nansy, Lucky Nansy." There are also similar sentiments in John Skinner's "Auld Minister's Song," for which see below, p. 321, n. 119.

[13] "A Slumber did my Spirit seal," ll. 7–8.

Jo" are formally parallel to one another, there are minute but significant differences between them which the reader or singer must bring out. The song is built up out of the unity between opposite concepts and feelings. As Professor R. D. Thornton says, it treats

> of marriage as a oneness, natural yet paradoxical; as a unity everywhere implying opposites from which it has been created and by which it has existed, opposites of man and woman, of husband and wife, of youth and age, of life and death, of solubility and dissolubility, of physical vigor and bodily weakness, of excitement and peace.[14]

And from it there emerges an exceptionally vivid conviction of the worth and beauty of life-long devotion. As in so many other works, what began as an exercise in tradition ends up as something new and revolutionary; quite easily and naturally, Burns here achieves a result which Wordsworth reached only with much theorising.

In "O, were my Love,"[15] where the poet expresses the conventional desire to be some object which the beloved has touched, only the first eight lines of introductory matter are by Burns; but they are poetically far inferior to its conclusion, which Burns inherited:

> O, gin my love were yon red rose,
>   That grows upon the castle wa',
> And I myself a drap o' dew
>   Into her bonie breast to fa',
> O, there, beyond expression blest,
>   I'd feast on beauty a' the night,
> Seal'd on her silk-saft faulds to rest,
>   Till fley'd awa by Phoebus' light!

The eight lines just quoted are amongst the loveliest in any volume of Burns's poems; and yet they were not composed by him, but by one of the anonymous poets whom he delighted to honour. Nothing could be more typical of the relationship between Burns and Scottish traditional song; he made the past his own, and the past—and his people—spoke through him.

---

[14] R. D. Thornton, *The Tuneful Flame: Songs of Robert Burns as He Sang Them*, Lawrence (Kansas) 1957. p. 7.　　　　[15] III. 279 (493).

"The Posie,"[16] written to a tune which he took down from Jean Armour's singing, is a beautiful exercise in the formal enumeration of flowers or other natural objects associated with the loved woman. Another lovely flower-song, not quite of the same type, is "Yon Rosy Brier" :[17] the second and third stanzas show what Scots-English can achieve in the lyric :

> Yon rosebuds in the morning dew,
> How pure among the leaves sae green !
> But purer was the lover's vow
> They witnessed in their shade yestreen.

> All in its rude and prickly bower,
> That crimson rose how sweet and fair !
> But love is far a sweeter flower
> Amid life's thorny path o' care.

"A Rose-bud, by my early Walk"[18] can also be treated here. The tune, by David Sillar, is in strathspey rhythm and is very difficult to sing.[19] The first two stanzas use eighteenth-century conventional diction, faintly qualified by the occasional Scotticism, to create the image of girlhood blossoming into womanhood :

> A rose-bud, by my early walk
> Adown a corn-inclosèd bawk,
> Sae gently bent its thorny stalk,
> All on a dewy morning.

> Ere twice the shades o' dawn are fled,
> In a' its crimson glory spread
> And drooping rich the dewy head,
> It scents the early morning.

---

[16] III. 122 (386). In addition to H. & H.'s source for this song, namely the blackletter broadside "A Posie of Rare Flowers gathered by a Young Man for his Mistress;" Ritter (pp. 230–2) notes similarities in : "Queen of the May," in Herd, *Scots Songs*, I. 279 ("Among the young lilies, my JENNY, I've stray'd, | Pinks, daisies, and woodbines I bring to my maid ; | Here's thyme sweetly smelling, and lavender gay, | A posy to form for my Queen of the May") ; "Since Jenny thinks mean," in *Vocal Magazine*, 1784 ; Carey, "I'll range around the shady Bowers," st. i (which Burns would know from *The Tea-table Miscellany*, II. 34) ; Prior, "The Garland" ; "A Nosegay," in the *Scots Magazine*, Jul. 1788 ; the well-known line (by [?] Robert Guy), "Love will find out the Way" ; Shenstone's "Pastoral Ballad," pt. II ; Thomson's *Spring*, ll. 709 ff. ; and Thomas Carew, "Ask me why I send you here | This firstling of the infant year ? . . . | This primrose . . ."

[17] III. 263 (486).   [18] III. 33 (329).   [19] Dick, *Songs*, p. 362.

In particular, the third and fourth lines of the second stanza, which concentrate the routine anxieties and devotion of motherhood in a precise visual image, show Burns again using the lyric to arouse a vivid *perception* :

> Within the bush her covert nest
> A little linnet fondly prest,
> *The dew sat chilly on her breast*
> *Sae early in the morning.* . . .

The last stanza is not so good, but even here Burns's mastery of the sound-values of Scots-English does not desert him. The pattern of alliteration and assonance is as evocative as that of "Man was made to Mourn," so that it almost (but not quite) effaces the impression conveyed by the hackneyed diction :

> So thou, dear bird, young Jeany fair,
> On trembling string or vocal air
> Shall sweetly pay the tender care
> That tents thy early morning !
> So thou, sweet rose-bud, young and gay,
> Shalt beauteous blaze upon the day,
> And bless the parent's evening ray
> That watch'd thy early morning !

In "To Miss Cruickshank,"[20] the symbols of flower and bird are both present; in other songs, the lover addresses a plaintive bird alone, in the tradition of all European complaints to the nightingale. For an example I have taken "O, stay, sweet warbling Wood-lark,"[21] with its moving final quatrain :

> Thou tells o' never-ending care,
> O' speechless grief and dark despair—
> For pity's sake, sweet bird, nae mair,
> Or my poor heart is broken !

When sung to the tune that was in Burns's mind when he wrote them, these lines are quite overpowering. Thomson set them to *Loch Erroch Side*, with Burns's consent; but they were originally intended for *Whare shall our Gudeman lie?*—the melody which, in quicker tempo, goes with "O, wha my Babie-clouts will buy?"[22] That two such contrasting songs could be sparked

[20] I. 292 (447).   [21] III. 223 (457).   [22] Dick, *Songs*, pp. 393–4.

off by the same tune is yet another testimony to the varied
emotional possibilities inherent in Scottish popular song.

In "The Banks o' Doon," which here must stand for a whole
class of songs in which Burns indulges in a favourite habit, the
mingling of landscape and sentiment—the expression of
emotion *through* pastoral description—the images of the rose
and the singing bird recur. It is interesting to trace the genesis
of the song, of which Burns wrote no less than three versions;
the first of these appears in a letter of 11 Mar. 1791,[23] in which
Burns states that it should be sung to the reel of *Ballendalloch*.
The second set, "Ye flowery Banks,"[24] retains the tune—and
the ballad style—of the original:

> Thou'll break my heart, thou bonie bird,
>   That sings beside thy mate:
> For sae I sat, and sae I sang,
>   And wist na o' my fate!
>
> Aft hae I rov'd by bonie Doon
>   To see the woodbine twine,
> And ilka bird sang o' its luve,
>   And sae did I o' mine.
>
> Wi' lightsome heart I pu'd a rose
>   Frae aff its thorny tree,
> And my fause lover staw my rose,
>   But left the thorn wi' me.

All critics have agreed that this second version is, *poetically*, far
superior to the third set, "The Banks o' Doon."[25] It is simpler,
and the extra adjectives and adverbs add nothing to the intensity of the emotion. In version III, the lines "That wantons
thro' the flowering thorn," "And fondly sae did I o' mine,"
for example, are much weaker than the corresponding lines in
version II, "That sings upon the bough," "And sae did I o'
mine." But I cannot hold with Henley and Henderson's
snobbish judgment[26] that the third set is the worst of the three
because it is popular. As a matter of fact, when it is sung to the
melody for ever associated with it, the extra syllables cease to
be redundant, and the song emerges as quite different in

---

[23] To Cunningham, in *Letters*, II. 65; H. & H., IV. 27 (94)— "Sweet are the
banks."   [24] IV. 28 (94).   [25] III. 124 (388).   [26] IV. 94.

mood from the other two. When considered as a *song*, and not merely as a verbal pattern, it becomes a beautifully poignant expression of love's melancholy, and the contrast between the bird's glee and the lover's pain emerges far more clearly than in either of the other versions :

> Thou'll break my heart, thou warbling bird,
> That wantons thro' the flowering thorn !
> Thou minds me o' departed joys,
> Departed never to return.

When associated with the music, the repetition of "departed" and the stock expression "never to return"[27] add immeasurably to the pathos. In a rather similar way, the somewhat stilted language of "The Lass o' Ballochmyle,"[28] when linked to the original melody, takes on an altogether new significance, so that the last four lines—quite good in themselves—become one of the finest realisations of the idea of pastoral in Scots-English, and equal to the very best Southron attempts in this manner :

> Give me the cot below the pine,
> To tend the flocks or till the soil,
> And every day have joys divine
> With the bonie lass o' Ballochmyle.

Some of the most interesting of Burns's songs belong to a group which features rustic courtship, and especially evening walks and meetings. "Ca' the Yowes to the knowes" achieves a satisfactory synthesis of the realities of Scottish country life on the one hand and traditional associations of love with shepherds and shepherdesses on the other. The first version,[29] containing six four-lined stanzas, appeared in the *Scots Musical Museum* in 1790. Stephen Clarke, the Edinburgh organist who acted as chief musical adviser to Johnson's *Museum*, took down the melody at Burns's request from the singing of a minister named

---

[27] Ritter, pp. 224–5, notes the parallel with Blair, *The Grave*, ll. 109 ff. ("Of joys departed, | Not to return, how painful the remembrance"), and compares Burns's last stanza with Matthew Parker, "The distress'd Virgin," in *The Roxburghe Ballads*, i. 278 ("I put my finger unto the bush, | thinking the sweetest Rose to find, | I prickt my finger to the bone, | and yet I left the Rose behind.") He also finds, in "The Banks o' Doon," possible echoes of Pinkerton, "Bothwell Bank," and of Gay, "The Wise Penitent."

[28] iv. 16 (87).   [29] iii. 65 (350).

Clunzie, who also supplied the words,[30] which Burns "mended"
by expanding the original first stanza into two and adding the
two final stanzas :

'If ye'll but stand to what ye've said,
I'se gang wi' you, my shepherd lad,
And ye may row me in your plaid,
And I sall be your dearie.'

'While waters wimple to the sea,
While day blinks in the lift sae hie,
Till clay-cauld death sall blin' my e'e,
Ye sall be my dearie.'

The song, as published in the *Scots Musical Museum*, is also an
example of that large and popular class which takes the form
of a dialogue between two lovers, and it is one of the few songs
in which Burns makes serious use of ballad conventions—
"clay-cauld death" and "blin' my e'e" come from that large
inherited stock of ballad expressions which are so reminiscent
of the *formulae* of Old English poetry or of the Homeric epics.

In the second set,[31] which appeared in Thomson's *Original
Scotish Airs* in 1805, the man alone is the singer ; there is no
dialogue, and the ballad touches have disappeared. They are
replaced by a pre-Romantic landscape of waves, ruined towers,
and fairies dancing in the moonlight, to which is added an
impression of protective tenderness suggested by the melody
itself :

Ghaist nor bogle shalt thou fear—
Thou'rt to Love and Heav'n sae dear
Nocht of ill may come thee near,
My bonie dearie.

But the best stanza is assuredly the last :[32]

Fair and lovely as thou art,
Thou hast stown my very heart ;
I can die—but canna part,
My bonie dearie.

When sung, these lines (which are surely by Burns himself)

---

[30] Cp. Burns to Thomson, [Sep. 1794], in *Letters*, II. 255; Dick, *Songs*,
pp. 389–90.   [31] III. 268 (488).
[32] This second version was also printed by Currie in 1800, IV. 161.

convey an intense and unalloyed emotion which all men have felt at some time or other; thanks to the tune which called them forth, they are as beautiful as anything else in Scots or English song.

Not all Burns's songs which feature evening trysts or meetings are as serious as "Ca' the Yowes to the knowes." There is, for example, the sly humour of "Comin thro' the Rye" :[33]

> Comin thro' the rye, poor body,
> Coming thro' the rye,
> She draigl't a' her petticoatie,
> Comin thro' the rye! . .

> *Chorus*

> O, Jenny's a' weet, poor body,
> Jenny's seldom dry :
> She draigl't a' her petticoatie,
> Comin thro' the rye!

There is also the unashamed physical passion of "Corn Rigs."[34] In the latter (an early song), the beauty of Nature and the humorous observation of feminine character—"wi sma' persuasion she agreed"—are united in a lyric which recreates a unique and *particular* moment of time—the kind of moment which, it is true, we have all experienced, but which can never occur again in exactly the same form :

> It was upon a Lammas night,
> When corn rigs are bonie,
> Beneath the moon's unclouded light,
> I held awa to Annie ;

[33] III. 151 (411).

[34] I. 180 (385). The song is ultimately based on a Scots folk original, "O, corn rigs and rye rigs, | O, corn rigs are bonie ; | And where'er you meet a bonie lass | Preen up her cockerncnie" (Dick, *Songs*, p. 353). Ritter, pp. 42–3, also finds reminiscences of "Nought but love," a popular song often ascribed to Gay, and of the folk-song "The Maid gaed to the Mill" (Herd, *Scots Songs*, II. 148) ; and he points out a decided resemblance between Burns's st. iii, ll. 5–7, and the *English* popular song, "The Girl I left behind me," st. ii ("Oh, ne'er shall I forget the night, | The stars were bright above me, | And gently lent their silv'ry light, | When first she vow'd to love me"). According to Chappell-Wooldridge, *Popular Music of the Olden Time*, 2 vols., 1893, II. 189, "The Girl I left behind me" dates from 1758. Thus *English*, as well as Scots, popular song has made its contribution to this eminently "vernacular" lyric.

The time flew by, wi' tentless heed;
Till, 'tween the late and early,
Wi' sma' persuasion she agreed
To see me thro' the barley.

Corn rigs, an' barley rigs,
An' corn rigs are bonie:
I'll ne'er forget that happy night,
Amang the rigs wi' Annie.

The best of all Burns's songs of this type is, in my opinion,
"The Lea-Rig."[35] Even when sung in the modern concert
version, where the tune has been slightly corrupted by Thomson,[36] it recreates both the overmastering passion and the
melancholy quality of love: there is, in the last stanza, a
strange but inevitable tension between the words "cheery, O,"
and "dearie, O!" and the sadness of their musical counterparts.
In "The Lea-Rig," as in so many of Burns's lyrical masterpieces, to the melody itself there is added an additional musical
element—the "tone-poetry" of the words themselves, the
harmonious blending of consonants and vowels:

When o'er the hill the eastern star
    Tells bughtin time is near, my jo,
And owsen frae the furrow'd field
    Return sae dowf and weary, O,
Down by the burn, where scented birks
    Wi' dew are hangin clear, my jo,
I'll meet thee on the lea-rig,
    My ain kind dearie, O.

Cross-alliteration of *m* and *r* combines with perfect choice of
individual words, both vernacular and Scots-English, to produce two of the finest couplets anywhere in Burns:

At midnight hour in mirkest glen
    I'd rove, and ne'er be eerie, O, . . .

The hunter lo'es the morning sun
    To rouse the mountain deer, my jo, . . .

[35] III. 284 (497). For the sources, in Fergusson and in popular tradition, see
H. & H.'s note.
[36] Dick, *Songs*, p. 397.

In this song, as in many others, the two kinds of tone-poetry[37] are interwoven into a composite pattern that does not exist for its own sake, but is strictly subordinate to the evocation of a *particular* emotion in a *particular* context.

Another favourite folk theme is that of the night visit to the girl at her window or in her room. One of the best examples in Burns is the vigorously impudent "Wha is that at my Bower Door,"[38] involving a dialogue between the lovers and a slyly observed contrast between the man's somewhat brutal insistence and the woman's apparently refined coyness. From the very start, despite all appearances to the contrary, she has wanted to let Findlay into the bower, and she ends as absolute mistress of the situation. Findlay has made a binding promise to her (to be secret)—that is, he has yielded to her femininity; and the joke is that he thinks that *he* has conquered her!

> 'Here this night if ye remain'—
>   'I'll remain!' quo' Findlay—
> 'I dread ye'll learn the gate again?'
>   'Indeed will I!' quo' Findlay.
> 'What may pass within this bower'
>   ('Let it pass!' quo' Findlay!)
> 'Ye maun conceal till your last hour'—
>   'Indeed will I!' quo' Findlay.

Findlay, one feels, is a man of the same stamp as Blazes Boylan in James Joyce's *Ulysses*; and the woman of the song is a Scottish Molly Bloom.

An even finer night-visit song is the irrepressibly gay "O, Whistle an' I'll come to ye, my Lad."[39] The singer is a young girl, and the lilting tune mirrors the bounding happiness of what today is termed "teen-age love," as well as her conviction that her own feelings, simply because they are so intense, must prove victorious over the cautious worldly wisdom of the "squares" who surround her. By themselves, the words are excellent—but, united to the tune, they are superb:

---

[37] The expression (applied originally to the union of poetry and vocal music) is taken from the sub-title of Dick, *Songs*—"*A Study in Tone-Poetry*." For the tone-poetry of combined song and verse texture, see below, p. 362.

[38] III. 102 (375). For the source, "Who but I, quoth Finlay," see H. & H.'s note.

[39] III. 5 (304). The chorus is in the Herd Manuscript, and the song seems to belong to that group in which everything, except the chorus, is Burns's.

But warily tent when ye come to court me,
And come nae unless the back-yett be a-jee;
Syne up the back-style, and let naebody see,
And come as ye were na comin to me,
And come as ye were na comin to me!

At kirk, or at market, whene'er ye meet me,
Gang by me as tho' that ye car'd na a flie;
But steal me a blink o' your bonie black e'e,
Yet look as ye were na lookin to me,
Yet look as ye were na lookin to me!

Ay vow and protest that ye care na for me,
And whyles ye may lightly my beauty a wee;
But court na anither tho' jokin ye be,
For fear that she wyle your fancy frae me,
For fear that she wyle your fancy frae me!

Chorus

O, whistle and I'll come to ye, my lad!
O, whistle an' I'll come to ye, my lad!
Tho' father an' mother an' a' should gae mad,
O, whistle an' I'll come to ye, my lad!

The night visit is in this case only mentioned in the first verse
and in the chorus; it is simply the occasion for a compressed
drama which extends to every hour of the day and yet involves
every one of the girl's waking thoughts, wherever she moves
in her contracted village world. In the last three lines of the
third stanza, the tempo slows down a little in order to hint at
another characteristic of teen-age love—its brittleness, and the
bitter pangs of jealousy which so often accompany it. A skilful
singer ought to bring out this sudden change of mood—and
immediately afterwards efface it in her joyous rendering of the
chorus.

It is only a step from the night visit to another, somewhat
coarser mood—that of the songs of gross popular drollery, as
Angellier calls them, presenting love as seen through the exclusively masculine eyes of the Tarbolton Bachelors' Club, and
the Edinburgh Crochallan Fencibles. One of the best of these,
admirably fitted to one of Burns's favourite tunes, *Clout the
Cauldron*, is "The Fornicator,"[40] a piece which is surely far

[40] *Merry Muses*, pp. 52–3.

more genuinely personal, far closer to the *real* Burns (in one of
his moods), than the Highland Mary songs :

> But for her sake this vow I make,
> And solemnly I swear it,
> That while I own a single crown
> She's welcome for to share it ;
> And my roguish boy his Mother's joy
> And the darling of his Pater,
> For him I boast my pains and cost,
> Although a Fornicator.

In this song, Burns identifies his sexual prowess with the con-
querors of history—an association similar to that which, in
"Louis, what reck I by Thee ?", led him to claim his superiority
to contemporary monarchs :

> Your warlike Kings and Heros bold,
> Great Captains and Commanders ;
> Your mighty Caesars fam'd of old,
> And conquering Alexanders ;
> In fields they fought and laurels bought,
> And bulwarks strong did batter,
> But still they grac'd our noble list,
> And ranked Fornicator ! ! !

In some of his other bawdy songs, Burns links sex with Biblical
figures, as in "The Patriarch,"[41] which features a spiritedly
irreverent conjugal debate between Jacob and Rachel, or in
"The bonniest Lass," a version of "For a' that" which occurs in
The Merry Muses.[42] In the latter piece, he says of King David :

> For a' that an' a' that,
> To keep him warm, and a' that,
> The daughters o' Jerusalem
> Were waled for him, an' a' that.

> Who wadna pity thae sweet dames
> He fumbled at, an' a' that,
> An raised their bluid up into flames
> He couldna drown, for a' that.

> For a' that an' a' that ;
> He wanted pith, an' a' that ;
> For, as to what we shall not name,
> What could he do but claw that.

[41] *Merry Muses*, pp. 67–8.   [42] Pp. 69–70.

In the sixth stanza, Burns returns to a favourite figure in his
own personal pantheon, King Solomon, to whom, the reader
will remember, allusion is also made in "Green grow the
Rashes, O" :

> King Solomon, prince o' divines,
> Wha proverbs made, an' a' that,
> Baith mistresses an' concubines,
> In hundreds had, for a' that.
>
> For a' that, an' a' that,
> Tho' a preacher wise, an' a' that,
> The smuttiest sang that e'er was sung,
> His Sang o' Sangs is a' that.

In these two songs, as in "The Holy Fair,"[43] the vigour of
physical passion is counterposed to the absurd pretensions to
sexual purity of "the rigidly righteous"—and, in the second
one, a contemporary comment is made :

> The bonniest lass that ye meet neist,
> Gie her a kiss an a' that,
> In spite o' ilka parish priest,
> Repentin' stool, an' a' that.
>
> For a' that an' a' that,
> Their mim-mou'd sangs an' a' that,
> In time and place convenient,
> They'll do't themselves for a' that.

It is the same point that is made in "Holy Willie's Prayer,"[44]
but raised from satire to the level of pure comedy by the ex-
uberant and vigorous tune, which should be taken more
lightly (and, of course, more quickly) than in "Is there for
honest Poverty."

From bawdry (albeit with a strong undercurrent of religious
and social criticism) it is natural to pass to songs on the comedy
of love and marriage, and to do so by way of "The Tailor fell
thro' the Bed,"[45] which some would no doubt class under the
former heading. It contains four stanzas, two of which are
traditional and two—the two best—by Burns, as follows :

[43] I. 36 (328) ; above, pp. 67–76.
[44] II. 25 (320) ; above, pp. 52–61.   [45] III. 44 (336).

The sleepy bit lassie, she dreaded nae ill,
The sleepy bit lassie, she dreaded nae ill;
The weather was cauld, and the lassie lay still:
She thought that a tailor could do her nae ill! . . .

There's somebody weary wi' lying her lane,
There's somebody weary wi' lying her lane!
There's some that are dowie, I trow wad be fain
To see the bit tailor come skippin again.

They serve to introduce a hint of the girl's character, and to communicate an *attitude*—the poet's gently smiling compassion for all young people tormented by desire. Ironically enough, the air is none other than the *March of the Corporation of Tailors* —and a spirited one it is, too.

"What can a young Lassie"[46] takes the conventional situation of the young wife married to an old man and makes of it yet another lyric of character grafted on to a reel-tune:

He hums and he hankers,
He frets and he cankers,
I never can please him
　　Do a' that I can.
He's peevish an' jealous
Of a' the young fellows—
O, dool on the day
　　I met wi' an auld man!

My auld auntie Katie
Upon me taks pity,
I'll do my endeavour
　　To follow her plan:
I'll cross him an' wrack him
Until I heartbreak him,
And then his auld brass
　　Will buy me a new pan.[47]

"Had I the Wyte?"[48]—based, like a set in *The Merry Muses*, on a fragment which is also preserved in the Herd Manuscript— is fitted to a reel-tune until recently popular in both Scotland

---

[46] III. 93 (368). In their note, H. & H. mention several popular sources.
[47] H. & H., III. 368, note that this stanza "is influenced by the set of *Auld Rob Morris* in Ramsay's *Tea-table Miscellany*," as follows: "Rob Morris, I grant, is an elderly man, | But then his auld brass, it will buy a new pan . . ."
[48] III. 149 (410).

and Northumberland. It deals with an equally popular folk-comedy (and art-comedy) situation—adultery—but in the third stanza Burns strikes a more compassionate note than elsewhere in the song :

Could I for shame, could I for shame,
Could I for shame refus'd her?
And wadna manhood been to blame
Had I unkindly used her?
He claw'd her wi' the ripplin-kame,
And blae and bluidy bruis'd her—
When sic a husband was frae hame,
What wife but wad excus'd her!

Among the best songs on the comedy of love, courtship and marriage are "Last May a braw Wooer,"[49] the second set of "Duncan Gray,"[50] and what is surely the most beautiful of all the many lyrics in which Burns penetrates the mind of a young girl—"Tam Glen."[51] In the first of these Burns pokes fun at the Scottish fondness for understatement, at our reluctance to communicate our feelings to others.[52] But he does not do so in a *general* way, as the writers of the early eighteenth-century would have done; he does so by putting his words in the mouth of a real girl—a shrewd, intelligent hussy who is yet able to laugh both at herself and at her suitor. There are only forty lines in the whole song; and, since the last line of each stanza is repeated, the content is expressed in a mere thirty-two lines. Yet into them Burns pours not only a criticism of one aspect of the Scottish character, but some spirited thrusts at the language of sentimental love. We can almost hear the girl's laughter at her wooer's inanities :

He spak o' the darts in my bonie black een,
And vow'd for my love he was diein.
I said, he might die when he liket for Jean :
The Lord forgie me for liein, for liein—
The Lord forgie me for liein!

There are only thirty-four words in that stanza, if we exclude repetitions—and twenty-nine of them are monosyllables. Where else in literature can one find the interplay of character, motive and mask, expressed with such ruthless economy?

[49] III. 242 (470).
[50] III. 215 (452).   [51] III. 84 (363).   [52] Cp. Dick, *Songs*, p. 419.

The suitor brings forward certain very weighty and material arguments to reinforce his gallantry. Jean (attractive little realist that she is) is by no means oblivious to them—but she pretends the contrary :

> A weel-stocket mailen, himself for the laird,
> And marriage aff-hand were his proffers :
> I never loot on that I kenn'd it, or car'd,
> But thought I might hae waur offers, waur offers—
> But thought I might hae waur offers.

In the fourth stanza the tone changes to one of excited indignation ; it is the very perfection of conversational song :

> But what wad ye think? In a fortnight or less
> (The Deil tak his taste to gae near her !)
> He up the Gate-Slack to my black cousin, Bess !
> Guess ye how, the jad ! I could bear her, could
> bear her—
> Guess ye how, the jad ! I could bear her.

But when she meets him at "the tryste o' Dalgarnock," all she needs to do is to give him an almost imperceptible glance ("Lest neebours might say I was saucy"—and not, of course, because she was in any way interested in him) :

> My wooer he caper'd as he'd been in drink,
> And vow'd I was his dear lassie, dear lassie—
> And vow'd I was his dear lassie !

To this her response is a piece of calculated "bitchery" which merely makes her more lovable still :

> I spier'd for my cousin fu' couthy and sweet :
> Gin she had recover'd her hearin?
> And how her new shoon fit her auld, shachl'd feet?
> But heavens ! how he fell a swearin, a swearin—
> But heavens ! how he fell a swearin !

The suitor retains his affected love-language to the end, while Jean never loses the sharpness of "the Scotch sarcastic humour" :

> He beggèd, for gudesake, I wad be his wife,
> Or else I wad kill him wi' sorrow ;
> So e'en to preserve the poor body in life,
> I think I maun wed him to-morrow, to-morrow—
> I think I maun wed him to-morrow !

If "Sleep'st thou" represents the Scots-English of the lyric,
then "Last May a braw Wooer" may be taken as stylistically
parallel to the supple vernacular of "Death and Doctor
Hornbook."[53]

The second set of "Duncan Gray" is very like similar
versions preserved in *The Merry Muses*, and it also resembles a
fragment in the Herd Manuscript, beginning

> 'Can ye play wi' Duncan Gray
> (Hey hey, the girdin o't),
> O'er the hills and far away
> (Hey, hey, the girdin o't)?
> Duncan he came her to woo
> On a day when we were fou',
> And Meg she swore that she wad spew,
> If he gaed her the girdin o't.'[54]

Burn's "respectable" version is indeed inseparable from the
merry and attractive tune, on which Burns himself passed the
best comment:

> Duncan Gray is that kind of light-horse gallop of an air, which
> precludes sentiment.—The ludicrous is its ruling feature.[55]

It is instructive to notice how Burns *concentrates* the words of his
original as he sets the scene for his own version; the vague "on
a day" becomes a very special occasion, in a line where every
word counts:

> On blythe Yule-Night when we were fou.

With the fifth line we are given a vivid image of the skittish girl
as she tosses her head and looks disdainfully amused:

> Maggie coost her head fu' high,
> Look'd asklent and unco skeigh,
> Gart poor Duncan stand abeigh—
> Ha, ha, the wooing o't!

The rhythm of the tune, the choice of words, and the tone-
poetry of vowels and consonants all combine in a remarkably
lively impression of the girl's mood and gestures. Unlike the

---

[53] Above, pp. 118-22.
[54] Cp. "Duncan Gray," first set, III. 215 (452); and *The Merry Muses*, pp. 98-9.
Hecht's text, p. 208, reads "Can ye play me Duncan Gray? | High, hey the
girdin o't," etc.   [55] To Thomson, 4 Dec. [1792], in *Letters*, II.135.

"braw wooer," Duncan does not seem to know the language of gallantry, but he sighs and sheds a tear just the same, and even (in a line which has justly been praised[56] as a masterstroke)

> Spak o' lowpin o'er a linn—
> Ha, ha, the wooing o't!

At this point, too, a skilful singer will bend the melody in the service of the words, illustrating by means of vocal inflexion and abruptly quickened rhythm the actual motion of an imagined leap over a waterfall.

In the third stanza the mood changes; the rhythm slows down; and the melody begins to take on faintly melancholy undertones:

> Time and Chance are but a tide
> (Ha, ha, the wooing o't):
> Slighted love is sair to bide
> (Ha, ha, the wooing o't!).

Then in the second half Duncan experiences a vigorous reversal of feeling, expressed alike in the racy colloquialism of the diction, in the expressive alliteration of *f* and *h*, and in yet another change of rhythm:

> 'Shall I like a fool,' quoth he,
> 'For a haughty hizzie die?
> She may gae to—France for me!'—
> Ha, ha, the wooing o't!

The fourth stanza, in which the singer describes the second *peripeteia* of his little tale ("Meg grew sick, as he grew hale") is wholly in the slower and sadder mood of the first half of the third stanza—but even the melancholy is intertwined with humour, as in the concluding couplet:

> And O! her een they spak sic things!—
> Ha, ha, the wooing o't!

In the nineteenth century, much was said about Burns's allegedly "Shakespearian" qualities. Actually—and "Duncan Gray" is a case in point—it is in his comic love-songs that Burns approaches most closely to Shakespeare. As in Shake-

---

[56] By the Hon. Andrew Erskine, in the postscript to a letter from Thomson to Burns, 20 Jan. 1793, in C. & W., III. 392.

speare's love-comedies, the action of the song centres in "ob-
structions in the love-relationship,"[57] which, in "Duncan Gray,"
are the natural result of the lovers' characters, and not of an
artificial and impossible plot. As in Shakespeare, too, there is a
reconciliation at the end. The sparkle of "Duncan Gray" reminds me of nothing so much as the sparkle of *Much Ado about
Nothing*, Duncan, like Benedick, *wills* his devotion :

> Duncan could na be her death,
> Swelling pity smoor'd his wrath ;
> Now they're crouse and canty baith—
> Ha, ha, the wooing o't !

It is impossible to mention Burns's remarkable success, at
the comic level, in writing dramatic lyrics in which the singer
is a young girl, without considering "I'm o'er young to Marry
yet,"[58] "Jamie, come try me,"[59] and "O, for Ane-and-twenty,
Tam."[60] In the first of these, the words and music combine to
give us a girl's mood shortly after puberty—shy, blushing, yet
full of the knowledge of what she is and what she must become :

> I am my mammie's ae bairn,
> Wi' unco folk I weary, Sir,
> And lying in a man's bed,
> I'm fley'd it make me eerie, Sir . . .[61]

> Fu' loud and shrill the frosty wind
> Blaws thro' the leafless timmer, Sir,
> But if ye come this gate again,
> I'll aulder be gin simmer, Sir.[62]

> *Chorus*

> I'm o'er young, I'm o'er young,
> I'm o'er young to marry yet !
> I'm o'er young, 'twad be a sin
> To tak me frae my mammie yet.

[57] For a theory of comedy in which this is the central concept, see J. Y. T.
Greig, *The Psychology of Laughter and Comedy*, London 1923, *passim*.
[58] III. 6 (305).   [59] III. 52 (342).   [60] III. III (382).
[61] Ritter, p. 182, notes the similarity to Ramsay, "Where wad bonny Annie
lie ?", st. ii : "Can a lass sae young as I | Venture on the bridal-tie, | Syne down
with a goodman lie ? | I'm flaed he keep me wauking."
[62] Ritter, *loc. cit.*, cites "The silly Maids," in D'Urfey, *Pills to Purge Melan-
choly*, IV. 95 : "Winter Nights are long you know . . . | Then who's so fond to lie
alone, | When two may lie together?"

In "Jamie, come try me"[63] the girl is slightly older, and the song calls up a picture of someone "just waiting to be asked"—breathless with desire, and almost beseeching Jamie to take the first step. The words are of the simplest—and yet the poetry is of the highest sort :

> If thou should ask my love,
> Could I deny thee?
> If thou would win my love,
> Jamie, come try me!

It is the translation into song of a long, meaningful, agonised look. The heroine of "O, for Ane-and-twenty, Tam", we feel, is older still—and yet the song tells us that she is only eighteen :

> They snool me sair, and haud me down,
> And gar me look like bluntie, Tam;
> But three short years will soon wheel roun'—
> And then comes ane-and-twenty, Tam!

She is the feminine equivalent of "the man o' independent mind," of whom Burns said on another occasion :

> . . . it is on such individuals as I, that for the hand of support & the eye of intelligence, a Nation has to rest.—The uninformed mob may swell a Nation's bulk; & the titled, tinsel Courtly throng may be its feathered ornament, but the number of those who are elevated enough in life, to reason & reflect; & yet low enough to keep clear of the venal contagion of a Court; these are a Nation's strength.—[64]

The singer of "O, for Ane-and-twenty, Tam", has some property of her own—that is the economic basis of her independence—but yet her family want her to marry for money. Here we have, in the lyric, the same opposition between love and money that appears in the early epistles. This is, of course, a commonplace of popular stall-balladry, but here it has become concretely embodied in a flesh-and-blood lass who is very much her lover's equal and symbolically shakes hands to close her bargain, just like a man :

---

[63] Ritter, pp. 204–5, agrees with H. & H. that the form of this song is traditional and quotes the following stanza from *The Roxburghe Ballads*, iii. 421 : "Thomas, why come you not | often to see me ? | I fear you have forgot | your vows to free me."

[64] To [John Francis Erskine *of Mar*, Apr. 1793], in *Letters*, ii. 171.

They'll hae me wed a wealthy coof,
  Tho' I mysel hae plenty, Tam ;
But hear'st thou, laddie—there's my loof:
  I'm thine at ane-and-twenty, Tam !

Chorus

An' O, for ane-and-twenty, Tam !
And hey, sweet ane-and-twenty, Tam !
I'll learn my kin a rattlin sang
An I saw ane-and-twenty, Tam.

The girl in "Tam Glen"[65] is a little less self-reliant ; perhaps a little younger, though the situation is similar. Gentler, she does not like the idea of causing her family distress :

My heart is a-breaking, dear tittie,
  Some counsel unto me come len'.
To anger them a' is a pity,
  But what will I do wi' Tam Glen?

Conflict is essential in any good play or story ; and conflict is present in "Tam Glen"—an emotional tug-of-war of a kind which afflicts millions of girls every day :

My minnie does constantly deave me,
  And bids me beware o' young men.
They flatter, she says, to deceive me—
  But wha can think sae o' Tam Glen?

The struggle is the familiar one between the claims of love and money ; but, in the next stanza, by using the diminutive form "daddie," Burns conveys that it is no tyrant of melodramatic or stall-ballad convention with whom the girl has to deal, but an ordinary, prudent, decent father sincerely concerned for his daughter's wordly welfare. Ironically, she brings forward against him the concept of Fate—which in Scotland is one that must always have theological undertones. Love's predestination, however, is guaranteed not by any subjective certainty of election, but by the objective witness of popular superstition :

Yestreen at the valentines' dealing,
  My heart to my mou gied a sten,
For thrice I drew ane without failing,
  And thrice it was written 'Tam Glen' !

[65] III. 84 (363).

And at Halloween, when she hung her wet "sark-sleeve" before the fire, what came up to turn it but her own lad's likeness? One can only marvel at Burns's mastery of feminine psychology, and at the understanding humour with which he makes the girl *bribe* her sister to give her the only advice that she wants to hear :

> Come, counsel, dear tittie, don't tarry !
> I'll gie ye my bonie black hen,
> Gif ye will advise me to marry
> The lad I lo'e dearly, Tam Glen.

Here, too, the comedy (though miniature) is Shakespearean in spirit—there is the same gentle smile at human foibles, the same deep sympathy, the same fundamental respect for people as people that is found in *As you like it* and *Twelfth Night*.

The last group of love songs we shall examine are amongst the loveliest of all those in which Burns had a hand—songs of pure passion almost devoid of intellectual content, and approximating to the primitive emotional cry. Burns's songs of this category are not only set to a definite tune, but the words themselves, considered in isolation, produce something of the effect of instrumental music. If music—or some music at any rate—embodies abstract emotion, purged of all such cramping particulars as must be associated with even the most general of statements in a national language, then Burns on occasion, and especially in songs of this type, comes as near to music as it is possible for poetry to come :

> O, wilt thou go wi' me, sweet Tibbie Dunbar?
> O, wilt thou go wi' me, sweet Tibbie Dunbar?
> Wilt thou ride on a horse, or be drawn in a car,
> Or walk by my side, O sweet Tibbie Dunbar? [66]

Psychologically, the basis for this song is the lover's infatuation

---

[66] "Sweet Tibbie Dunbar," III. 42 (335). There are many parallels in older popular songs, some of which are noted by Ritter, pp. 205–6, as follows : Ramsay, "Cock Laird," st. i, ll. 5–6 ("Wilt thou gae alang | Wi me, Jenny, Jenny?"), and "Now wat ye wha I met yestreen?", st. ii, l. 1 ("O, Katy, wiltu gang wi me" ; Percy, "Fairest o' the Fair," st. i, l. i ("O Nancy, wilt thou go with me") ; and "The Highland Lassie," in Ramsay's *Tea-table Miscellany*, II. 157, st. ii, ll. 3–4 ("I'd tak my Katy but a gown, | Bare-footed in her little *coatie*".)

with everything about his sweetheart, including her name, together with his simple delight in repeating it over and over again. The same trait is also found in "My Eppie Macnab"[67] and "Eppie Adair" :[68]

> An' O my Eppie,
> My jewel, my Eppie !
> Wha wadna be happy
> Wi' Eppie Adair ?

One of these songs, "For the Sake o' Somebody"[69]—especially when sung to its lovely tune—is the artistic expression of a love-lorn sigh :

> My heart is sair—I dare na tell—
> My heart is sair for Somebody :
> I would wake a winter night
> For the sake o' Somebody.
> O-hon ! for Somebody !
> O-hey ! for Somebody !
> I could range the world around
> For the sake o' Somebody.

"Thou hast left me ever, Jamie"[70] has all the immediacy of a piercing cry of anguish. It is written to the tune of *Fee him, Father, fee him*, which Burns heard played by Thomas Fraser, "the Hautboy player,"[71] in Sep. 1793. His own comment sums up the mood which the melody induces :

> I inclose you Fraser's set of this tune when he plays it slow ; in fact, he makes it the language of Despair.—I shall here give

---

[67] III. 101 (375). "My Eppie Macnab" is folk-material worked over by Burns : cp. *Songs from David Herd's MSS*, p. 113.

[68] III. 72 (356). Angellier, II. 282, notes the same trait in Tennyson's *Maud*, XII.

[69] III. 158 (416). In addition to Ramsay's verses on "Somebody" in *The Tea-table Miscellany*, Ritter, in *Neue Quellenfunde zu Robert Burns*, (henceforth cited as *N.Q.*, Halle 1903), pp. 21–2, notes another "Somebody" in D. Sime, *Edinburgh Musical Miscellany: A collection . . . of Scotch, English, and Irish Songs*, 1793, II. 43. He also points out that "I could range the world around" is a common folk-song *motif*, and that "Ye powers that smile on virtuous love" occurs in Robert Crawford's song "My Deary, if you die," and a similar line in "As early I walk'd" in *The Tea-table Miscellany*.

[70] III. 254 (480). It, too, is completely in the folk-tradition ; H. & H. note its resemblance to an older lyric, "Thou art gane awa frae me, Mary."

[71] To Thomson, 30 Jul. [1793], in *Letters*, II 179.

you two stanzas, in that style; merely to try if it will be any improvement.—Were it possible, in singing, to give it half the pathos which Fraser gives it in playing, it would make an admirably pathetic song.—[72]

The song must be quoted in full :

> Thou hast left me ever, Jamie,
> Thou hast left me ever !
> Thou hast left me ever, Jamie,
> Thou hast left me ever !
> Aften hast thou vow'd that Death
> Only should us sever ;
> Now thou'st left thy lass for ay—
> I maun see thee never, Jamie,
> I'll see thee never !
>
> Thou hast me forsaken, Jamie,
> Thou hast me forsaken !
> Thou hast me forsaken, Jamie,
> Thou hast me forsaken !
> Thou canst love another jo,
> While my heart is breaking—
> Soon my weary een I'll close,
> Never mair to waken, Jamie,
> Never mair to waken !

One is reminded of a magnificent passage just before the end of Conrad's *Nostromo* :[73]

> Linda's black figure detached itself upright on the light of the lantern with her arms raised above her head as though she were going to throw herself over.
> "It is I who loved you," she whispered, with a face as set and white as marble in the moonlight. "I ! Only I ! She will forget thee, killed miserably for her pretty face. I cannot understand. I cannot understand. But I shall never forget thee. Never !"
> She stood silent and still, as if collecting her strength to throw all her fidelity, her pain, bewilderment and despair into one great cry.
> "Never ! Gian' Battista !"

Both Burns and Conrad succeed in conveying a woman's

[72] To [Thomson, Sep. 1793], in *Letters*, II. 203. [73] *Ad fin.*

harrowing cry of grief; both recapture the confusion that follows emotional shock; and both do it by means of repetition, the mind's natural response to something it can hardly believe to be true. Burns's song, too, evokes a mood of pain, bewilderment and despair; it, too, is "a true cry of love and grief." But it does not depend on context or plot for its full effect; and, unlike the Conrad passage, it contains no hint of false romanticism, such as that found in the very last sentence of the novel,[74] which follows the extract just quoted. "Thou hast left me ever, Jamie," is as faultless as anything Burns ever wrote, or had a hand in.

The same can also be said of "Ay Waukin, O."[75] Like "For the Sake o' Somebody" and "Thou hast left me ever, Jamie", it is a woman's song; like them, it is one of the greatest dramatic lyrics that we have. It is the very voice of hopeless passion and frustrated desire, and perhaps, in its absolute transparency of language, the nearest thing to Sappho in the whole of Scottish or English literature. As Dick says, "the melody is remarkable for its brevity and simplicity."[76] Here Scottish folk-song,[77] refined and polished by Burns, has created what may well be its masterpiece:

---

[74] "In that true cry of undying passion that seemed to ring aloud from Punta Mala to Azuera and away to the bright line of the horizon, overhung by a big white cloud shining like a mass of solid silver, the genius of the magnificent Capataz de Cargadores dominated the dark gulf containing his conquests of treasure and love."

[75] III. 45 (337).   [76] *Songs*, p. 402.

[77] Ritter, *N.Q.*, pp. 1–3, quotes the stanza
    Ay waking oh!
    Waking ay and wearie;
    Sleep I canna get
    For thinking o' my dearie,
which appeared in W. Tytler, *Dissertation on the Scottish Music*, 1774. For Burns's st. iii, cp. "My Daddy forbad" (in *The Tea-table Miscellany*, II. 96), ll. 1–3 ("When I think on my lad, | I sigh and am sad, | For now he is far frae me.") ; and "The Day begins to peep" (in *Songs from David Herd's MSS*, p. 238), st. iii ("when a' the lave's at rest | . . . My heart's wi greif oppress't, | I am dowie, dull and wearie") : cp. Ritter. *Quellenstudien*, henceforth cited as *Q*., pp. 185, 208. Burns's role here evidently is not that of the creator or "maker"—but, rather, that of the humble folk-singer who passes on what he has heard from others, altering it slightly in the process. To emphasise the international and universal character of "Ay Waukin, O," Ritter, *N.Q.*, p. 3, quotes the following quatrain from A. Elwert, *Ungedruckten Resten alten Gesanges*, 1784 : "Ich kann und mag nicht fröhlich seyn | Wenn alle Leute schlafen | So muss ich wachen | Muss traurig seyn. . . ."

Simmer's a pleasant time :
Flowers of every colour,
The water rins owre the heugh,
And I long for my true lover.

When I sleep I dream,
When I wauk I'm eerie,
Sleep I can get nane
For thinkin on my dearie.

Lanely night comes on,
A' the lave are sleepin,
I think on my bonie lad,
And I bleer my een wi' greetin

Chorus

Ay waukin, O,
Waukin still and weary :
Sleep I can get nane
For thinking on my dearie.

There are two types of Burns's songs which overlap the
love-song *genre* proper—namely, what may be called rhetorical songs, in which there is a certain element of declaration and
bravado; and Jacobite songs. In the rhetorical songs,[78] the
singer is often a man; and the group as a whole tends to look
forward to a side of Romanticism not always appreciated
today—the glorification of adventure and the "glamour" of
the past which is found in Scott's poetry and in certain of the
Waverley Novels. "McPherson's Farewell,"[79] "The Silver
Tassie,"[80] "My Lord a-hunting,"[81] "Lord Gregory,"[82] and "My
Heart's in the Highlands,"[83] are songs in which some of these
characteristics are present; yet each is different, and each has
an attractiveness of its own.

Dr Daiches has recently reminded us of the *élan* and
vitality of "McPherson's Farewell,"[84] which is itself based upon

[78] One song which might conceivably be classified here, "Behold the Hour the
Boat Arrive," has been proved by Ritter to be no more and no less than a translation (by David Dalrymple) of Metastasio's song "La Partenza." Cp. *Archiv für
das Studium der Neueren Sprachen*, CVIII (New Series VIII), Brunswick 1902, p. 140.
[79] III. 9 (307).　　　[80] III. 53 (343).　　　[81] III. 198 (443).
[82] III. 220 (455).　　　[83] III. 62 (348).　　　[84] Daiches, p. 336.

popular originals like "The Last Words of James Mackpherson, Murderer."[85] Already, in the character of Burns's McPherson, a folk hero, we can see some of the Byronic superman's characteristics—his noble heart, his criminality, his utter fearlessness, his contempt for the laws of God and man :

> I've liv'd a life of sturt and strife ;
> I die by treacherie :
> It burns my heart I must depart,
> And not avengèd be.
>
> Now farewell light, thou sunshine bright,
> And all beneath the sky !
> May coward shame distain his name,
> The wretch that dare not die !

Though the guilt and the gloom of *Cain* and *The Corsair* are missing, Burns's chorus expresses a fierce joy in wrongdoing which makes its own appeal to "humanity's unofficial self" :

> Sae rantingly, sae wantonly,
> Sae dauntingly gaed he,
> He play'd a spring, and danc'd it round
> Below the gallows-tree.

Such a mood is not "dated" ; it has affinities with the feelings of the present "Beat Generation" in America, or—to take a slightly earlier example—with the third marching song in Yeats's *Last Poems*, where "grandfather," standing under the gallows, proclaims that "good strong blows are delights to the mind." In "McPherson's Farewell," as also in "My Lord a-hunting" and "Lord Gregory," Burns draws on ballad conventions ; but the best song in which he uses these devices, "Open the Door to me, O,"[86] does not quite belong to the

[85] Cp. H. & H., III. 307 for a note on this, and even earlier sources. Ritter, *Q.*, p. 183, says that Burns, by cutting out the strongly moralistic sentiments which occur at the end of the original broadside, has actually brought the song *nearer* to the tone and spirit of genuine folk-song. Burns does the very same thing elsewhere —*e.g.* in his ruthless contraction of the original of "Charlie, he's my Darling," from sixteen stanzas to five. Cp. Ritter, *N.Q.*, pp. 8–12. In these instances, Burns is, as it were, *creating* a folk-song out of inferior materials ; he is being "more folk than the folk."

[86] III. 211 (450). For sources, see Ritter, *N.Q.*, pp. 4–8. No one, so far as I know, has been able to find a *single* source for the magnificent st. iii :

rhetorical group. In "The Silver Tassie,"[87] the words are independent of the music to a greater extent than is usual with Burns. The lines were at first intended to go to a tune called *The Stolen Kiss* or *The Secret Kiss*; but in Sep. 1793 he suggested that they might well be fitted to *Wae's my Heart that we should sunder*, which implies that he was dissatisfied with the original melody. Thomson, however, set them to a third tune, *The Old Highland Laddie*, to which they are usually sung today.[88] Brilliantly compounded of borrowed and original elements, this song of parting is completely in line with what was to become the taste of the next generation. In some ways, even, it anticipates both the Tennyson of "Blow, Bugle, blow" and the Browning of the *Cavalier Lyrics*. The first four lines, which most critics have persisted in regarding as Burns's own, despite his express statement that they are "old,"[89] are certainly the best in the song:

> Go, fetch to me a pint o' wine,
> And fill it in a silver tassie,
> That I may drink before I go
> A service to my bonie lassie!

But the next quatrain, where the sound of the verse helps to build a precise picture of ship and weather, is also good. Burns here makes Romantic poetry out of his favourite contrast between a warm interior and a hostile outer world. It is the same opposition as that which underlies the opening paragraphs of "Tam o' Shanter"—with this difference, that now the room and the storm outside are alike pervaded by an air of aristocratic enchantment:

> The boat rocks at the pier o' Leith,
> Fu' loud the wind blaws frae the Ferry,
> The ship rides by the Berwick-Law,
> And I maun leave my bonie Mary.

The wan moon sets behind the white wave,
And Time is setting with me, O :
False friends, false love, farewell! for mair
  I'll ne'er trouble them nor thee, O !

As Ritter notes, there is, however, a Shakespearian parallel for st. iii, l. 2, in *Julius Caesar*, v. iii. 64 : "So in his red blood Cassius' day is set."

[87] iii. 53 (343).   [88] Dick, *Songs*, p. 402.

[89] Interleaved *Museum*, quoted by Dick, *loc. cit.*

Although the sprinkling of "the old Scots" here is not particularly archaic, the scene depicted in the first half of the second stanza most certainly *is*:

> The trumpets sound, the banners fly,[90]
> The glittering spears are rankèd ready,
> The shouts o' war are heard afar,
> The battle closes deep and bloody . . .

The menacing otherness beyond the room is suddenly no longer bleak, as in the second half of the first stanza, but *warm*—a frenzy of fanfares, hoarse cries, and spurting blood. Burns's technique ensures that conflict pervades the very texture of individual lines; for example, the stirring heroic quality of "The trumpets sound, the banners fly," is followed by "The glittering spears are rankèd ready," where short and long *i* vowels enhance an image of cold, blinding light, and, at the same time, the trilled *r . . . r* and broad vowels of "rankèd" and "ready" are suited to muscular vigour and martial ardour. "The battle closes deep and bloody" is not so much prosaic[91] as poetic in a significantly discordant way; by its sound alone it qualifies the glorification of war implicit in the three preceding lines. War, it reminds us, is really a matter of severed limbs and mangled intestines—something that is even further removed from the atmosphere of a cosy inn than is the windswept "pier o' Leith." Finally, the two main themes are summed up before being overlaid by the emotion of parting:

> It's not the roar o' sea or shore
> Wad make me longer wish to tarry,
> Nor shouts o' war that's heard afar:
> It's leaving thee, my bonie Mary![92]

[90] Ritter, *Q.*, p. 197, compares this line with one in the song "How stands the Glass around?" in Chappell-Wooldridge, ii. 135: "The trumpets sound, the colours they are flying, boys."   [91] C. Keith, p. 143.

[92] The antecedents of this stanza illustrate the complexities of literary history. The song as a whole is "forward-looking" and "Romantic"; yet, as Ritter (*Q.* pp. 196–7) demonstrates, the sources of the last stanza are old. The most immediate of them seems to be Ramsay's "Farewell to Lochaber": "These tears that I shed, they are a' for my dear, | And no for the dangers attending on weir, | Though bore on rough seas to a far bloody shore . . . | Though loudest of thunder on louder waves roar, | That's naething like leaving my love on the shore." Ramsays' lines are, of course, mere doggerel: Burns's sheer poetry. Behind

One song, "The Lass that made the Bed,"[93] which is difficult to assign to any particular category, may perhaps be treated here. Though the piece is poetically rather uneven, and seems to echo broadside ballads where a bed-maker marries her seducer and lives happily ever after, in the fourth and fifth stanzas we come face to face with a sensuousness that looks forwards to Keats and Swinburne, and backwards to the Song of Solomon :

> 'Haud aff your hands, young man,' she said,
>   'And dinna sae uncivil be ;
> Gif ye hae onie luve for me,
>   O, wrang na my virginitie !'
> Her hair was like the links o' gowd,
>   Her teeth were like the ivorie,
> Her cheeks like lilies dipt in wine,
>   The lass that made the bed to me !
>
> Her bosom was the driven snaw,
>   Twa drifted heaps sae fair to see ;
> Her limbs the polish'd marble stane,
>   The lass that made the bed to me !
> I kiss'd her o'er and o'er again,
>   And ay she wist na what to say.
> I laid her 'tween me an' the wa'—
>   The lassie thocht na lang till day.

In "The Lass that made the Bed," Burns's sprinkling of Scots words and phrases *does* include some quite archaic language, which produces—in the stanzas quoted—a kind of poetry that is closer to that of the Makars, or of some of their later imitators, such as Lewis Spence, than one usually expects from Burns.

It is only a step from "The Silver Tassie" and "The Lass that made the Bed" to the songs which were the product of Burns's sentimental Jacobitism.[94] They show exactly the same dependence on tradition as do all his other lyrics : that is, they

Ramsay lies Dryden—cp. the following couplet from *The Indian Emperor* : "My heart unmov'd can noise and horror bear, | Parting from you is all the death I fear." Thus there is direct continuity between the heroic drama of the Restoration and Scott and Tennyson, *via* Ramsay and Burns.

[93] III. 162 (419). One source is "The Cumberland Lass," D'Urfey, IV. 133–5.
[94] Burns's other political lyrics have been considered above, pp. 239–56.

may be either editings or revisions of previous songs, or new work, interspersed (as always) with reminiscences of older pieces. They have much in common with his rhetorical songs ; and, since they sometimes seize upon amorous incidents with a Jacobite flavour (here anticipating Scott), one or two of them could equally well be classified as love-songs. Burns's Jacobite songs bear much the same relation to the whole body of his lyrics as do the neo-classical imitations of the Edinburgh period to the whole body of his poetry. They are, however, of far higher quality than, let us say, the "Elegy on the Death of Sir James Hunter Blair,"[95] for the simple reason that they are *songs*, and that they do not disdain the use of Scots-English or the vernacular. Burns, when he had a tune in his head, never sank to the very lowest depths of bathos. In one of the songs of this group, "The lovely Lass of Inverness,"[96] set phrases drawn from the ballads combine to produce a moving lament for a father and three brothers slain at Drumossie Moor by Butcher Cumberland's men. The first stanza, in particular, reminds one of the effects Wordsworth was shortly to achieve in *Lyrical Ballads* :

> The lovely lass of Inverness,
>   Nae joy nor pleasure can she see ;
> For e'en to morn she cries 'Alas !'
>   And ay the saut tear blin's her e'e :—

In the third and fourth stanzas, with unerring instinct, Burns subordinates the song's political implications to the stylised evocation of a people's and a woman's grief :

> Their winding-sheet the bluidy clay,
>   Their graves are growin green to see,
> And by them lies the dearest lad
>   That ever blest a woman's e'e.
>
> Now wae to thee, thou cruel lord,
>   A bluidy man I trow thou be,
> For monie a heart thou hast made sair
>   That ne'er did wrang to thine or thee !'

Jacobite fervour is dominant in "The bonie Lass of Al-

[95] II. 218 (413) ; above p. 238.　　[96] III. 142 (401).

banie,"[97] said to have been written "immediately after the receipt of the news of the supposed marriage of Miss Walkinshaw with Prince Charles Stuart, who declared the legitimation of his daughter by a formal deed, registered in France in Dec. 1787."[98] Behind the song's mock-medieval trappings one senses a real contemporary yearning for national liberation. The "bonie lass" is a symbol for enslaved Scotland, and the "false usurper" is England:

> Alas the day, and woe the day!
> A false usurper wan the gree,
> Who now commands the towers and lands,
> The royal right of Albanie.

> We'll daily pray, we'll nightly pray,
> On bended knees most fervently,
> The time may come, with pipe and drum
> We'll welcome hame fair Albanie.

Only a few years later, under the stimulus of the French Revolution, Burns was to use a similar fiction—"Scotland's King and Law"—in the noblest of all his national songs, "Scots, wha hae."[99]

As songs, "Charlie he's my Darling,"[100] "O'er the Water to Charlie,"[101] and "It was a' for our rightfu' King"[102] are among the best of all Burns's Jacobite pieces. The last of these is apparently meant to be sung to *Mally Stuart*, a variant of the seventeenth-century English tune, *The Bailiff's Daughter of Islington*;[103] and, at the tragic level, it employs exactly the same "impressionistic" technique which Burns used in "My Love, she's but a Lassie yet."[104] The first two stanzas reproduce the cavalier's dignified resignation as he explains why he must go into exile; yet in the background, behind his words, one senses the full bitterness of defeat:

[97] IV. 22 (90). [98] Dick, *Songs*, p. 469.
[99] III. 251 (474). [100] III. 154 (414).
[101] III. 32 (328). [102] III. 182 (433).
[103] Dick, *Songs*, p. 470.

[104] Above, p. 275. In their note, H. & H. imply that in "It was a' for our rightfu' King" Burns uses the same sort of *montage* technique as in "A red, red Rose."

Now a' is done that men can do,
And a' is done in vain,
My Love and Native Land fareweel,
For I maun cross the main,
My dear—
For I maun cross the main.

The third stanza is a narrative one, in which the pattern of vowels and consonants and the rhythm of the verse reproduce, first, an abrupt and symbolic turning of the body ; secondly, the noise of sharply moved harness and jangling metal accoutrements ; and, thirdly, the actual moment of parting :

He turn'd him right and round about
Upon the Irish shore,
And gae his bridle reins a shake,
With adieu for evermore,
My dear—
And adieu for evermore !

In the last two stanzas the point of view shifts to that of the woman, and the verse loses its aristocratic colouring, at the same time as it becomes less restrained. Precisely because it is qualified by the "stiff upper lip" of his class and sex, the warrior's emotion comes through to us all the more intensely ; in contrast, the woman's is simpler : yet it, too, is qualified by a similar consciousness of inevitability. Her language is different from his : it has the universality, the absolute simplicity, of "Ay Waukin, O"[105] and "Thou hast left me ever, Jamie" :[106]

The soger frae the wars returns,
The sailor frae the main,
But I hae parted frae my love
Never to meet again,
My dear—
Never to meet again.

When day is gane, and night is come,
And a' folk bound to sleep,
I think on him that's far awa
The lee-lang night, and weep,
My dear—
The lee-lang night and weep.

[105] Above, pp. 310–11.   [106] Above, p. 309.

The occasion of this parting is unique, and it is brought before us vividly, without generality and without unnecessary detail; but, at the same time, Burns infuses into it the essence of every military and political defeat, and of every irrevocable separation. From the point of view of literary history, "It was a' for our rightfu' King" looks *away* from Burns's own generation, and away from the Scots literary tradition, towards the Romantic poetry of the two decades after his death.[107]

Burns was the author or arranger of a number of drinking-songs (including Masonic songs), from the early "John Barleycorn"[108] to "Auld Lang Syne":[109] and in this group, the positive values of love (and especially friendship) are stressed just as strongly as in his less lyrical pieces. In "Theniel Menzies' Bonie Mary,"[110] for example, social drinking is combined with the praise of a fine girl:

> In comin by the brig o' Dye,
> At Darlet we a blink did tarry;
> As day was dawin in the sky,
> We drank a health to bonie Mary.

> *Chorus*

> Theniel Menzies' bonie Mary,
> Theniel Menzies' bonie Mary,
> Charlie Grigor tint his plaidie,
> Kissin Theniel's bonie Mary!

The chorus shows the same delight in repeating a girl's name to music that we found in some of Burns's serious love-songs; as usual, the words are perfectly wedded to the tune, *Ruffian's Rant*, or *Roy's Wife*, as it is now generally called.[111] In "Willie Brew'd a Peck o' Maut,"[112] Burns celebrates a meeting with his schoolmaster friends William Nicol and Allan Masterton which took place at Moffat in the autumn of 1789. Never has the sheer joy of drunkenness been so well expressed as in the third and fourth stanzas:

---

[107] And also, perhaps, backwards—towards the seventeenth century. Cp. above, p. 314, n. 92.
[108] I. 243 (409).   [109] III. 147 (407).
[110] III. 20 (320).   [111] Dick, *Songs*, p. 442.
[112] III. 80 (359).

It is the moon, I ken her horn,[113]
That's blinkin in the lift sae hie :[114]
She shines sae bright to wyle us hame,
But, by my sooth, she'll wait a wee !

Wha first shall rise to gang awa,
A cuckold, coward loun is he !
Wha first beside his chair shall fa',
He is the King amang us three !

Then follows the canny understatement of the chorus :

We are na fou, we're nae that fou,
But just a drappie in our e'e !
The cock may craw, the day may daw,
And ay we'll taste the barley-bree !

Another instance of the normal Burnsian association
between drink and friendship is provided by the stanza which
the poet added to the traditional "Rattlin, roarin Willie,"[115]
in honour of William Dunbar, Esq., Writer to the Signet,
Edinburgh, and Colonel of the Crochallan Corps, "a club of
wits who took that title at the time of raising the fencible
regiments." The eight brief lines call up a vivid picture of one
of Edinburgh's convivial clubs, with Dunbar at the table
among a select gathering of bawdy, hard-drinking city notables :

As I cam by Crochallan,
I cannily keekit ben,
Rattlin, roarin Willie
Was sitting at yon boord-en' :
Sitting at yon boord-en',
And amang guid companie !
Rattlin, roarin Willie,
Ye're welcome hame to me.

But the best of Burns's Drinking Songs is the one which for
all Anglic-speaking peoples has become the traditional expression of good fellowship and group solidarity—"Auld Lang
Syne."[116] That the song celebrates both friendship between

---

[113] Cp. "Death and Dr Hornbook," st. iv, ll. 3–4 : "To count her horns, wi' a'
my pow'r | I set mysel. . . ."
[114] Cp. "Ca' the Yowes to the knowes" first set, st. vi, l. 2 : "While day blinks
in the lift sae hie."
[115] III. 35 (330).   [116] III. 147 (407).

man and man and affection between man and woman is suggested by one manuscript,[117] where the last word of the first line of the chorus ends with the untranslatable monosyllable "jo", a term of endearment roughly equivalent to the French "*mie.*" English "sweetheart" does not quite convey all the *nuances* of "jo", neither does the "dear" of the version Burns sent to Thomson : [118]

> And for auld lang syne, my jo,
> For auld lang syne,
> We'll tak a cup o' kindness yet,
> For auld lang syne.

The third and fourth stanzas are Burns's "*Recherche du temps perdu.*" But it is not to "the sessions of sweet silent thought" that he "summons up remembrance of things past"; in this song, memory is a social faculty, and the recollection is *shared* :

> We twa hae run about the braes,
> And pou'd the gowans fine,
> But we've wander'd monie a weary fit
> Sin' auld lang syne.

> We twa hae paidl'd in the burn
> Frae morning sun till dine,
> But seas between us braid hae roar'd
> Sin' auld lang syne.

In the fifth stanza, Burns's companion is addressed as "fiere" and not as "jo" or "dear." By the choice of this one word the poet calls up the values of masculine friendship[119] and unites

---

[117] That of a holograph by Burns in the interleaved *Museum*, printed in Dick, *Songs*, p. 208.

[118] *Op. cit.*, p. 209 ; this is also the reading of H. & H., III. 147.

[119] The earliest "sources," as cited by H. & H., III. 408, are a set in Watson's *Choice Collection of Comic and Serious Scots Poems*, Edinburgh 1711 ; a broadside ballad in the Laing Collection, Dalmeny; and a version by Allan Ramsay. All three feature *love* relationships. Ritter, *Q.*, p. 195, thinks that the main difference between Burns's and Watson's and Ramsay's sets consists in this, that Burns's song features two old *friends*, the others two old *lovers*. But if our analysis is correct, Burns's reminiscence includes *both* love and friendship. Ritter, *Q.*, pp. 194–5, draws attention to the Rev. J. Skinner's "Auld Minister's Song," which, he claims, is nearer to the original *folk*-source than the Ramsay or Watson versions. But, as Ritter himself notes, there is no evidence that Skinner's song is older than Burns's. It does, however, feature an exclusively masculine friendship : "What though

them to the tenderer and more personal ties referred to in the
chorus—it is of *comradeship* that he is singing here :

> And there's a hand, my trusty fiere,
> And gie's a hand o' thine,
> And we'll tak a right guid-willie waught
> For auld lang syne!

"A right guid-willie waught" is much more than a good "stiff
one," as Professor Thornton translates it :[120] it is the masculine
equivalent of the "cup o' kindness," which calls up an image
of a pledge between man and woman ; it means a drink shared
as a token of mutual good-will, with undertones of mingled
hospitality and ceremony. In "Auld Lang Syne" Burns brings
together two different types of nostalgia for past shared
happiness, and makes of them a single, compound emotion.
Thus our feelings *develop* as we sing it, until by the end of the
song we seem to experience a distillation of all the mutual
loyalty, all the partnerships between individuals that have
existed since the world began.

Although humour is a prime ingredient in a large number
of Burns's songs, there are certain lyrics which revel in comedy
of a peculiarly whimsical sort ; and it is these which must be
considered now. The charge is sometimes made that Burns
lacks the very highest kind of poetic imagination—the kind
which transforms reality and makes of it a self-consistent world
of the poet's own creation. It is often forgotten, however, that
he wrote—or had a hand in—such songs as "Scroggam,"[121]
"The Cooper o' Cuddy,"[122] "Willie Wastle,"[123] "The Deil's
awa wi' th' Exciseman,"[124] and "On Captain Grose"[125] ; and
that these songs of fantastic humour exuberantly pull and twist
reality out of shape in a fashion that makes us think of those
great Victorians Dickens, Lewis Carroll, and Edward Lear.
As in so many of his pieces, whether serious or comic, Burns
works by means of a series of rapid sketches which the reader
has to complete in his own mind :

these locks, ance hazel brown, | Are now well mix'd with gray : | I'm sure my
heart nae caulder grows, | But as my years decline. | Still friendship's flame as
warmly glows, | As it did langsyne."

[120] *The Tuneful Flame*, p. 22.   [121] III. 192 (440).   [122] III. 157 (416).
[123] III. 125 (388).   [124] III. 141 (399).   [125] II. 62 (352).

The guidwife's dochter fell in a fever,
  Scroggam!
The priest o' the parish fell in anither:
  Sing Auld Cowl, lay you down by me—
  Scroggam, my dearie, ruffum!

They laid the twa i' the bed thegither,
  Scroggam!
That the heat o' the tane might cool the tither:
  Sing Auld Cowl, lay you down by me—
  Scroggam, my dearie, ruffum!

"Willie Wastle" exaggerates the woman's objectionable features with all the enjoyment of a medieval or Gaelic "flyting," but it is only superficially in the style of medieval attacks upon Woman: it is not woman in general that the song pillories, but one particular specimen of the class. Furthermore, Burns is not completely serious; it is all part of a rather unpleasant rustic game.[126] In "The Cooper o' Cuddy," overtones of cruelty and contempt for the village cuckold are swept away by the fantasy, which is generated as much by the irresistible motion of its grand old tune, *Bab at the bowster*,[127] as by the dance of the words themselves:

The Cooper o' Cuddy came here awa,
  He ca'd the girrs out o'er us a',
An' our guidwife has gotten a ca',
  That's anger'd the silly guidman, O.

He sought them out, he sought them in,
  Wi 'Deil hae her!' an 'Deil hae him!'
But the body he was sae doited and blin',
  He wist na where he was gaun, O.

They cooper'd at e'en, they cooper'd at morn,
  Till our guidman has gotten the scorn:
On ilka brow she's planted a horn,
  And swears that there they sall stan', O!

In "The Deil's awa wi' th' Exciseman" Burns's favourite supernatural figure takes a hand in a wild dance which is

[126] But cp. above, p. 126.   [127] Dick, *Songs*, pp. 429–30.

almost a mass orgy, the artistic form being suggested by its magnificently light-hearted tune:

> The Deil cam fiddlin thro' the town,
> And danc'd awa wi' th' Exciseman,
> And ilka wife cries :—'Auld Mahoun,
> I wish you luck o' the prize, man !
>
> 'We'll mak our maut, and we'll brew our drink,
> We'll laugh, sing, and rejoice, man,
> And monie braw thanks to the meikle black Deil,
> That danc'd awa wi' th' Exciseman.'

Despite its miniature quality, this song is surely as worthy as is Beethoven's Seventh Symphony of Wagner's criticism—"the apotheosis of the Dance" :

> There's threesome reels, there's foursome reels,
> There's hornpipes and strathspeys, man,
> But the ae best dance ere cam to the land
> Was *The Deil's Awa wi' th' Exciseman.*

"The Deil's awa" is a blend of the medieval and the modern. One thinks of old pictures in which an entire populace are seen dancing, hand in hand, one after the other, in capering procession, of legends like "The Dancers of Kölbigk,"[128] or of the folk utopia of Cokaygne, where the walls are made of pasties "and all rich meat," and there are rivers of oil, honey, and wine.[129] But one also thinks of Rabelais's *"Fais ce que vouldras,"* *laissez-faire* economics. The emotion behind this little song is quite in harmony with libertarian ideas of freedom from governmental interference; it is a world without bureaucrats that Burns's singer imagines.

"On Captain Grose" transports the "chield . . . amang you takin notes"[130] into a world that never was, on sea or land, yet it makes us feel that we know the jovial antiquary all the better :

---

[128] Cp. E. K. Chambers, *English Literature at the Close of the Middle Ages*, Oxford 1947, p. 75.

[129] Cp. A. L. Morton, *The English Utopia*, London 1952, pp. 217–22.

[130] "On the late Captain Grose's Peregrinations thro' Scotland collecting the Antiquities of that Kingdom," l. 5 : H. & H., I. 289 (445).

Is he slain by Hielan' bodies?
Igo and ago
And eaten like a wether haggis?
Iram, coram, dago

Is he to Abra'm's bosom gane?
Igo and ago
Or haudin Sarah by the wame?
Iram, coram, dago. . . .

So may ye hae auld stanes in store,
Igo and ago
The very stanes that Adam bore!
Iram, coram, dago

So may ye get in glad possession,
Igo and ago
The coins o' Satan's coronation!
Iram, coram, dago

Geniality and grotesquerie, warm-hearted friendship, the humour of character—all are featured in this unconstrainedly natural comic lyric, which, as Dick points out, is an adaptation of "Sir John Malcolm," a song found in *The Charmer* (1764) and in Herd's *Scots Songs* (1769).[131] "Sir John Malcolm" is funny in an everyday, pedestrian manner at the expense of the Knight and his crony Sandie Don, who were apparently in the habit of boring their friends to death with their travellers' tales :

'Keep ye weel frae Sir John Malcolm, *Igo and Ago*,
If he's a wise man I mistak him, *Iram, Coram, dago*,
Keep ye weel frae Sandy Don, *Igo, and ago*,
He's ten times dafter than Sir John, *Iram, Coram, dago.*'

Nothing could be more typical of Burns's handling of inherited material than the way he transforms rustic name-calling into the humane presentation of a somewhat Falstaffian *character*. In any full assessment of Burns's humour, one would have to include not only the manifold tone-manipulation of "Tam o' Shanter," the bizarre distortions of "Death and Doctor Hornbook," the rustic high jinks of "Halloween," the gentle kindliness of "Tam Glen" and the pawky proverbial understanding of "In Simmer, when the Hay was mawn"—but also

---

[131] Dick, *Songs*, p. 479.

the turbulent, fanciful gaiety of the group of songs we have just been considering.

From our examination of Burns's songs category by category and type by type, it is now necessary to proceed to an estimate of their place in the whole of the poet's *œuvre*. No-one can study them without being impressed by their enormous variety. True, there are only some three hundred and fifty of them[1] as compared with the thousands collected by Bartók in Hungary, Rumania, and elsewhere; but they touch on almost every emotion of ordinary men and women, and their moods are wonderfully diverse. In his songs, Burns is more genuinely the Poet of Scotland than in the works of his Edinburgh period; indeed, he is more profoundly national than when he wrote "The Vision," or "The Cotter's Saturday Night," or "Tam o' Shanter." The reason is not far to seek; it lies in the fact that music is the most national of all the arts—at the same time as (within a given musical system, such as that of Europe, or of China) it is also the most universal. We do not have to be Czechs or Russians or Italians or Finns in order to respond to Smetana or Mussorgsky or Verdi or Sibelius; these composers speak impartially to us all; and yet we feel, behind their every note, all that their countrymen have experienced over the centuries. It is the same with Burns's songs, when these are regarded not merely as poems, but as unities of music and words. Before there were nations, there existed feudal or semi-tribal units with a consciousness of their own identity, which we may call "nationalities"; and of the three groups, Celtic, Anglic and Scandinavian, that came together to form the Scottish Nation, Celtic and Anglic each made its own distinctive contribution to the music of Burns's songs. The majority of his tunes are Highland, or Lowland Scottish crossed with Highland influence: but a fair number are of English origin.[2] Burns's words, however, are Scottish vernacular or Scots-English; in a somewhat wider sense, they are therefore, in either case, a variety of English, since Scots itself is historically an offshoot of

[1] The 361 in Dick, *Songs*, include many of which Burns was simply the transmitter, and many which he hardly altered at all. Perhaps the *true* total, including those which Burns mended and patched as well as those which he made, is nearer 250 than 350.   [2] Cp. Dick, *Songs, passim.*

Northern English. Where Burns uses Gaelic tunes, or Lowland ones in the Highland mode, there develops an incongruity between words and melody which the poet must regulate if he is to be artistically successful. Angellier noticed this long ago, in a passage which begins with the speculation that there might well be a latent connexion between a nation's language and its music.[3] In Angellier's opinion, Highland airs are, at some deep and primitive level, the result of a Celtic fashion of speaking; whereas the words Burns fitted to them were those of a Germanic language. Had Burns's diction been mellifluous and infinitely plastic, the task of setting words to traditional Highland melodies would have been much easier than it was. But Burns's style is above all compact, and a pithy brevity is one of its main virtues; his words are both "solid" and full of action.[4] However, the fact that he so often succeeded in the task of wedding Celtic or semi-Celtic music to Scots-English words is not really so extraordinary as Angellier supposed. In this he was merely following the example of the nameless folk-poets he admired so much, and of lesser predecessors and contemporaries, such as Jane Elliott ("The Flowers of the Forest"), Lady Barnard ("Auld Robin Gray"), the Rev. John Skinner ("Tullochgorum"), Robert Riddell [5] Gavin Turnbull,[6] and many others. Such attempts were surely inevitable,

[3] Angellier, II. 37. "Il est probable qu'il y a un rapport, non encore noté, entre le parler d'un peuple et ses mélodies. Ces airs, pour la plupart d'origine celtique, se dérobent à un langage d'une autre origine, ou se cabrent contre lui; leur rhythme secoue et disloque son accent. Encore ces obstacles sont-ils atténués pour les écrivains dont la langue est molle, s'étend et se plie comme de la glaise. Mais le style de Burns est compact et court; il est tout composé de mots solides. Comment les réduire à accompagner ces détours ondoyants? Que d'essais! De combien de façons il faut les placer, les déplacer, les réplacer, les essayer, pour en arracher le chant désiré?"

[4] Naturally enough, Burns was himself aware of the problem. Cp. his letter to Thomson, 8 Nov. 1792, in Letters, II. 129: "If you mean . . . that all the songs in your Collection shall be Poetry of the first merit, I am afraid you will find difficulty . . . more than you are aware of.—There is a peculiar rhythmus in many of our airs, and a necessity of adapting syllables to . . . what I would call the *feature notes*, . . . that cramps the Poet, & lays him under almost insuperable difficulties."

[5] Cp. Letters, II. 367.

[6] Cp. Burns to Thomson, 29 Oct. [1793], in Letters, II. 214-5; "By the by, Turnbull has a great many songs in M.S.S. which I can command, if you like his manner . . ." It was a very *English* manner. For other Ayrshire song-writers of Burns's own day, cp. [J. Paterson], *The Contemporaries of Burns, and the more recent Poets of Ayrshire*, Edinburgh 1840, pp. 17 ff.

because of the difference between the two of the three main
nationalities out of which Scotland arose. The tension between
words and music which underlies and supports the best of
Burns's songs reflects the racial composition of the Scottish
people, as well as that subliminal opposition between the
claims of reason and of passion which exists, as we have already
noted,[7] in every Scottish heart, together with other complementary struggles between day-dreaming and narrow practi-
cality, and between stolidity and fire. And just as, on the level
of language, the discordance between English and vernacular
words which had brought many a minor writer's purposes to
wreck, became for Burns a means of controlled modulation
from one kind of Scottish speech to another, so too, the tension
between Germanic words and part-Gaelic music enabled
Burns to make *other* transitions and shifts of mood beneath the
surface of his simplest lyrics.

Moreover, the "undulating bypaths" traversed by some of the
slower Scottish airs go far towards explaining Burns's fondness
for pastoral description in a song like "Where are the Joys" :[8]

> Nae mair a-winding the course o' yon river
> And marking sweet flowerets sae fair,
> Nae mair I trace the light footsteps o' Pleasure,
> But Sorrow and sad-sighing Care.

As poetry, and apart from its lovely tune, the verse may seem
trite and second-rate ; but when *sung* it achieves the same sort
of miracle as many of Schubert's settings of inferior German
lyrics.[9] It comes as close as Burns, with the resources available
to him, could get to the "mellifluous" language which Angellier
felt was the natural concomitant of such a tune.

The melodies with which Burns was most at home were
dance-tunes—strathspeys and reels which, by a simple alteration of tempo, could turn abruptly from gaiety into sadness
and back again, linking harshness with *rêverie*, and wild impetuosity with a quality at once plaintive and caressing.[10] It is
tunes like these which are the foundation of most of his best

---

[7] Above, pp. 41–3.   [8] III. 264 (486).

[9] Cp. M. J. E. Brown, *Schubert: A Critical Biography*, henceforth cited as *Schubert*,
London 1958, pp. 40–2, and *passim*.

[10] Cp. Angellier, II. 33 : "Il y a dans ces mélodies étranges une union de
rudesse et d'inexprimable rêverie, quelque chose da farouche et d'impétueux,

songs, and they express—as nothing else can—the inner nature of the Scottish mind. When Burns translated the very spirit of such melodies into vernacular or Scots-English words, he was, as it were, fashioning a body for a nation's soul : and the soul and the body are complementary.

There is yet another way in which Burns's lyrics are supremely national—in their realtionship to previous Scottish folk-song. They take over the older folk tradition and sum it up, at the same time as, in certain respects, they negate it. In the words of the *Handbook of Suggestions for the Consideration of Teachers* (1905) :[11]

> National or folk songs . . . are the expression in the idiom of the people of their joys and sorrows, their unaffected patriotism, their zest for sport and the simple pleasures of a country life. Such music is the early and spontaneous uprising of artistic power in a nation, and the ground on which all national music is built up ; folk songs are the true classics of a people, and their survival, so often by tradition alone, proves that their appeal is direct and lasting. . . .

Acting partly in the spirit of earlier folk-poets who had themselves changed inherited words to suit the conditions of their own times, and partly in the spirit of later folksong-collectors like Baring-Gould, Alfred Williams, and even, on occasion, Cecil Sharp himself, who all "revised" folk-song words in the interests of decency and grammatical decorum,[12] Burns, as we have seen, made slight alterations in many of the songs which he recorded and transmitted. On the great majority of the songs which he wrote or mended, however, he set the stamp of his own personality ; and it follows, therefore, that they have elements which differ in some respects from the components of "true" folk-songs—that they are, in part, "art-songs."

The American music-critic Sidney Finkelstein[13] has summed up the relation between "national" composers and the folk-

en même temps que de plaintif et de très caressant. Ces expressions paraissent et disparaissent, par notes soudaines, où la mélodie glisse avec une souplesse infinie, un instant saccadée et rauque, et tout d'un coup s'échappant fluide et limpide."
   [11] Quoted in *The Idiom of the People: English Traditional Verse . . . from the Manuscripts of Cecil J. Sharp*, ed. J. Reeves, London 1958, intro., p. 5. The passage, of course, ignores the extent to which the previous "art-songs" and "educated" poetry influence folk-song and poetry.   [12] *Op. cit.*, intro., *passim*.
   [13] In *How Music expresses Ideas*, London 1952, pp. 73–4.

music of their respective countries in terms which can well be applied to both the words and the music of Burns's songs:

> The composer may be called an intermediary, who returns in enriched form the material he has gotten from the people, reflecting in the process the conditions of life of the nation in his own time. By so doing, he is only repeating on a far higher level of formal development the process of creation of folk art itself, for folk art was the product of innumerable anonymous individuals of talent, each contributing something new to the common cultural possessions.

These words are true, not only of composers like Bartók, Vaughan Williams, Dvořák and Tchaikowsky; they apply also to Handel's, Bach's and Haydn's use and development of material drawn from the Lutheran chorales.[14] In so far as they are the result of conscious artistry (and the foregoing analysis of individual songs has surely demonstrated how careful and intelligent a song-writer Burns was), the best of Burns's songs should be compared with the work of Schubert and Hugo Wolf as well as with the folk-songs of other nations. Yet it should never be forgotten that what makes their author the most genuinely *national* of all poets is the way they bestride the two worlds of art-song and folk-song, including and, in a sense, transcending both.

In Elizabethan madrigals,[15] and in practically all art-songs before Burns, the words were composed first, the music second —a situation which Dryden summarised in a rather arrogant sentence: "It is my part to invent, and the musician's to humour that invention."[16]

In German *Lieder*, the relationship between words and music is formally similar, in that Schubert's and Wolf's songs are settings of *poems*, and the composer's conscious aim was to give musical form to the poet's ideas; but what emerges is in practice much more than a mere emanation of the poem. It is an entirely new creation, often far better as art than the original; and a great song, as we have seen, may quite well

---

[14] *Ibid.*

[15] Cp. W. Mellers, "Words and Music in Elizabethan England," in *Pelican Guide to English Literature*, Harmondsworth 1955, II. 386–415.

[16] Pref. to *Albion and Albanius*, in *Dramatic Essays*, Everyman edn., p. 180. But such a musician as the Elizabethan Dowland left the words far behind him.

be the offspring of second-rate words. Schubert, Wolf, Brahms, Richard Strauss, and Mahler may have *intended* to humour the poet's invention; what they actually did, in their finest songs, was something different. Thus, as Maurice Brown points out,[17] in Schubert's early setting of Goethe's "Rastlose Liebe," "the tempestuous beat of the music tells us more clearly what is in the poet's mind than his words dare do," and such songs as "An den Tod," "Die Forelle," and "An die Musik" rise far above the undistinguished verses of Daniel Schubart and Schober[18] on which they are based.

Burns's songs are rather to be interpreted in terms of Thomas Moore's dictum, "A pretty air without words resembles one of those *half* creatures of Plato, which are described as wandering in search of the remainder of themselves through the world";[19] he approached the problem of words and music from the opposite angle to Schubert or Dryden or Dowland, yet what he produced was in its own way as great as the masterpieces of German *Lieder*. In order to illustrate this point, let us briefly compare "Thou gloomy December"[20] with Schubert's "Gretchen am Spinnrade,"[21] and "O May, thy Morn"[22] with Wolf's "Das Ständchen."[23] To weight the comparison in favour of the Germans, I have chosen two of their very best pieces—and two of Burns's more mediocre (though far from contemptible) lyrics.

In "Thou gloomy December," one of the songs written for Clarinda, and to the melody of *Thro' the lang Muir I followed him Hame*,[24] which Burns himself described as "a charming, plaintive Scots tune," the words and music of the second stanza create an almost unbearable feeling of sorrow:

> Fond lovers' parting is sweet, painful pleasure,
> Hope beaming mild on the soft parting hour;
> But the dire feeling, O farewell for ever!
> Anguish unmingled and agony pure!

---

[17] *Schubert*, p. 49.   [18] *Op. cit.*, pp. 76–7.
[19] Advt. to *National Airs*, VOL. IV, quoted in V. C. Clinton-Baddeley, *Words for Music*, Cambridge 1941, p. 101.   [20] III. 185 (437).
[21] Cp. R. Capell, *Schubert's Songs*, 2nd edn., New York and London 1957, pp. 84–6.   [22] III. 170 (427).
[23] Cp. F. Walker, *Hugo Wolf: A Biography*, henceforth cited as *Wolf*, London 1951, pp. 238–9.   [24] Dick, *Songs*, p. 379.

This effect, surely, is not really different in *kind* from "the painful return of everyday sensation after the tranced numbness of the girl's body" that Maurice Brown finds in "Gretchen am Spinnrade" :[25]

> My peace is gone,
> My heart is sore,
> I find it never,
> And nevermore.[26]

When Burns's song is sung, a very slight quickening of tempo in the second line of the second stanza ("Hope beaming mild on the soft parting hour") conveys an impression of past *voluptuous* happiness ; in the fourth line, a further slowing-down evokes the piercing quality of "Anguish unmingled and agony pure."

In his analysis of "Gretchen am Spinnrade," Brown points out that there is a "sense of rapid heartbeats, almost of excitement, in the lines which Gretchen speaks. One could imagine an actress uttering them breathlessly."[27] In "Thou gloomy December," the comparable quality is a sense of storm (which Schubert also infused into many works, such as "Der stürmische Morgen"[28] in *Die Winterreise*), mirroring the storm in the poet's heart :

> Wild as the winter now tearing the forest,
> Till the last leaf o' the summer is flown—
> Such is the tempest has shaken my bosom,
> Till my last hope and last comfort is gone !

Just as there is in the middle section of "Gretchen am Spinnrade" a "powerful emotional and musical climax," and a "similar rise and relaxation" in each of the other two sections,[29] so Burns makes the third stanza the poetic and emotional climax of "Thou gloomy December," and here, too, both the second stanza and the first (which is repeated, with very slight modifications, as the fourth, thus indicating a cyclical development within the song—a return to the starting-point) have their own

---

[25] *Schubert*, p. 28.
[26] Goethe, *Faust*, PT. I, sc. xv, tr. Swanwick, London 1892 ("Meine Ruh' ist hin, | Mein Herz ist schwer ; | Ich finde sie nimmer | Und nimmermehr.")
[27] *Schubert*, p. 29.
[28] Cp. Capell, *Schubert's Songs*, p. 238.   [29] Brown, *Schubert*, p. 29.

rise and fall, in spite of the fact that the last line of the second stanza could by no stretch of the imagination be termed "relaxation." Considered as a song, then, the poetically uninteresting "Thou gloomy December" is worthy of serious comparison with one of Schubert's greatest songs; and—also considered as a unity of words and music—its mere existence makes one doubt the commonly held opinion that Burns was oblivious to "the deeper notes of sorrow."[30]

"O May, thy Morn" (another Clarinda song) was originally intended by Burns to go to the tune which is now always associated with "The wee, wee German Lairdie."[31] The first stanza, if taken slowly, calls forth a similar feeling to that which underlies "Auld Lang Syne,"[32]—only, this time, it is a more private, almost secret, emotion :

> O May thy morn was ne'er sae sweet
> As the mirk night o' December !
> For sparkling was the rosy wine,
> And private was the chamber,
> And dear was she I dare na name,
> But I will ay remember.

In "Das Ständchen" (a setting of one of Eichendorff's poems) Wolf gives us the following picture :

A student sings to the lute before his sweetheart's door. An older man, from a window near by, gazes over the moonlit roofs and overhears the student's song, which recalls to him his own lost youth and love. Many years ago he himself had sung out his heart in just this fashion. The left hand of Wolf's piano part sketches in the idealization of a lute accompaniment, while the right hand suggests nothing so obvious as the actual song of the student, but the half-forgotten melody of long ago as it hovers elusively in the consciousness of the onlooker. The voice part is wholly concerned with the older man's soliloquy. His present loneliness and his memories are exquisitely blended against the background of another's happiness. The vocal line is absolutely free, reflecting with the utmost subtlety every turn of the man's thoughts and every inflection of his voice. All semblance of a formal melody is abandoned ; phrase follows phrase of ever-new counterpoints to the instrumental framework of the song ; each

[30] C. Keith, p. 149.   [31] Dick, *Songs*, p. 379.   [32] Above, p. 322.

phrase is moulded to express the sentiment of each line of the poem.[33]

"Das Ständchen," in its confrontation of past and present, is closer to "In Simmer when the Hay was mawn"[34] than to "O May, thy Morn," but the first stanza of the latter song is faintly reminiscent of the nostalgia of the Wolf right-hand piano accompaniment. Burns's emotions, however, are by no means so evanescent or so tentative as those of Wolf's "older man" : the impression Clarinda has made upon Burns is a definite one, which he will, quite consciously, "ay remember." In Burns's second stanza, the pace quickens and the mood coarsens : we are in the present, perhaps in an alehouse, surrounded by men :

> And here's to them that, like oursel,
> Can push about the jorum !
> And here's to them that wish us weel
> May a' that's guid watch o'er 'em !

But in the concluding couplet, a serious note returns—and so, too, does the theme of secrecy :

> And here's to them we dare na tell,
> The dearest o' the quorum !

The changes of mood, the modulation between past and present and back again, are not nearly so refined as Wolf's—but they are there, just the same. Burns, it is true, has nothing to match the restless, romantic questing of Schubert's *Die Winterreise* cycle,[35] or the symbolic incoherence of Wolf's "Der Feuerreiter,"[36] but he can equal the light-heartedness of "Die Forelle,"[37] or the earthy humour of Wolf's "Storchenbotschaft" (according to Frank Walker,[38] "perhaps the finest piece of broad comedy in all music").

Finally, there is yet another point which Burns has in common with the great masters of *Lieder*. It has often been pointed out[39] that, with Schubert, and still more so with Wolf, the piano accompaniment adds enormously to the total musical

[33] Walker, *Wolf*, pp. 238–9.   [34] Above, p. 279.
[35] Cp. Capell, *Schubert's Songs* pp. 227–40.
[36] Cp. Walker, *Wolf*, pp. 234–5.
[37] Cp. Capell, *Schubert's Songs*, pp. 135–6.   [38] *Wolf*, p. 235.
[39] *E.g.*, in Capell, *Schubert's Songs*, pp. 38–9.

impression, for it is both a commentary upon, and a qualification of, the melody and the words. Burns does not have a piano to rely upon, but he has an equally noble instrument at his command—the sound-values of the words themselves, alliteration and assonance, and what elsewhere, adapting Dick's phrase, we have called "the tone-poetry of language." Again and again, in the course of the present chapter, we have come across instances where Burns uses verse-texture to qualify the meaning of a song; and it is the effects which he derives from this means that are most nearly analogous to the German composers' use of the pianoforte.[40]

We are now, perhaps, in a position to make some statement concerning the value of Burns's songs in relation to the rest of his work. Song-writing, which draws on the resources of both poetry and music, is an art in itself; and songs and poetry give different kinds of satisfaction—sometimes one values one more than the other, depending on one's mood. Yet Burns's genius was such that he was master of both arts. It is surely a matter for sheer wonderment that the man who wrote "Holy Willie's Prayer" could also write "A red, red Rose": yet he did, and both have been so long familiar to us, so much a part of our way of looking at the world, that we rarely stop to think how improbable it is that they should both have sprung from the mind of a single artist. Few men have achieved so much, in quality if not in quantity, in both poetry and song-writing; yet, when all is said and done, the songs give more lasting pleasure than even the very best of his poetry can supply. Taken *en masse*, as a single entity (and here the extent of Burns's individual authorship of particular songs is quite irrelevant), they recreate and preserve for all time the commonest feelings of an entire people; yet they are also the most international of all Burns's works—and, therefore, they are among the most universal works of art to have been created in the British Isles.

[40] If Burns's songs *must* be sung with accompaniment, perhaps the best instrument is the violin. Cp. A. Keith, p. 24: " 'Bonie Wee Thing,' sung to the violin's accompaniment, is more than a mere melody. The alternation of open and closed vowel sounds joins with the slurs and runs of the music." A similar close connexion between verse texture and music is noted in Capell, *Schubert's Songs*, p. 41: "The sound of words, and hence, too, the sense, are indeed to be reckoned as the more or less distant kinsmen of musical tones, and not alien allies."

Even *Hamlet's* universality is more limited than that of Burns's songs, for *Hamlet's* appeal is, one imagines, greatest for countries (including Russia) with a European culture: it would have to be preceded by a very lengthy explanatory talk indeed if it were ever acted in a Chinese village. But Burns's songs would require little beyond translation to appeal to a Chinese audience; the tunes would do the rest, and a little repetition would soon familiarise the audience with the conventions of our folk-music. In any case, the words themselves, if well translated, would find an echo in all their hearts.[41]

Burns's best songs fulfil the ideal of *universale in re* to an even greater extent than do his poems. Not only do they speak to all men everywhere, but they are dramatic lyrics which give the thoughts of unique and individual human beings at particular moments of time—either of Burns himself, or of some imagined person. Though rooted in the past, like all Burns's work, they are more forward-looking than any of his poems: in various ways, they anticipate Wordsworth, Scott, Keats, Tennyson, Browning and Yeats. However mysterious the process whereby their ultimate clarity is reached, their greatest quality is their simplicity; they are "maybe as cold and passionate as the dawn"—or as warm and passionate as a kiss, or, for that matter, of the cries of the crowd on the way to storming the Bastille. When Carlyle says that in his songs Burns "found a tone and words for every mood of man's heart,"[42] he is clearly exaggerating: there are moods in Marvell and Donne and Sir Philip Sidney and Schubert and Wolf which he did not know. But when Carlyle goes on to rank him as "the first of all our song-writers," meaning by "our" English as well as Scottish, then it is necessary to agree with him. In view of the tremendous achievements of nineteenth-century German *Lieder*, however, it is today impossible to accept his aggressive rider, "we know not where to find one worthy of being second to him"; Schubert and Wolf are at least Burns's equals.

[41] Cp. Dr Wen-Yuan-Ning, quoted above, p. 260.
[42] [Carlyle], review of Lockhart's *Burns*, in *Edinburgh Review*, XLVIII (1828), 287.

X

Conclusion

BURNS'S poetry exhibits both development and the repetition of early themes and attitudes. The two processes are in reality part of the increasing concentration and universalisation of his central interests and positive values. The first of these was physical desire, together with the commonest emotions that arise upon that foundation. Burns often equated love with instinct, and figured it sometimes as the heart, at other times (for example, in songs of the *Merry Muses* type) as the sexual organs. His second most absorbing interest was comradeship between man and man, symbolised in certain poems and songs by "boozing at the nappy" and "social glee," which was sublimated at Tarbolton and Mauchline into Freemasonry, and at Dumfries into the revolutionary yearning for fraternity that underlies "Is there for honest Poverty?"

A third theme to which Burns returned again and again was the uniqueness and sanctity of individual human beings—a spontaneous and passionate democratic humanism which extends to the whole of society the values of the family. Mme Raït-Kovaleva, in the course of a recent biographical essay, sums up this characteristic in the following terms :

> He was able to describe the finest and most truly human feelings and experiences of the simple people—not as a detached philosopher, not as a critic, but as a brother and friend, as a passionate lover to whom nothing human was foreign.[1]

There are, however, exceptions—in "Halloween,"[2] for example, Burns examines popular customs *de haut en bas*, but as a rule when he puts the people at a distance it is not in order to sneer at them but in order to sympathise with the large number

---

[1] Introduction to Marshak, *Robert Burns in Translation*, Moscow 1957, henceforth cited as Raït-Kovaleva, p. 66.   [2] Above, pp. 123–30.

of characters which his vantage-point has enabled him to bring
within his view. His kindly humour when dealing with the
ordinary foibles of mankind, as well as his satirical thrusts at
snobbery, meanness and hypocrisy, can also be related to his
stretching of family values until they enclose the entire community. Brothers and sisters, parents and children esteem one
another for their eccentricities and even for their weaknesses—
or at least, they ought to; they can laugh in the actual moment
of loving, in the very way in which Burns smiles at William
Creech or Tam Samson or Captain Grose.[3]

A fourth major characteristic of Burns's was his cult of the
"Honest Man," which was a common concept of the Enlightenment all over Europe, and in Burns's case was closely connected with the idea of fraternity. For Burns, one feels, the
ideal society was composed of independent tenant-farmers and
the owners of one-man businesses, all exchanging their products
"in equilibrium" according to the amount of labour that went
towards their making—in other words, the kind of society that
was taken as a demonstration model by Adam Smith and the
Scottish political economists of the late eighteenth century.
Even aristocrats like Lord Daer and Glencairn are "honest"
only in so far as they approximate to the norm of the free
producer; the "honest ploughman" to whom Burns compares
Lord Daer[4] is a real ploughman and not a courtier mas-
querading as a shepherd, or a peasant who somehow or other
manages to obey a conception of nobility that is feudal in
origin. Burns's honest man is of necessity "independent," and
when he comes together with other men it is almost as a member
of a coalition of free and equal states; only occasionally, in
works like "The Tree of Liberty" (that is, if Burns wrote the
poem) and "Scots, wha hae" does the poet identify himself
with a mass-movement. Even his misfits, his outcasts and
anarchistic beggars are in one sense simply lower-middle-class
men placed beyond the law by accident or chance; in another,
they form a grotesque caricature of the society from which they
are exiles, and in which a struggle of all against all also prevails.
The diplomatic analogy is again helpful; coalitions are con-

---

[3] II. 53 (344); above, pp. 122–3, 324–5.
[4] "Lines on Meeting with Lord Daer," II. 49 (340), st. vii.

tinually breaking down, and war is the continuation of politics by other means just as much in Scottish villages and towns as in the Concert of Europe.

These last two elements in Burns's thought are, in the final analysis, incompatible. Every independent producer is the father of a family within which it is at least possible for humane and brotherly relations to prevail. But each independent producer is in competition with all the rest, and if the values of the family are to dominate the social scene, then the freedom of the independent producer must be curtailed; for, despite the contrary assertions advanced by "Liberal" economists, the general good is *not* the inevitable and necessary consequence of each man's pursuing his own self-interest. Burns never resolved the conflict between fraternity and free competition, though in his later years he sometimes attempted to bring them together by means of abstract political moralising. On occasion he expressed the point of view of another class besides that of the petty artisans and small tenants; he sometimes identified himself with the agricultural labourers. But this was a special instance of his imaginative sympathy with all oppressed persons, and in no sense the embodiment of a permanent attitude. He is our supreme poet of Agrarian Revolution, as Goldsmith is perhaps the second; indeed, this side of his work is remarkably similar in content to some of the anonymous Scottish Gaelic folk-songs of the eighteenth and nineteenth centuries dealing with themes of exile and dispossession. Thus Burns, pre-eminently the poet of Lowland Scotland, touches the Highlands not only by his fondness for fitting words to Gaelic tunes; he is also linked to the Celtic north by the subject-matter of such pieces as the "Address of Beelzebub," "Will ye go to the Indies, my Mary?" and "My Highland Lassie, O."[5]

Although some recent critics have tended to underestimate the political poems, it is important not to fall into the equal and opposite error of assigning them too large a place in our judgment. I cannot go the whole way with Mme Raït-Kovaleva, who appears to interpret Burns's development in almost partisan terms. She sees him as moving onwards from

---

[5] II. 154 (388); IV. 15 (36); III. 10 (308). And cp. J. Ross, "A Classification of Gaelic Folk-song," in *Scottish Studies*, I (1957), p. 111.

the early, non-political songs to "The Twa Dogs," which she describes as "a protest against the landlords, but not yet a revolutionary protest."

Here, [she goes on], he speaks primarily about social injustice and the intrinsic worth of man, but these themes are not imbued with the prophetic strain that comes out in "Is there for honest Poverty?" and "The Tree of Liberty," though all these elements can be already felt in it. Increasingly, he employs national themes in his poetry, until he ends up as a truly revolutionary people's poet.[6]

Mme Raït-Kovaleva appears to underestimate the revolutionary side of "Man was made to Mourn", the early epistles, and "The Jolly Beggars," at the same time as she converts the left-wing Whiggery of Burns's later years into a more consistent adherence to revolutionary doctrines than is perhaps warranted by the evidence. She says much about his Scottish nationalism, but little about his praise of British victories in the Pittite poems; and so far is she from facing up to the "bourgeois-nationalist" implications of "Does haughty Gaul invasion threat?," that she does not even mention it.[7]

The ideas that Burns considered of especial worth exist in constant conflict with the forces that would destroy them— the pretensions of the "unco guid," the political domination of the aristocracy, the citizens' love of money, "the sober, gin-horse routine of existence."[8] The typical Burns poem or song establishes a circuit between these warring principles and qualities. In the satires, the surface meaning may involve the triumph of the negative element; but what Burns is really doing is to state his positive values by means of his irony, his humour, and his scornful annihilation of those who merely *seem* to "bear the gree." In the non-satiric poems, the negatives are explicitly dismissed, and the positive values directly and

---

[6] Raït-Kovaleva, pp. 28 ff.

[7] Cp. above, pp. 17 ff., 144 ff., 255. Mme A. E. Elistratova, *Robert Burns*, Moscow 1957, p. 142, *does* face this difficulty by claiming that, by the time Burns wrote "Does haughty Gaul invasion threat?", the Revolution had begun to develop reactionary features. She says: "The hopes which the poet held out for the French Revolution were literally trampled by its enemies [within France itself]. French politics revealed not liberating but bourgeois traits."

[8] Burns [to Thomson], 19 Oct. [1794], in *Letters* II. 265.

overwhelmingly stated. The major exception is of course "Tam
o' Shanter," where the total meaning is the result of a rather
subtle interaction between symbol and tone, and there are
minor works which also follow the same pattern. But, by and
large, conflict, tension, and the overcoming of negative forces
and ideas lie behind almost every one of Burns's masterpieces.

A similar sort of movement can be observed not only in
many individual poems and songs but also in the rhythm of
Burns's life and the pattern of his poetic development when
considered as a whole. The great conflict behind all Burns's
life and work was that between the desire for a "life of literary
leisure," which was the goal of all his efforts in the Excise, and
the desire to be a national poet, which was only possible if he
did not stray too far from the traditions of the countryside. It
appears in his poetry as far back as the Kilmarnock Edition,
at the level of sensibility ("refined" *versus* "folk") ; at the level
of thought (Pittite and Foxite, Jacobite and Jacobin, freethinker and moderate Christian) ; and at the level of language
(Scots and English, poetic diction and the racy speech of the
people). The attainment of an absolutely simple and beautifully moulded statement of his basic attitudes involved both a
narrowing and a deepening of his range. That poetry of the
surface of things about which Angellier[9] and Miss Keith[10] have
spoken belongs essentially to his early work ; as time went on,
it was sacrificed in favour of a unity of words and music that
tries to communicate the experience suggested by the melody.
During these same later years Burns wrote the rhetorical
political prophecies which Mme Raït-Kovaleva considers the
summit of his achievement. They are good, they are even
magnificent—much better than some of the present generation
of academic Burnsians are prepared to admit ; but they are
still inferior to his finest love-songs. It is as if, at the end of his
life, reason had separated itself out from emotion more completely than in the work of almost any other Scottish or English
poet. The letters and the political poems give us the thoughts
of which an Average Man is capable in a period of political
change ; the best of the songs embody the intensified feelings
of such a Jock Tamson. If one concentrates on broad outlines

[9] Angellier, II. 395.   [10] Pp. 175–80.

only, ignoring temporary upsets and setbacks, Burns's development as a poet was from the local to the national to the universal. His political evolution should surely be regarded as part of that wider progress, and not *vice versa*.

The question of the ultimate value of Burns's songs is inseparably bound up with a second problem—that of his use of sources. Another topic, closely connected with the first two, concerns his relation to the Scots literary tradition. Burns's sources were of four main kinds: previously existing works which he used as models to be emulated and, if possible, surpassed; songs which he patched and mended, or hardly altered at all; ideas and attitudes which were part of the thought-idiom of his age; and, stock expressions, turns of phrase, and, sometimes, whole lines, which he took over, with little or no change, from previous poets, from the Bible, or from the lips of the people.[11] These categories cut right across the division between Scots and English, or the distinction between folk-song and art-song. For example, "The Cotter's Saturday Night" imitates models which are ultimately English, but it contains echoes of both English and Scottish writers;[12] "The Holy Fair," "The Ordination," and the familiar epistles have *Scottish* prototypes, but use ideas which are both Scots-English and European;[13] "Holy Willie's Prayer" is in a tradition with English as well as Scottish roots;[14] "Green grow the Rashes, O" has links with both Scottish bawdry and the first chapter of Sterne's *Tristram Shandy*;[15] "The Posie," written for a tune taken down from the singing of that most Scottish of women, Jean Armour, has verbal connexions with a number of eighteenth-century art songs,[16] and so forth. It is surely inconsistent to condemn Burns's borrowings from neo-classic English in "The Vision,"[17] and at the same time to go into ecstasies over the use he makes of a score of traditional phrases in "A red, red Rose."[18] Far from being different, the processes are at bottom the same.

Again, the question of the exact amount of inherited

---

[11] Cp. Ritter, *N.Q.*, pp. iv–v.
[13] Above, pp. 62–5, 67–76.
[15] Above, p. 282, n. 4.
[17] Above, pp. 182–92, nn. 83, 85, 89, 91. 92.

[12] Above, pp. 175–6.
[14] Above, p. 58, n. 19.
[16] Above, p. 288, n. 16.
[18] Above, pp. 278–9.

material incorporated in each individual song is an important one, but the precise nature of that importance has sometimes been misconceived. To critics who are still bound by the late eighteenth-century fetishes of "genius" and "original composition" (concepts which, as we have seen, had a great effect upon Burns himself and his fortunes), it may seem to be a matter of separating what is Burns's own from what belongs to someone else. One possible comment on this is to repeat Molière's retort to an accusation of plagiarism: "*Il m'est permis de reprendre mon bien où je le trouve.*" Another is to point out that when his songs are considered as a whole, Burns transcends the limits of personality and becomes both the voice of a nation and the voice of humanity itself, at the same time (and this is the paradox of all great art) as he remains inalienably himself. In the last analysis, it simply does not matter how much is Burns's and how much comes from elsewhere: what matters is the song itself, as a work to be sung and listened to.

Burns's use of folk-poetry is like the treatment of folk-melodies by such twentieth-century musicians as Stravinsky and Bartók; and Bartók's own comments on the subject[19] are so important (not only for himself, but, by analogy, for Burns) that they deserve summary here. Bartók says that there are three possible ways of transmuting peasant music into modern music. The first method is to adopt a peasant melody unchanged, or to alter it to only a slight degree by writing an accompaniment, "and possibly some opening and concluding phrases." This kind of activity, he says, is similar to Bach's handling of the Lutheran chorales.[20]

Within this method of using folk-material, Bartók distinguishes two subsidiary types of composition. In the first of these, "accompaniment, introductory and concluding phrases are of secondary importance, they only serve as an ornamental setting for the precious stone: the peasant melody"[21]—exactly as in Burns's treatment of the folk-poetry of "Ay Waukin, O." But in the other variant, "the melody only serves as a 'motto'

---

[19] In an article, "The Influence of Peasant Music on Modern Music," in S. Moreux, *Béla Bartók*, tr. G. S. Fraser and Erik de Mauny, London 1953, Appendix, pp. 238–47.   [20] *Op. cit.*, p. 239.   [21] *Op. cit.*, p. 240.

while that which is built round it is of real importance"[22]—
again, exactly as in those of Burns's songs in which only the
chorus is old. In a statement which, *mutatis mutandis*, can be
made to apply to *both* the words and the music of many of
Burns's lyrics, Bartók continues :

> All shades of transition are possible between these two extremes
> and sometimes it is not even possible to decide which of the
> elements is predominant in any given case. But in every case it
> is of the greatest importance that the musical qualities of the
> setting should be derived from the musical qualities of the
> melody, from such characteristics as are contained in it openly
> or covertly, so that melody and all additions create the im-
> pression of complete unity.[23]

The modern composer's second way of approaching folk-
motifs is, according to Bartók, the method whereby a musician
"does not make use of a real peasant melody but invents his
own imitation of such melodies. *There is no true difference between
this method and the one described above.*"[24] This, in different circumstances, was precisely Burns's practice in many of his best
songs ; and it also bears a resemblance to what was involved
in writing some of the poems—for example, "The Twa Dogs"
and "The Brigs of Ayr."

Finally, there is the case where "neither peasant melodies
nor imitations of peasant melodies can be found [in a composer's music]. In this case, we may say, he has completely
absorbed the idiom of peasant music which has become his
musical mother-tongue."[25] Burns, too, has parallels to this
third method : in poetry pure and simple, such pieces as
"Death and Doctor Hornbook," and in song, lyrics like "Tam
Glen" and "O, wert thou in the Cauld Blast."[26]

When Bartók's remarks about the creative use of folk-music
are taken over by the literary critic they suggest, first, that
Burns employed analogues of all three of Bartók's methods ;
secondly, that he was in the habit of modulating from one to the
other in the course of a single work ; and, thirdly, that all

[22] *Ibid.*   [23] *Ibid.*   [24] *Op cit.*, p. 242 ; my italics.   [25] *Op. cit.*, p. 243.
[26] Just as, at the level of language, he was accustomed to modulate from the
vernacular to Scots-English and (sometimes) to an imitation of neo-classic "English
English."

methods, including the first, have a real artistic value. Speaking of Stravinsky, Bartók quite unequivocally maintains that

> it does not matter a jot whether a composer invents his own themes or takes his themes from elsewhere. He has a right to use musical material taken from all sources. What he has judged suitable for his purpose has become through this very use his mental property. . . . In maintaining that the question of the origin of a theme is completely unimportant from the artist's point of view, Stravinsky is right.[27]

This is categorical enough; and it is as true of poetry (and of Burns's poetry in particular) as it is of music.

As befits a writer whose best works usually show traces of conflict and whose whole life was a struggle, Burns's qualities are often those one might not at first sight expect to find together.[28] He was at one and the same time a master of colloquial language and conventional poetic diction; the impressionist of a folk tradition who somehow or other produced bounding lines as clear and definite as those advocated by William Blake; and the poet of a village and small-town culture expressing in particular characters and images that opposition between reason and emotion, illusion and reality which one finds throughout both seventeenth and eighteenth-century literature. He was, in the French sense of the term, a "naturalist" who happened to develop into a great songwriter; but his lyricism transformed naturalism into the romanticism of everyday life, just as in "Tam o' Shanter" his symbolism penetrated beyond the surface of daily things to the inner conflicts of all Scotsmen, and of many Englishmen, Americans, Canadians, Australians and New Zealanders. The poet of the great commonplaces, he was nevertheless capable of thought, using sharply focussed allegorical personages as his means of understanding society. In some works he explored

---

[27] Bartók, *op. cit.* (above, n. 19), p. 242.
[28] This point has been made by many writers—and by none more persuasively than by F. B. Snyder, *Robert Burns: His Personality, his Reputation, his Art*, Toronto 1936, *passim*.

the very boundary between poetry and music, at the level where language fuses with melody and becomes indistinguishable from it ; in others, he produced the poetry of rapid motion as it appears in everyday society and in the mind of the ordinary person. Furthermore, he was perhaps able to convey this sense of movement so convincingly because he had worked with his hands on farms and knew the racy speech of those who were directly engaged in physical labour. At first sight a poet of the body rather than of the soul, of feeling rather than of thought, he was nevertheless one of the three or four greatest British verse satirists ; and satire is surely an intellectual thing. Although he never achieved tragic or epic stature, he was capable of both homely pathos and the everyday sublime. After Chaucer, he is the first of English and Scottish non-dramatic comic poets ; but his Muse is not so brilliantly witty as the Comic Spirit of Meredith's definition, nor is it so free of prejudice or passion. There may or may not be dissociation of sensibility in Burns's serious poems ; they may or may not be disfigured by mawkishness and sentimentality. His humour, however, is generally free from such taints ; it is a sunlight not of the mind only but of the whole being irradiating for us every corner of his experience. Burns's humour, like his satire, is often concerned with incongruities between appearance and reality, practice and belief ; and it manages to do two apparently incompatible things at the same time, for it can make us identify ourselves with his characters in the very moment of standing back and contemplating them from a distance. Burns achieves a criticism of life more often than Matthew Arnold was prepared to admit, and at more than one level ; but his most characteristic and most far-reaching criticism is a comic one.

Nothing that has happened in the past fifty years can remove Burns from the place which the best nineteenth-century critics were disposed to give him. Though he is not of the same stature as Chaucer, Shakespeare and Milton, he ranks with the best of the Scots, English and Irish poets who come immediately behind them—Henryson, Dunbar, Gavin Douglas, Marlowe, Donne, Dryden, Pope, Blake, Wordsworth, Coleridge, Byron, Keats, Shelley, Tennyson, Browning, Hopkins, Yeats, and a few others whom one might perhaps be tempted to include among the great poets of the second rank. He has his faults and his failings, but then so have all the other poets I have mentioned—including the fashionable Donne, Blake, Hopkins and Yeats. European critics have likened him to such national bards as the Polish Mickiewicz, the Hungarian Petöfi, and the Ukrainian Shevchenko, and though I have no means of judging the validity of the last three comparisons, he undoubtedly has points in common with such diverse poets as Sappho, Catullus, Villon and Heine, with the whole European pastoral tradition, and with prose-writers so different from each other as Rabelais, Rousseau, and the Tolstoy of the peasant idylls. Burns's language is a barrier for the majority of English-speaking people, including many Scots; but the linguistic obstacles are no greater than those that separate us from Chaucer or the anonymous author of *Sir Gawayne and the Green Knight*. When once the effort has been made, and we have mastered the unfamiliar words, Burns appears as a regionalist only up to a point. In his finest works he is a writer who belongs not to Scotland only, but to the whole world ; and in his songs he looks forward—not merely to such diverse poets of the next generation as Scott, Wordsworth, Byron and Keats, nor merely to such Victorians as Tennyson and Browning—but, in addition, to the greatest masters of German *Lieder*, and to such twentieth-century musicians as Stravinsky and Bartók, who, in their creative use of folk-songs, were thorough-going revolutionaries and ardent traditionalists at one and the same time.

Appendixes

NOTE

Having made so much of the difference between vernacular Scots and Scots-English, I felt that it was incumbent on me to give some concrete examples showing how I personally would be inclined to pronounce certain typical Scots and Scots-English passages. "Sc.-Eng." here means English as pronounced by a Scots vernacular speaker, *e.g.* when reading aloud from the newspaper, or from the Bible. As regards details, there cannot, of course, be any finality, and the transcriptions themselves are only approximate. Thus, even though in Scots the vowel in an unstressed syllable usually retains some trace of its proper quality, such vowels (*e.g.* in pɑ·rʃəl, juˑθfəl) are often here represented by the symbol ə. Again, in rhetorical utterance, and especially in reciting poetry, Scottish (like English) speakers permit themselves more variation in vowel length than would probably occur in ordinary conversation; and the tentative indications of vowel length given in the transcriptions must not be regarded as in any sense a standard. Finally, in transcribing Scots-English, I have indicated certain pronunciations (*e.g.* pliʃˑʒər, əpiˑnjənz), now perhaps rather old-fashioned, but still sometimes used in reciting Burns.

I am especially grateful to Mr David Murison for all the assistance that he so generously has given me in compiling this appendix.

T. C.

PHONETIC VALUES IN BURNS'S SCOTS AND SCOTS-ENGLISH POEMS AND SONGS

The following extracts may prove helpful in assessing the texture of Burns's vernacular and Scots-English poetry, as pronounced by a Scot. No attempt has been made to reproduce historical or dialectal pronunciation—that is, to indicate the Ayrshire speech of Burns's own day ; the extracts follow what might be called "General Scottish," which permits of a number of alternative pronunciations, some of which are given in the transcriptions. The system followed is that of the alphabet of the International Phonetic Association with certain modifications, and substantially as set forth in *The Scottish National Dictionary*.[1] The sign = should here be taken to mean "as in," and the symbols used themselves have the following values :

Vowels[2]

ɑ = Sc. l*a*ss ; Eng. f*a*ther.

e = Sc. w*a*me, h*a*me ; Fr. *été*.

ε = Sc. t*e*ll ; Eng. b*e*t.

ə = Sc. or Eng. *a*bout.

i = Sc. p*i*ty, fr*ie*nd ; Sc. or Eng. f*ee*t.

ɪ = Sc. m*i*ther ; Eng. f*i*t.

o = Sc. th*o*le ; Sc.-Eng. t*oa*d.

ǫ = (Ayrshire) Sc. f*a*r ; Sc.-Eng. s*a*w.

ø = Fr. p*eu*.

u = Sc. br*oo*, t*ou*n ; Sc.-Eng. gr*ew*.

ʌ = Sc. or Eng. b*u*t.

---

[1] Vol. i [1931], pp. xlii ff. ; in addition to which, I have also freely consulted Sir James Wilson, (1) *Scottish Poems of Robert Burns in his Native Dialect*, henceforth cited as Wilson, London 1925, which contains versions of a number of Burns's poems in simplified spelling designed to show how they would have been pronounced by an Ayrshireman of the first half of this century ; and (2) *Dialects of Central Scotland*, London 1928 ; and D. D. Murison, "The Speech of Ayrshire in the Time of Burns," henceforth cited as D. D. Murison, in *Ayrshire at the Time of Burns*, Ayrshire Archaeological and Natural History Society, 1959, pp. 222 ff.

[2] The English pronunciations given under this heading are of course only approximately equivalent to the Scottish pronunciations, which do not diphthongise the long vowels. On ø, see esp. D. D. Murison, pp. 223–4.

Diphthongs

aı = Sc. f*i*ve, k*ye*.
əi = Sc. b*oi*l, k*i*nd, n*i*ne, t*i*me.
ʌu = Sc. g*ow*k.

Consonants

b = Sc. or Eng. *b*ed.
d = Sc. or Eng. *d*id.
f = Sc. or Eng. *f*ill.
g = Sc. or Eng. *g*ang.
h = Sc. or Eng. *h*it.
j = Sc. or Eng. *y*ou.
k = Sc. or Eng. ro*ck*.
l = Sc. *l*ull; Eng. lu*ll*.
m = Sc. or Eng. *m*e.

n = Sc. or Eng. *n*ot.
p = Sc. or Eng. *p*in.
r = Sc. *r*un (strongly "trilled").
s = Sc. or Eng. *s*ee.
t = Sc. or Eng. *t*ime, ho*t*.
v = Sc. or Eng. *v*an.
w = Sc. or Eng. *w*ine.
z = Sc. or Eng. *z*one.

Note also the following :

ç = Sc. *h*euk, li*ch*t, hei*ch*; Ger. i*ch*, ni*ch*t.
ð = Sc. or Eng. *th*en.
dʒ = Sc. *j*ouk; Eng. bri*dg*e.
hw = Sc. *wh*ite.
ŋ = Sc. or Eng. ga*ng*.
ʃ = Sc. or Eng. *sh*ut.
tʃ = Sc. or Eng. *ch*eap.
θ = Sc. or Eng. *th*in.
x = Sc. lo*ch*; Ger. la*ch*.
ʒ = Sc. poi*s*on; Eng. plea*s*ure.

Other Symbols

ˑ indicates half-lengthening of vowel.
: indicates double-lengthening of vowel.

§ 1. "Man was made to Mourn"[3]

As pronounced by a Scot, the effect of the second-last stanza is as much a matter of the sound-patterns produced from the interplay of the back vowels ʌ and o, as of the strongly-voiced trilled r, and alliteration of s, st, and ʃ. The importance of this last sound is often obscured by the spelling, for it is found in both "surely" (ʃeˑrlı) and "partial" (þeˑrʃəl) :

[3] Cp. above, pp. 17-24.

jıt lɛt nʌt ðıs tu mʌtʃ mɑı sʌn
Yet let not this too much, my son,

iˑ
dıstʌrb ðɑı juˑθfəl brɛˑst
Disturb thy youthful breast :

eː
ðıs pɑːˑʃəl vjuˑ əv çjuˑmən-kəind
This partial view of human-kind

ız ˑʃeːrlı nʌt ðə lɛˑst
Is surely not the last !

uː
ðə pɛːr oprɛsıd onıst mɑˑn
The poor, oppressèd, honest man

həd nıvər ʃeːr biˑn boːrn
Had never, sure, been born,

həd ðer nʌt biˑn sʌm rɛkʌmpɛns
Had there not been some recompense

ə
tɛ kʌmfərt ðoˑz ðat moːrn
To comfort those that mourn !

When read as Scots-English, the vowels ʌ and o (the latter often lengthened to oː) ; the trilled r so pronounced as to be sometimes almost syllabic ; the voiced consonants m, n and l—often the media of alliteration—all occur again and again throughout the whole poem, like the tolling of a funeral bell.

§ 2. "Holy Willie's Prayer"[4]

In "Holy Willie's Prayer," polysyllables with theological connotations ("generation, exaltation, damnation, creation, mercies, temporal, divine, glory,") seem particularly impressive when set beside the hammer-strokes of short words, such as "Thou might hae plung'd me deep in hell," and "That I for grace an' gear may shine." Miss Keith[5] has noted the predominance of monosyllables in the poem as a whole ; it should perhaps be added that as pronounced by a Scot the so-called "weak" stresses often carry extra emphasis, so that in these thirteen syllables, there are eight strong stresses ('), two half stresses (`), and only three really weak ones (ˣ) :

[4] Cp. above, pp. 52–6.   [5] Pp. 76–7.

˟Or ꞌelse, ꞋThou ꞌkens ꞋThy ꞌserꞋvant ꞌtrue
ꞋWad ꞌne˟ver ꞌsteer ˟her

with the result that the lines quoted are almost as solid as an ordinary pentameter and trimeter respectively. It would be superfluous to comment at length on the excellence of the rhymes. Generally, Burns rhymes upon stressed monosyllables of full meaning; but the flexibility of his favourite stanza form allows him to vary this pattern by fairly often ending with a polysyllable or a weak-stressed monosyllable. This makes it possible for him to rhyme trochaic feet on occasion : "dishonour—upon her," "near her—steer her" are two examples.

As we have seen, Willie is a supremely paradoxical figure, and the opposing sides of his nature are mirrored in the very sound and texture of the verse. Burns instinctively chooses nasal consonants to convey sonority, and plosives and velar to reflect either strength, or conflict, or both together, as in the fifth stanza with the magnificent rhyme and assonance of

     ɑ   ɑ
sɛmpəl ɛmpəl tɛmpəl əgzɛmpəl
sample, ample, temple, example,

and including also the alliterative "*g*race" and "*g*reat," and the interacting voiced and voiceless velars "*g*uide, bu*ck*ler" and "flo*ck*." Patterns of dignified and rolling sound alternate with sequences in which the prevailing consonants are sibilants and the voiceless fricative f, varied by occasional play with other consonants, such as l, as in the sixth stanza ("con*f*e*ss*; mu*st*; *f*a*sh*'d; *f*le*sh*ly; lu*st*; *s*ometime*s*; tru*st*; *s*el*f*; get*s*; de*f*iled; *s*in"). It is surely impossible to imagine a more creative use of assonance and alliteration than in :

          ə
te (g)nɑːʃ mɑ gømz ən(d) wiꞏp ən(d) weꞏl
To gnash my gooms, and weep and wail

                 ŋ
ɪn bʌrnɪn leꞏks
In burning lakes,

                             eꞏ
hwǫr dɑmnɪd diꞏvəlz roːr ən(d) jɛl
Whare damnèd devils roar and yell,

                   ə
tʃəind te ðər steꞏks
Chain'd to their stakes.

Burns's alliteration is not the mannered device that it sometimes was for such nineteenth-century poets as Tennyson or Swinburne, but the instinctive use of a traditional resource of Anglic-speakers for ensuring emphasis or memorability. "*W*eep and *w*ail," "*d*amn*è*d *d*evils," "*l*ift a *l*awless *l*eg," "*h*ingin lip . . . *h*eld up his *h*ead," "*m*e and *m*ine"—such phrases are close to the expression of the people, as reflected in proverbs, old saws, weather lore, and girls' singing games; and they serve to remind us yet again what a master of language Burns was.

§ 3. "The Ordination"[6]

Vernacular Scots and Scots-English

bʌt ðerz mʌralɪtɪ (h)ɪmsɛl
But there's Morality himsel,

    o
ɪmbre·sɪŋ ǫ·l əpi·njənz
Embracing all opinions;

hi:r hu (h)ɪ gi:z ðə tɪðər jɛl
Hear, how he gies the tither yell

    a·
bɪtwi·n hɪz twǫ kəmpe·njənz
Between his twa companions!

    ɪ
si: hu ʃi pi:lz ðə skɪn ən fɛl
See, how she peels the skin an' fell,

əz jɪn wər pi·lɪn ʌnjənz
As ane were peelin onions!

        ə
nu ðe·r ðər pa:kɪt af tə hɛl
Now there, they're pack*è*d aff to hell,

ən ba·nɪʃt ur dəmi:njənz
An' banish'd our dominions,

             hɛnsfo·rθ ðɪs de:
             Henceforth this day.

[6] Cp. above, pp. 62–5.

§ 4. "The Holy Fair"[7]

The sound-patterns of "The Holy Fair" are so completely integrated with the content that they never obtrude on the reader's consciousness. As in "Holy Willie's Prayer," sibilants, voiceless f, and close vowels are opposed to nasals, voiced l, and open vowels. The former group convey hatred, meanness or contempt, while the latter emphasise both the sonority of Scottish preaching and Burns's affirmation of life. The main types of consonant are already present in the first two lines, like the statement of a theme which is to be infinitely varied before the end :

> ʌpoˑn ə sɪmər sʌndɪ moˑrn
> Upon a simmer Sunday morn,

> ʌ
> hwən neːtərz feːs ɪz feːr
> When Nature's face is fair . . . .

The very last line of the poem contains a hiss and two fronted half-close vowels :

> sʌm ɪðər deː
> Some ither day.

But it is of the nature of a "dying fall," a reminiscence of the hypocrisy which has been negated by the poem's comic development, and is present in the conclusion only as a memory. A single isolated sibilant is by no means enough to annihilate the glorious confidence of the two preceding lines, in which voiced nasals and open or half-open vowels predominate in stressed syllables :

> ən mʌnɪ dʒoˑbz ðat deː bəgɪn
> And monie jobs that day begin,

> meˑ ɛnd ɪn hǫxmagaˑndɪ
> May end in houghmagandie . . .

§ 5. "Epistle to J. Lapraik"[8]

Scots-English

> eˑ
> bʌt jiˑ hum soˑʃəl pliˑʒər tʃaˑr(ə)mz
> But ye whom social pleasure charms

[7] Cp. above, pp. 74–5 ; Wilson, p. 87.
[8] Cp. above, pp. 91–2.

huˑz heˑrts ðə təid əv kəindnəs waˑr(ə)mz
Whose hearts the tide of kindness warms,

huˑ hoːld juˑr biˑɪŋ on ðə teˑr(ə)mz
Who hold your being on the terms

       ˈ
iˑtʃ eˑd ðə ʌðərz
Each aid the others,

     ʌu   eˑ
kʌm tə ma boːl kʌm tə ma aˑr(ə)mz
Come to my bowl, come to my arms,

   iˑ   ˈ
ma frɛnz ma brʌðərz
My friends, my brothers.

§ 6. "The Brigs of Ayr"[9]

(a) *Vernacular Scots and Scots-English*

                   ʌ
twʌz hwʌn ðə staks gɛt on ðər wɪntər hap
'Twas when the stacks get on their winter hap,

ən(d) θak ən(d) rep sɪkjuˑr ðə təil wʌn krap
And thack and rape secure the toil-won crap;

   ˈ   ˈ
pɪtatə-bɪŋz ər snʌgɪt ʌp fre skeˑθ
Potatoe-bings are snuggèd up frae skaith

     n ʌ   n
əv kʌmɪŋ wɪntərz bəitɪŋ froˑstɪ breˑθ
O' coming winter's biting, frosty breath. . . .

(b) *Scots-English*

         i
hɪz hoːrɪ hɛd wɪ(θ) wǫtər-lɪlɪz krʌund
. . . His hoary head with water-lilies crown'd,

hɪz maˑrlɪ lɛg wɪ(θ) gaˑrtər taˑŋ(g)əl bʌund
His manly leg with garter-tangle bound . . .

---

[9] Cp. above, pp. 195–8.

§ 7. "ELEGY ON CAPTAIN MATTHEW HENDERSON"[10]

Onomatopoeic effects in Scots-English,
with faint admixture of the vernacular

                             ʌ
moˑrn suˑtɪ kuˑts ən spɛkəlt tiˑlz
Mourn, sooty coots, and speckled teals ;

       ɛː ə   n
jiː fɪʃər heːrʌnz wǫtʃɪŋ iˑlz
Ye fisher herons, watching eels ;

jiː dʌk ən dreːk wɪ eːrɪ hwiˑlz
Ye duck and drake, wi' airy wheels

                n
       sɪrklɪŋ ðə leˑk
       Circling the lake ;

 ʌ
jiː bɪtər(ə)nz tɪl ðə kwaˑgməir riˑlz
Ye bitterns, till the quagmire reels,

           ə
      reːr fʌr hɪz seˑk
      Rair for his sake !

§ 8. "TAM O' SHANTER"[11]

(a) *Scots-English, which, for its full effect to be realised, has to be pronounced*
somewhat as follows :

          ʌ
bʌt pliːʒʌrz ər ləik poːpɪz sprɛd
But pleasures are like poppies spread :

                 ø
ju siːz ðə flʌuər ɪts bluˑm ɪz ʃɛd
You seize the flow'r, its bloom is shed ;

ər ləik ðə snoː fǫˑlz ɪn ðə rɪvər
Or like the snow falls in the river,

ə moˑmənt hwəit ðɛn mɛlts fər ɪvər
A moment white—then melts for ever . . .

[10] Cp. above, pp. 212–15.   [11] Cp. above, pp. 217–36.

ər ləik ðə bo·rɪɑːlɪs reːs
Or like the borealis race,

ðət flɪt er ju kɑn pəint ðər pleːs
That flit ere you can point their place;

ər ləik ðə reːnboˑz lʌvlɪ foˑr(ə)m
Or like the rainbow's lovely form

iˑvɑ·nɪʃɪŋ əmɪd ðə stoˑr(ə)m
Evanishing amid the storm.

(*b*) *Onomatopoeic vernacular Scots, with initial couplet in Scots-English* [12]

ðə pəipər luˑd ən(d) luˑdər bluˑ
The piper loud and louder blew,

ðə dɑ·nsərz kwɪk ən(d) kwɪkər fluˑ
The dancers quick and quicker flew,

ðe riˑld ðe sɛt ðe kroˑst ðe klikɪt
They reel'd, they set, they cross'd, they cleekit,

tɪl ɪlkʌ keˑrlɪn swɑt ən rikɪt
Till ilka carlin swat and reekit,

ən kɪst hər dʌdɪz tə ðə waˑrk
And coost her duddies to the wark,

ən lɪŋkɪt ɑt ɪt ɪn hər sɑˑrk
And linket at it in her sark!

(*c*) *Scots contrasted with Scots-English* [13]

ðər wɪz (j)eˑ wɪnsʌm wɛnʃ ən wǫːlɪ
There was ae winsome wench and wawlie,

ðɑt nɪçt ənlɪstɪt ɪn ðə koː(ə)r
That night enlisted in the core. . . .

[12] Cp. Wilson, p. 119.   [13] Cp. Wilson, pp. 121-3, 125.

ən ʃʌk beˑθ mʌk(ə)l koˑr(ə)n ən biːr
. . . And shook baith meikle corn and bear,

      ɪ   ɑ
ən(d) kɛpt ðə kʌntrɪ-səid ɪn fiːr
And kept the country-side in fear . . .

hər kʌtɪ sark o peˑzlɪ haːr(ə)n
Her cutty sark, o' Paisley harn,

ðət hwəil ə laˑsɪ ʃiˑ həd woˑr(ə)n
That while a lassie she had worn,

     tød ð
ɪn loˑndʒɪtjud θo soːrlɪ skaˑntɪ
In longitude tho' sorely scanty,

  ʌ   ʌ
ɪt wɪz hər bɛst ən(d) ʃi wɪz vǫˑntɪ
It was her best, and she was vauntie. . . .

tam tɪnt (h)ɪz riˑzən ǫˑ ðəgɪðər
Tam tint his reason a' thegither,

ən(d) roːrz ut wiˑl dɪn kʌtɪ-saˑrk
And roars out: 'Weel done, Cutty-sark!'

əˑn(d) ɪn ən ɪnstənt ǫˑl wəz daˑrk
And in an instant all was dark;

ən(d) skeˑrslɪ həd (h)i magɪ raˑlɪd
And scarcely had he Maggie rallied,

  ʌ ʌu
hwɛn uˑt ðə hɛˑlɪʃ liˑdʒən saˑlɪd
When out the hellish legion sallied. . . .

   ə   ɪ   ɛ   u
az iːgər rʌnz ðə markɪt-krʌud
As eager runs the market-crowd,

  ʌ   unz   u
hwɛn kaˑtʃ ðə θif rəzʌundz əlʌud
When 'Catch the thief!' resounds aloud,

        ʌ   ʌ
so magɪ rɪnz ðə wɪtʃɪz foˑlə
So Maggie runs, the witches follow,

  ɪ
wi mʌnɪ ən ɛldrɪtʃ skriːç ən(d) hoˑlə
Wi' monie an eldritch skriech and hollo.

ðə keˑrlɪn klǫxt hər bɪ ðə rʌmp
The carlin claught her by the rump

ən(d) lɛft peˑr magɪ skeˑrs ə stʌmp
And left poor Maggie scarce a stump.

§ 9. "O, SAW YE BONIE LESLEY?"[14]

Scots-English with sprinkling of the vernacular

o sǫː ji boːnɪ lɛzlɪ
O, saw ye bonie Lesley,

      az ʃiˑ geˑd ʌu(ə)r ðə boːrdər
      As she gaed o'er the Border?

ʃiz geːn ləik alɪgzaˑndər
She's gane, like Alexander,

      iˑ   ǫˑ d
      te spɛd hər koːnkwɛsts faˑrðər
      To spread her conquests farther.

te siˑ hər ɪz te løˑv hər
To see her is to love her,

an(d) løˑv bʌt hər fər ɪvər
And love but her for ever;

fər neˑtər meˑd hər hwʌt ʃi ɪz
For Nature made her what she is,

an(d) nɪvər meˑd ənɪðər
And never made anither!

14 Cp. above, pp. 270–1; Wilson, p. 327.

§ 10. "THE LEA-RIG"[15]

Tone-poetry

When united with the melody, the words of st. i produce an effect comparable to that which results from the interplay of melody and piano-accompaniment in German *Lieder*. Vowels not normally stressed when the song is read aloud as poetry are here given the same values as when it is sung; but extra indeterminate vowels (ə), employed by singers, *e.g.* in their pronunciation of "time" (təiəm) are not shown.

      ʌ   ǫ˙
hwɛn ʌur ðə hɪl ðə iːst(ə)rən staˑr
When o'er the hill the eastern star

tɛlz bʌxtɪn təim ɪz niˑr mɑɪ dʒoˑ
Tells bughtin time is near, my jo,

an(d) ʌuzən freˑ ðə fʌroˑd fiːld
And owsen frae the furrow'd field

riˑtʌr(ə)n se dʌuf and wiːriˑ oˑ
Return sae dowf and weary, O,

                   ǫ
dun bɑɪ ðə bʌr(ə)n hwer sɛntɪt bɪrks
Down by the burn, where scented birks

  ɪ dj
wi dʒu ar haŋɪn kliːr mɑɪ dʒoˑ
Wi' dew are hangin clear, my jo,

              iː
aˑl miːt ðiˑ on ðə ləi rɪg
I'll meet thee on the lea-rig,

  ɑː
mɑɪ eːn kəin diːriˑ oˑ
My ain kind dearie, O.

[15] Cp. above, pp. 294–5; Wilson, p. 339.

APPENDIX II

SOME PARALLELS

§ 1. "HOLY WILLIE'S PRAYER"[1]

This poem has the following parallels with the Authorised Version:

BURNS	A.V.
A burning and a shining light . . . [ii. 5]	He was a burning and a shining light. . . [Jn. v. 35]
Thou might hae plung'd me deep in hell | To gnash my gooms, and weep and wail | In burning lakes . . . [iv. 2–4]	(1) . . . and shall cast them into a furnace of fire: there shall be wailing and gnashing of teeth. [Mt. xiii. 42] (2) These both were cast alive into a lake of fire burning with brimstone. [Rev. xix. 20; cp. also xx. 10]
Where damnèd devils roar and yell . . . [iv. 5]	The young lions roared upon him, and yelled . . . [Jer. ii. 15]
. . . a pillar o' Thy temple [v. 3]	Him that overcometh will I make a pillar in the temple of my God . . . [Rev. iii. 12]
But Thou remembers we are dust . . . [vi. 5]	. . . he remembereth that we are dust. [Ps. ciii. 14]
Maybe Thou lets this fleshly thorn | Buffet Thy servant e'en and morn, | Lest he owre proud and high should turn | That he's sae gifted . . . [ix. 1–4]	. . . there was given to me a thorn in the flesh, the messenger of Satan to buffet me, lest I should be exalted above measure. [ii Cor. xii. 7]

[1] See above, pp. 52–61.

Frae God's ain Priest the people's hearts He steals awa. [XI. 5–6]	. . . so Absalom stole the hearts of the men of Israel. [II Sam. xv. 6]
Curse Thou his basket and his store . . . [XII. 5]	Cursed shall be thy basket and thy store . . . [Deut. XXVIII. 17]
Lord, hear my earnest cry and pray'r. [XIII. 1]	. . . hearken unto the cry and to the prayer which thy servant prayeth before thee today. [I Kings VIII, 28; cp. also II Chron. VI. 19]
Thy strong right hand, Lord, mak it bare | Upo' their heads! [XIII. 3–4]	The Lord hath made bare his holy arm in the eyes of all the nations. [Is. LII, 10]
My vera heart and flesh are quakin . . . [XIV. 2]	. . . my heart and my flesh crieth out for the living God. [Ps. LXXXIV. 2]

Burns's stylistic genius here consists in making creative use of the idiom of the people—in this case, the Biblical language of the Auld Lichts, thoroughly assimilated to Scottish phrase and intonation—by selecting from "the real language of men," in *exactly* the same way as he selects from the give-and-take of peasant conversation in "Death and Doctor Hornbook." See above, p. 121.

§ 2. "EPISTLE TO A YOUNG FRIEND"[2]

This epistle has at least three parallels with Young's *Night Thoughts*:

BURNS	YOUNG
. . . th' important end of life [iv. 3]	. . . which answers life's great end. [Night v, 773]
. . th' illicit rove . . . [vi. 3]	In thy nocturnal rove . . . [Night IX, 673]
A correspondence fix'd wi' Heaven. [x. 7]	. . . all correspondence with the skies . . . [Night II, 342]

[2] Above, p. 102, n. 49.

§ 3. "Is there for honest Poverty ?"[3]

Cp. T. Paine, *Rights of Man* :

Burns	Paine
Ye see yon birkie ca'd 'a lord,' Wha struts, an' stares, an' a' that ? Tho' hundreds worship at his word, He's but a cuif for a' that. For a' that, an' a' that, His ribband, star, an' a' that, The man o' independent mind, He looks an' laughs at a' that.	The French Constitution says, *There shall be no titles* ; and, of consequence, all that class of equivocal generation which in some countries is called "aristocracy," and in others "nobility," is done away, and the *peer* is exalted into Man . . . [Love of titles] talks about its fine *blue ribbon* like a girl, and shews its new *garter* like a child. (*Rights of Man*, Everyman Edn., p. 59).
A prince can mak a belted knight, A marquis, duke, an' a' that ! But an honest man's aboon his might— Guid faith, he mauna fa' that ! For a' that, an' a' that, Their dignities an' a' that, The pith o' sense an' pride o' worth Are higher rank than a' that.	The patriots of France have discovered in good time that rank and dignity in society must take a new ground. The old one has fallen through. It must now take the substantial ground of character, instead of chimerical ground of titles. . . . The artificial Noble shrinks into a dwarf before the Noble of Nature. . . . (*Op. cit.*, pp. 60, 63).

Burns's last stanza ("Then let us pray . . .") is most closely paralleled by Paine's statement : "For what we can foresee, all Europe may form but one great Republic, and man be free of the whole" (*op. cit.*, p. 211). It also represents the transformation of the Masonic concept of Brotherhood into the French revolutionary ideal of Fraternity.

[3] Above, p. 245, n. 89.

ANGELLIER'S CLASSIFICATION OF BURNS'S LOVE-SONGS

The following classification of Burns's love-songs has been extracted from Angellier, II. 235–313.

1. Songs on Love itself, and on its Mutability: I. 251 (414), "Green grow the Rashes, O"; III. 219 (455), "Let not Women e'er complain."

2. Impersonal pieces, often Complaints uttered by Girls: III. 269 (488), "How can my poor Heart be glad?"; III. 184 (436), "The Highland Widow's Lament."

3. Extremely "light" love-songs, often mere elaboration of a refrain, with little content: III. 48 (339), "The Gard'ner wi his Paidle."

4. Compressed Narratives: III. 198 (443), "My Lord a-hunting."

5. Imitations of old Ballads (very few): III. 211 (450), "O, open the Door"; III. 126 (388), "O, Lady Mary Ann"; III. 220 (455), "Lord Gregory."

6. Dialogues between Lovers: III. 277 (493), "O Philly, happy be that Day"; III. 212 (451), "When wild War's deadly Blast"; III. 281 (495), "There was a Lass."

7. Songs on Married Love, or on Lifelong Faithfulness: III. 109 (381), "I hae a Wife o' my ain"; III. 63 (349), "John Anderson, my Jo."

8. Songs on such conventional themes as (a) a Lover's desire to be some object which the Beloved has touched, or (b) a simple Enumeration of Flowers, or (c) a Lover's Address to a Plaintive Bird: (a) III. 279 (493), "O, were my Love yon Lilac fair"; (b) III. 122 (386), "The Posie"; cp. III. 263 (486), "O, bonie was yon rosie Brier"; (c) III. 223 (457), "O, stay, sweet warbling Wood-lark."

9. Personal Pieces, of a specially "refined" character: I. 183 (388), "From thee Eliza, I must go"; cp. III. 264 (486), "Where are the Joys?"

10. Songs mingling Landscape with Sentiment; III. 167 (424), "O, wat ye wha's in yon Town?"; cp. III. 124 (388), "Ye Banks and Braes c' bonie Doon."

11. Songs showing an almost Petrarchan obsession with a Girl's Eyes, which Angellier compares to Heine : III. 248 (473), "O, this is no my ain Lassie" ; III. 29 (326), "Blythe was She" ; and esp. III. 82 (362), "The Blue-eyed Lassie."

12. Songs dealing with Rustic Courtship (especially with Evening Walks and Meetings), in which there is often a mixture of amorous and pastoral poetry : III. 151 (411), "Comin' thro' the Rye" ; III. 65 (350), 268 (488), "Ca' the Yowes" ; III. 284 (497), "The Lea-rig" ; I. 180 (385), "Corn Rigs."

13. Graceful Compliments and Declarations of no importance, thrown out in passing : III. 103 (378), "Bonie wee Thing" ; III. 202 (444), "O, lay thy Loof in mine Lass."

14. III. 34 (330), "And I'll kiss thee yet"—one song on the age-old theme of a kiss, in which the chorus (when sung) is perhaps equal to Catullus's "Quaeris, quot mihi basiationes" :

And I'll kiss thee yet, yet,
And I'll kiss thee o'er again,
And I'll kiss thee yet, yet,
My bonie Peggy Alison.

15. Songs of Melancholy and Sadness, so simple as to seem, almost, the literary expression of a sigh : III. 158 (416), "For the Sake o' Somebody" ; III. 232 (463), "Canst thou leave me ?"

16. Songs of Artificial Compliment, *e.g.* the earliest lyrics to Clarinda.

17. Songs about Parting, Separation, or the Death of a Loved One : III. 105 (379), "Ae fond Kiss" ; cp. IV. 15 (86), "Will ye go to the Indies, my Mary ?" ; III. 10 (308), "My Highland Lassie, O" ; III. 255 (480), "Ye Banks and Braes and Streams around."

18. Songs of Pure Passion, almost devoid of intellectual content, and approximating to the primitive emotional cry—*i.e.*, where the very language itself is on the borderline between poetry and music : III. 42 (335), "Sweet Tibbie Dunbar" ; III. 72 (356), "Eppie Adair" ; III. 45 (337), "Ay waukin, O" ; III. 254 (480), "Thou hast left me ever, Jamie."

19. Songs of Brutal and Urgent Desire: iv. 25 (92), "Yestreen I had a Pint o' Wine"; and some of those of the songs preserved in *The Merry Muses of Caledonia* which are now generally recognised to be Burns's.

20. Songs of a more Refined and Luxurious Desire, *e.g.* the songs to "Chloris" (Jean Lorimer).

21. Songs of Hopeless Longing: iv. 43 (102), "O, wert thou in the Cauld Blast."

22. Songs on the theme of the Night Visit (to a girl's house or room): iii. 5 (304), "O, whistle an' I'll come to ye, my lad"; iii. 102 (375), "Wha is that at my Bower Door?"; iii. 274 (492), "O let me in this ae Night"; cp. iii. 170 (427), "O May, thy Morn." Although Angellier treats this group as a subsidiary of 23 (The Comedy of Love and Marriage), in reality it includes serious as well as comic songs.

23. Songs on the Comedy of Love and Marriage: iii. 194 (440), "Robin shure in Hairst"; iii. 23 (231), 215 (432), "Duncan Gray"; iii. 242 (470), "Last May a braw Wooer"; iii. 84 (363), "Tam Glen"; iii. 93 (368), "What can a young Lassie?"; iii. 239 (469), "Husband, Husband, cease your strife"; iii. 139 (398), "The Deuk's dang o'er my Daddie."

24. Songs on Adultery: iii. 149 (410), "Had I the Wyte?"; and cp. many of the songs in *The Merry Muses.*

25. Songs of Gross Popular Drollery: iii. 44 (336), "The Tailor fell thro' the Bed"; iii. 157 (416), "The Cooper o' Cuddy"; and many of the songs in *The Merry Muses.*

Abbreviations used in Citation of Works mentioned frequently in the Footnotes

Angellier = A. ANGELLIER, *Robert Burns: la vie, les oeuvres*, 2 vols. Paris 1893.

Bronson = B. H. BRONSON, "Some Aspects of Music and Literature in the Eighteenth Century," in *Music & Literature in England in the Seventeenth and Eighteenth Centuries*. Los Angeles 1954.

C. & W. = *The Life and Works of Robert Burns*, ed. ROBERT CHAMBERS, revised by WILLIAM WALLACE, 4 vols. Edinburgh and London 1896

Calvinism = J. T. McNEILL, *The History and Character of Calvinism*. New York. 1954.

Chambers = *Life and Works of Burns*, ed. R. CHAMBERS, 4 vols. Edinburgh and London 1856.

Commonplace Book, see R. B.'s *Commonplace Book*.

Craigie = W. A. CRAIGIE, *A Primer of Burns*. London 1896.

Cromek = R. H. CROMEK, *Reliques of Robert Burns*. London 1808.

Currie = *The Works of Robert Burns*, ed. J. CURRIE, 4 vols. Liverpool 1800.

Daiches = D. DAICHES, *Robert Burns*. London 1952.

Dick = *The Songs of Robert Burns*, ed. J. C. DICK. London 1903. Also referred to as *Songs*. See also *Notes*.

Essays = *Collected Essays of W. P. Ker*, ed. C. WHIBLEY, 2 vols. London 1925.

Fairchild = H. N. FAIRCHILD, *Religious Trends in English Poetry*, 2 vols. New York 1939–42.

Ferguson = J. DE LANCEY FERGUSON, *Pride and Passion*. New York 1939.

Gebbie = *Complete Works of Robert Burns (Self-interpreting)*, ed. G. GEBBIE, 6 vols. Philadelphia 1886; reissued 1908 and 1909.

Graham = H. G. GRAHAM, *The Social Life of Scotland in the Eighteenth Century*, 2 vols. London 1899.

H. & H. = *The Poetry of Robert Burns*, edd. W. E. HENLEY and T. F. HENDERSON, (the "Centenary Edition"), 4 vols. Edinburgh and London 1896–7.

Hately Waddell = *Life and Works of Robert Burns*, ed. P. HATELY WADDELL. Glasgow 1867.

369

Hecht = HANS HECHT, *Robert Burns*, 2nd (revised) edn. London 1950.

Inst. = CALVIN, *Institutes of the Christian Religion* (tr. Beveridge). London 1949.

Johnson = *The Scots Musical Museum*, ed. JAMES JOHNSON, 6 vols. Edinburgh 1787–1803.

Keith, A. = A. KEITH, *Burns and Folk Song*. Aberdeen 1922.

Keith, C. = CHRISTINA KEITH, *The Russet Coat*. London 1956.

Ker, W. P., see ESSAYS, and ON MODERN LITERATURE.

Letters = *The Letters of Robert Burns*, ed. J. De Lancey Ferguson, 2 vols. Oxford 1931.

Manual = [? WILLIAM BURNES], *Manual of Religious Belief in the Form of a Dialogue between Father and Son*. Kilmarnock 1875.

Merry Muses = *The Merry Muses of Caledonia: A Collection of Favourite Scots Songs Ancient and Modern; selected for the use of the Crochallan Fencibles*, edd. James Barke, Sydney Goodsir Smith, and J. De Lancey Ferguson. Auk Society, Edinburgh 1959.

New Judgments = *New Judgments: Robert Burns*, ed. W. Montgomerie. Glasgow 1947.

Notes = J. C. DICK, *Notes on Scottish Song by Robert Burns*. London 1908.

N.Q. = O. RITTER, *Neue Quellenfunde zu Robert Burns*. Halle 1903.

On Modern Literature = W. P. KER, *On Modern Literature*, ed. T. S. Spencer and J. Sutherland. London 1955.

Q., see RITTER.

R. B., His Associates = *Robert Burns, his Associates and Contemporaries*, ed. R. T. Fitzhugh. N. Carolina and Oxford 1943.

Raït-Kovaleva = S. MARSHAK, *Robert Burns in Translation*. Moscow 1957.

R. B.'s Commonplace Book = *Robert Burns's Commonplace Book 1783–1785*, edd. J. C. Ewing and D. Cook. Glasgow 1938. Also referred to as *Commonplace Book*.

Ritter = O. RITTER, *Quellenstudien zu Robert Burns 1773–1791*. Berlin 1901. Also referred to as *Q*. See also *N.Q.*

Roughead = *Trial of Deacon Brodie*, ed. W. Roughead, in Notable Scottish Trials. Glasgow and Edinburgh 1906.

Schubert = M. J. E. BROWN, *Schubert: A Critical Biography.* London 1958.

Scots Songs = *The Ancient and Modern Scots Songs, Heroic Ballads, etc.* ed. D. HERD, 2 vols. Edinburgh 1769.

Scottish Songs = *Ancient and Modern Scottish Songs, Heroic Ballads, Etc.,* ed. D. HERD, 2 vols. Edinburgh 1776.

S.N.D. = *The Scottish National Dictionary.*

Snyder = F. B. SNYDER, *The Life of Robert Burns.* New York 1932.

Speirs = J. SPEIRS, *The Scots Literary Tradition.* London 1940.

Strawhorn = J. STRAWHCRN, "The Background to Burns," in *Ayrshire Archaeological and Natural History Society Collections,* 1950–4.

Thompson, H. W. = H. W. THOMPSON, *A Scottish Man of Feeling: Some Account of Henry Mackenzie, Esq. of Edinburgh and of the Golden Age of Burns and Scott.* London and New York 1931.

Thomson = *Select Collection of Original Scotish Airs,* ed. G. THOMSON, 6 vols. London and Edinburgh 1793–1841.

Waddell, Hately, *see* HATELY WADDELL.

Whale = J. S. WHALE, *The Protestant Tradition.* Cambridge 1955.

Wittig = K. WITTIG, *The Scottish Tradition in Literature.* Edinburgh 1958.

Wolf = F. WALKER, *Hugo Wolf: A Biography.* London 1951.

Glossary

According to a statement printed at the beginning of the Glossary to the first edition of Burns's *Poems, chiefly in the Scottish Dialect* (Kilmarnock 1786, p. 236), ". . . the participle present . . . ends, in the Scotch Dialect, in *an* or *in*; in *an*, particularly, when the verb is composed of the participle present, and any of the tenses of the auxiliary, *to be*." And at the beginning of the Glossary to the second edition (Edinburgh 1787, p. 345) there is the following statement: "The *ch* and *gh* have always the guttural sound. The sound of the English diphthong [*sic*], is commonly spelled *ou*. The French *u*, a sound which often occurs in the Scotch language, is marked *oo*, or *ui*. The *a* in genuine Scotch words, except when forming a diphthong, or followed by an *e* mute after a single consonant, sounds generally like the broad English *a* in *wall*. The Scotch diphthongs, *ae*, always, and *ea* very often, sound like the French *e* masculine. The Scotch diphthong *ey*, sounds like the Latin *ei*."

A', *adj., sb., adv.* :   all.
abeigh, *adv.* :   off, to one side.
aboon, *adv., prep.* :   above.
acquent, *past pple.* :   acquainted.
ae, *adj.* :   one, only ; *before superl., adds emphasis.*
aff, *adv., prep.* :   off.
aff-loof, *adv.* :   *lit.* off-hand ; extempore.
aft, aften, *adv.* :   oft, often.
agley, *adv.* :   awry.
aiblins, *adv.* :   perhaps.
aik, *sb.* (aiken, *adj.*) :   oak.
ain, *adj.* :   own.
air, *adv.* :   early.
airn, *sb.* :   iron.
airt, *sb.* :   direction.
aith, *sb.* :   oath.
ajee, *adv.* :   ajar.
amaist, *adv.* :   almost.
amang, *prep.* :   among.

an', *conj.* :   and, if, when.
ance, *adv.* :   once.
ane, *num. adj., pron.* :   one.
anent, *prep.* :   concerning.
anither, *pron., adj.* :   another.
asklent, *adv.* :   askance.
aspar, *adv.* :   with open legs.
asteer, *pred. adj.* :   astir.
atween, *prep.* :   between.
aught, *num. adj.* :   eight, eighth.
aughtlins, *adv.* :   in any way.
auld, *adj.* :   old.
Auld Licht, *sb., adj.* :   *lit.* Old Light, *term applied to orthodox Calvinists in Scottish Churches during 18th cent.*
aumous, *sb.* :   alms.
ava, *adv.* :   at all.
awa, *adv.* :   away.
ay, aye, *adv.* :   always.

Bab, *vb.* :   bob.

bailie, *sb.*, *usually pron.* bylie: magistrate of a Scots burgh.

bairn, *sb.*: child.

baith, *adj.*, *pron.*: both.

bane, *sb.*: bone.

barefit, *adj.*, *adv.*: barefoot.

bashing, *pres. pple.*: *lit.* abashing; bashful.

baudrons, *sb.*: the cat, "pussy."

bauld, *adj.*: bold, cheerful.

bawk, *sb.*: unploughed ridge, boundary strip, field-path.

beas', *sb. pl.*: *lit.* beasts; lice.

beat, *past pple.*: beaten.

beet, *vb.*: add fuel to, feed (flame).

behint, *prep.*: behind.

beir, *vb.*: bear.

belang, *vb.*: belong.

ben, *adv.*: inside. *Sb.*: parlour.

benmost, *adj.*: inmost.

besouth, *prep.*: south of.

bicker, *vb.*: make a noise (*esp. of water*).

bide, *vb.*: wait, endure.

bield, *sb.*: protection.

bing, *sb.*: heap.

birdies, *sb. pl.*, *dim.*: maidens, girls.

birk, *sb.*: birch.

birr, *vb.*: whirr.

bit, *adj.*: small.

bizz, *vb.*: buzz.

bizzard, *sb.*: buzzard.

blae, *adj.*: blue.

blather, *sb.*: bladder.

blaw, *vb.*: blow.

bleer, *vb.*: blear.

bleeze, *vb.*, *sb.*: blaze.

blethers, *sb. pl.*: nonsense.

blink, *sb.*: glance, moment, trice. *Vb.*: leer.

bluid, *sb.*: blood.

bluidy, *adj.*: bloody.

bluntie, *sb.*: stupid person.

boddle, *sb.*: farthing, "properly two pennies Scots, or one third of an English penny" (H. & H.)

body, *sb.*: person.

bogle, *sb.*: hobgoblin.

bo(n)nie, bo(n)ny, *adj.*: handsome, beautiful.

boord-en', *sb.*: table-end.

boor-tree, *sb.*: "the shrub-elder, planted much of old in hedges of barnyards" (R.B.)

boot, *sb.*: "payment made to equalise an exchange" (*Eng. Dial. Dict.*). O' boot: freely, into the bargain.

bore, *sb.*: hole; opening (*in game of curling.*)

bot, *prep.*: *see* BUT.

bow-hough'd, *adj.*: bandy-legged.

bowster, *sb.*: bolster.

brachens, *sb. pl.*: bracken.

brae, *sb.*: hill-face.

braid, *adj.*: broad.

braid-claith, *sb.*: broadcloth.

brak, *vb. pret.*: broke.

branks, *sb. pl.*: wooden curb *or* bridle.

brattle, *sb.*: clattering noise.

braw, *adj.*, *adv.*: fine, handsome (-ly).

brawlie, *adv.*: finely.

bree, *sb.*: brew.

breastit, *vb. pret.*: brought strain of harness on (horse's) breast.

breed, *sb.*: breadth.

breeks, *sb. pl.*: breeches.

brent, *adj.*: "straight, steep [*i.e.* not sloping from baldness]" (H. & H.)

brig, *sb.*: bridge.

brither, *sb.*: brother.

browster-wives, *sb. pl.*: ale-wives.

brugh, *sb.*: burgh, borough.

brulzie, *sb.*: broil, brawl.

bughtin, *pres. pple.*: folding (*of sheep*).

bum, *vb.* : hum.

burn, *sb.* ; burnie, *dim.* : stream.

but, *prep.* : without.

butt, *sb.* : kitchen.

by, *prep.* : round. *Adv.* : past.

byke, *sb.* : bees' nest (*alse*, ants' *or* wasps').

byre, *sb.* : cowshed.

Ca', *vb.* ; ca'd, *pret. and past pple.* : call, drive.

ca', *sb.* : knock, blow.

cadger, *sb.* : hawker.

caird, *sb.* : tinker.

cairn, *sb.* : pyramid of rough stones.

callet, *sb.* : trull.

cam, *vb. pret.* : came.

canna, *vb. +neg. part.* : cannot.

cannie, canny, *adj., adv.* : gentle, careful, cautious(ly).

cantie, canty, *adj., adv.* : joyful(ly).

cantraip, *sb.* : magic, witchcraft, spell.

carl-hemp, *sb.* : male-hemp.

carlin, *sb.* : middle-aged or old woman; coarse, vigorous woman of the lower classes.

carmagnole, *sb.* : "violent Jacobin" (H. & H.).

cartes, *sb. pl.* : playing cards.

cattle, *sb. pl.* : animals (*in general*).

cauld, *adj., sb.* : cold.

causey, *sb.* : street laid with cobblestones.

chapman, *sb.* : pedlar.

cheeks o' branks, *sb. phrase* : sides of ox's bridle.

chiel, *sb.* : fellow.

chuck, *sb.* : dear one.

claes, *sb. pl.* : clothes.

claithing, *sb.* : clothing.

clamb, *vb. pret.* : climbed.

clark, *adj.* : scholarly.

claught, *vb. pret.* : clutched.

claut, *sb.* : clutch, grip.

claw, *sb.* : scratch.

cleek, *vb.* : link hands.

clink, *vb., sb.* : rhyme. *Sb.* : money.

clish-ma-claver, *sb.* : idle gabble.

clockie, *see below*, p. 387.

cloot, *sb.* : hoof.

clout, *sb.* : piece of cloth, rag, patch (*of any material e.g. metal*). *Vb.* : patch.

cock, cockie, *sb.* : good fellow.

coof, *see* CUIF.

cookit, *vb. pret.* : darted "in and out of hiding" (S.N.D.)

coost, *vb. pret.* : cast off, tossed.

cootie, *adj.* : leg-plumed.

core, *sb.* : corps.

couldna, *vb. +neg. part.* : couldn't.

couthy, *adj.* : affable.

crack, *sb.* : talk.

craik, *sb.* : corncraik, landrail.

crap, *sb.* : crop.

craver, *sb., cant* : beggar.

crambo-jingler, *sb.* : rhymer.

craw, *sb., vb.* : crow.

creel, *sb.* : osier-basket. *Metaphorically*, in a creel : perplexed.

creepie-chair, *sb.* : stool of repentance.

crib, *sb.* : rack, manger, stall.

crood, *vb.* : coo.

croon, *sb.* : subdued murmur, lowing.

crouchie, *adj.* : hunchbacked.

crouse(ly), *adj.* (*adv.*) : cocksure(ly), proud(ly), confident(ly).

crummock, *sb.* : staff with a crooked head.

crump, *adj.* : crisp.

cry, *vb.* : call.

cuif, *sb.* : dolt.

cushat, *sb.* : wood-pigeon.

cutty, *adj.* : short.

Daez't, *vb. pret.* : dazed.

daft, *adj.* : foolish, mad.

darg, *sb.* : day's work, task.

dashing, *pres. pple.* : "peacocking" (H. & H.)

daur, *vb.* : dare.

daw, *vb.* : dawn.

deave, *vb.* : deafen.

deep-lairing. *adv. +pres. pple.* : *lit.* deep-layering; piled high.

deevil, deil, *sb.* : devil.

descrive, *vb.* : describe.

deuk, *sb.* : duck.

dine, *sb.* : dinner-time, *i.e.* noon.

ding, *vb.* : be beaten.

dinna, *vb. +neg. part.* : don't.

dochter, *sb.* : daughter.

doited, *adj.* : stupid, senile.

dool, *sb.* : woe.

douce(ly), douse(ly), *adj.* (*adv.*) : sedate(ly).

dought, *vb. pret.* : could; downa, *vb. +neg. part.* : cannot.

dowf, dowie, dowy, *adj.* : dull, gloomy.

doytin, *pres. pple.* : doddering.

draigle, *vb.* : draggle.

drap (-pie), *sb.* : drop.

drouk, *vb.* : droukit, *past pple.* : soak.

dub, *sb.* : puddle.

duds, duddies, *sb. pl.* : clothes, rags.

dunt, *sb.* : blow.

durk, *sb.* : dirk, dagger.

dusht, *past pple.* : touched, pushed against.

dyke, *sb.* : wall, ditch.

dyvor, *sb., adj.* : bankrupt.

E'e, *sb.* (*pl.* e'en, een) : eye.

e'en, (1) *sb.* : evening. (2) *Adv.* : even.

eerie, *adj.* : frightened, "particularly the dread of spirits" [R.B.]; awe-stricken.

eikit, *past pple.* : added.

eild, *sb.* : age.

eldritch, *adj.* : uncanny, unearthly.

elf-candle, *sb.* : "spark or flash of light thought to be of supernatural origin" (*S.N.D.*)

eneugh, enow, *adj.* : enough.

evanish, *vb.* : vanish.

Fa', *vb., in "Guid Faith, he mauna fa' that," is so printed in most edd. but the verb should presumably be "fa," without apostrophe* : snatch at, pretend to, claim.

factor, *sb.* : agent, manager (of heritable estates in Scotland).

fae, *sb.* : foe.

fain, *adj.* : fond, glad.

fairin, *sb.* : present from a fair, deserts, a beating.

fairy, *sb. as adj.* : tiny.

faith ye yet!, *asseveration* : "bless you always!," good for you!

farl, *sb.* : "the quarter of a round cake of oatmeal" (H. & H.)

fash, *vb.* : trouble. Dinna fash your thumb : don't care a rap.

Fasten-e'en, *sb.* : the evening before the first day of Lent.

fattrils, *sb. pl.* : ribbon-ends, loose pieces of trimming.

faught, *sb.* : fight, struggle.

fauld, *sb.* : fold.

fause, *adj.* : false.

faut, *sb.* : fault.

fautor, *sb.* : transgressor.

fawsont, *adj.* : good-looking (*in "Address of Beelzebub"*), respectable.

fechtin, *vbl. sb.* : fighting.

feg, *sb.* : fig.

fell, *sb.*: (1) hill. (2) Flesh under the skin. *Adj.*: cruel, deadly. *Adv.*: very.

ferly, *sb.*: marvel.

fidge, *vb.*: fidget, wriggle. Fidge fu' fain: wriggle ecstatically. Fidgin fain: quivering ecstatically.

fient, *sb.*: devil, *in attrib. exprs.* fient a: devil a, *and* fient hae't: devil take it.

fier, *adj.*: hearty, sound.

fiere, *sb.*: companion, comrade.

filcher, *sb., cant*: thief.

filer, *sb., cant*: robber, cheater.

fit, *sb.*: foot.

flaff, *vb.*: flap.

fley'd, *past pple.*: scared.

flie, *sb.*: fly.

fling, *vb.*: kick, caper.

flingin-tree, *sb.*: flail.

forgie, *vb.*: forgive.

fou, fu', *adj.*: full, drunk. *Adv.*: fully, quite.

frae, *prep.*: from.

fud, *sb.*: short tail, scut.

fuff, *vb.*: puff.

fu-han't, *adj.*: full-handed.

Furich-Whiggs, *apparent, sb. pl.*: pro-probably *from Gaelic* fuirich, *vb.*: stay, remain, stop. *The line should presumably be punctuated,* Furich! Whiggs awa, man!: Stop! (*a command addressed to the fugitives, cp.* "*Stop, thief!*") Whigs away, man! (*general information for the Highlanders*).

fyke, *sb.*: fret, commotion.

fyle, *vb.*: soil.

Gab, *sb. vb.*: mouth; talk.

gaberlunzie, *sb.*: wandering beggar.

gae, *vb.* (gaun, *pres. pple., vbl. sb.*; gaed,

pret.; gaen, gane, *past pple.*): go. *But see also* GIE.

gait, gate, *sb.*: way, road.

gane, *see* GAE.

gang, *vb.*: go.

gar, *vb.* (gart, *pret.*): make (somebody do something).

gartened, *past pple.*: gartered.

gash, *adj.*: dignified, self-important.

gat, *vb. pret.*: got.

gate, *sb.*: *see* GAIT.

gaun, *see* GAE.

gear, *sb.*: possessions.

geck, *vb.*: "lift the head proudly" (*S.N.D.*)

geds, *sb. pl.*: pike (fish).

get, *sb.*: issue.

ghaists, *sb. pl.*: ghosts.

gie, *vb.* (gae *pret.*; gien, *past pple.*): give. Gie's: give us.

gif, *conj.*: if.

gin, *conj.*: if. *Prep.*: against, by.

girdin, *vbl. sb.*: saddling (girth); with, *in* Ha, ha, the girdin o't, *extra sense from* gird, *vb.*: strike, push.

girr, *sb.*: hoop.

giz, *sb.*: wig.

gled, *sb.*: hawk, kite.

glower, *vb.* (glowrin, *pres. pple.*): stare.

glunch, *sb., vb.*: frown, grimace.

gooms, *sb. pl.*: gums.

gos, *sb.*: goshawk.

gowan, *sb.*: wild daisy.

gowd, *sb.*: gold.

gowdspink, *sb.*: goldfinch.

graith, *sb.*: equipment, gear.

grane, *sb.*: groan.

grapple-airn, *sb.*: grappling-iron.

grat, *see* GREET.

graunie, *sb.*: granny.

gree, *vb.* (greet, *past pple.*): agree. *Sb.*: prize, victory.

greet, *vb.* (grat, *pret.*) : weep.

grumphie, *sb.* : grunter, *pet name for pig.*

gruntle, *sb.* : grunt, mouth.

gudame, *sb.* : grandmother.

gude, guid, *adj.* : good.

gudesake, *euph. for* God's sake.

guidman, *sb.* : husband, master of the house.

guidwife, *sb.* : mistress of the house.

guid-willie, *adj.* : full of good will.

Ha', *sb.* : hall.

ha'e, hae, *vb.* : have.

hafflins, *adv.* : half, partly.

haggis, *sb.* : "a special Scots pudding, made of sheep's entrails, onions, and oatmeal boiled in a sheep's stomach [the *pièce de resistance* at Burns Club Dinners, and an esteemed antidote to whisky]." (H. & H.)

hail, *sb.* : shot.

hainch, *sb.* : haunch, hip.

hain'd, *past pple.* : saved, preserved, looked after.

hairst, *sb.* : harvest.

haith, "a mild oath or exclamation or asseveration of surprise" (*S.N.D.*)

hald, *sb.* : holding, possession.

Halloween, *sb.* : All Hallow's Eve, 31 Oct.

Hallow-fair, *sb.* : fair held at Hallowmas, *the season of All Hallows, normally in the first week of November.*

hame, *sb.* : home.

hamely, *adj.* : familiar, home-loving, friendly.

hand-breed, *sb.* : hand's breadth.

hand-waled, *past pple.* : hand-picked, choicest.

haud, *vb.* : hold.

hauf, *sb.* : half.

ha(u)ffet, *sb.* : temple; side-lock.

haughs, *sb. pl.* : low-lying flat lands by a river.

havins, *sb.* : good behaving, restraint, moderation.

hawse, *sb.* : throat.

heft, *sb.* : haft.

heich, *adj.* : high, lofty.

held awa', *vbl. phrase* : held forth to.

hellim, *sb.* : helm.

hem-shin'd, *adj.* : bandy, *with a shin shaped like a* hame, *i.e. like* "one of the two curved pieces of wood or metal forming or covering one-half of the collar of a draught horse to which the traces are fastened" (*S.N.D.*)

herd, *sb.* : cowherd, shepherd.

herryment, *sb.* : spoliation.

heugh, *sb.* : pit, ravine, crag.

hie, *adj.* : high.

high-flier, *sb.* : one who runs into extravagance of opinion or action; *often synonymous with* Auld Licht, *q.v.*

hilchin, *pres. pple.* : hobbling.

hing, *vb.* (hingin, *pres. pple.*) : hang.

hizzie, *sb.* : hussy.

hoast, *sb.* : cough.

hoddin, *pres. pple.* : jogging, making "the motion of a sage countryman riding on a cart horse" (R.B.)

hog-shouther, *vb.* : to indulge in "a kind of horse-play by justling with the shoulder, to justle" (R.B.)

hoodie-craw, *sb.* : carrion crow.

hoodock, *adj.* : grasping.

hooker, *sb., cant* : trickster.

hool, *sb.* : sheath, outer case.

hoolie, *adv., interj.* : softly.

houghmagandie, *sb.* :   fornication.

hur nane sell, *pron. phrase* :   *lit.* her own self (nane *being due to wrong division of similar phrase* mine ain sel), *i.e., in this context,* we Highlanders.

hurdies, *sb. pl.* :   buttocks.

Ilk, ilka, *adj.* :   each, every.

ingle, *sb.* :   fire, fireside.

ingle-lowe, *sb.* :   firelight.

I'se, *contr. vb.* :   I shall.

ither, *adj.* :   other.

Jad, *sb.* :   jade.

jaw, *vb.* :   dash, spurt, jet.

jee!, *interj.*, (*cp.* ajee, *adv.* :   ajar), *used in* And jee! the door gaed to the wa' ; *not equivalent to Amer.* gee!

jimp, *adj.* :   small, slender.

jink, *vb.* :   escape.

jinkin, *pres. pple.* :   sporting.

jo, *sb.* :   sweetheart.

Johnie Ged's Hole, *sb. phrase* :   the grave.

jook, *vb.* :   duck.

jorum, *sb.* :   large drinking-bowl.

jowler, *sb.* :   large-jowled hunting dog *such as beagle.*

jundie, *vb.* :   "to justle" (R.B.), "ply the elbows" (H. & H.)

justle, *vb.* :   jostle.

Kail, *sb.* :   kale, cabbage.

kail-blade, *sb.* :   cabbage-leaf.

kail-runt, *sb.* :   cabbage-stalk.

kail-yard, *sb.* :   kitchen garden.

kebars, *sb. pl.* :   "cabers," rafters.

keek, *vb.* :   peep, peer (through). *Sb.* :   peep, stolen glance.

keepit, *past pple.* :   kept.

kelpie, *sb.* :   water-sprite (*usually evil*).

ken, *vb.* (kend, kent, *pret. and past pple*) :   know. *Sb.* :   knowledge.

kinchin co(v)e, *sb., cant* :   one of "the Sixteenth Rank of the Canting Tribe, being little Children whose parents are Dead, having been Beggers ; as also young Ladds running from their masters, who are first taught Canting, then thieving" (*New Dict. of the Canting Crew*).

kind, *adj.* (kin *misspelt as* kind) :   sort of.

kintra-wark, *sb.* :   country work, field work.

kirk, *sb.* :   church.

kist, *sb.* :   chest, money-box.

kittle, *vb.* :   tickle.

kittlin, *sb.* :   kitten.

knaw, *vb.* :   know.

kye, *sb. pl.* :   cows, kine.

kin', *adj.* :   kind.

Lade, *sb.* :   load.

laird, *sb.* :   landlord.

lalland, *adj.* :   lowland.

lammer-bead, *sb.* :   amber bead.

lane, *adj.* :   lone, alone. *And, with poss. adj. prefixed,* her lane, my lane, thy lane :   by her-(my- thy-) self.

lang, *adj., adv.* :   long.

lap, *vb. pret.* :   leapt.

lapfu', *sb.* :   lapful.

lat, *vb. pret.* :   let.

lave, *sb.* :   rest, remainder.

lav'rock, *sb.* :   lark.

lays, *sb. pl.* :   leas.

lea'e, *vb.* :   leave.

lea rig, *sb.* :   *lit.* meadow ridge ; grassed strip of the infield.

lear, *sb.* :   learning.

lee-lang, *adj.* :   live-long.

leesome, *adj.* :   allowable ; lawful.

leeze me (on), *vbl. phrase*:   *lit.* lief is me, dear is to me; *i.e.*, I am pleased with; blessings on . . . !

leuk, *vb.*:   look.

licht, *sb.*:   light.

lift, *sb.*:   sky.

lightly, *vb.*:   disparage.

link, *vb.*:   spring, leap furiously.

linn, *sb.*:   waterfall.

lintwhite, *sb.*:   linnet.

longsyne, *adv.*:   long ago.

loof, *sb.*:   palm, hand.

loon, loun, *sb.*:   fellow.

loot, *vb. pret.*:   let.

loup, lowp, *vb.* (luppen, *past pple*):   leap.

lowe, *sb.*:   flame.

lug, *sb.*:   ear.

lum, *sb.*:   chimney.

luppen, *see* LOUP.

Mae, *adj.*:   more.

mailen, *sb.*:   farm.

mair, *adj., adv.*:   more.

maist, *adv.*:   almost.

mak, *vb.*:   make.

makar, *sb.*:   poet.

manteele, *sb.*:   mantle.

mark, *sb.*:   old Scots coin, equivalent to 13⅓ pence stg.

maskin-pat, *sb.*:   teapot.

masons, *sb. pl.*:   freemasons.

maukins, *sb. pl.*:   hares.

maun, *vb.*:   must.

maunder, *sb., cant*:   beggar.

maunna, *vb. + neg. part.*:   must not.

maut, *sb.*:   malt.

mawn, *past pple.*:   mown.

meikle, *see* MUCKLE.

menseless, *adj.*:   indiscreet, indecorous.

mim, *adj.*:   "prim, affectedly meek" (R.B.)

mim-mou'd, *adj.*:   prim-mouthed.

mind, *vb.*:   pay attention to, remember.

minnie, *sb.*:   mother.

mirk, *adj.*:   dark.

mistak, *vb.*:   mistake.

mither, *sb.*:   mother.

monie, mony, *adj.*:   many.

moorlan', *adj.*:   moorland.

mort, *sb., cant*:   wench. Walking mort, *sb. phrase, cant*:   prostitute.

moss, *sb.*:   bog.

mou('), *sb.*:   mouth.

mowe, *sb.*:   sexual act. *Vb.*:   have sexual intercourse.

muckle, *adj.*:   much, great, big. Muckle House, the: the House of Commons.

muir, *sb.*:   moor.

mutchkin, *sb.*:   Sc. liquid measure of 4 gills, *forming ¼ of a Sc. pint, or ¾ of an imperial pint.*

-Na, *neg. particle*:   not.

nae, *adj.*:   no (*so in* naebody, naething).

naig, *sb.*:   nag.

nane, *pron.*:   none.

nappy, *sb.*:   ale.

near-hand, *adv.*:   almost.

neebor, *sb.*:   neighbour.

neist, niest, *adj.*:   next.

neive, *sb.*:   fist.

neivefu', *sb.*:   fistful.

neuk, *sb.*:   nook, corner.

New Licht, *adj. + sb.*:   New Light, *term applied to moderate party in 18th-cent. Scottish Church.*

nieve, *see* NEIVE.

no, *adv.*:   not.

nocht, *sb.*:   nothing.

nor, *conj.*:   than.

nowte, *sb. pl.* :   cattle.

O' boot, *see* Boot.
och !, *interj.* :   oh !
o(c)hon !, *interj.* :   alas !
ochrie !, *interj.* :   alas !
onie, ony, *adj.* :   any.
ourie, *adj.* :   "shivering, drooping" (R.B.)
out-cast, *sb.* :   quarrel.
outler, *adj.* :   outside, in the open fields.
out-owre, *adv.* :   *lit.* out over ; head over heels.
owre, *prep.* :   over. *Adv.* :   over, too.
owsen, *sb. pl.* :   oxen.

Paidle, *vb.* :   paddle, wade.
paitricks, *sb. pl.* :   partridges.
palliard, *sb.*, *cant.* :   one of "the Seventh Rank of the Canting Crew, whose Fathers were Born Beggers, and who themselves follow the same Trade, with Sham Sores, making a hideous Noise, Pretending grievous Pain, to extort Charity" (*New Dict. of the Canting Crew.*)
park, *sb.* :   field.
paughty, *adj.* :   haughty.
pauky, *adj.* :   artful, sly.
perreiss, *vb.* :   perish.
pirkis, *vb. pres.* :   perches.
pit, *vb.* :   put.
plack, *sb.* :   four pennies Sc., *equivalent to* ⅓ *of an English penny.*
plaidie, *sb.*, *dim.* :   plaid.
plainstanes, *sb. pl.* :   pavement.
plaisters, *sb. pl.* :   plasters.
plenishings, *sb. pl.* :   furniture.
pleugh, plew, *sb.* :   plough.
pliver, *sb.* :   plover.
poortith, *sb.* :   poverty.

pou, pu', *vb.* :   pull.
pouther, powther, *sb.* :   powder.
prancer, *sb.*, *cant* :   horse.
prigger, *sb.*, *cant* :   thief.
puir, *adj.* :   poor.

Quaick, *sb.* :   quack.
quat, *vb.* :   quit.
quean, *sb.* :   lass.
quey, *sb.* :   heifer.
quha, *pron.* :   who.
quhair, *adv.* :   where.
quhilk, *pron.*, *adj.* :   which.
quhy, *adv.* :   why.

Rade, *vb. pret.* :   rode.
rair, *vb.* :   roar.
ram-stam, *adj.* :   impetuous, reckless.
randie, *sb.* :   scoundrel, rascal.
rape, *sb.* :   rope.
rash, *sb.* :   rush.
rash-buss, *sb.* :   clump of rushes.
rattan, ratton, *sb.* :   rat.
raucle, *adj.* :   hasty, indisciplined, coarse.
raw, *sb.* :   row.
rax, *vb.* :   stretch ; wring (neck). Raxin, *pres. pple.* :   "elastic" (H. & H.)
ream, *sb.* :   foam.
rede, *sb.* :   counsel. *Vb.* :   advise.
red-wat-shod, *adj.* :   red-wet-shod, *i.e. walking in blood.*
reek, *sb.* :   smoke. *Vb.* :   smoke, steam.
reft, *past pple.* :   torn.
reif, *adj.* :   thieving.
remead, *sb.* :   remedy.
rig, *sb.* :   ridge.
rig-woodie, *adj.* :   like a rig-woodie, *i.e.* a "back withy," *twisted withies used as back band of a cart-horse,* hence stringy, wizened.

rin, *vb.* (rinnin, *pres. pple.*) : run.

ripp, *sb.* : handful of corn from the sheaf.

ripplin-kame, *sb.* : wool- *or* flax-comb.

rive, *vb.* (riven, rivin, *pres. pple.*) : split tear.

roose, *vb.* : rouse, inspire ; praise.

roosty, *adj.* : rusty.

routhie, *adj.* : well-stocked.

row, *vb.* : roll, wrap.

rowte, *vb.* : low, bellow.

rowth, *sb.* : plenty.

ruffler, *sb.*, *cant* : one of "the first Rank of Canters ; also notorious Rogues" (*New Dict. of the Canting Crew*).

rung, *sb.* : cudgel.

runt, *sb.* : stalk.

rys, *sb.* : twig, branch.

Sae, *adv.* : so.

saft, *adj.* : soft.

sair, *adj.*, *adv.* : sore, sorely.

sair, *vb.* (sair't, *past pple*) : serve.

sall, *vb.* : shall.

sang, *sb.* : song.

sark, *sb.* : shirt, shift.

saul, *sb.* : soul.

saunt, *sb.* : saint.

saut, *sb.* : salt.

saw, *vb.* : sow.

sawmont, *sb.* : salmon.

sax, *num. adj.* : six.

scaur, *sb.* : cliff.

scho, *pron.* : she.

scrievin, *pres. pple.* : careering.

sels, *sb. pl.* : selves.

set, *vb.* : "take up a position and perform a number of steps with one's face to one's partner or to the dancer on one's right or left" (*N.E.D.*)

settlin, *vbl. sb.* : *lit.* settling, *i.e.*, punishment.

shachl'd, *pple. adj.* : shuffling, slip-shod.

shavie, *sb.* : trick, prank, ill-turn.

shaw, *vb.* : show. *Sb.* : wood.

sheep-shank bane, *compound sb.* : "sheepshank bone," person of no importance.

sheuk, *vb. pret.* : shook.

shiel, *sb.* : shed.

shoon, *sb. pl.* : shoes.

shore, *vb.* : offer.

shouldna, *vb. + neg. part.* : shouldn't.

shouther, *sb.* : shoulder.

sic, siccan, *adj.* : such.

sickir, *adj.* : sure.

siller, *sb.*, *adj.* : silver.

simmer, *sb.* : summer.

skaith, *sb.*, *vb.* : damage, harm.

skeigh, *adj.* : skittish.

skelp, *vb.* (skelpin, *pres. pple.*) : slap, resound, hurry.

skirl, *vb.* : shriek, squeak.

sklent, *vb.* : squint.

skriegh, *vb.* : screech, whinny.

slae, *sb.* : sloe.

slap, *sb.* : breach in fence, opening.

slee, *adj.* : sly, ingenious.

sleekit, *adj.* : sleek.

sma', *adj.* : small.

smeek, *sb.* : smoke.

smoor, *vb.* : smother.

snakin, *pres. pple.* : sneaking.

snaw, *sb.* : snow.

sned, *vb.* : cut, crop.

snick, *sb.* : latch.

snirtle, *vb.* : snigger.

snool, *vb.* : snub.

so(d)ger, *sb.* : soldier.

some, *adv.* : a little.

sonsie, *adj.* : pleasant, jolly.

soom, *vb.* : swim.

soor, *adj.* :   sour.

souple, *adj.* :   supple.

souter, *sb.* :   cobbler.

spail, *sb.* :   splinter.

spak, *vb. pret.* :   spoke.

spavie, *sb.* :   spavin.

spean, *vb.* :   put a foal off its milk by frightening it.

speel, *vb.* :   climb.

speet, *vb.* :   spit.

spier, *vb.* :   ask.

splatter, *vb.* :   splash about.

spontoon, *sb.* :   "weapon carried by soldier-officers instead of a half-pike" (H. & H.)

sprattle, *vb.* :   scramble.

spunk, *sb.* :   touchwood, tinder, spark.

spunkie, *sb.* :   will-o'-the-wisp.

squatter, *vb.* :   fly from surface of water.

squattle, *vb.* :   squat.

stacher, *vb.* :   stagger.

stack, *vb. pret.* :   stuck.

stane, *sb.* :   stone.

stang, *vb.* :   sting. *Sb.* :   long pole.

stank, *sb.* :   pond.

stark, *adj.* :   strong.

starnie, *sb.* :   star.

stauk, *vb.* (staukin, *pres. pple.*) :   stalk.

staumrel, *adj.* :   half-witted.

staw, *vb. pret.* :   stole.

steek, *vb.* (steekit, *past pple.*) :   shut, close in.

sten, *sb., vb.* (sten't, *pret.*) :   leap.

stents, *sb. pl.* :   tax-assessments.

stented, *past pple.* :   set up, exalted.

stir, *sb., term of address* :   *lit.* master ; sir.

stirk, *sb.* :   young bullock.

stoor, *adj.* :   harsh.

stoure, *sb.* :   blown dust.

stown, *past pple.* :   stolen.

stownlins, *adv.* :   surreptitiously.

straik, *vb.* :   stroke.

strampant, *pres. pple.* :   treading heavily.

strang, *adj.* :   strong.

stude, *vb. pret.* :   stood.

stumpie, *sb.* :   quill pen, worn down to a stump.

sturt, *sb.* :   obstinate contentiousness.

sugh, *sb.* :   "sough," moan, swish.

swankie, *sb.* :   strapping fellow.

swat, *vb. pret.* :   sweated.

swatch, *sb.* :   "a strip of cloth used as a sample" (Chambers) ; sample.

swats, *sb. pl.* :   new ale.

swinge, *vb.* :   flog.

swith !, *adv. with imperat. force* :   quickly, at once !

swoor, *vb. pret.* :   swore.

syne, *adv., sb.* :   since, ago, thereafter.

Taed, *sb.* :   toad.

ta'en, *see* TAK.

tak, *vb.* (ta'en, *past pple*) :   take. Takin, *pres. pple.* :   captivating.

takin, *see* TAK.

tald, tauld, *vb. pret., past pple.* :   told.

tap, *sb.* :   top.

tarrow, *vb.* :   weary.

tassie, *sb.* :   goblet.

teet-bo, *sb.* :   peep-bo.

tent, *sb., vb.* :   heed, notice.

tentie, *adj.* :   attentive, watchful.

thack, *sb.* :   thatch.

thae, *adj.* :   those.

thairm, *sb.* :   gut ; (fiddle) string.

thane, *sb.* :   *in Sc. hist.*, chief of a clan who became one of the King's barons ; *in Burns*, lord.

thegither, *adv.* :   together.

thiggin, *pres. pple.* :   begging.

thought, *conj.* :   though.

thocht, *vb. pret.* :   thought.

thrang, *sb.* :   throng. *Adj.* :   thronged ; busy.

thraw, *vb.*: twist, turn; oppose, thwart.

thrissle, *sb.*: thistle.

thusgat, *adv.*: in this way.

tight, *adj.*: (*of a woman*) shapely.

till, *prep.*: to.

timmer, *sb.*: "timber", wood.

tine, *vb.* (tint, *pret.*): lose.

tinkler, *sb.*, *adj.*: tinker.

tip, *sb.*: tup.

tippeny, *sb.*: (twopenny) ale.

tither, *adj.*, *pron.*: other.

tittie, *sb.*: sister (*as term of endearment*).

toom, *adj.*: empty.

toop, *sb.*: tup.

toun, *sb.*: group of farm buildings; village; (*rarely*) small town.

tousie, touzie, *adj.*: shaggy.

tozie, *adj.*: intoxicated (*from prec.*).

trashtrie, *sb.*: small trash.

trews, *sb. pl.*: "close-fitting trousers, or breeches combined with stockings, formerly worn by Irishmen and Scottish Highlanders, and still by certain Scottish regiments" (*N.E.D.*)

trogger, *sb.*: packman.

troggin, *sb.*: wares.

trouth, *sb.*: truth; *as asseveration*, in truth.

trow, *vb.*: believe, think.

tryste, *sb.*: fair, cattle-market.

trysted, *pple adj.*: appointed, agreed upon.

trystin, *vbl. sb.*: assignation, "date," meeting.

tulyie, tulzie, *sb.*: squabble.

twa, *num. adj.*: two.

Ulzie, *sb.*: oil.

unco, *adj.*, *adv.*: strange(ly), unusual(ly), extreme(ly).

unsicker, *adj.*: uncertain.

upo', *prep.*: upon.

usquebae, *sb.*: whisky.

Vend, *vb.*: "vend," offer, utter, express.

vera, *adj.*, *adv.*: very.

Wa', *sb.*: wall.

wabster, *sb.*: weaver.

wad, *vb.*: would. Wad been: would have been. Wadna: wouldn't.

wae, *sb.*, *adj.*: woe; sad.

waft, *sb.*: weft, woof.

waft an' warp, *vbs.*: interlace weft with warp, weave.

wait, *see* WAT.

wale, *sb.*, *vb.*: pick, choice; choose.

wa(w)lie, wa(w)ly, *adj.*: choice, large.

walking Mort, *see* MORT.

wame, weym, *sb.*: belly.

wan, *vb. pret,*: won.

wark, *sb.*: work.

warldly, warly, *adj.*: worldly.

warlock, *sb.*: sorcerer, wizard.

warsle, *vb.*: wrestle, flounder.

warst, *adj.*: worst.

wast, *sb.*, *adj.*: west.

wat, wait (*arch.*), *vb.* (wist, *pret.*): know.

waught, *sb.*: draught.

wauk, *vb.* (waukin, *pres. pple.*): (stay a) wake; watch.

waur, *adj.*: worse.

wean, *sb.*: child.

wee, *adj.*, *sb.*: little.

weel, *sb.*: benefit.

weel, weill, *adv.*: well.

weel-gaun, *adj.*: well-going.

weel-hained, *adj.*: well-stored, well protected.

weel-stocket, *adj.*: well-stocked.

weet, *adj.* :   wet.

weym, *see* WAME.

wha, *pron.* :   who.

whang, *sb.* :   large slice.

whaup, *sb.* :   curlew. *So in* Whaup's i' the nest : There's an intruder in the nest (*cp. Sc. prov.* There's a whaup i' the rape : Something's wrong).

whar, whare, whaur, *adv.* :   where.

whase, *poss. adj.* :   whose.

whid, *sb.* :   lie.

whid, *vb.* :   scud.

whids, *sb. pl.* :   gambols.

Whig, *sb.* :   Covenanter, extreme Presbyterian, *as well as usual political sense. Vb.* :   behave like a Whig (*from above, sense 1*).

whiggish, *adj.* :   Presbyterian, moralistic.

whin, whinnet, *sb.* :   gorse.

whinge, *vb.* :   whine.

whipjack, *sb.*, *cant* :   one of "the Tenth Order of the Canting Crew ; Counterfeit Mariners Begging with false Passes, pretending Shipwrecks, great Losses at Sea, &c. narrow escapes ; telling dismal Stories, having learnt *Tar-terms* on purpose, but are meer Cheats" (*New Dict. of the Canting Crew*).

whisht, *sb.* :   silence, peace.

whissle, *vb.* :   whistle.

whittle, *sb.* :   knife.

whup, *sb.* :   whip.

whyles, *adv.* :   sometimes.

wi', *prep.* :   with.

wick a bore, *vbl. phrase, technical expression from game of curling* :   "drive a stone dexterously through an opening between two guards" (Jamieson).

wicker, *sb.* :   withy, pliant twig.

wiel, *sb.* :   eddy.

wight, *sb.* :   man.

wight, *adj.* :   strong, stout.

wimple, *vb.* (wimplin, *pres. pple.*) :   fold, curl, wind.

winna, *vb.* + *neg. part.* :   will not, won't.

winnock, *sb.* :   window.

wintle, *sb.* :   somersault.

withouten, *prep.* :   without.

woo', *sb.* :   wool.

woody, *sb.* :   withy, halter.

wrack, *vb.* :   rack, torture.

wrang, *adj.* :   wrong.

writer, *sb.* :   attorney, lawyer, law-clerk.

writer-chiel, *sb.* :   lawyer fellow.

wyle, *vb.* :   entice.

wyte, *sb.* :   blame.

Yestreen, *adv.* :   last night.

yett, *sb.* :   gate.

yill, *sb.* :   ale.

yon, *adj.* :   yonder.

yont, *prep.* :   beyond.

yook, *sb.* :   itch.

yowe, *sb.* (yowie, *dim.*) :   ewe.

yschit, *vb. pret.* :   issued, came out.

Explanatory Index of Proper Names and Special Phrases

Auld Cowl :   *nickname for parish priest.*

Baldy :   Archibald.

Berwick-Law :   "North Berwick Law, *a conspicuous height in Haddingtonshire overlooking the Firth of Forth*" (H. & H.)

Cassilis Downans :   "Certain little, romantic, rocky, green hills in the neighbourhood of the ancient seat of the Earls of Cassilis." (R.B.)

clockie :   *prefixed to clockmaker's name, as nickname.*

Coila :   *personification of Kyle, a district in Ayrshire.*

Colean :   Culzean House.

Crochallan Fencibles :   Edinburgh convivial club of the late 18th cent.

Eppie :   *dim. of* Elspeth.

Gate-Slack :   *defile through which a road passes, in Durisdeer Parish, Dumfriesshire.*

Heck :   Hector.

Hornie :   the Devil.

Hughoc :   *dim. of* Hugh.

Humphie :   *prop. n. from adj. meaning* hump-backed.

Land o' Cakes :   Scotland.

Leezie :   Lizzie.

Mahoun :   Mahomet ; *i.e.*, the Devil.

Mailie :   Molly.

Merran :   Marian.

Nick, Nickie-ben :   the Devil.

Thrillwall :   Thirlwall (*in Barbour's "Bruce," governor installed by the English in James of Douglas's castle, in Douglasdale*).

Index

EXPLANATORY NOTE

As the entry for Burns in Part I is necessarily long, it has been divided into six sections: (1) Biography; (2) Women and girls; (3) Outlook and views; (4) Language; (5) R. B. as poet, (a) technical characteristics of his poetry (b) general; (6) Songs. Critics and editors of Burns are indexed alphabetically under Critics; and writers and works discussed as sources or parallels for Burns's writing are indexed under Sources and parallels.

Individual works of Burns are listed separately in Part II.

Index

I. General

II. Burns's Works